Changing the World

POLITICS AND SOCIETY IN TWENTIETH-CENTURY AMERICA

ঞ্জ

Series Editors
WILLIAM CHAFE, GARY GERSTLE, LINDA GORDON, AND JULIAN ZELIZER

A list of titles in this series appears at the back of the book

Changing the World

AMERICAN
PROGRESSIVES
IN WAR AND
REVOLUTION

ALAN DAWLEY

PRINCETON UNIVERSITY PRESS
PRINCETON AND OXFORD

COPYRIGHT © 2003 BY PRINCETON UNIVERSITY PRESS

༝ৡৢৢ

Published by Princeton University Press, 41 William Street,
Princeton, New Jersey 08540
In the United Kingdom: Princeton University Press, 3 Market Place,
Woodstock, Oxfordshire OX20 1SY
All Rights Reserved

LIBRARY OF CONGRESS CATALOGING-IN-PUBLICATION DATA
Dawley, Alan, 1943–
Changing the world : American progressives in war and revolution / Alan Dawley.
p. cm.—(Politics and society in twentieth-century America)
Includes bibliographical references and index.
ISBN 0-691-11322-X (alk. paper)
1. United States—Politics and government—1913–1921. 2. United States—Politics
and government—1921–1923. 3. United States—Foreign relations—20th century.
4. Progressivism (United States politics) 5. Internationalism—History—20th century.
6. Social movements—United States—History—20th century. 7. Political activists—
United States—History—20th century. 8. Social reformers—United States—History—
20th century. 9. World politics—1900–1918. 10. World politics—1919–1932.
I. Title. II. Series.
E766.D38 2003   973.91'3—dc21   2002030732

British Library Cataloging-in-Publication Data is available

This book has been composed in Palatino
Printed on acid-free paper. ∞
www.pupress.princeton.edu

Printed in the United States of America

10 9 8 7 6 5 4 3 2 1

For Dr. Katy

Contents

Acknowledgments

᭖

While writing is a solitary experience, scholarship is more collaborative. Good readers of manuscripts save authors from the things they say but don't mean and, more important, from the things they mean to say which just aren't so. I have been fortunate in having good readers. Gary Gerstle displayed his discerning editorial talent in perceptive comments, and Emily Rosenberg offered penetrating and beneficial comments, as well. I am also grateful to Brigitta van Rhineberg, Senior Editor at Princeton University Press, for her unfailingly astute advice and infectious enthusiasm for the project. In addition, I wish to thank the following for comments on parts of the manuscript: John Chambers, Nancy Cott, Katy Dawley, Leon Fink, Lloyd Gardner, Tom Knock, Art Schmidt, Chips Sowerwine, and the following members of the Philadelphia Twentieth Century Reading Group: Walter Licht, Wendell Pritchett, and David Watt. In addition, I have learned much from conversations with other colleagues, as well as with practitioners of progressive politics. Over the years of research, I have benefited from responses of colleagues to material presented at conferences and seminars in the following venues: the Rutgers Center for Historical Analysis, 1992–93; the Historiale de la Grande Guerre, Peronne, France, 1996; the Sixth International Polanyi Conference, Montreal, 1996; the conference on Capitalism and the State, Emory University,

Atlanta, 1997; the Social Science History Association, Washington, 1997; the conference in honor of Marianne Debouzy, Paris, 1998; the Organization of American Historians, Toronto, Canada, 1999. At a critical point in formulating the analysis, I was introduced to the project on Internationalizing the Study of American History, and I want to thank its director Tom Bender for inviting me to participate in the La Pietra conference, a feast of lucidity in Florence, Italy, 1999.

Authors would be lost without archivists, and I wish to thank the many helpful staff members at the National Archives, where I first laid eyes on War Plans White as long ago as 1979; the Library of Congress, with its numerous relevant collections; the Swarthmore College Peace Collection; and Mudd Library at Princeton University. In addition, the library staffs at The College of New Jersey and the University of Pennsylvania, where I enjoyed the privileges of a Visiting Scholar, facilitated the research. At The College of New Jersey, my colleague Stuart McCook was most generous with his technical skills, as was Joann Manto with secretarial skills. I also wish to acknowledge support from The College of New Jersey in the form of released time over the years this book was in preparation and from the National Endowment for the Humanities for a year-long fellowship, 1993–94.

Changing the World

FIRST STEPS IN SELF-GOVERNMENT.

Making the World Safe for Democracy: A confused Russia is pulled
in different directions by "democracy" in Grecian garb and "violence"
brandishing the torch of anarchy, while a German soldier implores him
to betray the Allies. The image evokes an American mission to a troubled
world at the time of the Great War and the Russian Revolution. Rollin
Kirby, "First Steps in Self-Government," New York *World*, May 9, 1917.
(Reprinted with permission of American Newspaper Repository)

Introduction

༈

"We dedicate ourselves to Peace!"

With this vow ringing in their ears, women from some twenty countries gathered in Zurich, Switzerland, in May of 1919 hoping to free the world from the death grip of war. Yet peace was not the only thing on their minds. Most of the delegates were also veteran campaigners for social causes ranging from women's suffrage to labor standards. When one of them proclaimed, "Only in freedom is permanent peace possible," they knew they had found the right name for the Women's International League for Peace and Freedom.[1]

The women's league was a perfect example of the new internationalism that arrived on the scene in the early twentieth century. At a time when visions of social progress were clouded by violent upheavals on the world stage, a growing body of reformers came to believe that cooperation among the peoples of the world was part and parcel of the quest for social justice. What was the point of making a better world if it was only going to be blown to smithereens?

To American reformers in this period, changing the world always carried the double meaning of combating the evils afflicting their own society, while also improving the wider world. That was the view of the growing group of social reformers such as Jane Addams and reform politicians such as Theodore Roosevelt who started calling themselves "progressive" around 1910. "The adjective 'progressive' is what we like," wrote young journalist Walter Lippmann, "and the word 'new.' "[2]

No sooner had the founding generation of American progressives come on the scene than revolutionary movements began to shake the earth in the vast agrarian belt from Mexico to Russia, while simultaneously the empires and nations of Europe began to lunge at each others' throats in what became the Great War. For American progressives, there was no escaping these world-historical events, and from that time forward, the dual quest for improvement at home and abroad was at the heart of what it meant to be a progressive.

The dual effort of American progressives to change the world is the subject of this book. Starting in the years before the Great War, I have followed the progressives through the turbulent years of war and revolution into the conservative 1920s. I have tried to make sense of their responses to the major questions of the day—social injustice, economic inequality, war and peace, imperial intervention—in an effort to better understand the past. At the same time, I have also tried to link past and present in a way that might help a later generation think about the relation between American reform and world affairs in the twenty-first century.

Certainly, the founding generation of progressives has given us much to ponder. In a hectic round of activity, they set out to regulate big business, rid money-driven politics of corruption, secure a place for industrial workers in American life, and give the New Woman room to grow. As if dealing with issues of class and gender were not enough, they also tried to improve relations among ethnic groups—what they called "races"—with mixed results. Although a good many progressives were ready to include Catholic and Jewish immigrants in the American family, others tried to impose narrow Protestant values on immigrants, or else exclude them altogether. Despite some achievements in civil rights, including the formation of the flagship National Association for the Advancement of Colored People, white progressives fell woefully short in pursuing racial equality.

Although this eclectic collection of reforms hardly made for a unified movement, progressivism found a certain cohesion in three overlapping aims: winning social and economic justice, revitalizing public life, and improving the wider world. We will take them in turn. In addressing the social evils of the day, progressives pursued such reforms as wage and hours laws, the prohibition of child labor, and the regulation of business, all in an effort to bring order to the unregulated marketplace. It is important to recognize the international dimension of this effort. In a world knit together by far-flung markets and the international state system, progressives confronted social problems that crossed national boundaries, and their solutions did the same. Whether battling for women's suffrage, temperance, or labor standards, they commonly joined forces with their counterparts from Europe to Australia.[3]

In the process, they drew many ideas from the left. The left is defined here as the political stance, whether Marxist or not, that blamed inequalities in wealth and power on the workings of the capitalist system. That serves to distinguish leftists from progressives, who, for the most part, did not see capitalism behind every wrong, but it also establishes points of overlap between them. During the prewar heyday of socialism, many progressives could be found supping at the socialist table, sampling ideas of municipal ownership, social legislation, and redistribution of wealth. In some ways, American progressives resemble England's Fabian socialists and what were later called social democrats. European social democrats were partisans of mixed economy who combined support for private ownership with public regulation of business and modest redistribution of wealth, and many progressives did the same.[4]

The quest for social justice shaded over into a second aim—the revitalization of public life. In a host of ways from women's suffrage through public commissions, progressives aimed at replacing the existing politics of patronage and power with a new politics of civic engagement. In the process, they drew heavily on republican ideas. Heaping scorn on selfish private interests,

they embraced, instead, the republican principle of civic engagement in service to the public interest. In progressive campaigns
for good government, direct election of senators, and, most important, women's suffrage, the republican emphasis on active
citizenship was very much to the fore.

Progressives wanted to believe that the republican revival at
home was part of a worldwide movement toward greater self-
government. In the vast belt of agrarian societies that ringed the
globe, sleeping giants were awakening in Mexico, China, and
Russia in sprawling social revolutions aimed at throwing off imperial yokes. It is important to note that prior to the Bolshevik
revolution, rebel movements in the developing world commonly set their sights on a whole panoply of republican ideals,
including popular sovereignty, written constitutions, representative parliaments, and freedom of expression. Although social
revolutions could seem alien and threatening, American progressives stoked their own convictions by extending sympathy
to republican movements overseas.

The key to understanding the political philosophy of American progressivism is to see it as a quarrel with liberalism. The
liberal component in progressive thought is easy to spot. The
terms "progressive" and "liberal" were often used more or less
interchangeably, and progressives typically mounted the battle-
ments in defense of such quintessentially liberal ideas as civil liberty and limited government. Certainly, progressives preferred
modest government regulation to state ownership. Emphasizing
such liberal associations, an earlier generation of scholars treated
progressivism as part of the liberal tradition, which was seen to
be the *only* viable political tradition in the United States.[5]

The fact is, however, that progressives had serious objections
to laissez-faire liberalism. In a revealing turn of phrase, Walter
Lippmann, then at the start of a distinguished journalistic career,
spoke for his generation in rejecting the "drift" of the market
in favor of the "mastery" of social control.[6] While accepting the
general framework of capitalist property relations, progressives
had lost faith in the capacity of the free market to create social
justice. Setting out to bring the market under social control, but

suspicious of coercive bureaucracy, they fashioned compacts in civil society and imposed regulations in the public sphere that went beyond the old liberalism. Although lacking a well-developed body of doctrine, progressivism was a trenchant—and still pertinent—critique of laissez-faire.

Progressives braided together republican, socialist, and liberal strands to create something new. Dissatisfied with social and economic inequalities that arose under laissez-faire, they developed a distinct set of practices pitting social justice against class rule, civic engagement against patronage, and international cooperation against balance-of-power politics.

The last point needs to be emphasized. The critique of laissez-faire was not intended solely for domestic consumption. It also applied to world affairs, the third arena of progressive action. Although many commentators have noted that reform did not stop at the water's edge, they have often missed the fact that progressive thinking took shape in response to events overseas. Having come of age in an era of empire, progressives attributed the things they did not like, such as "dollar diplomacy," to the same plutocratic "special interests" that had corrupted American life, and they often turned around to bless U.S. overseas expansion as social and economic progress for the less fortunate.

Likewise, they attributed the misbehavior of the European great powers to the same pursuit of raw self-interest they despised in Gilded Age Robber Barons. Rejecting the materialism of balance-of-power politics, they embraced, instead, the idealism of making the world safe for democracy as they marched off on a wartime crusade to save the world. American reform did not stop at the water's edge, but neither did world affairs stop at the U.S. border. To the contrary, revolutionary upheavals and the clash of empires and nation-states worked their way into American reform at every turn.

The fact that internal and external matters were so deeply entwined did not make life easier for the progressives, or their historians. Examining American reform in the context of world affairs requires innovative methods. If social reform and foreign policy were important to one another, then they must be included, one with the other, inside the same frame of analysis. It is necessary to study interactions between social movements and political elites within and across national boundaries. Social history and international relations—history from the bottom up and history from the top down—must be combined in a way that incorporates both social movements and nation-states.

One fruitful result of such a method is that ordinary people take their rightful place alongside elites as history's decision makers. Every generation is forced to make decisions in circumstances not of its own choosing. That is the nature of history. But the burden of choice on the founding generation of American progressives was unusually great. Questions of war, empire, and revolution would have been immensely difficult taken one at a time, but in these years, all three arrived at once. Forced to make hard choices, progressives had to decide whether to join forces across national boundaries or let other peoples work out their own destinies in their own ways.

To understand choices made in the past, it is necessary to recover the full range of options, the paths forsaken, as well as the paths taken. Only by recovering lost options is it possible to accord a degree of freedom to historical actors, who would otherwise be mere prisoners of destiny. In the case at hand, that means we must remember those who lost the arguments over U.S. military intervention as well as those who won, out of fidelity to the historical record and to remind ourselves that things might have turned out differently.

As the United States sailed out on to the high seas of world affairs, progressives were deeply divided over which course to take. The most prominent figures—the ones best remembered a century later—went full steam ahead for intervention. Theodore Roosevelt, the nominee of the nation's first Progressive party, and Woodrow Wilson, who came to lead progressive forces after 1912, outdid one another in sending U.S. troops abroad. Roosevelt was an unabashed imperialist, and, if anything, Wilson was even more active overseas. In what has been called "missionary diplomacy," Wilson intervened in the Mexican and Russian revolutions and in several Latin American republics, and with his famous Fourteen Points, he brought the United States to the pinnacle of world leadership at the end of the Great War.[7]

At the same time, many other progressives—ones that deserve to be better remembered—wanted to steer clear of military interventions in all these places. Instead, they set a course toward the "new internationalism" of cooperation with other peoples in pursuit of world peace and social justice. No one was more important in that regard than Jane Addams. Not only was she the venerable queen of social reform, she also devoted her considerable talents to criticizing interventions in the Caribbean and holding back support for intervention in the Great War. For her courageous stands, she was honored at Zurich in 1919 with the presidency of the Women's International League, and later, on a much bigger stage, she would become the first American woman to receive the Nobel Peace Prize, fitting tribute to the prominent role women played in the movement for world peace.[8]

Progressive internationalism[9] found its main political champion in Robert La Follette. More than anyone else, the feisty senator from Wisconsin held the rightful claim to being the father of progressive politics. Near the end of his illustrious career in 1924, he mounted the second major presidential bid under a Progressive party banner. Having stood against the gale of superpatriotic support for the war, he also opposed imperial intervention and came out against the League of Nations. Indeed, in the troubled aftermath of the Great War, when most elites abandoned progressivism both at home and abroad, progressive internationalism was left in the safekeeping of the likes of Addams and La Follette.

In examining progressivism early in the century, we are thrust immediately into the larger realm of world history. American progressives were not the only ones wrestling with the unwanted consequences of the unregulated capitalist market and the unhappy results of nationalism run amok. Indeed, the entire world was caught up in an epoch-making conjuncture that began in the 1910s. The violent events of that decade were symptoms of a convulsive transformation in the pattern of power both within and between societies that saw the overthrow of ancient dynasties, challenges to modern structures of authority, and the beginning of the end of European hegemony. What began then was not completed until the de-colonization movements after the Second World War.

In the early stages of this conjuncture, in a moment sandwiched between the armistice of November 1918 and the conclusion of the Versailles peace conference seven months later, the United States rose briefly to the pinnacle of world leadership behind Woodrow Wilson. It was the first American moment[10] in world affairs, and it was no coincidence that the first world leader to come from the United States was also the preeminent progressive in the country. Besides U.S. economic clout, what gave Wilson moral leadership was his appeal to countless millions around the world as a reformer, a fresh answer to corruption, oppression, and militarism.

From that day forward, progressive ideas were bound up with the question of U.S. hegemony. Although hegemony rests, fundamentally, on economic and military power, the cultural element is essential, too. America won prestige for its high-consumption economy, but it also stood out to war-weary and oppressed peoples for its ideals of freedom and self-government. The attraction was not only Model Ts but also model schools.

As it turned out, the American moment was fleeting, because the national establishment reversed course in 1919. Uneasy about wearing the crown, which, in any case, Britain was not eager to relinquish, American elites retreated from world leadership at the same time as they abandoned reform. Their retreat was due, in part, to fear that events were spinning out of control in a moment of millennial excitement as movements for labor and women's rights flooded back onto the world stage, colonial peoples rushed forward to claim the right of self-determination, and the threat of revolution spread westward out of Russia. In the face of all this discontent, American elites feared that entanglement overseas would somehow worsen the class and racial conflicts that wracked their cities back home. Although progressivism retained a few staunch supporters in Congress, the Wilson administration was jailing dissenters, suppressing strikes, and spurning calls for postwar reconstruction, and, as a result, progressivism at the top collapsed in a heap.

Contrary to many historical accounts of the period, however, that did not mean the death of progressivism. Instead, it was born anew in movements for world peace and economic justice. Universal revulsion against war laid the moral foundation for the most significant peace movement of the twentieth century, and, despite some lingering sentimentality, the movement contained more hard-headed realism and vigorous anti-imperialism than its prewar predecessor. That was due, in part, to the economic turn of the postwar years, as progressives set aside moral crusades against drink and prostitution to focus on economic reforms of direct benefit to working people, including the right to organize unions, rural development, and production for use instead of profit. Reborn in the harsh environment of the 1920s, the new progressivism, leaner and tougher, was better positioned than the old would have been to address the problems of the Great Depression, enabling it to return to center stage in Franklin Roosevelt's New Deal.

All of this is laid out in the following chapters, followed by an epilogue that carries the story up to the turn of the twentieth century. As mentioned, one of my goals is the recovery of lost options in the past, and that does not mean recovering only the alternatives we like. Progressives had a very mixed record in dealing with the challenges of their time. In some respects, they rose to the occasion, took courageous stands, and fought the good fight. In other cases, they failed to heed the better angels of their nature, succumbed to fear, and betrayed causes they had once supported. There are many cautionary tales in their shortcomings and failures, including their zeal for solving political questions through military intervention, their excessive moralism, and their weakness on racial justice. Even participation in the First World War can be seen as a misguided attempt to improve the world.

At the same time, there are also positive lessons. Progressives were ready to take on the problems of the world because they believed local problems had international roots in the social conflicts of the marketplace and the militarized competition of the international state system. It takes an effort of the imagination to recapture all its bighearted vitality, but it is worth remembering the progressive vision at its best, of a world of interdependent peoples cooperating to promote justice and peace.

Remembering these historical options is not merely a scholastic exercise in reconstructing the past. My aim in recovering lost alternatives in the past is to better understand both past and present. In piecing together the documentary record, I have made every effort to reconstruct the era in a way that would be fully recognizable to participants. Yet historical narrative is, inescapably, a dialogue between past and present, and I have no wish to conceal the fact that this study is partly motivated by present concerns. At the beginning of the twenty-first century, globalization has brought back laissez-faire with a vengeance, helping to create global polarizations within and between nations on a scale the founding generation of progressives could not have imagined. Meanwhile, all eyes look to the United States, standing astride the world like a colossus, for leadership in addressing the explosive issues of the day.

At a time when other political philosophies are in retreat or, in the case of communism, in total collapse, progressivism has undergone something of a revival. Seeking some historical foundation for a more vibrant public life, a small army of American neoprogressives have rediscovered the civic ideals of the Progressive Era. For example, *Democracy's Discontent* by Michael Sandel calls for a return to the progressive spirit of civic engagement, and *Bowling Alone* by Robert Putnam argues that a civil society of the sort that flourished earlier in the century is the necessary precondition for a vibrant democracy.[11] Historians have contributed their share by setting aside an older view, in which progressives were seen as a technocratic elite bent on social control, in favor of a more friendly view which recognizes the founding generation as pioneers of social reform and participatory democracy.[12]

What is needed to extend such work is greater understanding of how world affairs worked their way into progressive ideas of social reform and civic engagement. If the founding generation of the 1910s established a progressive tradition in American politics, it is important to know why it originated and what it was all about, and that means looking at the full range of progressive practices, overseas as well as at home, and the full range of options, internationalist as well as imperialist, for bringing the United States onto the world stage.

I believe there is some urgency in recovering these options. In some ways, progressives faced choices a century ago that were quite different from ours. In others, the choices look quite familiar. In either case, the decisions made then have something to teach contemporaries seeking to be both good citizens of their own country and good citizens of a troubled world.

INTERNATIONALISM AND INTERVENTION: With war raging in Europe, a chivalrous Uncle Sam offers an umbrella of protection to a feminized South America in a highly favorable view of imperial paternalism. (Charles Bartholomew, *Minneapolis Journal*, ca. 1916)

1

The New Internationalism

At the dawn of the twentieth century in a climate of hope and promise a new internationalism took wing. After a long century of relative peace among the great powers, it was easy to believe that another century of even greater cooperation was in the offing. Growing connections among peoples around the globe seemed to be reducing ancient hatreds and national rivalries, while movements for the peaceful resolution of differences through mediation and arbitration were gaining wide support. In a 1905 book on "world organization," American social reformer Raymond Bridgeman took note of increasing "talk about the world getting together" and wondered whether this might bring about "world self-consciousness."[1]

World consciousness was embedded in many trends of the times. The openness of the world economy, for example, seemed to forecast a future of boundless economic growth. Under the protection of the British navy, money markets operated on an international gold standard in which local currencies were pegged to the British pound, and the pound, in turn, was said to be "as good as gold." More than at any time prior to the late twentieth century, capital circulated with relative ease across national boundaries to fund everything from African diamond mines to North American railways. Global commerce and investment, in turn, seemed to underwrite a more general global integration.

Labor also moved around with relative ease. In swirling migratory streams, Chinese workers arrived at Hawaiian pineapple fields, East Indians landed on Caribbean docks, and Italians showed up in Argentina. In the absence of significant legal barriers in the United States, upwards of a million Europeans passed the portals of Ellis Island each year, about a third of whom left again to continue their peregrinations or return home. By comparison to later years, migrants encountered few legal restrictions.

One reason labor was so footloose was the advent of big advances in transportation and communication. The spectacular sinking of the mighty *Titanic* in 1912 highlighted the growing scale of transatlantic passenger traffic, even if it left something to be desired in passenger safety. In addition, a thickening filigree of telephone lines overspread the globe, linked by undersea Atlantic and Pacific cables, while Marconi's new wireless radio was just beginning to span the Atlantic.

Before world war pressed down its boot, social solidarities were growing stronger every day. The New Woman, for example, was coming into her own all across the North Atlantic. Like a Cubist portrait in overlapping color facets, the bold model of modern womanhood was represented in the writings of Swedish feminist Ellen Key, Norwegian dramatist Henrik Ibsen, and American economist Charlotte Perkins Gilman. Sisters from across the seas linked arms in a number of women's organizations, notably the International Suffrage Alliance, whose biannual convention held in Budapest in the fall of 1913 heard an American deliver the presidential address and enthusiastically welcomed suffragists from China into the fold.

Internationalism was perhaps most readily identified with the working class movement. Ever since Marx and his comrades had organized the First International decades earlier, the left had posed as the champion of the workers of the world. The Socialist Second International, founded in Bern in 1889, had paid American workers the compliment of making May 1 the international workers' holiday in commemoration of the general strike for the 8-hour day which had rocked the United States three years earlier. That strike also produced one of the first great international *cause célèbres*—the defense of eight anarchists accused of a lethal bombing at Chicago's Haymarket Square.

Although the American Federation of Labor was not known for transnational solidarity, several other arms of the American labor movement signed on to internationalism from below. The Industrial Workers of the World, for example, had branches from Brussels to Brisbane, and the Socialist party was a member of the Second International. American socialism was entering its heyday in the years before the war under Eugene Debs, charismatic leader and three-time presidential candidate.

In this auspicious time, blueprints for progress normally reached across national boundaries. Among the educated middle classes of Europe and North America, not a week went by without one international gathering or another devoted to the cause of temperance, international arbitration, or public health. A heavy traffic in reform ideas clogged the sea lanes of the North Atlantic and, to a lesser extent, the South Pacific. American reform journals such as the *Survey*, brilliantly edited by Paul Kellogg, sent forth the most extraordinary outpouring of reform literature since the antebellum period, keeping tabs on child labor in southern textile mills and the hazards of Appalachian coal mining, while also tracking the latest developments in health insurance in Germany, public housing in Glasgow, and minimum wages in Australia. Overseas achievements inspired Americans to pick up the pace. All in all, modern conditions fostered the sense of an interconnected world.[2]

Although lagging behind their overseas counterparts in some respects, American reformers were notching successes of their own under the banner of a new "progressive" politics. To be progressive in what was later called the Progressive Era meant to support a politics of social justice and civic engagement over a politics of patronage and power, topics to be taken up in the next chapter. But it is important to emphasize at the outset the search by progressives for a new path in world affairs.

The new internationalism had no more enthusiastic champion than Jane Addams. Already famous as America's most illustrious social reformer, Addams was also gaining attention for championing the ideal of cooperation among the world's increasingly interdependent peoples. Her own life was something of a journey to diversity. Born to a Quaker family on the midwestern prairie, Addams had left behind the placid comfort of a small town to come to the brawling metropolis of Chicago and set up Hull House in 1891, the nation's first settlement house. Applying Protestant values and democratic principles to the harsh conditions of urban-industrial society, she become a pioneer in the quest for social justice.

It was not long, however, before she was overtaken by what she later called a "growing world consciousness." Casting off the dovish sentimentality of the old pacifism, she embraced a new moral realism, the view that the economic and social forces of modern life were making war obsolete. Writing in *The Newer Ideals of Peace*, she argued that as people from widely different backgrounds came together under the harsh conditions of modern industry, they were forced to cooperate willy-nilly in trade unions and reform movements. Just as these constructive movements were a peaceful substitute for the "primitive warfare" of class struggle, so Addams believed that social reform was pointing the world toward the path of peace. The epitome of the engaged citizen, Addams was equally an esteemed citizen of the world, and her twin quests for social justice and world peace would eventually be crowned with the Nobel Peace Prize.[3]

Addams' booming city of Chicago itself provided a rough-and-ready example of cosmopolitanism. Although located in the heart of the continent, the informal capital of the Midwest was a veritable crossroads of the world economy. It was the main rail hub of North America, an outlet for British capital, and an entrepot of world trade for all manner of commodities going to and from Europe and Latin America. The Windy City's great meatpacking facilities were famous the world over for turning thousands of lowing steers into canned beef every day through the efficiency of their celebrated "disassembly" line. Not for nothing did poet Carl Sandburg dub Chicago "hog butcher to the world."

Chicago was also a crossroads of world culture. Anyone who believed America lived in isolation needed only to visit the over-crowded neighborhood "back of the yards" to see an international bazaar of European peoples. Alongside a few remaining German and Irish enclaves, there was an increasing number of "new" immigrants from eastern and southern Europe, who somehow scraped together the money to build the same gold-domed Russian Orthodox churches they left behind in St. Peters-burg, support Roman Catholic churches which might as well have been in Naples, and install the Torah in Jewish synagogues that could have been in Kiev.

Variety was not limited to Europeans. Elsewhere in the city, there was also a Chinatown, a small Middle Eastern sector, and a handful of Mexicans whose numbers would mushroom after the war. In addition, African-Americans were leaving behind tar-paper shacks on Mississippi Delta plantations, climbing aboard the second-class cars of the Illinois Central railroad, and riding through the night into the uncertain promised land of the city's "black belt." All in all, Chicago contained an amazing con-fluence of cultures from the four corners of the globe.

Looking into the mirror of their own diversity, it was no won-der that American reformers saw an image of the new interna-tionalism in their teeming cities. Comprising about 14 percent of the total population at any given time, immigrants (and their children) made the United States into a conglomeration of peo-ple from other places, what young social critic Randolph Bourne dubbed "transnational America."[4] Watching the parade of im-migrants trudge past her front porch at Hull House, Addams concluded that the ethnic mixing she saw everyday in her rough-and-tumble Chicago neighborhood was itself a kind of in-ternational cooperation. "I believed," she affirmed, "that there was rising in the cosmopolitan centers of America, a sturdy and unprecedented international understanding which in time would be too profound to lend itself to war."[5] Emily Green Balch, the only other American woman besides Addams to win the Nobel Peace Prize, also held up America as a model society. Evoking the metaphor of an orchestra, Balch hailed the new social age in which ethnic groups—"races," in the language of the day—would be harmonized like the "wind and string instruments in a symphony." All in all, these social reformers held the most cosmopolitan attitudes of any generation of reformers yet to come along in American history.[6]

For many, however, the vision did not get past the color line. Although a few whites, Jane Addams among them, included "Negroes" in the orchestra, it must be noted that many who celebrated diversity also drew a color line that excluded the more than 10 percent of the population that was African-American. Unfortunately, the argument that America set an example to the world of multiracial harmony contained its own color-bound refutation.[7]

Even so, internationalists were often uncomfortable with what was called "the white man's burden." Ruling others without their consent, they believed, whether in Ireland or India, was the very antithesis of cooperation among diverse and interdependent peoples. They were not averse to criticizing their own government in this regard, pointing to the hypocrisy of a republic like the United States presuming to dictate how Cubans or Filipinos should be governed. In his anti-imperialist presidential campaign of 1900, William Jennings Bryan put his finger squarely on the problem: "A republic can have no subjects." The riddle of imperial republicanism teased Mark Twain, one of the more astute observers of his country's often curious conduct. Commenting on the United States' bloody suppression of the Philippine insurrection and the reduction of Cuba to an American protectorate, Twain suggested sardonically, "There must be two Americas: one that sets the captive free, and one that takes a once-captive's new freedom away from him."[8]

Another leading anti-imperialist was William James, pragmatist philosopher and pioneer psychologist. Revolted by the jingoism of the Spanish-American War, James protested vehemently against what he called "the idol of national destiny." He insisted, instead, that "angelic impulses and predatory lusts divide our heart exactly as they divide the heart of other countries." Objecting to the messianic impulse in American foreign policy, he demanded to know what gave Americans the right to "sow our ideals, plant our order, impose our God." Who said America needed to be the world's redeemer?[9]

Predatory lust posed a tough problem for opponents of empire. It was clear that no amount of tender-minded moralizing would ever overcome the predatory impulse. But James had a solution for that, too. What was needed, he argued, was a tough-minded morality that took account of men's propensity to aggression. In answer to both conservative realists and mushy-headed pacifists, James proposed "the moral equivalent of war." Instead of training young men to be soldiers, he recommended putting them to work subduing nature—clearing forests, cutting mountain roads, and otherwise engaging in the kind of hard labor that would satisfy the need for physical adventure.[10] James's "moral equivalent" has come down as the founding statement of moral realism in the critique of U.S. expansion.

The new internationalism faced many obstacles. Fear of foreigners and racial prejudice stood in the way of closer ties with other peoples. In addition, isolationists held up the Monroe Doctrine with its claim of a "separate sphere" in the Western Hemisphere as a kind of holy writ that precluded diplomatic alliances. Perhaps the strongest obstacle was nationalism. Given the division of the world economy into national units, every country did what it could to protect its domestic market against foreign competition. Only Britain practiced the free trade that everybody preached. In the United States, Republicans did the bidding of domestic manufacturers to push the tariff to ever higher levels, although the advent of Democratic control in Washington in 1913 resulted in some reductions.

Overall, internationalists had reason for optimism. International flows of capital, labor, and knowledge all seemed to point straight toward ever-greater cooperation among the peoples of the world. Widespread acceptance of that view is evident in the popularity of Norman Angell's pacifist tract *The Great Illusion*. Published in a dozen different countries in 1910, the book presented an antiwar version of social Darwinism. "War has no longer the justification that it makes for the survival of the fit-test," Angell contended, "it involves the survival of the less fit." To believe that progress comes about through war was the "great illusion." The truth was, said Angell, progress comes about through the peaceful exchanges of world trade and invest-ment. Since these were on the upswing, social evolution was making war obsolete. Right up until the terrible events that would tear the world apart in 1914, internationalism seemed to be the wave of the future.[11]

The New Imperialism

Easy assumptions of a world without conflict, however, were al-ready being undermined by the "new imperialism." Beginning in the last quarter of the nineteenth century, as the world econ-omy penetrated ever more deeply into less developed regions around the globe, the Great Powers engaged in an increasingly militarized scramble for colonies. Pursuing dreams of imperial glory, Europeans vied with one another for "a place in the sun," parceling out virtually all of Africa and large parts of Asia, all the while engaging in a dangerous arms race.

Alongside profit and power, imperial expansion was fueled by the self-serving belief in the necessity of empire. In contrast to the reform Darwinists, expansionists held to the view that human progress was driven by sometimes violent competition among races for the survival of the fittest. Not only did competi-tion strengthen the dominant races, it also brought the blessings of civilization to subordinate ones. In this he-man view of his-tory, war was not a calamity but an invigorating force. So said such military theorists as Germany's advocate of land war Count Bernhardi and America's arch-prophet of sea power Al-fred Thayer Mahan. The pugnacious Theodore Roosevelt weighed in at every opportunity with an ode to combat as the builder of manliness.[12]

In its own fashion, the United States acquired an empire in the tropics. It was based, first of all, on economic power. Having been a big importer of capital in the nineteenth century, the United States turned into a net exporter, with some $3.5 billion invested overseas before the war. Most of that money went to other developed countries, but there was growing investment in the economically dependent regions of the Western Hemisphere. As the hemisphere's major consumer of raw materials and rising investment banker, "the colossus of the North" replaced Britain by 1914 as the dominant economic power in Mexico and the Caribbean, a position that would expand after the war to cover all of South America. On top of this, the United States had acquired a collection of imperial possessions after the Spanish-American War running from Puerto Rico and Cuba in the Caribbean to the Philippines in the Western Pacific.

It is important to remember that the initial heavy lifting of empire was done mostly by conservatives, not progressives. The chief architects of empire were members of the northeastern establishment who joined forces after William McKinley's election in 1896 to promote overseas expansion. As Gilded Age realists, they viewed power as the bare-knuckled pursuit of self-interest in a dangerous world. In the waning moments of the century, they had won a war with Spain, acquired a string of colonies and protectorates from the Caribbean to the Western Pacific, elbowed their way into China, and otherwise thrust the United States fully into the great game of world power.

The same coterie of power mongers further expanded U.S. influence during the presidency of the remarkable Theodore Roosevelt. It takes a long yardstick to measure "TR." He was a pugilist, cowboy, police reporter, ward politician, husband, father, author, warrior, president, and statesman all rolled into one. Driven by some deep anxiety over masculinity, he pursued "the strenuous life" from dude ranches to African jungles, proclaiming his virility at every turn, as in his favorite saying, "bully," and his declaration of feeling "as strong as a Bull Moose." Teetering forever on the brink of self-parody, he was an easy target for satirical cartoonists, who loved to draw him with eyes bulging, mustache bristling, and military "big stick" slung over his shoulder.

Roosevelt captivated the public like no other political personality in the twentieth century, except his younger cousin Franklin. As the eponymous patron of Teddy Bears and the military hero of San Juan Hill, he was held in high regard. A complex figure with deeply conservative instincts that sometimes got expressed in progressive policies, he was the first president to stand up to big business by arranging a settlement of the 1902 anthracite coal strike and by initiating the antitrust Northern Securities case, though it has often been pointed out that his reputation as a "trust-buster" was greatly exaggerated and that Taft actually busted more trusts. Even before the term "progressive" came into use, Roosevelt had earned high marks from many reformers for backing regulations of big business, such as the Pure Food and Drug Act, and for his mediation of the Russo-Japanese War in 1905, which won him the first Nobel Peace Prize garnered by an American.

In retrospect, it seems odd that Roosevelt would be honored with a peace prize. After all, he has come down through history as a bellicose expansionist. Starting with unseemly enthusiasm for the white man's conquest of Amerindians, his imperial impulse carried on through military exploits as head of the Rough Riders in the Spanish-American War and support for the "large policy" of colonial acquisition. His most blatantly imperialist act was the seizure of the Panama Canal Zone. By dispensing lots of cash along with promises of military and diplomatic support, Roosevelt instigated a revolt in Central America that resulted in the creation of Panama in 1902, followed quickly by the cession of the Canal Zone to the United States and the famous boast "I took the Canal." Shortly thereafter, Santo Domingo's tardiness in making loan payments led to the arrival of U.S. gunboats and the proclamation of the Roosevelt Corollary to the Monroe Doctrine, by which the American president gave his country the right to intervene anywhere to exercise "an international police power" against "chronic wrongdoing."

America's outward thrust continued under President William Howard Taft, when the administration practiced what was known as "dollar diplomacy." A key figure in that pursuit was

Secretary of State Philander Knox. As attorney to the great steel magnate Andrew Carnegie, Knox had helped break the 1892 Homestead strike with Pinkertons and federal troops, proving he possessed the cunning and *sang froid* needed to stand guard over industrial millions. As Taft's secretary of state, Knox did not hesitate to send Marines into Nicaragua in 1912 when repayment of U.S. bank loans seemed in jeopardy.

Next to Roosevelt himself, the most influential figure among the ranks of conservative Republicans was Elihu Root. Before becoming successively secretary of state, secretary of war, and senator from New York, Root had been the foremost corporation lawyer in the land, whose clients included railroad magnates Jay Gould ("I can hire half the working class to shoot the other half") and E. H. Harriman, patriarch of the noted clan of influential public servants. To the likes of Root, with one foot in Wall Street and the other in the State Department, the realistic pursuit of U.S. business and national interests was its own justification, never mind all the fluff about uplift and benevolence. Despite his Gilded Age roots, Root was no fossil of a bygone era. Going beyond the confines of "dollar diplomacy," he concluded arbitration treaties with Latin American countries and the Root-Takahira Agreement with Japan, for which he was awarded the Nobel Peace Prize in 1912, following in the footsteps of his close friend Roosevelt.

Republicans like Root and Knox were the founding fathers of realism in modern American foreign policy. To these men of influence, "interest" was not a dirty word to be hurled at big business, but the legitimate driving force of national policy. As they saw it, the international system of competing nation-states was the diplomatic equivalent of the competitive market, just as national interests were the equivalent of business interests. Although foreign policy was not supposed to be for sale to any single enterprise, the wise statesman looked out for the general interests of the dominant businesses of the day, while also pursuing the strategic objectives of the state.

The more the United States sailed out onto the high seas of world power, the more Republican realists began to think in in-

ternational terms. As imperial administrators, seasoned statesmen, and architects of a leading role for the United States in the
international system, they were the prototype for all the managers of state power who have come along since, from the Stim-
sons and Forrestals of the 1930s and 1940s through the "Wise
Men" of the Cold War. Already, they glimpsed the kind of role
the United States would come to play as manager of the international system after World War II. Seeking the roots of U.S. hegemony, historians have given too much credit to Woodrow Wilson and too little to these Republican forerunners.

The new men of power had one foot in Washington, D.C., the
strategic capital of the Western Hemisphere, and another in
New York City, the financial capital. Although no record exists
of their feelings as they traveled back and forth between the
two centers, it is possible to imagine how they might have felt
by analyzing the great architectural monuments of their day.
As a form of cultural representation, architecture reveals much
about a society's deepest beliefs and values. In the age of empire, a Great Power was thought to require grand edifices, and
there were no grander buildings in all the hemisphere than
Union Station in Washington and Penn Station in New York,
twin symbols of the new imperial republic. Opened in 1907 and
1910, respectively, these imposing train stations marked the
advent of imperial America as surely as the classical structures
on which they were modeled marked the ascendancy of imperial Rome. Boarding the train in Washington, the traveler
passed through a grand imitation of the Baths of Diocletian designed by Daniel Burnham, famous for his visionary White City
at Chicago's 1893 Columbian Exposition. Arriving in New
York, the traveler disembarked in a majestic imitation of the
Baths of Caracalla, handiwork of Charles McKim, equally famous as the designer of Newport mansions and many other imposing edifices.[13]

To make way for construction in both cases, infamous slum
districts had to be cleared away—Swampoodle in Washington,
Hell's Kitchen in New York—in order to allow the gleaming
white columns of the *belle époque* palaces to rise unsullied by the

eyesore of poverty. With its barrel-vaulted ceiling rising 90 feet above floor level, Union Station's immense main concourse was the largest hall in the world, big enough to hold the entire U.S. army under the splendor of its Constantinian arches, coffered ceilings, and majestic skylights. No less vaulting, Penn Station was swathed with the same travertine marble that had been used to build the Roman Coliseum and St. Peter's Basilica. It was also graced with porticoed carriageways modeled after Berlin's famous Brandenburg Gate.

The esthetics of power built into in these two edifices were reinforced by edifying ethical teachings. In deference to Victorian notions of propriety, the sexes were segregated in separate men's and women's waiting rooms. There were also solemn sculptures by Augustus St. Gaudens, the leading sculptor of the day, whose classical allegories of Promethian Fire and Archimedean Mechanics would presumably elevate the weary traveler's mind. Harvard's president Charles Eliot was invited to choose uplifting inscriptions for Union Station, one of which mused enigmatically on the duties of empire: "He that would bring home the wealth of the Indies must carry the wealth of the Indies with him." No evidence exists to say for sure whether the new men of power swelled with pride at the nation's imperial greatness as they disembarked from the *Congressional Limited* after riding between the two stations, but surely, surrounded by such grandeur, they must have felt they had *arrived*.[14]

It is revealing to compare the imperial motif with the modern style being developed at the same time by midwesterners Louis Sullivan and his most prominent protege Frank Lloyd Wright. To Sullivan, grandiose Roman imitations violated the fundamental precept of "form follows function." Beginning in the 1890s, Sullivan had followed that precept in building clean-lined office buildings that expressed the principle of rational order associated with modern society, and they became the very architectural model of what was coming to be called "modern." Like Sullivan's vertical office towers, factories also exemplified modernism, with their clean horizontal lines of concrete platforms framing glass windows.

Sullivan's young Wisconsin apprentice went a step further.[15] When Wright laid eyes on Burnham's White City in 1893, he was utterly disgusted by its fake wedding-cake appearance, and he turned, instead, to the honest geometry of the Prairie style. Adapting international influences to his native Wisconsin, in 1911 he produced Taliesin, a masterpiece of republican architecture that stands squarely in the tradition of Jeffersonian small proprietors. Located near the town of Spring Green, Taliesin sits on a low hill overlooking a tranquil pond nestled among verdant hills near the Wisconsin River. With its dramatic horizontal lines and earth-tone colors, it seems to grow out of the hill like a natural rock outcropping. It was the perfect embodiment of "organic architecture" (the phrase was borrowed from Ruskin), a manifesto of revolt against the ostentatious display of the Victorian mansion, and a gauntlet thrown down to the abstract formalism that came to characterize the main line of modern architecture in the twentieth century.

The fact that many have seen Taliesin in patriotic terms, as an American challenge to European tradition, does not mean it was a monument to American isolation. To the contrary, Wright was resolutely cosmopolitan and included many foreign influences in his domestic design. He prided himself on bringing Mayan, Asian, and European influences to the American prairie. A trip to Japan in 1905 had expanded his repertoire of Asian motifs, and a visit to Florence revealed Italian villas clinging to the terraced hillsides of Tuscany and may very well have inspired the location of Taliesin—Welsh for "shining brow"—just below the crest. And so the dueling architectural styles of Burnham and Wright, Union Station and Taliesin, represented the opposition between an imperial mentality and a more republican, yet cosmopolitan frame of mind.

Despite their common aims in social reform, the Roosevelt imperialists parted company with the Addams internationalists in their vision of America's role in the world. To the one, the United States had a duty to project its growing power overseas and bring weaker peoples under its firm but benevolent rule; to the other, Americans had an obligation to join with other peoples in mutually beneficial cooperation. The difference was not between bellicose men and pacifist women, but between different sets of values in which gender helped to draw the contrast between patriarchal notions of authority, on the one hand, and egalitarian notions of power sharing, on the other. Both sides agreed the former was more masculine, the latter more feminine.

There was a time when the major division in foreign policy was seen to run between isolationism and internationalism. Especially after the Second World War, the architects of American Cold War expansion called themselves "internationalists" and went into battle against benighted "isolationists." The argument here is not that the United States lacked a tradition of diplomatic isolation. Rather it is that the opposition to isolationism came from two competing impulses, one unilateralist and imperialist, the other multilateralist and truly internationalist. In departing from America's isolationist past, they moved in different directions, with very different consequences for the place of the United States in world affairs.

Ludlow and Veracruz

To better understand the challenges facing both the new internationalists and the new imperialists, let us look closely at a pair of conflicts—one domestic, the other international—that converged on one another in the same week in April of 1914.

On the domestic side was the Ludlow Massacre. The infamous massacre of striking miners and their families on April 20, 1914, was only one of a ragged string of violent clashes in the mining regions of the Rocky Mountain West. Against the backdrop of spectacular mountain scenery, absentee owners waged economic war against their competitors over the broken bodies of their underpaid employees. In the clash between propertyless miners and the moguls of coal and copper, industrial relations were as rough and craggy as the Rockies themselves, producing some of the most infamous episodes in the annals of America's long and bloody labor wars at legendary places with the names of Coeur d'Alene, Cripple Creek, and Bisbee.

High on this list of dishonor was the massacre at Ludlow.[16] Situated on the banks of the Purgatory River in the rocky foothills of the Sangre de Cristo Mountains, the little mining town of Ludlow, Colorado, lay under a dark cloud in the spring of 1914. Backed by the United Mine Workers, the strongest industrial union in the country, the varied ethnic mix of striking coal miners had set up a tent colony to house families evicted from company homes of the Colorado Fuel and Iron Company, whose principal stockholder was none other than John D. Rockefeller, Jr.

After months of tension, authorities were eager to bring an end to the impasse. On the morning of April 20, with riflemen of the Colorado National Guard lining a ridge overlooking the tents, the commander of the Guard summoned George Tikas, a Greek mine leader to the top of the ridge for a parlay. Angry words were exchanged, and when the commander brought down his rifle butt on Tikas's skull, it seemed to be a signal for the shooting to begin. In a scene that resembled cavalry attacks on Indian tepees, Guardsmen raked the tent colony with indiscriminate gunfire and then hurled torches to set the colony ablaze. The grisly result was some 60 dead, mostly women and children, 11 of whom perished in a fiery pit below one of the tents where they had huddled in a desperate attempt to find safety.

No sooner had the smoke cleared than the battle of Ludlow was re-fought in the theater of public opinion. To counter the great public outcry created by press reports, "Junior" Rockefeller, who was just then assuming command of family interests from his father, took two highly publicized actions. The first was to improve industrial relations. In answer to labor's complaints that his employees were treated like serfs, he brought in former Canadian Prime Minister Mackenzie King to devise the Colorado Industrial Plan aimed at giving employees—though not their unions—some voice in the operations. The second step was to improve public relations. To win over the general public, he hired public relations expert Ivy Lee ("Poison" to his enemies) to transform the image of Rockefeller from Robber Baron into enlightened businessman. These improvements followed close on the heels of the establishment of the Rockefeller Foundation, whose benevolent bequests for public health and education also helped rehabilitate the family name. Thus began the Rockefeller clan's long effort to make industrial relations, public relations, and philanthropy serve the cause of corporate ascendancy.[17]

Progressives had their own uses for Ludlow. Labor advocates held up the outrage as proof of the need to curb the power of giant corporations. That was the central message of Frank Walsh, feisty chair of the U.S. Commission on Industrial Relations, which had been established two years earlier to investigate the causes of industrial violence. Turning the commission into a public theater and writing his own script, Walsh arraigned Rockefeller before the bar of public opinion in a scathing interrogation that exposed the tragic consequences of unregulated competition. Although Walsh was unable to win any national legislation as a direct result, the furor over industrial violence contributed to a climate that produced a good deal of state legislation and extensive wartime regulation aimed at labor peace.[18]

Progressive prescriptions shaded over into leftist plans for changing the world. Playing out their own script, radical demonstrators around the country denounced the Rockefellers in no uncertain terms as vicious plutocrats hiding behind hired guns. Taking outrage to an extreme, a tiny few plotted violent revenge. If big money was going to wage class warfare through bullet bargaining, then anarchists would answer in kind. In New York City, anarchist capital of the country, a veteran of "propaganda by the deed" planned an *attentat* at the sumptuous Rockefeller estate in Pocantico Hills north of the city, while a fanatical cell of bomb makers hidden in a Lexington Avenue tenement accidentally blew themselves up, along with one innocent bystander. This reckless, suicidal act was repudiated by most on the left. Emma Goldman, for example, heaped scorn on misguided idealists who built bombs in a congested tenement house: "I was aghast at such irresponsibility."[19]

Meanwhile, the first major overseas test for the new internationalism was posed by revolution in Mexico. The revolution began in 1910 with the overthrow of long-term dictator Porfirio Díaz by upper-class patriots angry that so much of the national patrimony had been sold to outsiders. At the time, U.S. capital investments in Mexico, direct and indirect, surpassed not only the British but the holdings of Mexicans themselves, allowing the proceeds of silver mining in the Sierra Madre and oil drilling along the Gulf of Mexico to be siphoned off by the foreign corporations who were fast making the country an economic colony of Wall Street and the City of London.[20] Better for Mexico's own prominent families—*haciendados*, bankers, and oilmen like the Madero family—to regain control of the country's destiny and install one of their own in the presidential palace. Accordingly, when Díaz fell he was replaced by Francisco Madero.

Given all that Yankees had at stake in Mexico, there were sure to be loud calls for intervention. In a strong echo of the rabid jingoism of the Spanish-American War, the Hearst press called for a march to retrace the steps of General Winfield Scott in the Mexican War of 1846–48 all the way to Chapultepec Castle, or even to follow the example of Hernán Cortés and conquer Mexico straight out. Business interests also demanded intervention, speaking through the mouthpiece of Republican Senator Albert Fall, whose future lay in the corruption scandal of Teapot Dome.[21]

Yet it was not just the jingo press or business interests who called for intervention, but many progressives, as well. Holding up the American occupation of the Philippines as a shining example of "progress in the education of a people for self-government," *The Outlook*, a journal close to Roosevelt, proclaimed that a U.S. military protectorate in Mexico "is the duty which lies before us."[22]

Not wanting to be identified with the crass "dollar diplomacy" of William Howard Taft or with the bellicosity of Roosevelt, President Wilson initially tried to let events play themselves out. But some of his closest advisors were urging intervention. Colonel Edward House, in particular, had a personal stake in protecting American lives and property, since his family was deeply invested in Mexican railroads, agriculture, and oil wells. When rebels pillaged the Tampico home of his cousin about the same time as others ransacked a silver mine owned by a close friend, House told Wilson the time had come to intervene.[23]

The president did not have to be coaxed to oppose the current Mexican leader, General Huerta. Because of his role in the assassination of his predecessor Madero, Huerta was seen in the Wilson administration as "a butcher." The fact that Wilson's personal emissary probably sanctioned the killing in advance was conveniently overlooked. Posing as a stern but progressive schoolmaster, the one-time president of Princeton University vowed to "teach the South American Republics to elect good men." Good men were defined as those who would establish a government "under which all contracts and business and concessions will be safer than they have been."[24]

The crisis came to a head in April 1914. Plying some of the most beautiful aquamarine waters in the world, U.S. naval patrols in the Gulf of Mexico were under orders from General Funston to be on the lookout for shipments of arms destined for Huerta. The trigger incident was the arrest of a small American party that had gone ashore at Veracruz for provisions. Although the local military commander apologized and Huerta did everything in his power to soothe American feelings, General Funston would not be mollified. Upon receiving word of the imminent arrival of another arms shipment, he gave the order. Beneath an azure sky with palm trees swaying in the breeze against a backdrop of rugged hills, American bluecoats stormed ashore on April 21. Seventeen fell, along with more than 100 Mexican defenders.

Progressives could not overlook the coincidence in timing that linked the Veracruz landing and the Ludlow Massacre. On several successive days at the end of April, reports of the grisly events at Ludlow competed for headlines with accounts of American forces splashing ashore at Veracruz. The coincidence of timing was painfully apparent to Colorado Governor Ammons ("Mammon" to his enemies), who journeyed to Washing-

ton to appeal for federal troops to end the bullet bargaining at
Ludlow. Arriving on April 20, the day of the massacre, he found
Washington abuzz with rumors of war and the Hearst press
screaming for U.S. troops, which, in fact, landed at Veracruz the
very next day.[25]

To many prominent progressives, reform at home and expansion overseas were two parts of the same process. Followers of
Roosevelt cheered Wilson's dispatch of federal troops to Veracruz and cheered again a week later when troops went to Ludlow. According to *The Outlook*, "The maintenance of social justice
in Mexico will inspire us to maintain social justice in Colorado.
The preservation of law and order in Mexico will help us to preserve law and order in New York."[26] In their view, to be a good
citizen meant also being a world policeman.

Other progressives were not so sure. Robert La Follette, the
Wisconsin senator who had the best claim of being the father of
progressive politics, had been a critic of Taft's "dollar diplomacy," complaining that it reduced the U.S. Marines to a collection agency for Yankee creditors. Now La Follette was critical
of Wilson's action in Veracruz. He believed that Mexicans and
Americans were both exploited by the same plutocratic system
that "makes so much money out of us that it creates a huge surplus. Privilege, never satiated, wants this surplus to be at work
bringing in still more profits." If profit was the driving force, it
was easy to predict the outcome. The flag would follow the dollar into Latin America because "weak and undeveloped (and
unexploited!) countries offer the biggest returns."[27]

The left had a similar view of the economic roots of expansion. American socialists gleefully pointed out that Rockefeller
was both the principle stockholder in the Colorado Fuel and
Iron Corporation and a major investor in Tampico oil wells close
to Veracruz. To Ohio socialists, it was obvious that the same corporate interests making an economic tributary of Mexico were
also coining fortunes out of labor in the United States: "The Capitalist Class of the United States are possessed of vast interests
in lands, oil fields, pipe lines, mines, factories and railroads in
Mexico by and through which they are robbing the Mexican

working class of their heritage the same as they are robbing the working class of the United States."[28] The remedy was for Wilson to withdraw troops from Mexico, where they had been upholding robbery, and send them into Colorado to defend miners and their families. The connection was underscored by the fact that troops sent to Ludlow on April 28 had to be transported from as far away as Georgia, because most of the troops normally stationed near the strike zone had been redeployed to the Mexican border.

If capitalists were exploiting Mexican and American workers with perfect impartiality, then it followed that an international struggle was necessary to promote both social revolution in Mexico and labor revolt in the United States. The main organization pursuing that strategy in 1914 was the Industrial Workers of the World. Thrilled about the outbreak of revolution so close to the United States, the IWW put international solidarity into practice in combating capitalist depredations on both sides of the border. The IWW, linked with the *Casa del Obrero Mundial*, supported their Mexican comrades the Flores Magon brothers during their U.S. exile, and welcomed Mexican-Americans into union ranks.

A good part of what Americans of all persuasions understood about insurgent Mexico came from the vivid on-the-scene reporting of John Reed. Eager to ride with the rebels, the dashing young reporter saddled up and headed south into the Mexican whirlwind. On the first leg of a global journey that would take him to the battlefields of France and the steppes of Russia, Reed's odyssey in search of living history is one of the most extraordinary entries in the annals of American radicalism. Seeking escape from the narrow confines of his hometown of Portland, Oregon, he had been something of a playboy in his undergraduate days at Harvard, and then had moved on to Greenwich Village in search of love and revolution. He found both in the company of the celebrated salon mistress Mabel Dodge and then moved on to team up with Louise Bryant, who had made her own journey from Portland to bohemian Greenwich Village. The two lovers became comrades in arms fighting bourgeois conventions of art, sex, and property. Although sympathetic to the workers' cause, Reed was not yet attached to any political party, and his pieces for *The Masses* had an *épater-le-bourgeoisie* quality. Along with his reporting, he achieved fame by bringing carnival to class struggle in the form of a theatrical pageant in Madison Square Garden which publicized the 1913 strike of silk workers in Paterson, New Jersey.

No sooner were the sets struck than Reed set off in search of "insurgent Mexico." Courageously dodging bullets, he made his way through the cactus and sagebrush of the Sonoran desert to join up with the swashbuckling peasant general Pancho Villa. Reed's widely read account of his Mexican adventures is almost a work of poetry, comparable to a great fresco, "a panoramic picture which reveals history in a thousand details," [29] in the words of an admirer. It reveals Reed's deepening commitment to the international workers' cause; and upon leaving Mexico, he headed straight for Ludlow, hoping that the dispossessed on both sides of the border might shake the earth with their bold steps toward emancipation. Like the example of Tom Paine in an earlier time of revolution, Reed's engagement with the worldwide forces of change practically defined for the left what being a world citizen was all about.

Yet it was not clear whether support for Villa was the best way to advance internationalism. For different reasons, Wilson, too, was backing Villa at this point. Did that make U.S. intervention a good thing? In a race where there were many horses, it was not clear which one outsiders should ride. Perhaps it was better not to ride at all. Was not opposition to any outside interference also a valid form of internationalism? These questions would agitate American progressives from that day forward. With the outbreak of war in Europe in the summer and the advent of revolution in Russia three years later, they would only take on greater significance as time went by.

Although American reformers were blinded to the dangers ahead by their own optimism, it is a mistake to cast them as naive "innocents abroad." Engaged with the realities of industrial society and with the world beyond America's shores, they were the most cosmopolitan generation of reformers to appear thus far in American history. They had yet to figure out whether internationalism called for solidarity across national borders or for keeping hands off; but when the Veracruz landing ended quickly, that choice was postponed to another day. As a result, on the eve of the Great War, it was still possible for progressives to believe that social reform and the new internationalism could march hand in hand toward a better future, and that they could be both good citizens of the United States and cosmopolitan citizens of the world.

The Collapse of Internationalism

Because internationalism seemed to be the wave of the future, nearly everybody was stunned to see the nations of Europe lunge at each other's throats at the beginning of August 1914. It quickly became clear that the prewar decades had been roiling with conflict—class warfare, ethnic disputes, imperial rivalries, and peasant revolutions, and, above all, the deadly divisions of nationalism. The contradiction at the heart of the international system was that its own organizing principle threatened to tear it apart. Despite its global reach, capitalism developed within the shell of the nation-state, and property rights were enforced, not through some universal code of international law, but through the courts and police forces of the various nation-states, each with its own national interests, flag-waving patriots, and military machines.

A foretaste of nationalist violence to come had already appeared in the bloody Balkan Wars of 1912–13. Restive under the rule of the Ottoman Turks on one side and the Austrian Habsburgs on the other, the peoples of the Balkans went to war with their overlords and with each other in a vicious cycle of attack and reprisal. Out of the latest round of violence stepped a fanatical Serbian nationalist to assassinate Archduke Francis Ferdinand, heir to the Austrian throne, in Sarajevo on the fateful day of June 28, 1914.

Over the next month, the world watched in horrified amazement as events hurtled toward a crash like a mountain train that had lost its brakes. First came the Austrian ultimatum to Serbia followed by Russian mobilization of troops; then came the German vow of assistance to its Austrian partner in the Triple Alliance (Germany, Austria, Italy), followed by British and French support for their Russian partner in the Triple Entente (Britain, France, Russia). Finally, the international system of competing sovereign states which had been introduced at the Treaty of Westphalia in 1648 and had passed through the heyday of balance-of-power politics now reached its unhappy culmination in rapid-fire declarations of war from August 1 through 4.

As soon as the major nations of Europe started shooting at each other, one-time internationalists rushed to the colors of their respective nations. No one had been a more ardent devotee of world peace than Norman Angell, author of *The Great Illusion*, but now he pointed the finger of blame exclusively at the Germans. Rushing into print with an impassioned call to arms, Angell urged Englishmen and their allies to crush the "evil influence of the German" before Prussian militarists had a chance to crush them.[30]

All sides were carried away by the illusion that war would somehow be redemptive. Looking back, it is little short of astonishing to see how French and German intellectuals alike hailed the coming of war as "the moral regeneration of Europe." Two leading French Catholics wrote a manifesto entitled *La guerre redemptive*; Thomas Mann, the great German writer, later recalled how on that never-to-be-forgotten fourth of August "a wave of deep moral feeling overwhelmed us." According to Romain Rolland, the French novelist who stood out as an early opponent of war, "Among the elite of each country, there is not one who does not proclaim and is not convinced that the cause of his people is the cause of God, the cause of liberty, and of human progress." Whatever the specific content, each nation had its own myths of national destiny—whether France bestowing enlightenment, Britain planting civilization, or Germany spreading *Kultur*. War would be redemptive, and everybody believed *they* would be the redeemers.[31]

Likewise, all sides exulted in the spirit of wartime unity as a kind of secular salvation. In England, said one commentator, "one beautiful result of the war is the union of hearts." In France, it was the *union sacrée* (sacred union); in Germany, the *Burgfrieden* (fortress truce). The war temporarily submerged class and political conflicts that had raged for decades. In a sermon preached on Pentecost, a German minister compared the spirit of unity to the original coming of the Holy Spirit on the first Pentecost: "The apostles of the Reich stood together united on the fourth of August, and the Kaiser gave this unanimity the most appropriate expression: 'I see no more parties, I see only Germans!' "[32]

Enjoying the luxury of being outside the battle, Americans harbored no such illusions, at least not for the time being. It was true that Americans could not resist sympathizing with one side or another as European commanders hastily threw their armies and navies into battle for the glorious defense of whichever fatherland they happened to represent. Hearts of the Anglophile upper crust immediately went out to plucky England, while German-Americans sympathized with their encircled homeland. In ethnic Milwaukee, parts of which amounted to outlying suburbs of the Balkans, 1,500 Serbs, Croatians, Slovenians, Slovaks, and Montenegrans met in Bohemian Turn Hall to express sympathy with Serbia and to offer thanks to Russia for coming to its aid against Austria-Hungary. Russian Jews and socialists, meanwhile, started counting the days until the fall of the tsar.[33]

And yet these ancestral sympathies were overshadowed by the dark clouds of war's brutality. When it came time to ring out the old year of 1914, there was a somber tone to the celebrations. The *New York Times* ruefully noted that Rheims, home of the New Year's champagne, had suffered major bombardment, and that the past year "did more damage than any of its predecessors since modern history has been keeping a record."[34] What the editors did not know was that the next year and the years after that would be worse.

What had begun in August 1914 as a war among the Great Powers rapidly escalated in a matter of weeks into what would soon be called the Great War. Everything about it was great—the biggest armies the world had ever seen; hundreds of thousands of civilians at work in munitions plants; some 10 million dead before it was all over. The war quickly became a giant vortex sucking in the whole world, leading to the Arab revolt in the Middle East, Japanese moves on China, and imperial battles in Africa. All told, this huge swirl of events marked the start of a major conjuncture in modern history, the opening of a thirty-year period of convulsion that destroyed old regimes, spawned struggles of nations and classes, killed millions, and, in a supreme example of unintended consequences, finally overthrew the global reign of the Europeans who had started it all.

For the time being, however, American progressives could stay out, condemning the "European war" as proof of the venality of the Old World. Nothing in their philosophy of gradual improvement enabled them to truly comprehend the volcano of fear and loathing erupting in Europe. To the partisans of civic engagement, war was not "politics by other means," in the famous dictum of Clausewitz, but the very negation of the politics of social compromise they held dear. To say they were unprepared for the war and the series of cataclysms that ensued over the next thirty years would be an understatement. But that is not the fault of any presumed American innocence. How could anyone have been prepared for the most violent and destructive century in human history?

Prepared or not, the more the United States became involved overseas, the more progressives were forced to choose between nationalism and internationalism. Facing that choice in 1914, European socialists on both sides (Italy excepted) had thrown in their lot with their respective countries at the outbreak of war, betraying their own internationalist principles and dealing a blow to their movement from which it would never fully recover.

As they were drawn into the vortex of world war, progressives also had to grapple with U.S. intervention in the revolutions taking place in Mexico and Russia. It would have been extremely difficult to deal with questions of war, empire, and revolution taken one at a time. But between the outbreak of the Great War and its aftermath in the early 1920s, American progressives were forced to confront all three at the same time. Before examining their responses, we should take a closer look at what made progressives tick.

Progressives v. Plutocracy: Thomas Powers, "The Monopoly Brothers Supported by the Little Consumer," New York American, April 2, 1912. The oppressed consumer is overburdened by bloated "trusts" and grafting politicians, while Teddy Roosevelt leads a shrinking parade of supporters. (Library of Congress, Prints and Photos Division)

2

The Social Republic

In the time before the Great War, all the reform efforts that later gave the "Progressive Era" its name seemed to come to a head. Scratching their itch to improve the world, the first generation to call themselves "progressive" began to regulate the trusts and adopted a spate of social reforms in the states. Writing in the spring of 1914, budding journalist Walter Lippmann captured the mood: "Our time, of course, believes in change. The adjective 'progressive' is what we like, and the word 'new,' be it the New Nationalism of Roosevelt, the New Freedom of Wilson, or the New Socialism of the syndicalists."[1]

Any definition of "progressive" has to begin with progress. The myth of progress is the River Jordan of American culture, as deep as the Reformation and as wide as the Enlightenment, sweeping along in its mighty current generations of immigrants and pioneers, practical builders and idealistic dreamers. Progressive reformers, too, swam in the stream, warmed by the belief that in their efforts to make the world a better place they would, one day, reach the other shore.

But beyond that, the subject is not so easy to define. Many a contemporary pencil was broken in the attempt, and, as time went on, plenty of typewriters and word processors, too. Was progressivism a cohesive movement, or merely a collection of scattered reforms? Did it emanate from the top, middle, or bottom rungs of society? Was it in the liberal tradition or on the left? Did it die in the war or survive to fight another day?

Actually, uncertainty on these questions is in the nature of the beast. Coming along in the era of ragtime, progressive reform took on a ragtime rhythm of its own. Unlike the steady beat of a John Philip Sousa march, the movement had something of the irregularity and openness of a syncopated rag. It hopped back and forth across all sorts of boundaries, grabbing political ideas here and there, and connecting diverse peoples across lines of class and culture. Such intermingling in political and social borderlands was possible because boundaries remained open before the war. There were, as yet, no bleak front lines marked by the impassable terrain of "no man's land." Nor were there any hard and fast divisions between revolutionaries and reformers on opposite sides of the political barricades. As time went on, those closures would reshape American progressivism, and subsequent chapters will examine that process. For now, we take a look at progressives on the eve of the Great War to establish a kind of baseline for comparison to what came later.

In the broadest context, American progressives were part of a worldwide reaction against the unwanted consequences of the unregulated market. From Central Europe to Central Africa, big business had come to seem like a marauding giant, a Gulliver trampling over ordinary people everywhere. Social critics of many stripes believed that giving free reign to the market was precisely what had caused the conditions that cried out for reform. Instead of producing a well-ordered society, the market under Adam Smith's "unseen hand" had given rise to extreme inequality, economic imperialism, and rampant acquisitiveness. Far from being a self-regulating sphere of exchange, the market was, in reality, a set of institutions embedded in society and entwined with the state. Laissez-faire was a conscious policy, not some fit of absence of mind. A new policy was needed, one that put public ahead of private interests.[2]

In that spirit, a new breed of scientific experts proffered their own benevolent hand to bring order out of the chaos of the market. Fresh from a stint with the socialist mayor of Schenectady,

New York, Walter Lippmann combined English Fabian socialism with feminist critiques of patriarchy to produce *Drift and Mastery* in 1914, one of the most trenchant commentaries of the young century. Tracing the causes of social disorder to the dislocations of the modern economy, Lippmann proposed to bring conflict under control through a set of government commissions combined with public-spirited trade unions and corporate managers. In place of the "drift" that characterized laissez-faire, he called, instead, for a new kind of "mastery."[3]

Lippmann put a technocratic gloss on what was a much broader reform movement. In a protective reaction of society against the market, Lilliputians on both sides of the Atlantic tried to lasso the giant to the ground with business regulations, social legislation, and labor reforms. In this widening effort, reformers and radicals may have grabbed separate lines, but they often wound up pulling in the same direction. Against the common enemy of big business, they joined in support of structural changes aimed at shifting power from private interests to public interests.

The "public interest" is one of the main themes that emerge from prewar progressivism. In a revival of the republican tradition in American politics, reformers attacked corrupt, money-driven politics where business interests sought only their own private gain. Instead, they rallied ordinary citizens to the banner of civic engagement to promote the public good. The latter parts of the chapter will take up this theme.

We begin, however, with the new social ethos. The most enduring contribution of the progressive generation to American reform was the invention of a *social* conscience. Coming to grips with the unwanted consequences of the market, progressives discovered that poverty and slums were the result of unhealthy economic and social conditions, not individual moral failings, and that improvement, therefore, had to come through economic and social change, not individual uplift.

The new social ethos was genuinely social, in the sense that it was not the expression of any single class or group, but the product of myriad exchanges among a variety of groups thrown together in what might be called the social borderlands of America's growing cities. In these border zones of class and culture, Yankee Protestants rubbed elbows with Irish and German immigrants and with newer arrivals from southern and eastern Europe, plus the first pioneers of the Great Migration of African-Americans. The result was a set of exceptionally fruitful cultural exchanges.

No one better exemplified the social ethos than Jane Addams. In her many manifestos of reform, Addams indicted the modern industrial system for its failure to bring about "social righteousness" and "social order," and as a remedy, she proposed "social democracy."[4] A quarter century earlier, she had left behind the placid comfort of a small town on the midwestern prairie to come to the brawling metropolis of Chicago and set up the country's first settlement house in a working-class district on the city's West Side. Inspired by Toynbee Hall in London's East End, Hull House was intended to bridge the gap between Wasp gentility and immigrant poverty, and Addams enlisted wealthy philanthropists and middle-class allies in crusades against the social evils that afflicted the poor. An intentional, cross-class community, the settlement house was a small but vital zone of engagement, a middle ground in the social borderlands.[5]

Hull House quickly rose to recognition as the premier center of social reform in the country, and it became a mecca for reformers from all over the world. English Fabian socialists Beatrice Webb and H. G. Wells and rubbed elbows with American progressives such as Lillian Wald of New York's Henry Street Settlement and John Dewey, already esteemed as the leading philosopher of pragmatism.

While relishing contact with such illustrious peers, settlement workers prided themselves on reaching outside their own circle. In a story that reveals an unexpected sense of humor, Addams described an encounter across the class divide with an elevator operator on her way to a ladies luncheon. With wry sarcasm, the elevator boy calmly inquired, "What are you eating with today—with garbage or with the social evil?" Struggling to muster "as much dignity as I could command under the circumstances," Addams replied, "Garbage." [6]

Reform campaigns arose from everyday experience in congested urban neighborhoods. As different groups met and mingled, each called out their favorite tunes for the others to dance to in what became a complex rhythm of call and response. Predictably, the loudest call came from Yankee Protestants. Reared on New Testament stories of the Sermon on the Mount and belting out "Onward, Christian Soldiers," missionaries of the new Social Gospel went forth to demand a whole slew of improvements they believed were called for in the Bible, including kindergartens and playgrounds, the closing of the saloons, the abolition of prostitution, and Americanization of the immigrants. Since Protestants were still the majority, these calls were sure to resound in city halls and state legislatures.

But Yankee Protestants were no more the sole voice of the new ethos than were the social engineers. Indeed, what was *new* was the mingling of non-Protestant voices—Jewish, secular, and Catholic—in the chorus of reform. The Jewish contribution was especially significant. Religious Jews called out their own tunes based on the stories of the Old Testament prophets, such as Moses leading the ancient Hebrews out of bondage, the most widely recognized allegory of emancipation in Western culture. There was also the enduring wisdom of Hillel, "If I am not for myself, then who will be for me? But if I am for myself alone, then who am I?"

Secular Jewish ideals were even more prominent in the schemes of reformers. For the first time in American history, the front ranks of reformers included such prominent figures of German-Jewish descent as Louis Brandeis, preeminent American Zionist and soon-to-be Supreme Court justice, alongside Felix Frankfurter, member of the Wilson administration, and Walter Lippmann, writer at the *New Republic*, weekly bible of progressive thought. Addams and her peers touted the contributions of the Amalgamated Clothing Workers union, headed by Russian-Jewish immigrant Sidney Hillman, as a model of industrial unionism, especially after it signed the Protocol of Peace agreeing to substitute arbitration for strikes.

Catholic and Eastern Orthodox immigrants had smaller roles in the reform chorus itself, and Catholic reformers such as Father Joseph Ryan, author of a faith-based call for social justice, were somewhat unusual. At the same time, Catholic immigrants were only a generation or two removed from the collective mentality of the peasant village, and they carried with them traditional Catholic social teachings on corporate solidarity and the reciprocal obligations of employer and employee which had been given new emphasis by Pope Leo XIII in his 1891 encyclical *Rerum Novarum*. Certainly, this heritage was much closer to the new ethos than Protestant individualism, and it had a major impact on mass acceptance of the social ethos.

Class also played a key role. The working-class way of life with its endless round of pooling, gifting, and lending was a far cry from Adam Smith's famous law of supply and demand, with its commandment to buy-cheap-and-sell-dear. In short, it was *in* the market but not *of* it. In the absence of much in the way of social welfare, the front line of defense against the rampant insecurity of the market was mutual aid. Under the motto "what goes around comes around," food and clothing were handed around through criss-crossing networks of mutual support, which included mutual benefit clubs, sickness and burial societies, trade unions, and neighborhood associations. Together these networks offset unemployment, injury, and low wages by redistributing whatever meager resources clung to the grass roots. Even community rituals and rites of passage—births, funerals, and, especially, weddings—were themselves grand occasions for pooling resources. Among the very poor, the basic institutions of civil society, such as the churches with their mutual aid societies, were also important centers of economic cooperation. For all these reasons, working people themselves deserve credit as the true pioneers of social reform.

This way of life with its mutualist ethic nurtured the labor movement. Under the autocratic leadership of crusty Samuel Gompers, the American Federation of Labor (AFL) looked to collective bargaining with employers rather than social welfare from the state as the best form of protection for independent workingmen. The AFL even stood opposed to state pensions and minimum wages, at least for male workers. At the same time, the labor federation came to the aid of society's dependents by opposing child labor, sweatshops, and the exploitation of women.

Responding to the question of what labor wanted, Gompers once blurted out, "More!" And then, in a burst of Victorian idealism, he went on to say he meant not only higher wages, but also "more schoolhouses and less jails; more books and less arsenals; more learning and less vice; more leisure and less greed; more justice and less revenge; in fact, more of the opportunities to cultivate our better natures, to make manhood more noble, womanhood more beautiful, and childhood more happy and bright."[7] All in all, the collective practices of working people in their everyday lives and their expressions of international solidarity cleared the way for a shift from individual to social conscience in society at large.

Although the middle classes were slower to develop a social conscience, reformers responded to the workers' call and forged other cross-class organizations to go along with the settlement houses. The National Women's Trade Union League, for example, brought the resources of middle-class allies to the cause of trade union organizing. Likewise, the National Consumers League under the indomitable Florence Kelley, second only to Jane Addams in the ranks of reformers, mobilized consumers to support social legislation and ethical consumption. Borrowing a tactic from the trade unions, they urged consumers to shop responsibly by looking for the "fair" or "white" label and by shunning the "foul" products of sweatshops, child labor, and anti-union employers.[8]

In another example of middle-class response, Upton Sinclair, an aspiring writer from a family of faded gentry, took his notebooks to a Chicago settlement house to gather material for *The Jungle*, the most influential piece of muckraking literature ever written. His description of the work environment—a dangerous

frenzy of flashing knives on a skating rink of blood and guts—
is the most vivid available to this day. Pouring out sympathy for
a family of long-suffering Lithuanians, Sinclair took his fictional
heroes through a series of heart-rending episodes in which they
were exploited at every turn by predatory packers, mercenary
merchants, and grafting politicians.

Sympathy for the plight of working people drew reformers
like Sinclair to the political left. At a time when political boundaries were relatively open, progressivism flourished in the border regions between liberalism and socialism. Although debate
was often fierce, the line between social reform and socialist revolution was not as hard and fast as it would become after the
Bolshevik revolution. Many American progressives were socialists at one time or another, including Walter Lippmann, Florence
Kelley, W. E. B. Du Bois, Walter Weyl, and Crystal Eastman. A
large portion of socialist party members would have been quite
comfortable with what a journalist described as the "advanced
positions" of the progressives: "public ownership and enfran-
chisement of labor, economic freedom, industrial cooperation,
and political equality for the black man with the white man, for
the alien with the citizen." Even Jane Addams did not quail at
using the term "socialism" to characterize these positions.[9]

The cross-fertilization of social reform and the left was personified by Frederick Howe, whose "confessions" captured the
essence of the progressive temper. "All of my activities," Howe
wrote, " have been part of a lifelong interest in the changing and
improving of conditions that result in suffering and injustice."[10]
Years earlier he had left Meadville, Pennsylvania, to begin his
lifelong journey as a pilgrim for progress. After he settled in
Cleveland as a member of Tom Johnson's reform administration,
Howe's itch to improve was transformed in the crucibles of
urban life. Determined to unlearn the Anglo-Saxon Protestant
values he had acquired growing up in a small town, he put together an eclectic mix of Henry George's Single Tax, Jeffersonian
distrust of special privilege, and, eventually, a belief that labor
held the key to future progress. He even did a stint in Greenwich
Village working for a radical publishing house, while being tu-

tored by his wife Marie Jenney on the latest ideas of sexual liberation. Like many of his fellow progressives, he inhabited the ideological borderlands between liberalism and socialism.

Ginger on the left was supplied by a small band of rebels out to overturn all the foundations of bourgeois society at once. Gathering in bohemian enclaves in every big city in the country, refugees from the suffocating provincialism of small-town America bumped into refugees from political persecution in Europe. In New York's Greenwich Village, for example, Crystal Eastman and her brother Max, children of two Congregational ministers in upstate New York, came into contact with the likes of Leon Trotsky, soon to become head of the Red Army in Russia. In this heady intellectual atmosphere, radicals grafted the ideas of Sigmund Freud on to utopian communism, while throwing out the whole complex of Victorian values. Out went property rights, individual competition, separate spheres for women and men, sexual prudery, and self-denial. In came collective ownership, "companionate marriage," sexual candor, and free love.

The goal of this astonishing revolt was to make "love and revolution" at the same time. So said Max Eastman, provocative editor of the avant-garde newspaper *The Masses*.[11] Just as Addams believed social reform was unfolding within the bosom of a new internationalism, so Eastman and his peers pursued personal freedom in the context of world revolution.

That was certainly the case with Margaret Sanger. Having quit Corning, New York, to work as a visiting nurse on New York's Lower East Side, Sanger quickly developed an admiration for the immigrants she met, contrasting their wholesome spirit of unrest with the complacency of Americans mired in prosperity and respectability. Under the anarchist battle cry "No Gods, No Masters," Sanger launched *The Woman Rebel* in March 1914. An uncompromising feminist, she complained that women were enslaved "by sex conventions, by motherhood and its present necessary child-rearing, by wage-slavery, by middle-class morality, by customs, laws, and superstitions."[12] Even someone as slow-witted as Anthony Comstock, special U.S. postal inspector in charge of smut, had no trouble figuring out that Sanger was attacking every principle of morality he was sworn to uphold. Within four months, Comstock indicted the rebel and had her journal shut down for obscenity.

Not one to submit quietly, Sanger jumped bail and fled to England and the waiting arms of pioneer sexologist Havelock Ellis. Together they tried to take the sin out of sex and put pleasure back in by honoring what Ellis called "the love rights of women." Moving on to France, Sanger discovered the contraceptive diaphragm with which she would be associated for the rest of her life. Although she would later abandon radical politics, at this stage in her lifelong crusade for birth control, her feminist and socialist goals were inseparable. By separating sex from procreation and freeing women from the burden of unwanted maternity, she hoped "family limitation" would lift the masses out of poverty.

Everyone who ever embraced love and revolution owed a debt to Emma Goldman. As central in the radical milieu as Addams was among reformers, Goldman was the most infamous ideological outlaw of the day. Born in Russia, she had escaped from an authoritarian father in Rochester, New York, to find refuge in a world of ideas that combined the anarchism of Peter Kropotkin with Freud's theories of libido and the modern drama of Henrik Ibsen. By linking women's freedom to the abolition of private property, she did more than anyone else to radicalize the women's movement. In a breathtaking view of the human prospect, she envisioned a world in which the freeing of sexuality from the bondage of property would unlock the whole range of human freedoms.

Goldman was not afraid to scandalize genteel reformers by denouncing their efforts to rescue fallen women. The idea of virtuous ladies uplifting debauched prostitutes was utter nonsense, she said, because "the traffic in women" ensnared respectable and disreputable alike. The same economic motives that drove working women into prostitution, she insisted, drove middle-class maidens into loveless marriages: "Thus it is merely a question of degree whether she sells herself to one man in or out of marriage, or to many men."[13]

The equation of marriage and prostitution horrified mainline social reformers. In *A New Conscience and an Ancient Evil*, Jane Addams called for the suppression of prostitution and other social evils in the name of preserving the social order built around monogamous marriage.[14] Although very much a New Woman in breaking free of the confines of home and hearth, Addams never dropped the decorum of a Lady. As a Victorian revisionist, not a sexual rebel, she updated the moral code without changing the fundamental reverence for motherhood as the highest of woman's duties and for chastity as the jewel in the crown of virtue. To the reckless devotees of love and revolution, she would have snorted a loud "Harrumph!"

On one thing Victorian revisionists and bohemians agreed: the heterosexual couple was the norm. Even though a number of New Women were involved in "Boston marriages," including Lillian Wald, head of the Henry Street Settlement in New York, and probably Jane Addams herself, they never dared argue for public acceptance of same-sex relationships. Likewise, the exploration of new forms of masculinity did not lead to the embrace of other men, at least not in terms of a public defense of homosexuality. Warming to the idea of equality between the sexes, Floyd Dell endorsed "feminism for men," but he treated same-sex liaisons with icy contempt. When bohemians brought eroticism out in the open, it was for heterosexuals only.

As it turned out, the new world of free love was no Garden of Eden, either. The critique of bourgeois marriage could become a convenient excuse for family desertion. That was the case with Frank Lloyd Wright, already one of the country's best know architects when he abandoned his wife and several children to run off with the first of a string of lovers. Wright had no patience for bourgeois marriage: "It grew upon me as a property institution always grows, with its mortgages and restrictions and absurd demands that one feel what others declare one ought. It is a barnyard institution. I am a wild bird—and must stay free."[15]

Free birds were chagrined to discover a big gap between theory and emotional reality. Slavish dependency wormed its way into Goldman's would-be free love, as revealed in anguished letters detailing the infidelities of one of her lovers. The double standard sneaked back into the companionate marriages of Greenwich Village bohemians. Max Eastman, for example, professed a desire for companionate marriage in the future egalitarian commonwealth where both partners were free to take lovers without jealousy or guilt. At the same time, he revealed his desire for a woman who would not only excite him in bed but also wash his dirty clothes and type his brilliant manuscripts.[16]

Yet for all their faults and failures, the rebels were a prophetic voice. In creating a new morality that separated sexuality from procreation, they fashioned a new conscience that gave moral sanction to what a growing number of people were actually doing in their everyday lives. Every subsequent leap intended to liberate sex from hidebound repression was indebted to them from the Roaring Twenties through the sexual revolution of the 'Sixties to the homosexual coming out of the 1970s. As the launching pad for everything that followed, it was the most significant sexual rebellion in American history to date.

The same could not be said of civil rights. The most glaring failure of the progressive generation came in the area of racial justice. Racial segregation narrowed the borderlands of contact between African-Americans and European-Americans, while Darwinian assumptions of racial hierarchy made it hard for any contact to take place on the plane of equality. Among the few white progressives who took strong positions against bigotry, Jane Addams stepped forward to help W. E. B. Du Bois and other black leaders found the National Association for the Advancement of Colored People in 1909, a glowing exception to the rule.

In its call for racial advancement, the NAACP exemplified two fundamental beliefs of the age—faith in progress and the belief that "race" was a prime vehicle for achieving it. Faith in progress—material and racial—went so deep that all the prominent African-American leaders of the day, including the otherwise feuding Du Bois and Booker T. Washington, could not help but speak its language. Du Bois saw racial uplift as the "most ingenious invention for human progress" and asserted that "race groups are striving, each in its own way, to develop for civilization its particular message."[17]

At the same time, more pernicious assumptions were also hard at work. Many progressives were caught up in the vogue for eugenics. A joke made the rounds about George Bernard Shaw, the brilliant English Fabian writer, and Isadora Duncan, the free-spirited pioneer of modern dance, in which Duncan offered to bear Shaw's child. "Imagine a child that would have your mind and my body," said Duncan. "Yes," replied Shaw, "but what if it had your mind and my body!" Despite the out-and-out racist uses of eugenic ideas to consign so-called lower races to permanent subordination, many reformers were beguiled by the idea of genetic manipulation and incorporated human breeding in their reform schemes.

The majority of white progressives tended to see the race problem as a problem of "the colored," not as a problem of the color line. They recoiled from the idea of "social equality," defined as the intermingling of black and white, and their otherwise probing social investigations, such as the flagship survey of Pittsburgh steel workers, raised no objection to segregation, either in law or in custom.

It would be wrong to blame progressives for the failings of American society as a whole. It was not Jane Addams's fault that the two greatest race riots of the era—East St. Louis in 1917 and Chicago in 1919—occurred in her home state of Illinois. Yet white reformers should be held to account for consigning racial justice to the margins of their larger quest for social justice. Because racial assumptions were stitched into the fabric of society at every point, their failure to combat stereotypes of white male benevolence significantly weakened assaults on gender and class inequalities, as well.

In a backhanded way, the near absence of sympathetic interaction across racial lines demonstrates the importance of social and political borderlands to the struggle for social protection against the unwanted consequences of capitalist development. Where people of diverse backgrounds learned to dance to each others' tunes, the new social conscience could be truly *social—*

not merely white middle-class morality masquerading as universal values. Conversely, where they did not, exclusion was the rule and middle-class values reigned supreme.

Although the progressives seemed moralistic to later generations, in the context of their times, they introduced a healthy dose of moral realism to a culture steeped in Victorian sentimentality. In contrast to hide-bound ideologues of all stripes, they tried to see the world as it actually was and to improve it step by step. Unlike earlier American reformers, they invented a truly social ethos by crossing all manner of social and political boundaries. The most cosmopolitan band of Americans yet to come along, the progressive generation influenced everyone who set out to change the world in the decades to come.

Variations on a Theme

Even as it was enfolded within world-historical patterns, progressivism was also shaped by distinctively American political traditions. The most important was republicanism, with its embrace of *res publica*, and, especially, the complex legacy of Thomas Jefferson. In its sunniest form, the Jeffersonian tradition glorified the man of small property, the yeoman farmer with a stake in society who bravely defended equal rights against special privilege. The trouble with Jefferson is that opposition to privilege always came burdened with class and racial inequalities exemplified in his lifelong ownership of African slaves, and it was always associated with territorial expansion exemplified in the Louisiana Purchase. When social reformers took up Jeffersonian republicanism, they were embracing a very mixed tradition.

Reformers won their first political victories, not in Washington, but in states and localities, where regional traditions shaped the outcome. Variations on the progressive theme are made clear in regional comparison. Progressivism was strongest in the West, where the Jeffersonian dream of liberty had not led to an egalitarian paradise of small holders but to the kind of class polarization that Jefferson had feared even more than slavery itself. It was weakest in the South, in part, because of the long-term legacy of slavery in preventing the dispossessed from meeting on any common ground. And it left its greatest legacy in the Midwest because, by contrast, farmers, workers, and consumers were able to cultivate a middle ground close to the sunny side of Jefferson.

Progressive politics had its biggest prewar impact along the Pacific coast and in the peaks and valleys of the Rocky Mountains. With the combined support of middle-class opinion and strong labor movements in a number of western cities, notably, Denver, Seattle, and San Francisco, progressive leaders succeeded in turning several western states into laboratories of reform. The most extensive regulation of hours and working conditions in mining and other hazardous occupations was found here. Moreover, California was the only state in the union in 1914 whose governor, Hiram Johnson, was actually a member of the Progressive party, and he owed his victory to a good number of labor votes.

Most striking was the widespread support for women's suffrage. In 1914 women voted in every state west of the Mississippi except New Mexico, and the West was the only region in the country where they enjoyed the vote. They had it because of support from opposite points on the spectrum, ranging from progressive elements in the labor movement to well-heeled conservatives who argued women voters would have a civilizing influence on lower-class men.

None of this made for racial enlightenment. To the contrary, many western progressives, including Progressive party figures such as Governor Johnson, were also prominent supporters of Chinese exclusion, prohibitions on Japanese land ownership, and other racist measures. Mexican-Americans, too, suffered discrimination at the hands of employers and mistreatment from white workers, to which progressives raised only minor objections. Radicals in the Industrial Workers of the World were more vocal in support of racial equality, but they had little influence over public policy.

If progressives had the highest profile in the West, they were much harder to find in the South. Southern conditions and customs—above all the class and racial inequalities at the heart of "the southern way of life"—made southern progressivism more southern than progressive.[18] It is not that the South had no need of reform. Even as textile factories and steel mills brought the New South part way into the heartland of the world economy, much of the region remained a part of the underdeveloped world, a land of tar-paper shacks and gunny-sack clothing where per capita income was on the order of a third below the national average. This, too, was a legacy of the Jeffersonian republic. The tangle of slavery and racism had combined with the plantation system and excessive reliance on the cash crop of cotton to create the poorest region in the country.

Southern progressives wrote a different prescription for these problems than their counterparts in the North and West. Although they endorsed government regulation of railroads and certain other restrictions on absentee corporations, they measured progress in terms of the number of new insurance offices in Atlanta and belching blast furnaces in Birmingham, southern bastion of the United States Steel Corporation. Their proposal for reducing poverty was a compound of moral uplift, better schooling, and improved public health.

Unlike their northern and western counterparts, southern progressives did not look to the social borderlands. There was nothing to compare with the host of activists pouring out of settlement houses and union halls elsewhere in the country. Instead, a lonely band of reformers, such as Alexander McKelway of the Presbyterian Church, Lucy Randolph Mason of the YWCA, and professors at the University of North Carolina, bravely campaigned against child labor, poverty, and overwork. They had little impact. The majority of the southern delegation in Congress even opposed federal restrictions on child labor.

In fact, social borderlands were hard to find, having been all but eliminated by racial segregation. While they disdained demagoguery and lynch mobs, southern progressives welcomed Jim

Crow as a reasonable solution to the race problem and endorsed disenfranchisement on the grounds that it would reduce the corrupt influence of the lower classes, black and white alike. To those who worried that women's suffrage would open the door to Negro voting, they promised that the South could trust "its Anglo-Saxon women as the medium through which to retain the supremacy of the white race over the African."[19]

White supremacy was intertwined with gender paternalism. Far from revolting against Victorian mores, the South remained the main bastion of gentility, separate spheres for men and women, and the sexual double standard. The southern belle on a pedestal weighed heavily on southern womanhood, and not even Scarlett O'Hara, Margaret Mitchell's scathing portrait of a shrewd, calculating New South businesswoman, could escape her hoop skirts. Deep South suffragists flew their banners low. The record is quite clear: left to southern states, the Nineteenth Amendment would never have been ratified.[20]

While the North and West were embracing a whole constellation of reforms, the New South was peddling the snake oil of prohibition. In 1907 Georgia became the first state in the country to go dry, and conversions did not stop until the Eighteenth Amendment was passed after the war. Although progressives elsewhere commonly supported temperance, in the South prohibition was a cure-all that was supposed to lead to all other forms of moral redemption. In calling for individual regeneration to eliminate the sins of drink, sex, and gambling, the chorus of Bible-based redeemers drowned out the Social Gospel of salvation through social reform.

In the North and West, progressivism absorbed elements from both populism and socialism to acquire a certain hard edge that cut toward the redistribution of wealth. In the South, however, the populist revolt bypassed progressivism altogether and degenerated into the rants of Democratic party demagogues. Southern voters rejected progressivism so thoroughly that the future Progressive parties of 1924 and 1948 ran *behind* even the hated Republicans. To those who carried the banner in these

elections, the southern version of progressivism was simply un-
recognizable. Anyone curious about the limits of progressive
politics in the United States should start by looking at Dixieland.

Progressive politics enjoyed its longest run in the Midwest.
The fact that midwesterners led both the second and third Progressive parties (Robert La Follette and Henry Wallace, respectively) points to the vitality of progressivism in the region. If any
state could be held up as a model of reform, it was Wisconsin.
Seeking a middle way between radicalism and reaction, the state
had adopted a slew of moderate reforms dear to progressive
hearts—the direct primary and referendum, railroad regulation
and rural road building, factory laws and workmen's compensation, hours limitations and "mothers' pensions" (state grants to
single mothers). No wonder reformers all over the country
pointed to "the Wisconsin idea" as the model for the country.

The leading figure in the state's republican revival was Robert
La Follette. Raised among Norwegian farmers in Dane County
near Madison, "Fighting Bob" made his reputation in well-pub-
licized battles with corrupt political bosses and self-seeking railroad tycoons. Starting as a committed Republican, he built the
organizational foundations for a family dynasty in his home
state and went on to become the leader of the "insurgents" in
the Senate. He was the rightful choice to lead the nation's first
Progressive party in 1912, but Theodore Roosevelt stepped in to
reap what his rival had sown.

With his leonine head and theatrical oratory—he loved Shake-
speare and had won debating prizes as a student—La Follette
made a much bigger impression on both friend and foe than his
5′ 5″ frame would have suggested. Like his fellow midwesterner
William Jennings Bryan, he stood in the shadow of Jefferson. De-
claiming against special privilege, he carried on a never-ending
crusade to end ""*the encroachment of the powerful few upon the
rights of the many.*" He saw politics as a moral melodrama in
which tribunes of the people battled the powerful. According to
a colleague, the irrepressible insurgent saw himself as "the central figure in a mighty conflict between right and wrong, truth
and hypocrisy, greed and altruism."[21]

His penchant for oratory led his critics on the left to complain that his campaigns against railroad combines, international banks, and industrial trusts were mostly rhetorical. The critics were right, in so far as he refused to launch a frontal assault on capitalist property and rejected populist demands for national ownership of mines and railroads. Yet La Follette was not just another windbag. Everyone agreed he had the courage of his convictions. In a revealing portrait drawn by John Dos Passos, he stands "lonely with his back to the wall, fighting corruption and big business and high finance and trusts and combinations of combinations and the miasmic lethargy of Washington."[22] On the principle that half a loaf is better than none, he waged legislative struggles in his home state and then in the Senate for stricter regulation of railroads and protections for working people, including a federal statute for maritime workers that bears his name.

In one important respect, he departed from Jefferson. In opposing the kind of spread-eagle expansion that had characterized the Louisiana Purchase, La Follette added a creative twist to the Jeffersonian tradition by making opposition to special privilege work against U.S. expansion. La Follette's role in developing a consistent anti-interventionist position has not gotten the attention it deserves. Unlike the fickle Bryan, whose anti-imperialism evaporated in the heat of Caribbean landings, La Follette consistently opposed U.S. expansion on the grounds that it only benefited a handful of big businesses. Beginning with his opposition to Latin American adventures, he went on to question U.S. intervention in the European war and then opposed the League of Nations as a tool of British imperialism.

If Wisconsin was a showcase of republican revival, it was the result of an unusual balance of social and economic forces in the state that favored a middle way. Turning different kinds of discontent against the common enemy of big business, progressive politicians cultivated common ground among middle-class consumers, small farmers looking toward agricultural improvements, and skilled workers in cities like Milwaukee, home to one of the most successful socialist political machines in the country.

Posing as champions of good order against the chaos of the market, German socialists sent stiff-necked Victor Berger to Congress (even when his colleagues refused to seat him during the postwar Red Scare), and pushed the state's progressives toward more extensive social welfare and labor reforms than they would have supported on their own.

If all the world were Wisconsin, the twentieth century might have been an age of the golden meridian in which small producers and industrial craftsmen used republican ideals of equal rights to moderate the special privileges that had been granted to big business under laissez-faire liberalism. On the larger canvass, midwestern progressives joined with their counterparts in the Rocky Mountain and Pacific states to press reform on the nation at large. But before progressives could move their agenda at the national level, they had to get past an oligarchy of wealth and privilege unprecedented in American history.

The National Establishment

With one foot in Wall Street and the other in Washington, the nation's leading men of affairs had a very different idea from the reformers of what it meant to be a good citizen. Shuttling back and forth between the offices of J. P. Morgan & Co. in lower Manhattan and the State Department in Foggy Bottom, the new oligarchs of the New York–Washington axis were eager to lead their country toward regional preeminence and world power. As we will see, regulatory legislation in the Wilson years began a process that eventually transformed a plutocratic oligarchy of the Gilded Age into a more bureaucratic national establishment. For now, let us search out the origins of the corporate class.

The economic foundations of the new class lay in giant corporations. Responding to intense competition and severe price deflation, Gilded Age businessmen fought the market at every turn. They tried pools, cartels, and several other devices before finding the secret of success in corporate concentration. Some corporations consolidated all the steps in the production process under one owner ("vertical integration," exemplified by the "beef trust"), while others fattened on the corpses of slain competitors ("horizontal integration"). The biggest usually did both, as in the cases of Rockefeller's oil empire and the United States Steel Corporation. Andrew Carnegie's holdings were already gigantic when he sold out in 1901 to the world's first billion dollar corporation financed by J. P. Morgan, the country's leading banker, prompting observers to remark on the advent of a new era of "finance capitalism."

To be sure, the vast majority of firms still operated in a Hobbesian environment where the life of the firm was nasty, brutish, and short. The irony was that cutthroat competition also promoted the very wave of mergers and consolidations that was turning the free market into its opposite. When the dust settled shortly after the turn of the century, most of heavy industry was dominated by corporate oligopoly, not small proprietary firms, and the leading businessmen increasingly thought in terms of managed markets, not free competition.[23]

These same men of affairs also conducted the serious business of America's rise to world power. With its immense domestic market, the United States had been the undisputed heavyweight champion of modern industry for more than a decade. Manufactured goods had replaced agricultural products as the country's major exports, allowing the United States to challenge Britain as the workshop of the world. On the eve of the war, it led the world in every major industrial commodity, producing more pig iron than the next three countries combined and using more energy from modern fuels than the next five.[24]

We have already seen how the rise of big business led to a new collaboration between business and government overseas. American business preferred the informal empire of the Open Door to outright acquisition of colonies, but Uncle Sam was not above wielding his own knife against the tottering Spanish Empire in 1898, acquiring colonies and protectorates and policing them with gunboat diplomacy. Under President Taft, economic domination of the hemisphere was underwritten by "dollar diplomacy."

Class did not rest on property alone. Family ties, breeding, education, and other aspects of what is called social reproduction played an equally important role in the formation of the national upper class. Drawing on the bank accounts of blue chip securities, the Gilded Age *nouveaux riches* gradually married into the old pedigreed elites of the northeast, pouring their money into the veins of several blueblood strains: Knickerbocker patricians, lovingly described as commercial and financial fossils of overrefinement in Edith Wharton's *Age of Innocence*; New England Brahmins, heirs to mercantile wealth headquartered in Boston, "the home of the bean and the cod, where the Lowells talk only to Cabots and the Cabots talk only to God"; and Philadelphia gentlemen, smug scions of a Protestant establishment who woke up one day to find they no longer carried economic weight. Before giving up the ghost, these local elites bequeathed to the national upper class their Wasp sense of moral superiority, something the elite never quite outgrew, and the firm belief that they, and not any immigrant intruders, were the true heirs of the national patrimony.

The Gilded Age upper crust were American provincials, in both senses of that term: proudly mired in localism while feeling inferior to the capital. Steeped in the optimistic beliefs and get-ahead values of American culture, they were, at the same time, obsequious imitators of Old World customs. Fawning over the faded glories of Europe's past, they conducted the Grand Tour of Vienna and Rome, gave themselves faux aristocratic pedigrees by marrying into European royalty, and consummated their marriages on a bed of riches plundered from Baroque palaces from Normandy to Lombardy. No Viking raiding parties ever looted as many medieval manuscripts or jeweled crowns as the legendary hunting expeditions of J. P. Morgan. In an example of ostentatious display that would have made earlier generations of American provincials blush, the newlywed Edith McCormick, nee Rockefeller, decorated her nuptial abode on Chicago's Lake Shore Drive with gilded chairs owned by Napoleon, a rug that belonged to Peter the Great, and a gold dinner service from the mysterious Princess Borghese.[25]

Provincialism was still in evidence in the celebrations that rang in the New Year of 1914. Bidding farewell to Father Time, party-goers in New York's theater district danced the "Spanish" tango, the latest imported dance craze, and popped corks on an abundant supply of French champagne. As the clock ticked down in a darkened room at posh Maxim's, heralds in ancient Germanic costume played a fanfare of trumpets, and at the stroke of midnight, lights blazed forth to reveal a young maiden cradling a cornucopia of flowers as she descended from the ceiling like a Roman goddess from heaven.[26]

Before the rich could become a national establishment, they had to convert their fabulous fortunes into the patrimonies that go with class power. In the decades after the turn of the century, a good deal of ill-gotten gains were melted down in the crucibles of breeding and education to be poured out as the golden ingots of old money, solid, polished, and legitimate. In such fashion did the great baronial families—Harrimans, Mellons, Rockefellers— seek to escape the taint of their Robber Baron forebears and become pillars of the establishment.

Recognizing the fickleness of fortune, they created institutions of biological and social reproduction intended to establish estimable pedigrees. Ivy League universities and their fancy feeder schools, such as Exeter and Choate, became the breeding ground of the next generation. After a good marriage alliance, the next steps were to join the Manhattan Club, enter the Social Register, donate a hospital wing, and endow a university chair, or, in the case of Rockefeller's University of Chicago, a whole new university. In place of old-fashioned private charity which sought to improve the world one soul at a time, newly founded philanthropic foundations, such as Carnegie (1911), Rockefeller (1913), and Commonwealth (1918), shared the general aim of the Russell Sage Foundation (1907) of insuring there would always be "an institution charged with improving the social conditions of the country."[27]

Corporate philanthropy represented the enlightened wing of the business establishment. Accepting the existence of social and economic problems, they offered a managerial approach to reform that offered alternatives to progressive proposals at every turn. In place of social ethos, managers substituted an ethos of *efficiency*. Instead of trade unions and collective bargaining, they proposed "scientific management" and industrial relations. Instead of social welfare, they touted "welfare capitalism." To counter social justice and labor organizations, corporate leaders had created reform organizations of their own, notably, the National Civic Federation (1895), a pressure group dominated by big business but including representatives of labor and the public; the U.S. Chamber of Commerce (1911), a pro-business lobby in Washington; and the National Industrial Conference Board (1916), a public relations arm of a consortium of employer associations. The overriding aim was to reshape the public sphere around corporate enterprise in the long Hamiltonian tradition of pro-business government.

Wherever progressives sought to reform society, they ran into the oligarchs of big business, enlightened or not. Progressives may have gone after the "trusts," but the "trusts" were ready for them. Out of the push and pull between reformers and business leaders, there emerged, under a succession of administrations from Theodore Roosevelt (1901–09) through William Howard Taft (1909–13) to Woodrow Wilson (1913–21), an ever-denser network of regulations linking the corporate and government bureaucracies. This so-called Fourth Branch of government helped transform a fragmented set of freewheeling Gilded Age entrepreneurs into a truly national establishment lodged in the New York–Washington power axis. It is time to look at what was happening in the nation's capital.

Republican Revival

Under the banner of progressivism, national politics was undergoing a republican revival. With the ghosts of Jefferson and Hamilton hovering overhead, national leaders from Wilson on down were championing the public interest over private interests and civic engagement over money making. In the complex political equation that was American democracy, many factors came into play. Feeling the hot breath of populism and socialism on their necks, moderate leaders used republican ideas to move American politics beyond laissez-faire. In terms of political geography, advanced progressives in the West and Midwest, sometimes backed by southern regional interests, did battle with the New York–Washington oligarchs. By the summer of 1914, they had notched some notable achievements in federal regulation of the market, and momentum was running their way.

Given the current occupant of the White House, that was something of a surprise. Woodrow Wilson began his career as a Victorian liberal who believed in the Jeffersonian prescription that the best government was the one that governed least. Raised as a southern Democrat, he took up agrarian opposition to tariffs on manufactured imports and embraced traditional Democratic support for free trade. A thoroughgoing Anglophile, he made his reputation in the academic world with a book on "congressional government" which praised the British parliamentary system for making the head of government responsible to the party in parliament, not to the people. The son of a Presbyterian minister and past president of the arch-Presbyterian university in Princeton, he entered politics in New Jersey determined to redeem a corrupt system by bringing virtue into politics, starting with his own election as governor.

The battle of virtue against corruption was nothing new. It had been a stock political stance of liberal reformers for decades. Nor was there much that was really new in the New Freedom, his 1912 campaign slogan. Vowing to restore equal opportunity, it called for free trade, a breakup of the trusts, and a return to the lost world of nineteenth-century competition. The New Freedom was the brainchild of Louis Brandeis, a brilliant lawyer, prominent Zionist, and future Supreme Court justice, who intended it as a call to latter-day Jeffersonians to battle against "bigness." For all its rhetorical bravado, the New Freedom was no populist battle cry. When Wilson said he was the champion of "the man on the make, not the man already made," he sounded more like Grover Cleveland touting the virtues of the free market. The fact that Teddy Roosevelt was calling for extensive government regulation only made Wilson seem like the staid Victorian liberal that he was at heart.

Wilson's main electoral asset was his ability to bridge North and South. His experience as the governor of a northern state attracted the urban branch of the Democratic party, while his southern upbringing at the family manse in Stanton, Virginia, reassured the "solid" Democratic South, perennially worried about challenges to white supremacy. As someone who identified civilization with the white races, Wilson endorsed disfranchisement of black voters on the grounds that Reconstruction in the South was a time of corrupt Negro rule that needed to be redeemed by the bold knights of the Ku Klux Klan, a biased version of events that also received his warm endorsement when it turned up in the1915 blockbuster movie *Birth of a Nation*. Owing his election to the lily-white southern wing of his party, he had no compunctions about supporting the introduction of segregation in the federal bureaucracy.

Wilson almost certainly would not have become president were it not for the split in the Republican party that launched the third-party candidacy of Teddy Roosevelt. If one event had to be singled out as the founding moment of progressive politics, it was the formation of the Progressive party in 1912. In the first of three campaigns for president under the Progressive banner (the others were for Robert La Follette in 1924 and Henry Wallace in 1948), the Progressive party earned its place in history by bringing demands for social justice into the political mainstream. Taking watered down ideas from the Socialist party, which won a million votes in 1912, the Progressives followed the lead of state legislatures from Massachusetts to California that were leapfrogging over one another to adopt such reforms as hours limitations, women's protections, and curbs on child labor. Most of the social justice planks in the platform had been drafted by Jane Addams, using the Social Creed adopted that year by the Federal Council of Churches as a guide.[28]

Addams's presence points to another historic aspect of the Progressive party. It was the first major national campaign to push for a constitutional amendment granting women the right to vote. Riding a swelling international wave, the Progressives were attempting to extend a string of victories for women's suffrage that included New Zealand, Norway, and a dozen western states in the United States. And when it came time to make history by having a woman second the nomination of a major presidential contender, the person who came forward was—who else?—Jane Addams.

At first, Roosevelt had attempted to rally Republicans to his reform standard, declaring to the faithful, "We stand at Armageddon and battle for the Lord." But when the Republican convention went ahead and renominated President William Howard Taft, a band of angry insurgents walked out on the Old Guard to mount their own crusade. Singing "Onward, Christian Soldiers," the Progressives unfurled the banner of the New Nationalism and went marching as to war with the cross of Jesus going on before. The new Progressive venture was also known as the "Bull Moose" party, in reference to Roosevelt's declaration after an earlier assassination attempt that he felt "as strong as a Bull Moose."

Roosevelt exemplified the embrace of public over private interests that was at the heart of the republican revival. Full of contempt for the sordid materialism of the Gilded Age, he denounced in no uncertain terms "that base spirit of gain and greed which recognizes in commercialism the be-all and end-all of national life." Unbridled commercialism was base in its own right, because there were higher purposes in life than mere material prosperity, and it was also harmful to the national interest, because it promoted class warfare, "a contest between the brutal greed of the 'have-nots' and the brutal greed of the 'haves.' "[29]

Running as the champion of the New Nationalism, Roosevelt loudly blew the bugle of reform. Consciously stealing ideas from the left, the "Bull Moose" called for government regulation of the trusts and some mild social justice measures. Always connected to his conservative roots, Roosevelt tried to persuade members of his class to assume responsibility for the less fortunate, a stance that made him America's only Tory socialist. Coming in second with 27 percent of the vote, he led the most important third party effort in the twentieth century.

Despite their differences, Roosevelt and Wilson both came to reject the drift of laissez-faire in favor of greater public control over the market, and their dual embrace of the public interest marked the resurrection of the republican tradition in American politics. The key thinker in this regard was Herbert Croly, whose long homage to Roosevelt, *The Promise of American Life* (1909), became its founding text. Like so many of his contemporaries, Croly began with the "social problem," defined primarily as "a morally and socially undesirable distribution of wealth," which he traced to "chaotic individualism." If the excessive individualism of the market had led to the prodigious concentration of wealth, then the solution lay in using Hamiltonian means—a strong central government—to achieve the Jeffersonian ends of equality.[30]

At a time when most of his fellow progressives were echoing Jefferson's attacks on special privilege and warning of the dangers of a corrupt alliance between business and government, Croly laid stress on the Hamiltonian side of the equation. In his embrace of a stronger national government, he pointed away from civil society, where most social reformers located their machinery of social control, and toward Washington, where he believed the public interest could best be served.

Croly's departure from nineteenth-century liberalism was an eclectic blend of American and European social thought. For the basic idiom, he drew on republican principles of the public interest, engaged citizenship, and opposition to special privilege. At the same time, he relied heavily on Saint Simon's "science of society" to justify notions of social control. The end result was a somewhat more democratic American counterpart to Fabian socialism. (Fabianism was popular among English intellectuals, such as George Bernard Shaw, who believed in the control of society by highly intelligent people such as themselves.)

To be in a position to engineer things in Washington, Croly helped found the *New Republic* in late 1914 with money from Willard Straight, an eccentric banker at the House of Morgan.

Croly assembled a team of highly talented journalists and would-be mandarins, including Walter Lippmann, who was just moving out of his socialist phase. From that time forward, *The New Republic* remained the prime journal of progressive opinion in the United States until its abandonment of progressive causes in the Reagan era.

To their great surprise, progressives were now looking to Wilson, not Roosevelt, as the vehicle of their Fabian aims. It turned out that the Victorian gentleman possessed ideological flexibility and considerable political skills. By 1914 Wilson had modified his own liberal views to support the most significant federal regulation of private enterprise yet enacted in the United States. He also recognized that the political balance had shifted in favor of regulation. The election of a Democratic majority in Congress had brought a number of friends of labor to Washington, two of whom would also be appointed to Wilson's cabinet, Secretary of Labor William B. Wilson and Attorney General A. Mitchell Palmer. (Palmer would later become famous as the sponsor of the notorious raids against radicals during the postwar Red Scare.) The election had also broken the stranglehold of the Republican old guard and permitted Republican "insurgents" led by Robert La Follette to gain unexpected leverage.

With Wilson's backing, Congress created the Federal Reserve System in late 1913. Bowing to regional banking interests in the South and elsewhere, legislators did not set up a true central bank but, instead, a hydra-headed system with no fewer than twelve regional boards. This decentralized system put public regulators at a disadvantage. Since private banking power remained centralized in Wall Street, it was clear from the beginning that the New York branch of the Fed would be the first among equals in making regulatory decisions and that the Fed chairman would answer to financiers, not popular interests. Still, there was some gain for the public interest.

Regulation took another major step forward with the Clayton Act in the summer of 1914. The Clayton Act outlawed interlocking directorates and otherwise laid down the rules of the game for the era of oligopoly. To administer those rules, the Federal Trade Commission was established in the fall of 1914. Behind the rhetoric of promoting the public interest against private wealth, the main body of supporters hoped the FTC would give medium-sized businesses a lever to use against the corporate giants. In the end, however, the Trade Commission's ability to enforce regulations was severely limited by an alliance between big business and southern conservatives.

Such regulatory measures were important in forging a truly *national* establishment. The new federal regulations undermined the old plutocratic nexus between palm-greasing magnates and compliant politicians and created a new bureaucratic nexus that linked corporate executives and public administrators in what later came to be called the Fourth Branch of government. The new structure of class rule featured a cadre of officials equally at home in Wall Street brokerage offices and Washington bureaus; a set of rules for business-government cooperation at home and abroad; and an underlying assumption that Washington had an essential role to play in the development of corporate capitalism.

The characteristics of this emerging political economy had a lot to do with America's geopolitical location. Americans live on a continent and think it is an island (unlike the English, who live on an island and think it's a continent). Protected by giant oceanic moats, the United States had little to fear from European powers and absolutely nothing to fear from its much weaker neighbors within North America itself. Not even the Civil War left much in the way of a military establishment, and there was little else in the nineteenth century to disturb the decentralized, federal character of America's relatively weak state. From the time of the Constitution, upper-class fear of popular majorities had kept the liberal state weak through a set of arrangements that chopped power into small pieces through internal checks and balances, federalism, and localized party structures.

As we have seen, however, recent developments were pushing the United States in a Hamiltonian direction toward a stronger state. Empire building required a stronger navy and marine corps for foreign interventions, a stronger army befitting a great power, an imperial administration to run the overseas colonies, and a more active state department to promote business interests overseas. At the same time, the rise of big business and the accompanying regulation of money, banking, and corporate practices had greatly expanded the federal bureaucracy.

As Croly predicted, Hamiltonian methods would eventually be turned to Jeffersonian ends. Although there was precious little social legislation on federal statute books in the spring of 1914, progressives were optimistic that the rash of state laws prohibiting child labor, limiting hours in hazardous occupations, protecting women workers, and providing for workmen's compensation would eventually lead to national action. Sure enough, within two years, Congress would enact federal prohibitions on child labor, along with protections for government employees, seamen, and railroad workers. To be sure, social legislation came in patches without uniform standards, but U.S. intervention in the European war would further the trend toward state intervention in the economy.

Progressives had to transcend both Hamilton and Jefferson if they wanted to improve the status of women. Sensitive to the balance of political forces, Wilson at this point refused to endorse the Anthony Amendment for equal suffrage. Needless to say, no national leader would touch the campaign for birth control and sexual freedom, since anyone who dared complain about the marauding of Special Postal Inspector Anthony Comstock was immediately pilloried for condoning immorality. Yet millions of women voted in 14 states west of the Mississippi, and the suffrage movement showed signs of revival that, under the impact of the war and with Wilson's tardy support, would make the Nineteenth Amendment the law of the land six years later.

When it came to racial equality, progressives would have to repudiate Jefferson altogether. Although progressives such as W. E. B. Du Bois were among the founders of the NAACP, the progressive generation did not make racial equality a top priority. To the contrary, most white progressives lined up behind Wilson in support of segregation, disfranchisement, the exclusion of Asian immigrants, and the pseudo-science of eugenics.

The record was mixed on public regulation of private property. Many on the left doubted that the republican tradition offered any serious opposition to the capitalist market. The left preferred to look elsewhere—to Germany, where state controls on business were more extensive and where republicanism was weak; to France, where republicanism was entangled with a strong state; to Britain, where the old republicanism of Paine and the Chartists was being rapidly transformed by the Labour party; or finally, to Russia, where Lenin viewed the democratic republic as "the best possible shell for capitalism" and where state controls were about to be imposed with a vengeance.

Yet these comparisons miss much of what was going on in American reform. The progressive generation gave America a social conscience and a more cosmopolitan outlook. Drawing on the best in the Jeffersonian tradition, they sought to place the public good ahead of private gain. Without opposing private property, they put up a vigorous fight against the excesses of big business. American progressives may have been more timid in approaching the Gulliver of world capital, but, like their European contemporaries, they, too, were attempting to restrain it. As we will see, every move in that direction was deeply affected by world affairs.

THE WHITE MAN'S BURDEN.

EMPIRE AND RACE: Rollin Kirby, "The White Man's Burden," New York *World*, January 14, 1916. President Wilson attempts to carry Mexico through the rocky terrain of its own revolution. Recalling Kipling's racist apology for empire, the belief that Mexicans were not fully capable of self-government led many American progressives to join conservatives in supporting Wilson's Mexican interventions in 1914 and 1916. (Library of Congress, Prints and Photos Division)

3

Empire and Reform

At the very moment when progressivism was cresting in national politics, great events were rocking the world. While the earthquake of revolution rumbled through old imperial regimes from Mexico to China to Russia, the Great War in Europe was opening an age of catastrophe that would continue through the bombing of Hiroshima. Progressives were deeply divided about how to respond to these epoch-making events. Seeking to limit the U.S. role overseas, many tried to adapt the "new internationalism" to the increasingly dangerous world. Social reformers such as Jane Addams cheered the collapse of old regimes, while struggling to hold back U.S. intervention in Latin America and to keep the United States out of the war in Europe. Their activism deserves more attention than it has received.

Yet reformers were powerless to stop the tide of U.S. expansion. In fact, most progressives in the national establishment were working hard to expand American power overseas. Theodore Roosevelt and Woodrow Wilson outdid one another in military interventions south of the border, and Wilson would soon take the country into the Great War. The fact that the two most prominent progressives in the land were equally ardent interventionists speaks volumes about the association between progressivism and imperialism. Evidently, the itch to improve the world, whether the world wants it or not, did not stop at the border.

For that reason, progressivism figures in most explanations of imperial expansion. When critics of empire assemble a lineup of suspects, it is likely to include the happy-faced reformer, armed only with blueprints for new schools and plans to combat tropical diseases. At the same time, it would be a mistake to hold reformers solely responsible, not when the lineup also includes the sabre-rattling militarist, the greedy investor, and the wild-eyed jingoist. What is safest to say is that neither progressivism nor imperialism in this period can be understood apart from the other.

Empire as Progress

Empire is one of the great contradictions of American history. In many ways, empire is at the center of American development. Starting with the Louisiana Purchase, the United States swept across the continent in the nineteenth century under the banner of Manifest Destiny, trampling over Amerindians, Mexicans, and anyone else who got in the way, and then embarked on overseas expansion in the Spanish-American War that continued in varying ways from that day forward. Yet, the selfsame United States was founded in revolt against the leading empire of the day, went on to issue the Monroe Doctrine promising support to other infant republics in the hemisphere against European colonialism, and prided itself as being an enemy of imperialism.

The contradiction was only deepened by the fact that outright colonialism was only the tip of the iceberg of informal empire. Expanding economically into the mostly agrarian regions of Latin America, the United States was well on its way by 1914 toward replacing Britain as the dominant power in the Western Hemisphere. The regional relationship fit the global pattern in which galloping development in the world's financial-industrial heartland—what was later called the global North—was leading to dependent development in the vast provincial regions of the global South.

Empire posed a special problem for progressives, because it contradicted their founding principles. How could they uphold international cooperation in the face of U.S. marine landings? What was the point of imposing social reform on unwilling recipients? What happened to republicanism when a republic acquired subjects? Progressives who supported U.S. expansion expended a good deal of effort trying to answer these questions, with mixed results.

The first recourse was to equate American expansion with progress. Since Americans liked to measure progress in terms of economic growth, it was not hard to make the case that the coming of railroads, banana plantations, and copper mines in Latin America benefited a desperately poor region, that is, if the possibility that the impoverished Latin laborers were being exploited by Yankee corporations was overlooked.

Reform-minded Americans *were* embarrassed, however, by a corollary to the economic argument. The idea that colonies, marine landings, and naval bases on foreign soil were necessary to achieve a stable climate for American commerce—the idea that the flag should follow the dollar—had an unsavory mercenary odor to it. Why should U.S. foreign policy be for sale to the highest bidder? At a time when muckraking journalists were going all out against "special interests," the practice of "dollar diplomacy" fell into disrepute.

Teddy Roosevelt was the key figure in putting a progressive face on hitherto conservative empire-building. Breaking ranks with the Republican Old Guard to fight for the New Nationalism in 1912, Roosevelt berated the crass materialism of profit-seeking businessmen at home and abroad and defended expansion in Darwinist terms of civilized Anglo-Saxons bringing order out of barbarian chaos. The argument about civilizing the unruly was heard often. For example, Herbert Croly, the closest thing to an official philosopher of the New Nationalism, disavowed Taft's pursuit of "selfish interests" and argued, instead, for the pursuit of both commercial and national goals through a Pan-

American system under U.S. auspices that would replace chronic unrest with "order and good government."[1]

Such justifications for intervention involved some breathtaking leaps of logic. In the Platt Amendment, for example, the U.S. Congress proclaimed a right to send troops into Cuba in defense of what was shamelessly said to be "Cuban independence." Just as the most brutal European imperialists could congratulate themselves on a civilizing mission, so American officials justified the suppression of self-government in Nicaragua under the tortured logic that they were out to maintain republican institutions. Twisting Lincoln's Gettysburg Address to imperial ends, the State Department solemnly vowed, "we are anxious that the experiment of a government of the people, for the people, and by the people shall not fail in any republic on this continent."[2]

The civilizing mission was often couched in terms of social uplift. Seeking "to advance the civilization of the United States," public health experts from the Rockefeller Foundation fanned out around the world to enhance "human progress" by ending the scourges of hookworm and yellow fever. Surely, there was something to be said for the arrival of schools, medicine, and sanitation in places where indoor toilets were an oddity. The fact that Wycliffe Rose, a leader in the effort to establish the International Health Board, worked closely with Rockefeller, the U.S. State Department, and the British Foreign Office does not diminish the achievement of reducing these debilitating diseases. The conquest of the tropics was not complete without the conquest of tropical diseases.[3]

Cuba under General Leonard Wood was a favorite exhibit of social uplift. During the U.S. occupation of the island from 1898 to 1902, the former Rough Rider turned imperial administrator performed a number of good works, including a new sewer system and the eradication of the yellow fever mosquito. Installing American-style good government proved a little more difficult, however. An American military occupation got underway again in 1906 and remained on and off for the next 16 years.[4]

It is revealing to see how much Roosevelt and Wilson had in common with respect to expansion. In some ways, the pugnacious proponent of "Big Stick" diplomacy could not have been more different from the prim Presbyterian schoolmaster. Certainly, there was little love lost between them in their bitter election battle of 1912. But in combining moralism and realism in foreign policy—the itch to uplift and the itch to control—they were a perfect pair. In proposing to teach Mexicans how to elect "good men," Wilson's interventions in Mexico (to be discussed in a later section) had the flavor of the Roosevelt Corollary to the Monroe Doctrine justifying intervention against "chronic wrongdoing." What Franklin K. Lane, Wilson's special emissary to Mexico, said about his boss—"there is a great deal of the special policeman, of the sanitary engineer, of the social worker, and of the welfare dictator about the American people" [5]— applied with equal force to Roosevelt. As Christian moralists, both thought of the U.S. role overseas as morally redemptive. Both would have agreed with Albert Beveridge, a close associate of Roosevelt, that the United States had a messianic mission as God's chosen nation to lead in the regeneration of the world.

Neither president walked softly in foreign affairs, but a comparison of their records clearly shows that Wilson carried a bigger stick and left his footprints in a good many more places. What Roosevelt began with the seizure of Panama, Wilson completed with the construction of the canal (1914), and Wilson went on to preside over a series of military interventions in Haiti (1915), the Dominican Republic (1916), Mexico (1914, 1916), and Cuba (1917). And that was only the beginning. Wilson went on to intervene in Europe (1917–18), first, to defeat the Central Powers and then to overthrow the Bolshevik regime in Russia (1918–20). It was a record even the "imperial presidents" of the high Cold War could not surpass.

The fact that the dominant figures from the Republican and Democratic parties outdid one another in overseas adventures gives American progressivism a certain resemblance to what has been called in Europe "social imperialism"—conquest overseas accompanied by social legislation at home. Social imperialism was pioneered in Germany by the autocratic Chancellor Otto von Bismarck, and Roosevelt is often called "the American Bismarck." But there is little of the autocrat in the general run of American progressives, and perhaps the closer parallel is to European liberals, such as L. T. Hobhouse in England and Max Weber in Germany, who sought to put a humane face on the capitalism of their day, while working toward liberal republican governments with overseas colonies intact.

One other factor deserves to be singled out for special consideration. Progressive imperialism was imbued with the racial ideology of the day. Under prevailing Darwinian doctrines, it was all right for a republic to rule others, so long as the others were thought to be biologically incapable of ruling themselves. Indeed, according to the notion of "the white man's burden," it was the *duty* of the supposed racial superiors to do so.

That helps explain the habit of intervention in places like Haiti and the Dominican Republic where Americans had little money at stake. Since the two republics shared the same Caribbean island, it was not surprising that intervention in Haiti in 1915 was followed the next year by a military occupation of the Dominican Republic. The strategic motive was easy to spot. The Wilson administration was eager to guard the approaches to the newly completed Panama Canal at a time when Europe was wracked by war. The fact that Europeans were otherwise occupied increased the temptation for U.S. intervention, while reducing Europe's ability to oppose it. Financial motives were also present. When the finances of both Haiti and the Dominican Republic went into a tailspin, American officials were able to impose arrangements advantageous to U.S. investors, including the transfer of Haiti's gold reserves to New York and supervision by U.S. economic experts.[6]

Yet cultural motives were also at work. The fact that American officials did not stop at economic supervision in Haiti but went on to dissolve the legislature at gunpoint, kill thousands, and install a puppet regime points to assumptions based in racial and gender ideology about the right of Yankees to rule a range of non-Europeans around the world. Such assumptions are evident in advertising images, world's fairs, and editorial cartoons, which could not help drawing the color line in support of expansion. In "The Cares of a Growing Family," for example, a stern-faced, fatherly President McKinley is shown with Cuba, Puerto Rico, and the Philippines sitting at his feet, depicted in stereotypical caricature as wide-eyed children with thick lips, knotty hair, and loincloths.[7]

Among progressives, racist ideology was not expressed as hatred but rather as paternalism. William Jennings Bryan, for example, had mounted an anti-imperialist presidential campaign in 1900, but now, as secretary of state, the selfsame Bryan championed intervention in Latin America on the grounds that the United States should play the role of benevolent tutor to backward peoples inexperienced in the arts of self-government. Borrowing imagery from the Negrophobic southern press, the national media imposed a mask of infantilized plantation pickaninnies on the rich admixture of Amerindians, Europeans, Africans, and East Indians who actually made up the peoples of the Caribbean. Editorial writers tossed logic to the winds in putting forth circular arguments which started by explaining the colonial dependency of Caribbean peoples in terms of a supposed racial incapacity for self-government and ended up by using the dependency of Caribbean peoples as proof of that same incapacity.

Racial paternalism shaded off into visions of empire as one big happy family. In newspaper cartoons, American presidents were frequently shown as father to their colonial dependents. Cartoonists like to portray Uncle Sam as a stern but benevolent parent of rambunctious Cuba and well-behaved Puerto Rico dressed in children's clothes. Uncle Sam often appeared in a classroom setting as a demanding schoolmaster trying to knock sense into the thick heads of his colonial pupils. The implicit message hardly needed spelling out: if the peoples of Latin America and the Caribbean lacked the capacity for self-government, then U.S. intervention was justified until they could be taught how to behave themselves.

Gendered assumptions of paternal authority were accompanied by notions of maternal duty to the race. When word got out that Anglo-Saxon birthrates were lower than rates among immigrants from southern and eastern Europe and among

Asians and Latin Americans, Roosevelt used the "bully pulpit" of the White House to sound the alarm about "race suicide" and called upon Anglo-Saxon women to wage "the warfare of the cradle" by increasing the number of their offspring.[8]

Comparing the nation's two most prominent progressives, racial paternalism once again united otherwise bitter adversaries. Roosevelt and Wilson both saw themselves as benevolent tutors to backward races. Roosevelt believed Latin Americans, Slavs, and Africans were all "in the childhood stage of race development," while Wilson used nearly identical language to describe "undeveloped peoples, still in the childhood of their political growth."[9]

Not only did white supremacy transcend partisan division, it also bridged North and South. Wilson's reinstatement of segregation in official Washington raised precious little protest among white Yankees. Playing out racial paternalism in Caribbean waters hastened the reunification of Wasp elites from opposite sides of the Mason-Dixon line. Sounding like a southern apologist for Jim Crow, a senator from rock-ribbed Vermont warned against Cuban self-rule by invoking the legend of black misrule during Reconstruction. "Let us avoid the criminal blunder made in the past," he said, "when we bestowed with unthinking liberality the highest privilege of Anglo-Saxon freedom upon an illiterate, alien race just emerging from bondage."[10]

In shaping race relations, empire affected basic concepts of citizenship, of who was qualified to enjoy the full blessings of liberty and who was not. Clearly, the fate of lighter and darker-skinned Americans was bound up with what happened elsewhere in the world, as W. E. B. Du Bois pointed out in his subsequently much-quoted comment of 1903 where he defined "the problem of the color line" in terms of "the relation of the darker to the lighter races of men in Asia and Africa, in America and the islands of the sea."[11]

True, racial arguments could be mounted against colonialism—some white southerners did not want to add to "the white man's burden" by acquiring new colonies in the tropics. But that could easily be turned into an argument in favor of informal empire, the kind that did not incur administrative costs but preserved economic benefits. Racial paternalism was one of the most effective ideological veils with which progressives could cover over the contradictions of empire. Combining all factors—racial, economic, strategic—the United States emerged with what later came to be called hegemony in the Western Hemisphere. According to most progressives, the result was progress. And as proof they held up the great achievement of the Panama Canal.

The Canal and the Exposition

One of the main proving grounds for progressive imperialism was the Panama Canal. Constructed between 1906 and 1914, in the same years that progressivism moved from city councils and state legislatures to the imperial capital in Washington, the canal opened for business in the fateful month of August 1914. The first vessel to traverse the system of locks and waterways that connected the Atlantic Ocean to the Pacific was a little cement boat, the *Cristobal*, whose humble voyage ended the quest begun four centuries earlier by European explorers searching the length and breadth of the continent for the fabled Northwest Passage.

The outbreak of war in Europe at exactly the same moment had forestalled any ceremony to mark the historic occasion, but soon it came time to celebrate, and for celebration there was nothing like a world's fair. The Panama-Pacific International Exposition opened in San Francisco on February 20, 1915. Like the other grand expositions from London's 1851 Crystal Palace onward, the central theme of the Panama-Pacific Exposition was progress. In a series of pavilions laid out along the Avenue of Progress, the exposition told the story of man's rise to civilization starting in the distant evolutionary mists of the lower animals and ascending through the sturdy pioneers of the Westward Movement to the modern master of the Palaces of Transportation and Machinery. Promoters of the exposition huffed and puffed about modern man's command of the machine: "Ten years ago, men walked bewildered among the machines they had built, and even the strongest hearted feared that the race had delivered itself up to a soul-less Superman made of steam and steel and chemicals. To-day, men have conquered these servants and freed their own spirits."[12]

The canal itself was held up as the greatest engineering feat of the age and a great advance for all humankind. Despite the absence of official pavilions from Germany, Russia, or Great Britain, who were otherwise occupied, the fair's managers truly sought to make the exposition an *international* event, according places of honor to the sister republics of Latin America, as well as Japan, China, and other Asian countries.

At the same time, the spirit of messianic Americanism shone through in the equation of world progress with the national greatness of the United States. Speaking on Roosevelt Day at the Panama-Pacific Exposition, the president who had seized the Canal Zone took the occasion to pump up America's fighting spirits. Roosevelt warned, "No nation ever amounted to anything if its population was composed of pacifists and poltroons, if its sons did not have the fighting edge, if its women did not feel as the mothers of Washington's Continentals felt."[13]

In most other speeches, the broader theme was U.S. economic strength. Had not American know-how driven the canal to completion after a French team under Lesseps faltered? Was not the United States already the greatest commercial and industrial nation in the world? To make sure fair-goers got the message, a working assembly line on fair grounds turned out actual Ford motor cars. In his keynote address, Vice President Marshall struck the theme of economic opportunity, combining references to the Spanish conquistadors with a pitch for California agriculture. He said the canal had been built by spiritual descendants of those "who looked not vainly for the Seven Cities of Cibola," and "whose vision foretold that the gold of the mountain would be excelled by the gold of the wheatfield and the multi-colored products of orchard and vineyard."[14]

Like other world's fairs, the exposition was much more than a trade fair. It was also a showcase of social progress. To civic boosters, the fair was a symbol of the city's rebuilding after the devastating 1906 earthquake. Located near the Presidio overlooking San Francisco Bay on one of the most beautiful sites on the continent, it was a veritable phoenix of civic pride to local leaders. To social reformers, on the other hand, it was a mecca of good causes, and advocates of all manner of betterment, including temperance, women's suffrage, and education, made pilgrimages to the World's Social Progress Congress held on exposition grounds in close collaboration with the Women's Congress of Missions, whose 2,000 delegates heard uplifting stories about Christianizing and civilizing the heathen from Alaska to China.

The exposition coincided with the heyday of California progressivism. Having adopted women's suffrage, railroad regulation, and numerous political innovations such as the referendum, California rivaled Wisconsin as the most progressive state in the union. Prominent among the fair's many dignitaries was Governor Hiram Johnson, currently the only governor in the union elected as a Progressive. Having been Roosevelt's running mate on the Progressive party ticket in 1912, Johnson forged a cross-class coalition based on hostility to grasping corporations and support for California's union labor.

As in La Follette's Wisconsin, progressive possibilities were greatly enhanced by the presence of a strong labor movement, which had brought the closed shop to San Francisco building trades and had actually captured control of city government under the Union Labor party. Economic and political power translated into jobs for union members at union wages in constructing the exposition, plus promises of future support from the state's Progressive leaders. At the 1915 convention of the American Federation of Labor, Governor Johnson assured delegates that "the concepts of labor described here today are the concepts of government."[15]

Yet respect for honest labor was not the only republican legacy California progressives built upon. Updating the powerful anti-Asian movement that had raged on the West Coast for decades, Johnson helped spearhead the drive to exclude Japanese and Chinese aliens from land ownership, thereby gaining wide support from San Francisco union leaders, who were as obsessed with the "Yellow peril" as he was. Whether the tried-and-true method of mobilizing voters against the supposed Asian menace reflected deep-seated ideology or sheer demagoguery, it pointed to the pervasive influence of white supremacy.

Darwinian notions of racial competition were built into the fair at every turn. One of the exposition's strongest boosters was future president Herbert Hoover, then a California mining engineer with a vision of history that hinged on the struggle for supremacy between the English and the Spanish races, or what he described as "the Northern and Southern branches of the Aryan race." Ignoring Amerindians altogether in retracing the history of North America, Hoover believed that struggle had culminated in California in the Mexican War, "the last great conflict of these races for the actual possession of the land. There the meekly religious Southerner vanished like a mist before the more virile Northerner."[16]

Such views were often found in the company of eugenics, the science (pseudo-science to its critics) of human breeding so popular among highly educated white Anglo-Saxon Protestants. Worry about their own "race suicide" in the face of what they saw as over-breeding among the "lower orders" brought strong attendance at the exposition's Race Betterment Congress, where experts on eugenics explained how the newly developed Stanford-Binet IQ test could be used to sort out higher and lower abilities (the same IQ test that would soon gain notoriety by labeling a large portion of U.S. Army recruits as "morons"). At the end of a hard day of scholarly addresses, supporters of race hygiene were treated to an elaborate theatrical pageant called "Redemption," an allegory of mankind's fall under the degenerate influence of Pleasure, happily followed by redemption, when "Mankind and Womankind, enlisting the services of Science, Faith and Enlightenment, overcame war and began a new race upon the solid foundation of physical perfection and mental enlightenment."[17]

If such high-minded pageantry grew tiresome, all the fun-loving fair-goer had to do was troop on over to the carnival midway for more lighthearted entertainment. Dubbed the Joy Zone in honor of the Canal Zone, the midway featured an ethnological panorama of human progress from the primitive ways of half-naked Samoans upward to a backward Mexican village and on to the Mysterious Orient. Whatever the intention, the treatment of non-Europeans as exotic circus acts could not help but reinforce the complacent view that Anglo-Americans and their north-European cousins were somehow higher up on the ladder of civilization.

That attitude was the implicit message in the biggest parade of the entire fair, led by Queen Zona, accompanied by a menagerie of elephants and camels sauntering along rather incongruously to the beat of a John Philip Sousa brass band, followed by a Pageant of Nations that included wild tribes from the Zone, Indians, cowboys, Orientals, and Levantine beauties. It all ended with a bang with the blowing up of a battleship in the harbor.[18]

At first, it might seem there was little to connect the highblown fantasy of the exposition with the biggest ditch in the Western Hemisphere, 43 miles of concrete locks and waterways through malaria-infested swamps across the Isthmus of Panama. Yet there was more of the exposition in the canal than first appeared, for assumptions about the superiority of Anglo-Saxon civilization had been transplanted to the soil of Central America to nurture the artificial society that grew up in the Canal Zone during construction from 1906 to 1914. The social order that developed there was an exotic hybrid, part temperate, part tropical, that combined capitalist division of labor, white supremacy, and military hierarchy with Panamanian and West Indian ways of life in a remarkable two-class system that segregated workers and their families into gold and silver payrolls.[19]

The Yankee chapter in the story of the canal begins with President Roosevelt's seizure of the Isthmus of Panama from Colombia in his landmark act of empire building. Inspired by Alfred Thayer Mahan's *The Influence of Sea Power upon History*, Roosevelt very much wanted to quicken the navy's ability to shuttle between the Atlantic and Pacific Oceans at one of the world's most vital choke points. A local coup d'etat under his sponsorship led, in astonishingly short order, to Panamanian secession, diplomatic recognition, a treaty ceding the Zone to the United States, and the famous boast, "I took the Canal." Plans were quickly drawn up under U.S. Army Colonel George Goethals for a system of double locks and gun emplacements to guarantee the navy rapid and safe passage.

What began as a strategic military undertaking turned into the greatest construction project in the world on a scale that compared with the pyramids. With a virtually unlimited supply of capital from the federal government and all the necessary technology already at hand, the biggest problem facing the Isthmus Canal Commission (ICC) was labor: how to recruit a labor force that would survive appalling working conditions, social isolation, and tropical diseases in the steaming jungles of Panama. In addressing the problem of labor scarcity, the ICC came up against the same basic problem that had plagued the Americas ever since Europeans had started prospecting for gold and wound up enslaving millions of African laborers on cash crop plantations. Although slavery was thankfully no longer an option, Uncle Sam had never undertaken such a vast construction project in his new tropical empire, and no one knew at the outset how the labor problem would be solved.

The labor force came from the four corners of the earth. The largest contingent was comprised of the West Indian offspring of African slaves, and there was a sizable group of mestizos of Amerindian and Spanish descent, along with a handful of Chinese and South Asians. Supervisory personnel were usually Yankees of German and other European backgrounds. The fact that this marble cake of many cultures could congregate in one small spot spoke volumes about global interconnections.

Some of the most advanced forms of labor discipline were not really suited to moving millions of tons of Panamanian rock with dynamite and shovel. Although military engineers were almost certainly familiar with the new techniques of scientific management, time-and-motion study, and the assembly line, it was not practical to apply the new work disciplines of the "second" Industrial Revolution to such a sprawling construction project. Instead, the ICC relied on other forms of control more familiar to the region's agriculture and railroad construction projects—the impersonal discipline of the labor market, the bark of the straw boss, and the white sheriff and his chain gang.

These class and racial forms of discipline were common to cash-crop agriculture in the Caribbean, Central America, and the American South, and the Army had some prior experience adapting these agrarian disciplines to large construction projects. In building and repairing dikes along the Mississippi River, the Army Corps of Engineers had used racially based plantation labor, and closer to hand, the railroad across the isthmus had been built with a racially divided labor force that bowed to the intense color-consciousness of Panamanian culture. In addition, the ICC relied on military authority, treating civilian supervisors as equivalent to military officers in charge of enlisted men. After some trial and error, the ICC assembled all these influences into what amounted to a 553-square-mile company town run by U.S. military authorities under what Goethals made no bones about calling "an autocratic government."

The most remarkable thing about this government-owned company town was the infamous two-class system of gold and silver payrolls. Gold workers were a privileged minority of white Americans in skilled or supervisory roles who had been recruited with promises of premium pay and authority; silver workers were a subjugated majority of mostly West Indian laborers brought in because the number of Spanish-speakers living in Colón and Panama City was inadequate to the task, and because European immigrants were prone to strikes.

A number of interests converged to create the gold-silver system. Although it bore strong resemblance to Jim Crow in the American South, most of the architects of the system were northerners, including Goethals (New York) and chief sanitary engineer William Gorgas (Maine). As one observer wrote, "Any northerner can say 'nigger' as glibly as a Carolinian, and growl if one of them steps on his shadow."[20] As military men, the engineers were also thoroughly familiar with racial segregation at a time when African-American units invariably came under the command of white officers. In addition, white workers set aside any notions of universal solidarity and used white supremacist arguments to reserve the gold roll exclusively for skilled whites, a demand for exclusion of both West Indians and Europeans that was consistent with AFL acceptance of racial segregation in the ranks of craft unions and its current nativist campaign for immigration restriction in the United States.

The gold-and-silver line ran through everything in the Zone. Like Jim Crow, it determined pay rates for silver workers (half), promotion opportunities (none), housing (inferior), and social life (segregated). It meant that silver children went to overcrowded, second-rate schools, and to add insult to injury, it meant that silver workers were required to pay for gold schools, because gold workers were exempt from taxation! Indirectly, it also killed West Indians at four times the rate of other workers through harsher working conditions and second-class medical treatment. All in all, the two-tier system harked back to slavery and looked forward to the apartheid regime of South Africa.

The fact that an apartheid system was being constructed in Panama under official U.S. auspices just as progressivism was coming into its own had a significant impact both on the canal and on American progressivism. With the American press eagerly reporting every blast through the Culebra Cut and each step to eradicate malaria, it was not enough to make the dirt fly; there was also pressure on the ICC to get in step with social progress. It had to become industrial relations expert, social engineer, educational administrator, and public health official all rolled into one. Goethals was frequently called upon to demonstrate American benevolence by pointing to improved sanitation and declining accident rates, even if the statistics did not always confirm the point. In response to criticism from moral reformers, Goethals was forced to defend the importation of West Indian women against accusations that American taxpayers were procuring prostitutes for canal employees. He sent affidavits to a congressional committee swearing that the women were of good moral character. The fact that imperial apartheid could be justified in *progressive* terms reinforced the self-image among America's leaders that Anglo-Saxon rule over darker peoples was in and of itself a step forward in the march of progress.

From the perspective of the silver roll, the idea of Canal-as-progress was a little harder to swallow. True, to the desperately poor migrant laborers from Barbados and Jamaica, the silver roll could seem like something of a step up. "Most of us came from our homelands in search of work and improvements," said one immigrant. "We turned out to be pioneers in a foreign land." Even so, the indignity of second-class status was etched deeply in popular memory, reappearing decades later in popular ballads lamenting the oppressive system, such as "West Indian Man," sung by Ruben Blades in the 1990s: "You got paid in silver, the white man in gold / And the yellow fever took everyone's soul."[21]

One immediate consequence of blatant discrimination was to swell support for the powerful upsurge of black nationalism that was about to catapult Marcus Garvey to leadership of the largest pan-African movement in history. To generations of Africans living in the New World, the Gulf of Mexico and the Caribbean constituted one giant sea of misery where the descendants of African slaves still suffered oppressive labor conditions, ranging from the dock labor of New Orleans to the lowland agriculture of Venezuela and from the banana plantations of Central America back to the sugar cane fields of the West Indies.

Setting out from his native Jamaica in 1909, Garvey sailed around this sea as an itinerant preacher of racial uplift among West Indian laboring communities from Honduras to Colombia. During a sojourn in Panama, he helped establish a newspaper to speak for the silver roll workers caught between the oppression of the Yankee authorities and the hostility of the Spanish-speaking Panamanians, who thought themselves superior to West Indians. As a subject of the British crown, he called upon British consuls to protect West Indian laborers, but to no avail, and, eventually, he gravitated to London, where he collaborated with other aggrieved colonials in projects aimed at imperial reform. Finally, on the eve of the war, he returned to Jamaica in July 1914 to establish the Universal Negro Improvement Association, a fitting close to his remarkable odyssey.

Garvey's journey was also a cultural one. Starting in the West Indian caste system where light skin and European connections were marks of high status, Garvey traveled across color lines to embrace the beauty of black Africa. Recalling his break with the pigmentocracy, he wrote, "I had to decide whether to please my friends and be one of the 'black-whites' of Jamaica, and be reasonably prosperous, or come out openly, and help improve and protect the integrity of the black millions, and suffer. I decided to do the latter."[22]

Over the next two decades, Garvey's UNIA became the primary vehicle for translating the experience of racial and class oppression into a black nationalist movement that spread out from the West Indies to touch the entire Atlantic littoral with the message of pride in African ancestry—"Back to Africa"—and uplift for the African race from Liberia to Colón to Harlem—"Up, you mighty race, you can accomplish what you will!" When Garvey moved his headquarters to Harlem in 1916, it was clear that colonial subjects were determined to avenge themselves for oppression epitomized by the gold-and-silver system.

Opponents of Empire and War

At the beginning of 1914, few Americans gave much thought to imperial conquest. The bitter disputes over colonial policy in the wake of the Spanish-American War were a fading memory, and there was, as yet, no intervention in Mexico or in Russia to divide the country. In that lull between wars, the common arguments for empire—national mission, white man's burden, economic interest, world progress—had little trouble carrying the day.

That does not mean there was no criticism of U.S. foreign policy. As we have seen, "dollar diplomacy" came under attack for putting American foreign policy up for sale, and a handful of progressives, most prominently, Robert La Follette, picked up the argument of the anti-imperialists that running the hemisphere from the deck of a gunboat was an unacceptable infringement of republican principles.

Yet even critics of "dollar diplomacy" had no clear vision of a division of the world into developed and dependent regions. Few Americans paid much attention to theories of imperialism being developed by J. H. Hobson and Karl Kautsky (let alone V. I. Lenin) in which the export of surplus capital was the lynchpin of empire. And although there was an active peace movement, the peace societies were honeycombed with pacifist sentimentality and wishful thinking about international law and arbitration.

That situation was about to change, however. Beginning with Mexico (1910), China (1911), and Russia (1917), Americans were forced to come to terms with revolution (to be discussed in the next section and in chapter 5). And at the same time, beginning in August 1914, they were forced to deal with war in Europe. At the outset of the European war, they were in a highly fortunate position. As a neutral people with few colonial claims outside the Western Hemisphere, their peace efforts seemed untainted by self-interest. When the increasing brutality of the war machine made mincemeat of the ideals of Western civilization, they could stand forth as the keepers of Western conscience, a role well suited to people who believed in redeeming the world by the force of moral example.

The earliest organized opposition to war came from the ranks of the women's rights movement. Before the month of August was out, New York suffragists had mounted a silent parade in somber protest against violence, and over the next several months American suffragists were galvanized into action by their European sisters, Rosika Schwimmer, Hungarian cofounder of the International Woman Suffrage Alliance, and Emmeline Pethick-Lawrence, a militant English suffragist. The budding peace movement took full advantage of internationalism in the women's movement. As long ago as the antislavery conventions of the 1840s, women had forged transnational alliances, which deepened through the struggles for temperance, social hygiene, and women's suffrage. In the fall of 1914, after national speaking tours, pacifist demonstrations, and an audience with the president (Wilson was polite), Carrie Chapman Catt, head of the International Woman Suffrage Alliance, was ready to enlist Jane Addams in a call for a women's peace convention.[23]

Meeting in Washington on January 10, 1915, the Woman's Peace party brought together suffragists, feminists, club women, and a striking array of organizations from the Socialist party through the Women's Christian Temperance Union to the Daughters of the American Revolution.[24] Confronting the question of why there should be a *woman's* peace organization, the delegates walked a fine line in feminist debate between equality and difference. Claiming to represent "the mother half of humanity," their speeches and manifestos exuded maternalist ideology. Appeals to motherhood were certain to stir powerful feelings of female virtue and maternal love. Certainly, the imagery of mother-protector helped make "I Didn't Raise My Boy to Be a Soldier" ("I brought him up to be my pride and joy") perhaps the most popular antiwar song of all time. If love ever had a chance to shape foreign policy, maternalism was its most promising avenue of influence.

Yet in good pragmatic fashion, the basis of their appeal was not sentimentality but *experience*. Instead of invoking some metaphysical concept of Mother, the Woman's Peace party emphasized women's biological and social roles as custodians of life. Speaking as human beings who were sometimes mothers, they emphasized the humanitarian values that grew out of their work in the care of the helpless and the unfortunate. Claiming no innate moral superiority, they professed a special moral passion of revolt against both the cruelty and the waste of war. In this spirit, they advanced a set of pacifist demands, including an immediate conference of neutral nations, universal disarmament, a concert of nations to supercede the balance of power, and, for good measure, women's suffrage. The New Woman had entered many realms formerly closed on the basis of sex. Why not diplomacy?[25]

Jane Addams put all of her considerable prestige on the line as she entered the male world of diplomacy to become a prime symbol of international peace (for which she would eventually win a Nobel Peace Prize in 1931). She led an American delegation to the women's peace convention in The Hague in the spring of 1915, braving official obstacles and nationalist hatreds to bring together women from both the Allied nations and the Central Powers. There was solemn discussion of a concert of nations, universal disarmament, and the rights of smaller nations, ideas that would all work their way into the major peace proposals over the next few years.

Although the Hague conference had no perceptible effect on European diplomacy, it was hailed by supporters such as Crystal Eastman as a great sign of progress: "The fact that women of the warring nations met and discussed the war problems sanely and in friendship while all their male relatives were out shooting each other is to my mind a great and significant event in history—significant in the history of human progress and . . . of women's progress." All the same, the best the Hague delegates could do was to promise to meet again after the war, which, in fact, they did in 1919 to found the Women's International League for Peace and Freedom.[26]

Meanwhile, social reformers tried to align peace with social progress. Concerned about rising demands for military preparedness, the cream of social reformers met in New York in November 1915 to counter what they regarded as a threat to social welfare and American democracy.[27] Key leaders all trod the borders between socialism and progressivism, including Lillian Wald, head of the settlement house, Paul Kellogg of the *Survey*, and Florence Kelley of the National Consumers League.

They chose the young Crystal Eastman to be the sparkplug of the new organization. Eastman personified the woman rebel of the Progressive Era. The child of *two* Congregational ministers, she grew up with the American creed of liberty and equality. Applying the creed to women's situation made her a feminist, and applying it to the brutal conditions of urban-industrial life made her a socialist. She won acclaim as a social investigator of industrial accidents and acquired a lifelong attachment to the emancipation of women and wage-workers. As a humanist-socialist-feminist-pacifist, she was a living embodiment of the hybrid quality of progressivism as a blend of liberalism and socialism.[28]

Frustrated by the shilly-shallying of the Wilson administration, pacifists latched on to an idea for a people's peace mission to war-torn Europe. The idea for a Peace Ship was hatched by the impetuous Rosika Schwimmer, and chief promoter Louis Lochner turned to Henry Ford for financial backing. Although more crackpot than critic, the Flivver King was thought to be sympathetic to social reform because of his well-known hostility to bankers and his famous $5 day. The quixotic peace quest appealed to the Detroit manufacturer, who once said he would sooner burn down his factories than see them used for war production (never mind the fact that the Ford plant in Britain was already producing vehicles used in the Dardanelles campaign).[29]

With a rag-tag band of peace crusaders aboard, including some of the Hague women, minus Jane Addams, the Peace Ship embarked from a New York pier in early December as the band played—what else?—"Onward, Christian Soldiers." Although the mission stirred some interest in Europe's tiny pacifist circles, it quickly fizzled. It would be the last time American reformers were permitted to intervene in the European conflict. The next time Americans intervened, it would be with bayonets.

The Mexican Revolution

Alongside war in Europe, Americans had to respond to revolution in Asia and Latin America. If the overthrow of the Manchu dynasty in China was at some remove, the overthrow of dictatorship in Mexico in 1910 and the subsequent social upheaval sent a shock wave throughout the Americas that could not be ignored. Seeking to shape the Mexican Revolution to his own design, President Wilson sent American troops into Mexico at Veracruz in 1914 and again in 1916 in the Punitive Expedition.

From this point until the last decade of the century, revolution entered deeply into American history as revolutionary upheavals convulsed eastern Europe and became pandemic in the colonial regions of the globe from Latin America to southeast Asia, where even the poorest of peoples in the most impoverished regions could make Yankees react.

The American response to revolution was shaped by the same divided legacy that had caused Mark Twain to wonder whether there were two Americas, "one that sets the captive free, and one that takes a once-captive's new freedom away from him."[30] In some ways, Americans carried on in the manner of imperial conquest and stood ready to oppose radical change in Mexico. In other respects, they followed the Spirit of '76 and welcomed the overthrow of autocrats like Porfirio Díaz. Although the United States would become the greatest counterrevolutionary force in the world after 1945, it would be a mistake to read that later stance into American actions of the early part of the century. From Sun Yatsen's China and Kerensky's Russia to the Weimar Republic, the line between reform and revolution was not a brick wall, and, under certain circumstances, many progressives, including President Wilson, supported republican revolution.

Mexico was the first testing ground of the American response to revolution. The long frontier between the two countries was both a barrier and a borderland, a zone of interaction between two quite different peoples who shared geography, ecology, economy, and history. Interpenetration of opposites was the very nature of borderlands along the Rio Bravo/Rio Grande, where Mexican and American ways intermingled. Much of the territory incorporated into the United States after the Mexican-American war of 1846–48 retained its Mexican flavor in everything from regional food to place names for Los Angeles and San Francisco. Even their cultural differences united the two peoples in a dialectic of opposites, as Anglo and Mexican, gringo and *tejano*, each found their identity against the other.[31] Like a family bond that could not be broken, Mexicans and Americans were forever tied to one another. Whether that was a blessing or a curse has always been debated. "Poor Mexico," moaned Porfirio Díaz, "so far from God, so close to the United States."

Economies were also interconnected. The same American-based mining corporations that dug copper from the cactus-covered foothills of the Rocky Mountains in southern Arizona also operated in Sonora, where the mountains were called Sierra Madre. Standard Oil, Phelps Dodge, and other hard-driving corporations exploited the labor and mineral wealth of both regions with sublime impartiality. For example, the Guggenheims' American Smelting and Refining Company paid $7 million more in dividends than in wages in 1916, with profits taken from both sides of the border. Nor did corporate executives hesitate to call upon the ruthless rifles of the Arizona Rangers on one side of the border and the notoriously brutal Mexican *Rurales* on the other.

In a regional variant of the global North-South divide, economic relations were anything but an equal exchange. U.S. investments in Mexico, direct and indirect, surpassed not only the British but the investment capital of Mexicans themselves. In addition, the huge U.S. domestic market absorbed fully 90 percent of exports from Mexico by 1920.[32] While Yankee capital flowed south, a gathering stream of dispossessed Mexican laborers flowed north. In what had been Mexican territory in their grandparents' day, Mexican immigrants comprised the majority of pick-and-shovel men on railroads and of common laborers in coal and metal mines in the southwestern United States. Immigration regulations were but an inconvenience to booming agribusinessmen and mine owners whose labor recruiting gave the main stimulus to the doubling of the Mexican-American population in the Southwest each decade between 1900 and 1930.[33]

Cross-border connections were especially vivid in twin towns, such as Tijuana and San Diego, and Ciudad Juárez and El Paso. Mexicans and Americans depicted the physical appearance of border towns in terms of the same polar opposites: cleanliness and order on one side, dirt and disorder on the other. Looking north with a half-admiring eye, Martin Luis Guzman confessed ruefully that Ciudad Juárez was a sad sight, especially when compared with "the bright orderliness of that opposite riverbank, close but foreign." To cross from Mexican Nogales to Nogales, Arizona, was to move from poverty to plenty, and Guzman reported he "fell under a kind of spell. It was the attraction of commerce, vitality." Roaming the Anglo stores, he reported, "We were fascinated by the rows of kitchen utensils, the shining

frying pans, the coal and wood stoves, the shotguns, the bicy-
cles, the automobiles." Even so, Guzman rejected Yankee materialism in favor of Latin pleasures. Always the return home
"made our hearts dance as we felt the roots of our being sink
into something we had known, possessed, and loved for centuries. . . . Not for nothing were we Mexicans."[34]

Looking south, Anglos painted essentially the same picture of
contrasts. According to one Anglo visitor, Juárez was "a city of
low adobe structures, with dirty and unsanitary streets, and with
few evidences of modern advances." But Anglos drew a different
moral. "Juarez is the most immoral, degenerate, and utterly
wicked place I have ever seen or heard of in my travels," complained the American consul. "Murder and robbery are everyday
occurrences and gambling, dope selling and using, drinking to
excess and sexual vices are continuous." No doubt, the consul
thanked his lucky stars he lived on the American side.[35]

The kaleidoscopic mixture of colors in the cribs, gambling
joints, and brothels of border towns was precisely what made
Anglo officials treat them as cesspools of moral degradation.
After touring the area in 1916 for the Army social hygiene unit,
Raymond Fosdick reported a flourishing sex trade with prostitutes of all descriptions—"white," "colored," "mulatto," "Mexican"—who were "flocking" to the border. In what turned out to
be a rehearsal for the campaign against VD among doughboys
in France, social hygienists tried unsuccessfully to prevent fraternization by putting Mexican towns and the Mexican quarter
of American towns off limits.[36]

The coming of commercial agriculture and industrialization
gave Yankee employers an economic stake in defining Mexicans
in racial terms. Drawing upon long-standing denigration of
"greasers," the Anglo builders of the new commercial order set
about painting Mexicans as an inferior race, "obedient and
cheap." With the large influx of Mexican labor 1910–30, both
sides in the debate over immigration restriction resorted to the
same derogatory stereotypes. Arguing in favor of unrestricted
immigration, a leader of the Los Angeles Chamber of Commerce
stated, "Much of California's agricultural labor requirements

consist of those tasks to which the Oriental and Mexican, due to their crouching and bending habits, are fully adapted, while the white is physically unable to adapt himself to them."[37]

The assumption of biological inferiority, in turn, became justification for mistreatment. Mexicans were paid a "Mexican rate" in the worst jobs; confined to segregated districts called "frogtown"; sent to segregated schools (if schooling was available at all); denied civil rights and access to the voting booth; made the target of vigilante attacks; and singled out for especially brutal treatment at the hands of company guards, local sheriffs, Texas and Arizona Rangers, and National Guardsmen. And then, in the typical circular logic of racial reasoning, after all this degradation, Anglos had the nerve to call Mexicans inferior for their poverty and lack of education.

In many respects, Mexican-Americans resembled African-Americans of the New South. Underpaid black labor was even more important to southern households, farms, and factories (except textile mills), and their presence made racial segregation *the* distinctive characteristic of "the southern way of life." Contemporaries drew the parallel to the Southwest. In the debate over Mexican immigration, the American Eugenics Society warned "Our great Southwest is rapidly creating for itself a new racial problem, as our old South did when it imported slave labor from Africa."[38]

Yet in the end, white supremacy did not fall as hard upon Mexican-Americans as upon African-Americans. Unlike Africans in the New World, Mexicans in the United States were not cut off from the material and cultural resources of their homeland. What was more, U.S. authorities had to contend with Mexico itself, which acted as an informal protector of its nationals across the border. No African colony could do the same. Thus Mexico had some influence over the destiny of its more powerful neighbor. In this respect, being in the borderlands had certain advantages.

Given all the border crossings, the Mexican Revolution was certain to become a major factor in American life.[39] As we saw in the first chapter, the revolution began with the overthrow of dictator Porfirio Díaz in 1910 by upper-class patriots, but it soon went beyond the typical palace coup to become the first of many social revolutions in the twentieth century where whole systems of property and ruling authority came under attack. As in the French Revolution of 1789, opposing social forces contended with one another over the direction of change. Rejecting patriarchal and authoritarian structures of the past, bourgeois nationalists, such as the "First Chief" Venustiano Carranza, leader of the Constitutionalists, sought a republican system based on a strong national constitution.

But with peasant armies roaming the countryside, events quickly overflowed these relatively safe channels. In the north, the dispossessed of Chihuahua and Sonora joined the roving armies of Pancho Villa, treacherous brigand or Robin Hood, depending on the viewpoint. In scenes reminiscent of the French Revolution, some of the more radical factions sacked haciendas and wrecked silver mines, and on several occasions, they strayed across the border to stage minor attacks on U.S. towns.

Amid the ruins of sacked haciendas arose extravagant hopes for emancipating the wretched of the earth. In the Plan of Ayala, the charismatic Emiliano Zapata put forth sweeping demands for the return of peasant land stolen by grasping landlords. Casting off the ancient burden of peonage, zapatistas transformed parts of the state of Morelos into a veritable workshop of land redistribution. Meanwhile, the air in industrial areas was full of talk about worker protections and the nationalization of oil and mineral rights.

Shock waves from the Mexican earthquake quickly spread across the border. The whole border region was shaking with banditry, strikes, riots, and radicalism of the IWW stripe. Oil and mining interests were as keen to have the military clamp down on industrial discontent in the southwestern United States as they were insistent on military intervention in Mexico.[40] Beset on all sides by rival military caudillos, warring moderates, and radical insurrectos, American businessmen placed their bets on whichever horse looked like a winner at any given moment.

Given all that was at stake in Mexico—money, principles, geopolitics—there were loud calls for intervention from business leaders. Although President Wilson was loathe to be identified with the "dollar diplomacy" of his predecessors, he was equally keen to shape Mexican events to his own design. Having intervened once at Veracruz in 1914 to little effect, he had grabbed hold of the proverbial tiger, which he could neither safely ride nor safely let go. He persisted in a vain search for the middle way between what he called "the reactionary class," on the one hand—the rich, the oligarchs, and the church hierarchy—and the *zapatista* radicals on the other.[41] He threw his support first toward Villa, then Carranza, then made enemies of both in 1916 by mobilizing the U.S. National Guard a second time and sending the American Expeditionary Force under General "Blackjack" Pershing on a so-called Punitive Expedition across the border.

Pursuing the elusive Villa ever deeper into the buckling and heaving terrain of the Mexican Revolution, Pershing had trouble seeing his way forward. What was the goal of the expedition? Where would it end? Wilson's second intervention only succeeded in throwing up a wall of anti-Americanism that prevented him from linking up with either the constitutionalist Carranza, or the rising figure of General Obregón, or any other leader who might have been compatible with progressive aims. Instead of controlling the revolution, all he got for his pains was a radical constitution in 1917 that proclaimed oil and other natural resources to be Mexico's national patrimony.

Far from uniting progressive forces, intervention in Mexico split them into three opposing camps. One group hailed Wilson's incursions between 1914 and 1916, not only in Mexico but also in Haiti and the Dominican Republic, as a boon to reform. All of these interventions had the blessing of Secretary of State William Jennings Bryan, nominal leader of the reform wing of the Democratic party. In 1900, Bryan had been the anti-imperialist candidate for president, but now any compunctions about intervening in Latin America were overridden by the assumption of a presumed Anglo-Saxon ability to manage the affairs of so-called lesser races.

A second group of New Nationalist Republicans called for full-scale intervention. Reverting to their roots as McKinley conservatives, men like Roosevelt and Root demanded that U.S. troops be sent in to defend property and order against revolutionary chaos. As in the Caribbean, they equated the restoration of financial stability with the progress of civilization. Far from worrying about undermining republican self-government, they believed they were coming to its defense.

The third group objected that war would kill reform. Fanning the flames of opposition, Lincoln Steffens, the foremost muckraking journalist in the country, roused large audiences against Wilson's misadventures, and midwestern progressives, such as La Follette, lambasted mercenary motives. The campaign saw the beginning of an analysis of economic interests behind intervention that would develop into a comprehensive critique of imperialism—including U.S. imperialism—after the Great War.[42]

Spearheading progressive opposition to intervention was the fledgling American Union Against Militarism, initially organized in opposition to preparedness for the European war, now focused intently on ending the threat of war with Mexico. Crystal Eastman and her colleagues flooded the main channels of mass mobilization—face-to-face mass meetings and mass circulation newspapers—with the message of peace. Eastman was especially effective with paid newspaper ads revealing that U.S. provocations lay behind an incident at Carrizal arising out of the Punitive Expedition where several U.S. soldiers had been killed. Telegrams poured into the White House, which historians credit with causing Wilson to stop short of war. In claiming victory, Eastman put her finger on the essence of people's diplomacy. "We must make it known to everybody," she wrote, "that the *people* acting directly—not through their governments or diplomats or armies, stopped that war and can stop all wars if enough of them will act together and act quickly."[43]

At the start of the presidential campaign in September 1916, it looked as if Mexico would be the dominant issue. While the Republican nominee Charles Evans Hughes berated Wilson for indecisiveness without offering any cohesive alternative of his own, progressive internationalists kept trumpeting the slogan that had emerged at the Democratic convention, "He Kept Us

Out of War." In later years, the slogan would be remembered in the context of U.S. entrance into the European war a scant five months later; at the time, however, it applied more to Mexico, where U.S. troops were already fighting on foreign soil. Several months after the election, as involvement with Europe deepened, Wilson withdrew from Mexico.

Wilson's interventions coincided with the high tide of progressivism at home. Two year earlier, when marines were splashing ashore at Veracruz, the Federal Reserve Board and Federal Trade Commission had come into being. Now, while General Pershing was chasing Pancho Villa through the rugged arroyos of Chihuahua, child labor was being outlawed in the Keating-Owen Act, and working hours on the railroads were being reduced by the Adamson Act. In so far as overseas intervention took place in the name of reform, the impact was to link progressivism to the idea that Anglo-Saxons were the vanguard of advancing civilization and to push antidemocratic, paternalist assumptions to the fore. Conversely, opposition to Caribbean and Mexican interventions tended to link progressivism to the ideal of mutual cooperation among peoples around the globe. Either way, everyone was compelled to take international affairs into account in defining what it meant to be a good citizen of the United States.

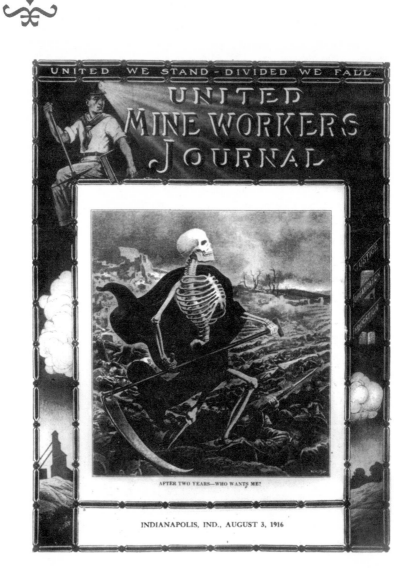

POPULAR OPPOSITION TO WAR: Front cover of the *United Mine Workers Journal*, August 3, 1916. Strong antiwar sentiment is evident in this grisly depiction of the Grim Reaper harvesting countless corpses in the furrows of northern France. (Wisconsin Historical Society, WHi–4246).

4

Messianic America

A merican intervention in the Great War is one of the key issues in the nation's history. Deciding whether to plunge into the European cauldron was not only a question of war and peace but of the role the United States would play in the epoch-making conjuncture that reshaped world history between 1914 and 1945. In becoming a great power, would the United States go it alone or support collective security? Expand its empire or reduce it?[1]

There is no way the United States could have remained aloof from the Great War. Home to the world's biggest economy, the country could not help being affected by economic changes that almost overnight turned it into the world's biggest money lender. As an empire among empires, it was also caught up in the same forces that had shattered prewar internationalism and driven Europeans into the fray—economic competition, imperial rivalry, and national ambition. No matter how hard Americans pretended they were outside history, they could not have escaped the choice between war and peace.

Being forced to choose, however, did not necessarily mean choosing war. What in retrospect may seem to be an inevitable outcome appeared at the time to have been an open question. There were other options. Admonished by President Wilson to be "neutral in thought and deed," Americans held fast for two and a half years to their isolationist moorings in Washington's

Farewell Address and the Monroe Doctrine. From their safe haven across the Atlantic, they watched in horrified disbelief, asking, with *The New Republic*, "Has war ever been more dreadful than now?"[2] Right down to the declaration of war on April 6, 1917, it is likely that a majority was against going in. Intervention was *not* a forgone conclusion.

In attempting to explain intervention, the emphasis here is on nationalism.[3] As one of the foremost ideologies of the modern epoch, nationalism is a system of meaning that marks out collective identity, legitimates ruling elites, and sets millions into motion in defense of country. Yet it is anything but a simple phenomenon. The contradictions in this complex ideology confound contemporaries and historians alike. In some respects, it was the very framework in which capitalist development took place. That is, nation-states furthered the aims of profit-making by upholding the legal framework of private enterprise, facilitating capital accumulation, promoting the interests of their respective businessmen abroad, and reigning in radical movements at home. In other respects, however, nationalism was the prime vehicle for combating capitalist abuses. National governments adopted labor standards, welfare measures, and economic regulations that defied the expressed wishes of business, even when they stopped short of socialist demands for the "nationalization" of the means of production.

The following pages trace the role of nationalism in the debate over intervention. Although political battle lines shifted between 1914 and 1917, it is possible to distinguish two main positions. At one pole, conservatives raised the American flag and argued for the unilateral pursuit of U.S. interests through military preparedness and, eventually, a declaration of war. At the other pole, progressives initially raised the banner of internationalism, arguing against intervention on the grounds that it would set back the quest for social justice. However, as U.S. involvement deepened overseas, many progressives convinced themselves that preparedness might have the benefit of increasing the role of the federal government in regulating the market. Besides, how could they watch Europe go to pieces and do nothing? Thus when the hour of decision struck in April of 1917, they were ready to join Woodrow Wilson's idealistic crusade to make the world safe for democracy.

Debate took place in an atmosphere increasingly charged with messianic Americanism. The belief that America has a God-given mission of redemption is one of the country's most powerful national myths. Myths are stories with high moral purpose pointing to some transcendent destiny. As ideology in narrative form, myth is fictional, but the fact that real people are acting out the plot means that myth is no less real for being fictional.[4]

In practice, the messianic myth has led Americans in opposite directions, sometimes inward in self-righteous isolation, at other times outward in jingoistic expansion, often in both directions at once. It could just as easily propel the country into a war as keep it out. It could also recoil back upon the United States, as everyone would soon find out in the ferocious wartime spirit of "100 percent Americanism" and in the postwar Red Scare.[5]

Nationalist fervor was hardly unique to the United States. As we have seen, all the nations of Europe had gone on a binge of patriotic feeling at the outbreak of war in 1914. All the same, the messianic form of American nationalism was especially important in propelling the United States into the fray. That was because there was only a remote possibility of a military attack on the United States and its interests in the Western Hemisphere. In the absence of a direct threat to American soil, the messianic myth provided a moral justification for intervention, one that held special appeal to reform-minded Protestants steeped in the notion of redemptive mission.

We will return to that point in the last section. For now the focus is on nationalism among conservatives.

Conservative Nationalism

Within weeks of the outbreak of war, conservative elites in the New York–Washington axis were campaigning to strengthen the nation against its enemies foreign and domestic. Calling for "100 percent Americanism," they began pursuing the twin goals of expansion overseas and social discipline at home through a set of interlocking measures that included military preparedness, immigration restriction, and a harsh form of Americanization for immigrants already here. We will look at each in turn.[6]

Leading the charge for preparedness were a number of New Nationalist followers of Teddy Roosevelt. The aim of Roosevelt's New Nationalism was to capture progressive reform for conservative purposes, but now that Wilson had grabbed the progressive banner, Roosevelt seemed to lose interest in social justice. Eyeing another run for the White House in 1916, he turned, instead, to an increasingly strident campaign against the twin menace of "hyphenated Americans" and military weakness.

For Roosevelt, fomenting bellicose nationalism was a reversion to type. Known as "the American Bismarck," the former Rough Rider had waged a lifelong campaign to elevate service to the nation above crass commercialism, and his proudest achievements came through imperial conquest. With characteristic ebullience, he embraced the martial virtues of honor, manliness, courage, and service to the state. Speaking to an audience of Civil War veterans, for example, he praised their scorn for material gain "when the crisis called for showing your manhood."

Now, with war raging in Europe, the time for showing manly courage had come round again. Roosevelt regarded Wilson as a contemptible coward for not being more forceful in defense of U.S. interests. Curling his lip at Wilson's pacifist rhetoric, he sneered, "Peace without victory is the natural ideal of the man who is too proud to fight." Fuming over the "flabby pacifism" of the neutrality period—it represented nothing less than "national emasculation"—he attributed this atrophy of will power to insufficient manhood on Wilson's part, plus a mood of effete materialism. There was too much "love of ease and undue regard for material success," he complained.[7]

Patriotic manhood had its counterpart in patriotic Motherhood. Women of the preparedness movement gave away nothing to social reformers in the glorification of Motherhood. Invoking the same maternal imagery as the reformers, conservatives turned it to their own ends in arguing that woman's duty to conserve life and defend the home somehow required support for a strong navy, the bigger the better. To the proponents of patriotic Motherhood, women could not guard the home unless they were themselves protected by male breadwinners and well-armed warriors. That was certainly the message of the newly created Women's Section of the Navy League, and it could be heard with increasing stridency among women's clubbers and the Daughters of the American Revolution.[8]

Picking up support among civilian lobbies for the military, the preparedness movement also won ringing endorsement from newly minted patriotic societies, such as the National Security League and the American Defense Society, which were closely linked to the effort of the New Nationalists to recapture the Republican party.

The movement found its most prominent military spokesman in General Leonard Wood. One of the new breed of imperial proconsuls, Wood personified the connection between expansion overseas and social discipline at home. As a former Rough Rider and military governor of Cuba, he rose steadily under Roosevelt's patronage to become army chief of staff, where he won support for increased military budgets and for a men's summer encampment at Plattsburg, New York, and a Woman's Preparedness Camp in Maryland. Following a string of Men on Horseback before him from William Henry Harrison to Ulysses S. Grant, he was riding the stallion of preparedness, hoping it would take him all the way to the White House.

Conservatives like Wood prided themselves on their diplomatic realism. To New Nationalists, as well as to conservative Democrats, beefing up the American military was a matter of simple prudence in a dangerous world. Moreover, the Monroe Doctrine needed to be defended against possible German incursions into the Western Hemisphere, especially now that the Panama Canal was open for business.[9] Standing in a long line of famous practitioners of *raison d'état* from Machiavelli to Talley-

rand, conservative realists sought to make *interest* the fundamental basis of diplomatic practice, in the process rehabilitating
a concept that had been discredited by progressives.

Pinstriped elites had plenty of company in stoking the fires
of nationalism. A good part of the mass media inflamed public
opinion with sensational stories about "German outrages."
Bombarding the public with banner headlines, the Hearst press
cultivated hatred for the Germans with stories about the use of
poison gas at Ypres (actually, the Allies used more poison gas
overall than did the Central Powers). In the resulting climate,
being pro-German seemed unpatriotic.

Being pro-British, however, was somehow a form of good
Americanism. Most of the big city dailies on the East Coast were
strongly Anglophile and opened their columns to the often hys-
terical propaganda shoveled in by British media mogul Lord
Northcliffe. As a result, a good deal of the imagery and sloganeering associated with World War I—hatred for "the Hun," contempt for "slackers," "the rape of Belgium"—were actually British imports.

A prime example of inflammatory media coverage came with
the sinking of the *Lusitania* by German torpedoes on May 7,
1915, killing 1,100 passengers, including 128 Americans. Although subsequent investigation showed the British Cunard
liner was carrying munitions deep in its hold, headlines
screamed about innocent civilians being killed in an unpro-
voked attack without warning by a sinister German U-boat. The
reason millions of Americans felt outrage over the sinking of the
Lusitania was that it occurred in a symbolic universe where total
strangers felt kinship with immediate victims because of the fic-
tion of a common national identity, which the mass media had
done so much to foster.

Another expression of the rising nationalist tide was the
movement to Americanize the immigrant. The perennial problem of forging a common American identity was made all the
more urgent in the early twentieth century by the arrival of millions of "new" immigrants from southern and eastern Europe.
Among Protestant patricians, worries about "balkanization" had

been rife for some time, never more so than during the Balkan wars of 1912–13, when Teddy Roosevelt was only one of many voices warning that a "Balkanized" American might somehow fall prey to internecine conflict, just as the Balkan peninsula had.

Calling for the restoration of a mythical homogeneous America, conservatives attempted to put the *unum* in the religious and ethnic *pluribus* by teaching immigrants the basics of English, civics, American values, and loyalty to the flag. Convinced that internal division would open the country to unwanted foreign influences, New Nationalists formed the National Americanization Committee in 1914. Backed by some of the greatest names in industry—Harriman, DuPont, Ford—the head of the Committee Frances Kellor promoted Americanization as "the civilian side of national defense."[10]

At its best, Americanization exemplified a tolerant kind of *civic* nationalism. In keeping with the Enlightenment tradition, some New Nationalists subscribed to a view of the nation as a social compact entered into by individuals of their own free choice. The nation was not chosen by God but by men and women who accepted the American creed of liberty and equality as inscribed in the founding documents of the Declaration of Independence and the Constitution. Citizens were made, not born. The nation was based on *consent*, not blood. The remedy for second-class citizens, such as women and racial minorities, was to appeal to these same republican values in pursuit of first-class status. For immigrants, the way in was through assimilation.

In practice, however, the Americanization movement turned out to be a good deal nastier. Instead of a mutual compact, the actual practice often was a one-way street where Protestant Americanizers insisted that newcomers immediately turn into English-speaking, teetotaling, clean-living, industrious, temperate, and frugal Americans like themselves. In this way, Americanization shaded over into an intolerant form of *cultural* nationalism keyed to white, Anglo-Saxon Protestants. Built around ethnic and linguistic affinities and rooted in nineteenth-century romanticism, cultural nationalism rested on a set of ingrained habits of thought and feeling. Instead of free choice and membership by consent, identity came from being chosen by others, and membership was determined by *descent*.[11]

More than its civic counterpart, cultural nationalism was imbued with the intense race consciousness of the day. The racialist bible was Madison Grant's *The Passing of the Great Race*, published in 1916, which divided European races into a hierarchy of Nordics, Alpines, and Mediterraneans, each with its distinctive inherited traits. While the Nordics were blessed with leadership ability, the unfortunate Mediterraneans were said to be mired in their low levels of intelligence. Such ideas were fodder for the broadly influential eugenics movement. Under the patronage of wealthy blue bloods, the self-described scientists of the Eugenics Record Office set out to establish a biological republic in which only those with the approved "germplasm" were deemed worthy citizens. The diametric opposite of civic nationalism, the racial nation was one of blood, not choice; of breeding, not education; of American birth, not Americanization.

Racial nationalism permeated the movement to restrict immigration, yet another expression of the conservative impulse. Looking down on "racial" groups from Asia and the wrong regions of Europe, restrictionists sought to reduce or eliminate the influx of "undesirables" on the grounds laid out in the Congressional Dillingham report of 1911 that the "new" immigrants from southern and eastern Europe lacked the virtues of the old.

The Boston-based Immigration Restriction League was the most effective of several lobbies for the cause, and the most eminent member of the League was Henry Cabot Lodge, distinguished senator from Massachusetts. To Lodge, immigration restriction was part of a package that included imperial expansion, the Monroe Doctrine, and 100 percent Americanism. Unlike his former Harvard classmate, Teddy Roosevelt, Lodge had no confidence in the ability of the country to assimilate its immigrants. As far as he was concerned, the only way to stop the balkanization of the United States was to cut off all immigration from the Balkans.

Nativism was another impetus behind conservative nationalism. Fear of foreigners had raised its head on several earlier occasions but now came on stronger than ever before. An odd nativist coalition rallied to the cause of immigration restriction. It included antilabor politicians such as Lodge and Albert Johnson of Washington, along with Samuel Gompers of the American Federation of Labor. Representing mostly old stock immigrants of British, Irish, and German ancestry who often shared the prevailing disdain for Slavs, Mediterraneans, and other "undesirables," the AFL was motivated by a combination of nativist prejudice and a misguided theory of low-wage "races" whose unfair competition needed to be kept out of the U.S. labor market.

The increasing strength of nationalism was registered in the passage of the Literacy Act of 1917. The Act excluded any would-be immigrants unable to read and write in their native tongue. To civic nationalists, illiteracy was a strong indication of the inability to learn essential civic values necessary to being a good America. To cultural nationalists, it was a sign of inferior biological or cultural heritage. To nativists, it was just another excuse to keep out the foreigners. The combined effect was enough to muster a two-thirds majority in Congress to pass the act over Wilson's veto. As a symbolic declaration of separation from Europe, the act marked a significant step away from the economic internationalism that characterized the prewar period and toward the nationalist controls on labor migration that would be expanded after the war.

The growing strength of nationalism of all types was also evident in gains for preparedness. The 1916 National Defence Act, for example, provided a large increase in the military budget, and the tax bill of the same year raised federal revenue to pay for it. Meanwhile, forced to respond to his Republican critics, Wilson set up the Council of National Defence (CND), whose job was to coordinate the country's response to the war in Europe. A halfway bureaucracy typical of progressive reform, it linked both the federal and state governments to civil society in a para-state nexus of public/private power.

As these measures indicate, the more Americans were drawn into the European vortex, the more nationalistic they became. Every month all through 1916 and early 1917 brought gains for preparedness, immigration restriction, and a conformist kind of Americanization. Even so, the fact that the country remained neutral was a sign that intervention was not inevitable. It is time to look at the other side in the battle.

Progressive Drift

Progressive opponents of war and militarism did their best to carry prewar internationalism into the increasingly nationalistic environment of the neutrality period. Against the formula of social discipline plus military preparedness they offered their own combination of social justice and world peace. By associating their ideas with the best American democratic traditions, they were able to counter the conservatives, limit defections in their ranks, and hold on to majority support right down to the declaration of war in April 1917.

Forced to engage the enemy on nationalist terrain, progressives battled back with more peaceable alternatives. First and foremost, they rededicated themselves to the *civic* brand of nationalism in the hope that it would reduce ethnic friction. If everyone could freely choose their own national identity, there might be no blood feuds or festering territorial disputes. According to John Dewey, America had separated language, cultural traditions, and "all that is called race" from the state. "Let this idea fly abroad," Dewey wrote, "it bears healing in its wings."[12]

Relishing the spice of America's cultural variety, they also offered a multiethnic alternative to 100 percent Americanism. In a 1916 essay on "What It Means to Be an American," Emily Green Balch envisioned the transformation of existing conflicts of class, race, and nation into an elegant "symphony" of differences. "The new age must be a social age," Balch wrote, "an age of more fraternal relations between men, an age in which exploitation of class by class is outgrown, an age in which brutal and greedy rivalry of nation with nation is outgrown." Proud daughter of New England, Balch had carved out a career as an iconoclastic economics professor at Wellesley College; her letter of dismissal for antiwar views proved it was getting harder to assert them.[13]

Balch was one of many contemporaries attempting to define American nationalism in internationalist terms. Her metaphor was probably inspired by Horace Kallen's hymn to the ethnic "symphony of civilization" which appeared in a widely discussed 1915 essay that championed pluralist democracy against the Melting Pot. Pluralism also found an echo in Randolph Bourne's idea of "transnational" America and in Jane Addams's many writings. In multiethnic America, Addams contended, "a South Italian Catholic is forced by the very exigencies of the situation to make friends with an Austrian Jew." The same could be said of Yankee Protestants such as herself. Not until after the war did such views gain the international honor of a Nobel Peace Prize, first for Addams (1931) and then Balch (1945). Somehow, it was fit compensation for the prewar Nobel prizes given to their countrymen Root and Roosevelt.[14]

In the view of these cultural pluralists, the very fact that America was a collection of minorities made it a model international society. With doors open to all comers, it was a refuge for oppressed nationalities. If America was to redeem the world, it would not be by force of arms, but by setting the example of a harmonious, multinational society. Here was a nationalism to end all nationalisms.

Progressives also had an answer to preparedness. Working through the American Union Against Militarism, reformers tried to persuade the public that the best way to oppose militarism was to remain true to hallowed American traditions going back to Lexington and Concord. That meant opposing a standing army, peacetime conscription, and anything smacking of military supremacy over civil authority. Under the energetic direction of Crystal Eastman, the American Union Against Militarism appealed to these traditions in its frequent antiwar rallies, countless leaflets and press releases, and a "War Against War" exhibit whose centerpiece was a huge armored dinosaur symbolizing the military establishment lumbering along with a pea-sized brain.[15]

The pacifist case against militarism was often combined with a populist attack on big business. Lambasting bankers and munitions makers for gouging huge profits out of war's misery, Frederick Howe, soon to be commissioner of Ellis Island, attacked "the privileges, profits, and immunities which the ruling classes enjoy." The same theme turned up in a constant stream of pamphlets, one of which contained "The Ballad of Bethlelem Steel," part of which read, "A fort is taken, the papers say, / Five thousand dead in the murderous deal. / A victory? No, just another grim day. / But up to five hundred goes Bethlehem Steel."[16]

This kind of economic determinism—the belief that wars happen because they are good for business—typified the thinking of progressives such as Robert La Follette. As the ringleader of a Senate filibuster in March 1917 against a bill to arm U.S. merchant ships, La Follette earned the hatred of Wilson, who reviled him as one of "the little group of willful men expressing no opinion but their own."[17]

In his unshakable conviction that he served a higher moral cause, La Follette resembled both of his chief rivals for progressive leadership, Roosevelt and Wilson. But La Follette did not fan the fires of nationalism. Instead, he aspired to be a tribune of the people, a representative of farmers, workers, and small businessmen, a Solon of social reform whose unswerving moral conviction gave him the courage to defy bosses, plutocrats, majorities, and presidents.

In their campaign against war, progressive internationalists were well armed with horrific stories of carnage. All doubt about the brutality of modern warfare was laid to rest by the epic battles of 1916 at Verdun and the Somme. Readers of popular journals came across eyewitness accounts: "Suddenly, as if at the tap of a baton the great orchestra of death crashed out. It is absurd to describe it; no words have been made for a modern bombardment of this intensity." In another first-hand account, a young French-Canadian immigrant returned from the trenches to tell his terrible tale of shrapnel, mines, poison gas, machine guns, and "rats, rats, rats—tens of thousands of rats." By the end of 1916, the American press was reporting a rate of killing three times greater than any war in the nineteenth century and was referring to "the greatest saturnalia of death and destruction of all time."[18]

Visual imagery reinforced that gruesome idea. Because British censors succeeded in suppressing all photographic evidence of the carnage, the reading public had to rely on the allegory of editorial cartoons for depictions of the awful truth. The grim reaper appeared everywhere from the *New York Tribune* to the *United Mine Workers Journal*, harvesting uncountable corpses in the trenches of northern France. In giving vent to imagination, the mind's eye of editorial cartoonists created stunning images that, ironically, proved to be more true-to-life than the censored products of the camera eye.

The grim reality of the trenches was also conveyed in narratives published by American volunteers before intervention. Unlike scholarly interpretations that stress either modernist irony or sentimental romanticism, the prevailing tone in the most popular narratives was closer to stoic realism.[19] In a journalistic account, Frederick Palmer emphasized the daily struggle to survive under dehumanizing conditions: "None had any sense of the glorious sport of war, only that of grim routine." The same attitude was captured from a nurse's perspective in Mary Borden's *The Forbidden Zone*, apparently written in 1916. In a tone of studied banality, Borden compares her work in a field hospital at the battle of the Somme to women's domestic labor mending clothes: "Just as you send your clothes to the laundry and mend them when they come back, so we send our men to the trenches and mend them when they come back again."[20]

The fact was that after numbing accounts of Verdun and the Somme, no one could hold on to romantic notions of modern warfare. Shortly after winning reelection in November 1916, while preparing his final attempt at mediation, President Wilson described the war in a private note as "this vast, gruesome contest of systematized destruction." He asked, "Where is any longer the glory commensurate with the sacrifice of the millions of men required in modern warfare to carry and defend Verdun?"[21] It is not hard to understand why most Americans wanted no part of it.

Progressive opponents were joined by many other antiwar voices. Radicals mounted demonstrations against preparedness, though it is not clear who threw a bomb into a 1916 preparedness rally in San Francisco. (Authorities took the opportunity to falsely convict labor radicals Tom Mooney and Warren Billings of the deed, and their innocence took two decades to vindicate.) German and Irish communities also opposed U.S. intervention. Pro-German newspapers, such as *The Fatherland*, highlighted the German contributions to American life, including university education and city planning, while the Irish-American press kept up a drumbeat of denunciation of imperial Britain, which only grew louder with Britain's bloody suppression of the 1916 Easter Rebellion.

Probably the biggest obstacle to intervention was the vague but widespread sentiment in favor of continued diplomatic isolation. It had the weight of a century of diplomatic practice behind it and the sanction of the most sacred texts of American diplomacy, Washington's Farewell Address, with its warning against entangling alliances, and the Monroe Doctrine, with its separate spheres of Old and New World diplomacy. Although isolationism ran counter to the progressive belief in international cooperation, all in all, so long as the United States remained neutral, progressives could credibly speak as if they represented the antiwar majority as against the preparedness minority.

Progressives had much to cheer about in the winter of 1916–17. They had held military training in the schools to a minimum and had defeated proposals for peacetime conscription. They were turning the equation of military preparedness and social discipline inside out by linking world peace and social justice. Unprecedented social legislation was being enacted at the federal level, including the newly minted Keating-Owen prohibition of child labor and the Adamson Act granting railroad workers the 8-hour day. Fresh from these victories, the American Association for Labor Legislation fully expected national health insurance to be the next conquest. (Almost a century later, progressives are still waiting.)

The Tax Act of 1916 also represented an important progressive victory in fiscal policy. On the theory that those with the most ability to pay should pay the most, the Act dramatically increased income taxes on the well-to-do, the first such levies under the Seventeenth Amendment, which had been adopted in the waning days of the Taft administration. Under the progressive rate structure, most ordinary incomes were exempt, and levies fell mainly on the rich. In addition, federal inheritance taxes were imposed on large estates for the first time. Together these taxes amounted to one of the greatest progressive achievements of the entire century. No wonder they elicited howls of protest from the rich.

Progressives also had reason to think they had a political friend and ideological champion in the White House. The cabinet included several of their ranks: Josephus Daniels, secretary of the navy from North Carolina, and Newton Baker, one-time reform mayor of Cleveland and now secretary of war, an odd position for a reputed pacifist. Although Wilson was astute enough to balance these with appointments of conservatives, such as Robert Lansing, and although he had gone out of his way to assure business of his honorable intentions, progressives had greater access to the highest circles of power than ever before.

Progressives were also successful in containing conservative advances at the ballot box. They were strong enough in the November elections to help Wilson defeat Charles Evans Hughes on the popular slogan "He Kept Us Out of War." Their peace efforts seemed to be crowned with success when President Wilson's made his landmark "Peace Without Victory" speech on January 22, 1917, which took up their own themes of world peace, disarmament, self-determination, and a concert of nations. All in all, progressive internationalism was holding the fort as the alternative to world war.

Yet the ground was eroding under their feet. Ironically, the very gains they celebrated were bound up with the coming of war, including hours regulation and progressive taxation. In addition, Wilson had responded to the preparedness movement by supporting an expanded military and setting up the Council of National Defence (CND). And as the Wilson administration drifted toward war, many progressives drifted along with it. The CND was soaking up leaders of mass movements like a sponge, including Carrie Chapman Catt and other leading suffragists. Having received a coveted CND appointment, Samuel Gompers, an English immigrant of Dutch-Jewish extraction, immediately began rallying the mostly Catholic members of AFL unions to the cause of preparedness under the banner of civic nationalism. "America is a symbol," Gompers wrote, "the hopes of the world can be expressed in the ideal—America."[22]

A lot of other progressives were drifting with the nationalist current. As early as March of 1915, *The New Republic* was calling for a more active role in the European war. Endorsing the idea of a "league of peace" that was making the rounds of international reform circles, the editors heaped scorn upon American provincialism. "Instead of thinking and acting as a self-contained democracy whose virtue depended upon its isolation," the editors admonished, "the American people must think and act as a democracy whose future depends upon its ability to play its part and assume its responsibility in a society of democratic nations."[23]

On the eve of U.S. intervention, progressivism was poised to become the dominant tradition in American politics. Having bested conservatives, laissez-faire liberals, corporate managers, and a variety of radicals and leftists, progressives held leading positions in the two major parties, claimed the legislative initiative in many states and the federal government, and gave voice to a new ethos of social responsibility and civic engagement that was making deep inroads on the marketplace ethos of individual competition.

But this national power came at a price. Seeking to reclaim the republic from upper-class conservatives, progressives believed they could enlist "the nation" on the side of "the people" in the battle against "the interests." They appealed to the swelling spirit of nationalism—what Herbert Croly called the New Nationalism and Walter Lippmann dubbed "mastery"—against the plutocratic interests that were attempting to steal the national patrimony. And especially as war approached, they became enamored of state institutions, such as the Council of National Defence and a stronger military establishment, as vehicles of progress.

The embrace of the nation-state marked a subtle but important shift away from civic-mindedness. In place of talk about the *public* interest, more and more was heard of the *national* interest. In place of civic associations, public commissions, and other voluntary associations of civil society, the emphasis now was on agencies in Washington backed by the threat of state coercion. In all, progressives spoke less about the public interest and a symphony of peoples and more about the good of the nation in a concert of nations. They did not foresee the cruel trick history had in store, that in seeking to capture nationalism for their own ends, instead, they turned out to be its captives.

Chosen Peoples

The appeal of nationalism was enhanced by the belief that the United States was a chosen nation with a God-given destiny to redeem the world. One of the most intriguing things about the chosen nation is the presence of so many chosen peoples within it. From Puritans to Mormons, many groups have entered American history with a deep memory of persecution and a sense of being singled out by providence for divine purposes. That was true of African-Americans and Jewish-Americans, pilgrim peoples in search of a Promised Land. In a different way, it was also true of many white, Anglo-Saxon Protestants and other descendants of north European immigrants seeking religious freedom in the New World. Comparison of the traditions of these three peoples serves to illuminate the messianic myth.

First a disclaimer. Because of the arbitrary nature of group definitions, comparison among them is always risky. The term Wasp has been applied to everyone from Yankee Protestant bluebloods to poor whites in the South and to virtually anyone with English, Scottish, Dutch, German, Scandinavian, or other north European ancestry. Comparison is also messy because normally there are as many differences within groups as there are between them. Let it be understood that the names used here apply to three internally varied cultural traditions, not to well-organized social groups.

Comparison among them serves to highlight the origins of messianic Americanism among what we are calling Wasps. Neither African-Americans nor Jewish-Americans could fully celebrate an America in which they remained subordinate targets of racial animosity. Immigrant descendants of north Europeans, on the other hand, were so closely identified with the America nation that it does not stretch the truth too far to say that messianic Americanism was the ethnic nationalism of the Wasp.

Differences were painfully apparent with respect to attitudes toward freedom.[24] For many Wasps, America itself was the Promised Land, and freedom was their birthright within it. Even lower-class whites around the country commonly felt entitled to this most precious possession and stood ready to defend it with riot and violence against any and all enemies. To African-Americans and American Jews, on the other hand, America was no less a land of bondage than a land of promise. The rise of Jim Crow, racist justifications for empire, and the spread racial nationalism all conspired to prove that freedom was a prize not yet won. That attitude helped initiate a period of unprecedented sympathy and cooperation between the two groups. Just as many African-Americans came to view anti-Semitism as another kind of racial prejudice, so many Jews fleeing persecution in Europe asked whether Negroes were not the Jews of America.

Despite their small numbers—never more than 4 percent of the total population—Jewish thinkers and writers were unusually important in the larger struggle for the American soul. Among Yiddish-speaking refugees from the terrors of eastern Europe were many utopians who saw America as the *goldene medinah*. Coming into New York harbor, one of the dreamers reported, "I fell in love with America. My heart told me that this is the greatest, the freest and the best country in the world."

Even the religiously Orthodox were tempted to believe that the historic quest for a homeland might have ended on American soil. One immigrant complained that his friends were asking, "What have we to do with Palestine? America is our Palestine and our Synagogue is our Temple. We don't believe in the coming of the Messiah."[25]

Especially to those who had come to regard America as a promised land, every protest against racism was a demand that America live up to its professed ideals. Emma Lazarus, a champion of Enlightenment rationalism and a strong advocate of assimilation, had set the tone in her famous poem "The New Colossus" in which the Statue of Liberty, "mother of exiles," lifts her lamp beside the golden door to welcome Europe's "huddled masses, yearning to breathe free." Taking these ideals to heart, Mary Antin gained celebrity for her 1912 autobiography *The Promised Land*, a classic story of assimilation in which the heroine moves from the medieval *shtetl* of Polotzk, Russia, to the enlightened world of Emersonian individualism.[26]

Yet the more they accepted this idealized America, the more they felt the contradictions of racism and anti-Semitism. No event did more to bring that home than the lynching of Leo Frank in 1915. Frank was falsely accused of sexually molesting and murdering a 13-year-old mill girl named Mary Phagan in the Atlanta pencil factory where he worked as superintendent. Convicted in an atmosphere seething with anti-Semitism and class hatred, Frank was subsequently pardoned by a progressive Georgia governor, only to be lynched by a vigilante mob calling itself The Knights of Mary Phagan.

Sending a shock wave around the country, the grisly crime revived ancient Jewish fears of persecution and forced even successful business and professional people to ask, was there any place in the entire world where a Jew could be safe? Combined with anxiety over the rising tide of racial nativism that would soon produce severe restrictions on immigration from eastern Europe, the Frank case went a long way toward kindling a spirit of sympathetic cooperation between American Jews and those who were the most common victims of lynch mobs.[27]

That cooperation was enhanced by social and economic forces which drew the Jewish and African diasporas closer together. Labor shortages caused by the cut-off in European immigration induced African-Americans to abandon the plantations of the South for the job-rich cities of the North, where they often moved into neighborhoods such as Harlem and into industries such as garment making where there were already heavy Jewish concentrations. Despite considerable differences in origin, the Jewish migration out of eastern Europe and the Great Migration from the South produced social and cultural worlds that intersected at countless points.

Contact produced a good deal of friction. Blacks complained about the hiring practices of Jewish merchants and gave vent to their share of anti-Semitic stereotypes. For their part, Jews often displayed a contemptuous or patronizing attitude tinged with racism toward "*schwartzes.*" By performing in blackface and so-called black dialect, Jewish entertainers such as Al Jolson mocked the original.

Yet Jewish imitation of Afro-American culture could also be intended as flattery. In vaudeville, silent movies, and Tin Pan Alley, Jewish entertainers appropriated many black idioms. As a former cantor, Jolson merged Jewish klezmer music and Afro-American jazz in the famous film *The Jazz Singer*. In another example, Irving Berlin borrowed (some said stole) enough from Scott Joplin to compose "Alexander's Ragtime Band." In responding to the syncopated rhythms of ragtime and the improvisational style of jazz, these Jewish musicians came to appreciate the way black music snatched fleeting moments of freedom from the racial tyranny that otherwise surrounded them.

Turning to African-Americans, the quest for freedom was replete with stories and symbols equally recognizable among Jews. No African-American religious service was complete without some reference to Hebrew deliverance from bondage. "Didn't my Lord deliver Daniel," asked one gospel song, "Then why not every man?" Likewise, the folklore of the Great Migration was replete with the imagery of Moses leading his people into Canaan. Repelled by poverty, disease, and lynching in the

South, and attracted by the demand for labor in the North, rural blacks began to move to northern cities in record numbers. Although most accounts stress economic and social factors, "Northern fever" was raging all over the South by 1916, as pilgrims pulled up stakes and headed for Beulah Land. In promoting the migration, the Chicago *Defender* pulled out all the Old Testament stops—it was the Exodus, the Hegira, the Flight out of Egypt, the Black Diaspora. Many migrants felt the same way. After crossing the Ohio River, a party from Hattiesburg, Mississippi, held a prayer service to celebrate "Crossing over Jordan" in which they sang "I done come out o' de land of Egypt; ain't that good news."[28]

The struggle for freedom was every bit as much a part of what it meant to be a Jew. Each year at Passover, Jews celebrated the release of the ancient Hebrews from Egyptian captivity. With the spirit of Moses looking on, the service concluded with the vow, "Next year in Jerusalem." Emancipation from civil and political disabilities in nineteenth-century Europe was regarded as a major turning point, but true freedom had no more come than had the Messiah. Jewish visionaries of one stripe or another—socialists, anarchists, Zionists—continued to search for their respective Promised Lands.

Given their status as outsiders, both Jewish-Americans and African-Americans were forced into what Du Bois termed "double consciousness." On the one hand, they warmly embraced the sunny side of the American creed of liberty and equality. On the other hand, they were too often victims of racism or anti-Semitism to equate the ideal with reality. What Du Bois said about the "twoness" of Negroes—part Negro, part American—applied in many respects to American Jews, as well. Just as the descendants of Negro slaves asked whether America was a house of bondage or of freedom, so Jews asked the same question. Was America the *goldene medinah*? Or just another vale of tears on the long road to Jerusalem?

The main point here is that ambivalence about America made it impossible for these oppressed peoples to fully embrace messianic Americanism. They knew that for all its redeeming qualities, the United States was often not on the side of freedom. Had Wasps learned this lesson, they, too, might have been more careful about succumbing to the siren call of saving the world.

As it was, in the spring of 1917, many white Protestants gave in to the messianic myth. The myth carried immense historical momentum. Starting with the Puritan search for a "cittie upon a hill," it ran through Tom Paine's vision of America as an "asylum for Mankind" and illuminated the epic migration of those "yearning to breathe free." It reached a pinnacle in the Civil War, when Enlightenment ideals were played out as Protestant allegory, with Lincoln as the American Christ who died for the sin of slavery, though not before he had hailed the United States in the Gettysburg Address as "last best hope on earth."[29] In the 1890s, it justified overseas expansion, in the words of Senator Albert Beveridge, of "*the* nation chosen to lead in the regeneration of the world." Later, it would resonate in the struggle against fascism during World War II and echo in the Cold War, when America was held up as the homeland of the "free world."

One great curiosity about this quintessentially American belief is that it originated outside the United States. For three centuries, a wide variety of Europeans had poured their hopes into the New World, viewing it as an asylum for persecuted minorities, a beacon of republicanism, a refuge for defeated liberals, and, for countless immigrants, a land of opportunity. Whenever they needed a state of Nature, a Promised Land, or some other place of presumed innocence, Europeans imagined it on the other side of the Atlantic in an allegorical country they found convenient to keep just beyond the horizon. At the dawn of the twentieth century, America continued to be a repository of hope. British writers such as Rudyard Kipling were already handing over the baton of Anglo-Saxon world leadership to their American cousins, and W. T. Stead was predicting "the Americanization of the world." Truly, the idea that the New World had been created to redeem the Old was a European invention.[30]

The key to understanding the messianic myth lies in its twofold character, secular in content, religious in form. The religious forms derived mostly from the Calvinist Reformation, with its story of fall and redemption and its vision of the apocalypse, or "end-time," when the seals of the Book of Revelation will be opened and all true believers will be saved. Pouring secular ideals into these religious forms resulted in a quasi-religious mission to redeem the world by spreading the ideals of the Jeffersonian Enlightenment—the creed of liberty and equality, the belief in progress, faith in human perfectibility.[31]

In other times and places—say, Puritan New England or modern Islamic theocracies—the process is reversed. Religious content is poured into secular forms, and the sword of the state conquers on behalf of Christ or Mohammed. But the dethronement of established religion and the decline of sacramental world views in the nineteenth century diminished the role of the church in public life, creating a thirst for meaning at the very time that religion lost its capacity to provide it. Far from being immune to this need for salvation, modern men and women are often ready to die for it. What can be more compelling to the isolated modern self than to be taken up in some grand scheme of destiny?

To such lost souls, socialism had a quasi-religious appeal. It enfolded atomized individuals within the warm embrace of a fictive community, offering solidarity with other pilgrims on the way to attaining heaven on earth. But nationalism did the same thing, and, in many ways, it did it better. At least in so far as it forged a common bond among all members of the nation, high and low, nationalism united otherwise antagonistic elements around a sense of common destiny. As the emotional equivalent of religion, nationalism was an exceedingly potent force. Unlike the mundane values of the marketplace, it could provide a set of principles worth dying for, a fact that was being demonstrated daily on the battlefields of Europe, sad proof of the proposition that the twentieth-century wars of nationalism were the awful equivalent of the seventeenth-century wars of religion.

In its messianic form, American nationalism had its strongest appeal to white, Anglo-Saxon Protestants. Occupying a relatively privileged position, they could fully identify with the story of America saving the world in a way that oppressed groups could not. According to Frederick Howe, a leading progressive reformer, the missionary mentality was the dominant influence on his generation. Having grown up in small-town Pennsylvania, Howe spoke from the heart of Protestant America in saying, "Missionaries and battleships, anti-saloon leagues and Ku Klux Klans, Wilson and Santo Domingo are all a part of that evangelistic psychology that makes America what she is."[32] At a time when evangelical crusades were underway against the saloon, the brothel, venereal disease, and slum conditions, the most astute part of Howe's observation was that redeeming America and redeeming the world were two sides of the same coin.

Although messianic Americanism was not just the ethnic nationalism of the Wasps, it owed more to them than to any other ethnic group. To the presumptive heirs of the national patrimony, the idea that the United States was the nation chosen by God to redeem the world was the very *telos*—the goal and justification—of American history. No heir of the Protestant Reformation was ever far removed from the sense of moral obligation to save the world. All the mainline Protestant denominations and most Protestant sects had proselytizing arms and overseas missions, and the message of redemption from sin was the very heart of moral teaching in Sunday schools, Bible study classes, religious revivals, and YMCA functions. Over many generations the metaphor of lifting up the fallen had become so deeply embedded in the culture that it was the very language in which people thought. The question that remains is how the messianic myth affected the debate over intervention.

Redeeming War

To understand the "why" of intervention, it is helpful to keep in mind that people make choices within a limited range of options. They choose their own destiny, to paraphrase Marx, but under conditions inherited from the past. So it was with the American declaration of war on April 6, 1917. The decision was the logical product of antecedent causes, which will be discussed shortly. But what is logical in retrospect is not necessarily inevitable in prospect. People face the future believing events can go in many different directions. That is the very precondition of hope. In approaching the question of intervention, it is necessary to remember that what ends up as a forgone conclusion begins as one of many open options.

Let us begin with the lost option of neutrality. As long as the giant moat of the Atlantic Ocean protected them from attack, Americans could have remained safely above the fray. In the increasingly heated debate over preparedness in early 1917, neutrality clearly held the upper hand. It had the deep-seated tradition of diplomatic isolation behind it, and the rise of strident, 100 per cent Americanism initially reinforced isolation, as did growing nativism in the movement against immigration and everything else European.

In addition, the churches—vital institutions of civil society—contained many vocal opponents of US entrance into the war. Among the country's 24 million Protestants, the peace churches spoke against war, and so did many evangelicals and fundamentalists who wanted no part of a secular crusade. The evangelical press campaigned vociferously against any military buildup; *The King's Business*, for example, warned against the pernicious modernist tendency to "substitute democracy for a divinely appointed plan of REDEMPTION."[33] Roman Catholics, the second largest religious group with almost 16 million members, had their own reasons for opposing an overseas crusade. Certainly, Irish and German communities were reluctant to join anything led by Protestant Anglophiles. The same was true of Jewish-Americans, who, at least until the Russian revolution in March, were horrified at the prospect of going in on the side of the tsar. All told, support for neutrality among so many segments of the population meant that there would be many reluctant crusaders when the nation finally went to war.

For now it meant there was widespread support for Wilson's peacemaking efforts. Since total noninvolvement was out of the question, Wilson tried to mediate between the warring parties. Immediately after his reelection, he went to both the Allies and the Central Powers in an effort to begin joint discussions that might lead to a negotiated settlement. Although rebuffed by both sides, he did not give up on the search for peace. To the contrary, he gave his landmark "Peace Without Victory" speech on January 22, 1917, in the spirit of progressive internationalism. Taking his cue from ideas circulating in peace and justice circles, he enunciated key principles—freedom of the seas, consent of the governed, collective security, a concert of nations—that would become central to the worldwide search for a just peace over the next two years. "These are American principles, American policies," he declared, "And they are also the principles and policies of forward-looking men and women everywhere, of every modern nation, of every enlightened community."[34]

As long as America was officially neutral, Wilson was able to reconcile Americanism and internationalism. He could reasonably pose as the impartial leader of world opinion and could sow the seeds of progressive internationalism on German as well as French soil. Had Wilson been able to continue his mediation efforts, who knows whether the exhausted parties might have reached a more equitable peace agreement than the unbalanced and destabilizing treaty that came out of Versailles.

Neutrality also had much to commend it in economic terms. Unprecedented sales of food and arms to the Allies had brought prosperity all around. Rescued from low commodity prices, manufacturers and farmers entered what they would later look back on as a golden age. With unemployment a little over two percent, workers entered the tightest labor market they had ever known. Rising incomes enabled consumers to go on a buying spree. All in all, neutrality brought Americans the best economic times of their lives, all the sweeter because it did not have to be purchased at the cost of American lives.

Nor is it clear that ordinary Americans, as opposed to merchants and financiers, had much of a long-term stake in an Allied victory. As it turned out, the extreme dislocations of the war led to difficulties for farmers in the 1920s when European markets collapsed, followed by trouble for everyone when the financial consequences of the war helped bring about the Great

Depression of the 1930s. Nobody could have known it at the time, but it is doubtful things would have been worse if the Germans had won.

As it was, the neutrality option increasingly lost ground in the late winter. Neither the Allies nor the Central Powers proved willing to give an inch. Even as Wilson delivered his "Peace Without Victory" speech, the German military was laying plans for the resumption of submarine warfare. When the renewed threat of attack was announced on February 1, the Germans knew that sinking American ships risked a U.S. declaration of war, but they hoped for final victory before the Americans could mobilize effectively.

Looking back on the resumption of U-boat warfare, it is easy to mark it as the turning point on the road to intervention. It led to the arming of U.S. merchant ships in an effort to keep the lucrative trade with the Allies going across the North Atlantic, and it also led to the reassertion of the principles of "freedom of the seas" and "neutral rights" as vital American interests. In short, armed neutrality looked a lot like war by another name.

Yet it is worth repeating that being forced to choose did not necessarily mean choosing war. What in retrospect is a logical progression of events does not rule out some other sequence. Even as options were being foreclosed, contrary forces were still in play. To understand why the events of February and March led to intervention, let us return to the subject of nationalism. The more that nationalism took hold of public discourse, the more attacks on American ships gained *meaning* as affronts to national honor. What finally cast the die for war was the convergence of national interests as defined by upper-class conservatives and the rising support for a messianic mission among progressives. Together, these two forms of nationalism, the one realist, the other idealist, overrode the objections of progressive internationalists, cut the country loose from its historic isolationist moorings, and shoved it into the maelstrom.

It was the combination of realism and idealism that did the trick. On the realist side, conservatives were increasingly alarmed about the possible consequences of a German victory.

They worried that the $2 billion in American loans to the Allies would become uncollectible and that the booming trade in food and manufactures would collapse. They also shuddered at the prospect of German interference in the Western Hemisphere. This was why the infamous Zimmerman Note set off all the alarm bells. On February 25 the cabinet received word that British secret service had decoded a message from the German secretary of state proposing an alliance with Mexico in the event of war with the United States. With incredible temerity, Germany promised to support Mexico's reconquest of territory lost in the Mexican-American War. The proposal was ludicrous on its face—Germany was in no position to come to Mexico's aid—but there was good reason to believe that a German victory in the war would lead to meddling in a U.S. sphere of influence. Most of all, conservatives worried about missing an opportunity to join the front rank of Great Powers. Unless the weight of the United States was felt in the scales of world power during the war, how could they expect to wield influence in the postwar world? As Wilson's mediation efforts stalled, conservatives became increasingly eager for intervention.

Here is where messianic Americanism came in. The more Americans contemplated intervention in the Old World, paradoxically, the more they defined themselves *against* Europe. Insisting that America was not just different from the Old World, but altogether exceptional, they held the United States to be a nation outside the limitations of history with a duty to redeem history's sins. As we have seen, the belief in moral superiority pointed in opposite directions, which helps account for the sudden flip-flops in American foreign policy. At times, it turned inward in the isolationism of "American First," fearing that foreign contacts were contaminating. At other times, it fueled overseas crusades, as with the jingoism of the Spanish-American War. In the fierce debates over intervention, the messianic myth played an increasingly critical role. It drowned out progressive internationalists, while firing up conservative nationalists. Especially among Anglo-Saxon Protestants, it turned the isolationist impulse outward against the foreign foe.

Meanwhile, the soon-to-be Allies were pumping up the myth, as well. When the British and the French came knocking on America's door, it was not only for munitions, but also for a badly needed boost in morale. As the battlefield stalemate ground on month after grisly month, one Frenchman flattered Americans by saying that "It is of the highest moral importance that the United States, the most progressive Power in the world, should be represented in this new army of crusaders." And from Britain's Viscount Bryce came a desperate plea for American troops on the grounds that "Even a small American force would have an immense moral effect." Hailing Wilson's proposed league of nations, a British journalist proclaimed that the mission of the New World was "to help the old find the way out of the wilderness."[35]

The call to a national mission of redemption met its strongest response among modernist Protestants who had long since abandoned the old-time religion in favor of the gospel of Americanism. Many of the early defectors from neutrality to preparedness came from well-heeled mainline churches where liberal theology had taken hold, especially from among 1 million Episcopalians and 1.6 million Presbyterians, who together made up a kind of informal Protestant establishment.[36] The "high church" link to preparedness was epitomized by Robert Lansing, appointed secretary of state in 1915 after Bryan resigned in protest over what he saw as Wilson's bellicose response to U-boat warfare. Out went the Great Commoner and antiwar fundamentalist; in came the international lawyer with Wall Street connections, elder of the Presbyterian Church, and vigorous proponent of checking German power.

There is a double irony here. Protestant modernists such as Lansing talked as if the moment of Armageddon was at hand, even though they had given up any genuine belief in the end-time. Meanwhile, Protestant fundamentalists who actually believed fervently in the Final Conflict between Christ and Satan at first refused to associate it with the Great War.

The climactic moment finally arrived in early April. Speaking to a hastily called joint session of Congress on April 2, 1917, Wilson summoned Americans to their destiny. As the son of a Presbyterian minister and as apostle of Anglo-American liberalism, he was well prepared to weave the twin legacy of the Calvinist Reformation and the Jeffersonian Enlightenment into his call to redeem humanity. Once again, he wrapped American commercial and diplomatic interests in the moral universals of freedom of the seas and neutral rights, while proposing a sacred democratic mission against the forces of autocracy and militarism. Asking the nation to take up arms in "the most terrible and destructive of all wars," he promised America would fight not for territory or gain, not even for martial glory, but for "a universal dominion of right by such a concert of free peoples as shall bring peace and safety to all nations and make the world itself at last free."[37]

The fact that it was impossible to top such lofty rhetoric did not prevent Congress from trying. The debate that followed over the next four days rang with the same themes. Everyone acknowledged the horror of war. Even supporters of intervention quoted General Sherman's famous "War is hell," and one went a step further to say, "modern war is *worse* than hell." Opponents called the European war a "catastrophe" and a "slaughter pen," and Senator George Norris used a term that would resound across the twentieth century: "holocaust."[38]

What else but a mission of salvation could make people go willingly into the holocaust of hell? Sounding the messianic trumpet, Henry Myers, Democrat of Montana, reminded his colleagues of America's divine destiny. "This country has been specially favored by Providence," he said. "It has had the privilege of setting the Statue of Liberty Enlightening the World in New York Harbor, bespeaking to all the world democracy, liberty, enlightenment in self-rule." Others picked up the message. Warning against pacifist naivete, Henry Ashurst, Democrat of Arizona, laid out a litany of evils that beset the world, from private envy to lust for world power. Fortunately, America was the one to defeat these evils in "her historic position as the leader and noble pioneer in the vanguard of progress and human liberty."[39]

Speaking for the conservatives, Henry Cabot Lodge, later Wilson's sworn enemy, weighed in with an ode to war as the Second Coming of the Nation. No longer would the country be torn apart by warring "race groups," Lodge said. In an echo of the nationalist fervor that gripped Europeans on all sides in 1914, he hailed the coming spirit of unity: "Instead of division into race groups, it will unify us into one Nation, and national degeneracy and national cowardice will slink back into the darkness from which they should never have emerged."[40]

It took a good deal of courage to stand against the nationalist tide. Senator Robert La Follette, the most prominent opponent, presented antiwar petitions, rebutted Wilson's war message point by point, invoked the millions of maimed victims, and, most tellingly, pointed to British imperialism as a standing refutation of Wilson's flowery notion of a democratic crusade.[41]

Another redoubtable opponent of war was George Norris. A Nebraska progressive with a strong populist streak, Norris decried the nefarious manipulations of munitions makers and Wall Street bankers that lay behind the drive to war. He provoked the harshest exchange of the entire debate when he dared to say, "We are going into war upon the command of gold." Condemning stockbrokers for their eagerness to coin the lifeblood of their countrymen into money, Norris brazenly declared, "I feel we are about to put the dollar sign upon the American flag." This presumed insult to the flag brought howls of protest from the normally congenial Senate. Rising to defend the honor of Old Glory, Senator Williams accused Norris of giving aid and comfort to the Hohenzollerns: "If it be not treason, it grazes the edge of treason."[42]

Apparently, it was only treason if talk about money came from the opposition. In fact, supporters of intervention were pounding the cash register as hard as they could. Forgetting that the country was prospering under neutrality, businessmen and diplomats furiously recalculated their position. Repeating the arguments they had made in response to the renewal of U-boat warfare on February 1, Elihu Root spoke for his fellow Republicans in declaring that a German victory would eliminate the British Navy as the first line of defense for the Monroe Doctrine, undermine U.S. supremacy in the Western Hemisphere, and jeopardize repayment of loans to the Allies.

Democrats took up the same theme. Senator Claude Swanson of Virginia calculated the future cost of acquiescing in Germany's attacks on Atlantic shipping at exactly $3,382,000,000. Losing exports to the Allies would result in being "precipitated from great prosperity to acute financial and industrial distress."[43] Moreover, if the United States stayed out of the war to end all wars, how could it claim a role in shaping the peace?

Senate sensitivity about mercenary motives reveals a deep ambivalence about commerce. From Yankee traders to compulsive shoppers, no people were more commercially minded than Americans, yet none recoiled more quickly from their own materialism. Even as they pursued commercial success, they regarded the market as a sordid realm of masculine vice set off from the chaste realm of feminine virtue. The same ambivalence was present in debates over intervention. Even as they chased after the dollar, they distrusted their own motives. In fact, precisely *because* their motives were partly commercial, their conscience would not rest until they had attached some higher purpose to intervention. That was why the flag could follow the dollar but could not be seen to have dollar signs on it.

Especially for Protestant elites, the messianic myth overcame moral qualms. Although Americans had died in U-boat attacks and U.S. interests were at stake, the case for just war was on shaky ground, since American soil had not been invaded. Another moral obstacle was the likely cost in human life. Even the bloodletting of the American Civil War paled in comparison. The beauty of the messianic myth was that it answered these moral objections. America would wage a war to end all wars.

The genius of Wilson's leadership at this moment lay in combining the seemingly opposed impulses of selfishness and salvation. Wilson took the realist ambition of making the United States a Great Power and gave it the force of an absolute moral imperative. It was a brilliant stroke. The combination of money and morality would sustain America's rise to power for the rest of the century and beyond.

Satisfied on both points—self-interest and moral purpose—national leaders closed ranks around the redeemer mission. According to a Unitarian minister from New York, "It is as plain as the light of day that our Republic now is engaged upon no less a task than the ransoming of humanity." Long-time supporters of Roosevelt, such as *The North American*, a highbrow journal of opinion, discovered unexpected nobility in Wilson and rushed to embrace his "great utterance of last week—'the world must be made safe for democracy.'" Reaching into the Book of Revelations, the editors hailed "the alliance of the democratic people of the world to meet at their Armageddon the confederated forces of autocracy." And then, in a quintessential expression of the savior myth, the editors said that never since the coming of Christ had there been an event of greater moment for humanity. "Like its great Teacher and Martyr," the editors wrote, "the cause of justice has had its grim Golgotha and its triumphant resurrection, promise and proof of a glorious immortality." Whether or not the modernist editors actually believed in Golgotha and resurrection, they knew how to turn Christian allegory to political uses.[44]

Five years earlier many of the same New Nationalists had sung "Onward, Christian Soldiers" at the Progressive party convention in 1912, and had thrilled to hear Teddy Roosevelt say, "We stand at Armageddon and battle for the Lord." Now they rallied to his nemesis Wilson as he led the nation on a messianic quest. Soon they would be singing "Onward, Christian Soldiers" to the departing soldiers of the American Expeditionary Force as they went off to a truly fearsome Armageddon in the trenches of northern France.

The fact that America mobilized in its own evangelical fashion did not make American mobilization exceptional. One of the most striking things about the belief that war would be redemptive is that Europeans had embraced it, too, in the first flush of enthusiasm in August 1914. What should we make of this? Does it point to a spiritual void in capitalist society, with its commercialism and alienation, which the coming of war seemed in a perverse way to fill? Clearly, something was amiss when modern, scientific people marched off on a medieval crusade of wanton destruction.

A few had sensed there was something wrong in the workings of modern life. Walter Lippmann, for example, had rung an alarm bell that the twentieth century was already in danger of becoming a Paradise Lost. Where nothing was sacred, Lippmann warned, pandemonium reigned: "The sanctity of property, the patriarchal family, hereditary caste, the dogma of sin, obedience to authority,—the rock of ages, in brief, has been blasted for us." Peering into the moral abyss, he warned, "The chaos is our real problem."[45] The danger was that if religious content had been drained out, but religious forms remained, then anything might fill the void—anti-Semitism, racial hatred, fascism, or, for now, hatred of the Hun.

Caught up in the worldwide convulsion, progressive America plunged into an era of extremes where the hyperrationalism of industrial efficiency went hand in hand with an orgy of fear and loathing. Against the backdrop of mechanized destruction, one observer wrote, "The world seems suddenly to have gone insane, a cold, calculating, scientific, merciless form of insanity which takes little count of human life."[46] Americans in 1917 were not the last ones to take this fearful plunge, or by any means, the worst example, but their decision points to one of the great tragedies of the twentieth century: in seeking redemption, people, instead, descended into the hell of modern war.

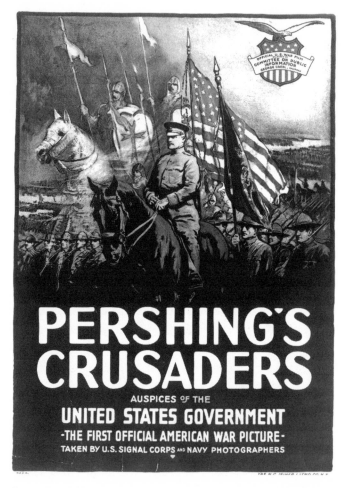

CRUSADING SOLDIERS OF DEMOCRACY: General John "Black Jack" Pershing, commander of the American Exeditionary Force, leads his men into battle with the ghosts of Christian crusaders hovering in the background. In this advertising poster for the first U.S. government war film, the Committee on Public Information draws a curious connection between modern-day republican warriors and medieval Catholics. (Library of Congress, Prints and Photos Division)

5

World War and Revolution

The declaration of war marked the opening of the most contentious period in twentieth-century American history. War fever directed against the foreign foe also turned inward against domestic dissent, while class and racial tensions exploded in western mining regions and booming industrial cities. As if that were not enough, waves from the earthquake of revolution in Russia came rolling across the Atlantic. Not until the middle of the 1920s would the tumult subside.

In the midst of these disturbances, Americans launched their crusade to make the world, America included, safe for democracy. Behind Wilson's famous battle cry, they set out to defeat the foreign foes of Prussian militarism and Old World corruption, as well as the domestic enemies of immorality and political dissension. For many, it was the most exhilarating time of their lives.

Changing the world, however, proved to be much more complicated than anyone imagined. For one thing, there were other crusaders in the field. Just a few weeks before American intervention, Russian revolutionaries had also mounted the world stage. The overthrow of the tsar in March 1917 was only the beginning of a struggle that continued through the second revolution in November, which brought the Bolsheviks to power proclaiming the dawn of a new era.

The combined effect of American entrance into the war and the ongoing revolution in Russia widened the conflict from a European to a truly world war and, at the same time, turned it into a quest for a new world order. Starting in the spring of 1917, the war was not just about who would control Alsace-Lorraine, or who would wind up with the most colonial possessions, or even about toppling hereditary dynasties. It was also about creating a whole new society and a new system of international relations.

That was why American progressives and Russian communists, Wilson and Lenin, found themselves competing. Although deeply divided over property and state power, both championed the principles of self-determination, popular government, and the open covenants of the new diplomacy. Wilson no less than Lenin appealed to the peoples of the world over the heads of their despotic governments and promised to sweep away old imperial regimes. To be sure, the ideological and geopolitical divisions between them would soon widen to a fateful chasm, but in the fluid period between the revolution in Russia in March 1917 and the Versailles conference, which ended in June 1919, the two rivals were running on the same track.

The fact that world war was thoroughly entangled with social revolution complicated the quest of America progressives to be good citizens in their home country and, at the same time, good citizens of the world. If they supported American intervention overseas in hopes of spreading their ideas of reform, how could they avoid imposing American ideas on others? If crusading Americanism was merely isolationism in reverse, what did true internationalism look like? And if internationalism meant solidarity across national boundaries, what if that conflicted with self-determination?

We will address these questions in due course. First we need to look at the range of American opinion following the declaration of war.

American Crusaders

Like their European counterparts three years earlier, many Americans indulged in "the moral exaltation of the war." According to Felix Adler of the Ethical Culture Society, they swelled with "the chevalier, romantic, idealistic spirit." Even the usually sober Secretary of the Treasury William McAdoo felt his heart beating faster: "It is a kind of crusade; and, like all crusades, it sweeps along on a powerful stream of romanticism." The crusading spirit ran deepest among Anglo-Saxon Protestants imbued with the messianic myth. Sounding Gabriel's trumpet, evangelicals tried to paint the American army as an avenging army of the Lord. *"We Must Win the War to Win the World,"* said the missionary board of the Congregational church. The YMCA set up Bible classes for army recruits before they went off to France as "reverent Crusaders for Democracy," and Christian hymns, such as "Onward, Christian Soldiers," were required singing in AEF training camps.[1]

Echoing Union troops marching off to battle against slavery, American doughboys also sang "The Battle Hymn of the Republic," the foremost anthem of messianic Americanism. To older lines about "the fateful lightning of His terrible, swift sword," new verses had been added: "We have heard the cry of anguish, / From the victims of the Hun, / And we know our country's peril/ If the war-lord's will is done. / We will fight for world-wide freedom / Till the victory is won. / For God is marching on." Having held back during the preparedness controversy, the evangelical churches now came forward in all their zeal. "This conflict is indeed a crusade," said one preacher, "the greatest in history—the holiest."[2]

The flood of crusading imagery pointed to the close relation between Protestantism and American nationalism. Many Protestants truly believed America was God's chosen nation to lead in the redemption of the world, and they immediately saw the war as a contest between evil and good, Old World corruption and New World innocence. "I tell you," said Reverend "Billy" Sunday, the greatest evangelist of the day, "it is Bill against Woodrow, Germany against America, Hell against Heaven." For Sunday and his many followers, this Manichaean mentality of Good-versus-Evil was rooted in the biblical book of Revelations, with its prophetic vision of the Apocalypse. Conjuring up images of the Beast of the Apocalypse, Sunday growled that the German people were "the pack of hungry, wolfish Huns, whose fangs drip with blood and gore."[3]

To a vast audience that included the common herd and upper crust alike, there was no more moving spectacle than an evangelical preacher like Reverend Sunday. About the time the first American troops were departing for France, Sunday entered New York City to launch a great revival before a throng of some 14,000 that included the eminently respectable Fifth Avenue Baptist Bible class and its illustrious leader, John D. Rockefeller, Jr. Moving on in the winter of 1917–18, Sunday waged the "Battle of Washington," a two-month crusade to save the soul of the nation's capital. Among the thousands who turned out to hear his message of hate for the Hun and redemption from the twin evils of sex and drink were cabinet members, U.S. senators, and numerous other pinstriped Washingtonians.[4]

Protestant moralists turned first to evils at home, and there was no greater evil than the demon rum. As the prime bastion of the redeemer mentality, the South had led the way toward prohibition before the war, and now prohibition became the law of the land in a series of steps that outlawed the manufacture and sale of intoxicating beverages with more than a small percentage of alcohol. Having authorized emergency wartime restrictions, Congress sent out the Eighteenth Amendment for ratification, and passed the Volstead Act to bridge the gap between the end of the war and ratification, which came in 1919.

The assault on commercialized sex was not far behind. As a journalist wrote, "John Barleycorn and the Woman of Babylon are partners," so it is not surprising that the country went off booze and illicit sex at the same time. Responding to pressures from both social hygienists, who focused on venereal disease, and evangelicals, who fretted about immorality, the federal government closed virtually every red-light district in the country that local authorities had not gotten to first.

Evangelical Protestants were not the only ones caught up in the messianic myth. Most progressives also enlisted in what they believed would be a two-front war, one for military victory and another for reform. Inspired by Wilson's grandiloquent rhetoric, progressives prepared to make America safe for democracy. "This is not merely a war of armies," declared John Dewey, echoing the president, "this is a war of peoples." Hitching reason to desire, they convinced themselves that American intervention was the best opportunity for reform to come along in their lifetime. Believing that the moment of mastery had arrived, Walter Lippmann accepted a string of government assignments in the hope that "we shall stand committed as never before to the realization of democracy in America."[5]

That belief was shared by other reformers who had taken positions in the Wilson administration, including Carrie Chapman Catt, suffrage leader and eager volunteer at the Women's Advisory Committee of the Council of National Defence, and Felix Frankfurter, who promoted industrial democracy at the helm of the War Labor Policies Board. Even W. E. B. Du Bois, convinced that the war would improve race relations, editorialized in *The Crisis* in favor of "closing ranks."[6]

Having gotten over their initial shock at the outbreak of the most terrible war in human history, progressives now tried to write it into the book of human progress. They took up the theme first sounded by H. G. Wells, the British writer, that this was "a war to end all wars." Somehow, out of the destruction would come a new concert of nations and a permanent peace. In the end, Progress would triumph. Another wrote, "Out of evil good may come—nay *must* come."[7]

Swept along on the same tide of romanticism, progressives contributed a good deal to the worst excesses of wartime propaganda. One example was the Liberty Loan drives under the direction of Secretary of the Treasury William McAdoo, a mild progressive from Tennessee. To raise money for the enormous costs of the war, McAdoo channeled patriotic emotion through a vigorous "selling campaign" that used every patriotic symbol in sight from Uncle Sam to Miss Liberty. According to McAdoo, "Women's clubs turned themselves into selling agencies. Factories and workshops stopped their plants and assembled their workmen so they might listen to Liberty Loan speeches and subscribe for bonds. The newspapers and billboard people contributed apace."[8]

The main engine of the propaganda machine was the Committee on Public Information, headed by former progressive journalist George Creel. Using the most advanced public relations techniques of the day, Creel besieged the public with tens of millions of pamphlets, posters, and news articles, along with thousands of so-called 4-Minute Men, who made patriotic speeches during the changing of reels in movie theaters. The Creel Committee also produced the first-ever government-made film, an anti-VD feature titled *Fit to Fight*, and commissioned the most extensive set of feature films yet produced, including *Pershing's Crusaders*, full of doughboys' derring-do, and *America's Answer*, a blockbuster which broke all distribution records by playing in nearly 6,000 theaters. In a fitting tribute to himself, the salesman-in-chief entitled his memoir "How We Advertised America."[9]

It is interesting to note that the equation was also being reversed. Advertisers at J. Walter Thompson, for example, were using the war to sell their products. In the case of Allen's Foot Powder, ads hailed the one-time balm for tired shoppers as the new "Infantrymen's Friend," a magic powder that would comfort the poor soldier subject to "irritating conditions" in the trenches: "Mail him a 3-cake box today and see what he says in his next letter." What took the cake for capitalizing on suffering was the ludicrous ad campaign of the Rat Biscuit Company. Getting into the spirit of the times, these patriotic purveyors of rat poison urged their customers to "Feed Belgians—not Rats," as if buying rat poison would somehow supply food to starving Belgians.[10]

In any case, Creel was second only to the president in defining the war in messianic terms. In Creel's countless pamphlets, it was a simple conflict between good and evil, freedom-loving American democracy and autocratic Prussian militarism. "Pershing's crusaders" were knights of democracy out to slay the Hun, portrayed in Creel's melodramatic posters as a malevolent beast whose claws dripped with the blood of innocent victims. Between these opposing poles of New World innocence and Old World corruption, there was no moral ambiguity.

Some of the most potent weapons in the selling campaign were gender images. Depictions of men ranged from virile soldiers and workers to helpless targets of foreign devils. Women were dowdy homemakers, voluptuous victims, and everything in between. Before the sexual sell had a name, Creel artists were evoking titillating images of clean-cut Wasp women in diaphanous gowns selling Liberty Bonds. At a time when women were putting on overalls to work in factories, artist Howard Chandler Christie loved to cross-dress his models in military uniforms. In one case, a coquettish brunette decked out in Navy blues looks out from a recruiting poster and coos, "Gee, I wish I were a man, I'd join the Navy." Other posters played on feminine innocence. In high-impact visuals designed to evoke the masculine protective impulse, posters showed the pornographic violence of Prussian gorillas ravishing fair damsels while perpetrating the infamous "rape of Belgium."

To sophisticated audiences, Creel's manipulation of gender imagery appeared crude and prurient, even laughable. His handiwork hardly measured up to the high standards of French Cubism, Russian Constructivism, and other brands of modern art that were put to use as propaganda at the same time. On the morning after, many progressives would wake up with a hangover. But for now, they gleefully indulged in the campaign to sell the war and, willy-nilly, swelled the tide of messianic Americanism that would engulf them at war's end.

Anyone wanting to believe that war would sweep aside Old World corruption was rewarded in early March with the overthrow of the Russian tsar. The fall of the four-hundred-year-old Romanov dynasty and its replacement by the Russian Republic under a Provisional Government of middle-class reformers and moderate socialists gave encouragement to reformers everywhere. Saluting the Russian people for being "democratic at heart," Wilson said in his April 2 war message that the revolution had made Russia a "fit partner for a league with honor."[11]

In fact, the tsar's ouster removed one of the major obstacles in the way of popular support for American intervention. With their new republican ally, American progressives could campaign for reform and come to the rescue of sister republics crying out for help—poor, abused Belgium and beleaguered, Third-Republican France. As for imperial Britain, did not the homeland of the Magna Carta and Parliament also deserve aid?

Wars have a way of upending expectations, however, and the Great War was no exception. The best laid plans of evangelicals, progressives, and statesmen alike were pushed aside by the troublesome reality of wartime events. Looking first at the military front, things did not go quite as planned. Initially, the expectation was for a defensive war in which the bulk of American forces would huddle safely behind the great moat of the Atlantic Ocean awaiting the impossible German invasion contemplated by U.S. contingency plans. Responding to Allied requests for a boost in morale, a relatively small number of troops would be ferried across the Atlantic largely for symbolic purposes, but America's main contribution would come in the forms of economic aid and diplomatic support.

What changed these plans was an urgent plea from the French commander Marshall Joffre that the war might be lost without hundreds of thousands of American troops.[12] Joffre's urgency was warranted by the military situation in the spring of 1917. The endless stalemate on the Western Front had led to exhaustion among the troops, evident in the French mutiny against General Nivelle, and to war weariness among civilians. Worse, the Eastern Front was collapsing. The overthrow of the tsar had not led to the hoped-for reinvigoration of Russian forces, but to exactly the opposite, an unstoppable hemorrhage of desertion, mutiny, and disintegration along the entire front, which the Provisional Government was powerless to reverse.

Responding quickly to these dangers, the Wilson administration laid plans to assemble the American Expeditionary Force (AEF), the largest army the country had ever seen. Within weeks of the April 6 declaration of war, Secretary of War Newton Baker was scrambling to recruit volunteers while preparing for mass conscription to begin on June 5. Eventually, some 4 million men were mobilized, of whom 2 million were ferried across the Atlantic, along with a handful of nurses and other female support

personnel. To lead American forces into battle, Secretary of War
Baker chose General "Black Jack" Pershing. Having demonstrated political loyalty to the president in the controversy
around Mexican intervention a year earlier, Pershing was a soldier's soldier who had served in imperial campaigns from Cuba
to the Philippines. He represented the new type of no-nonsense
professional suitable for policing an empire and now fit to enter
the lion's den of the Great Powers.

In mobilizing the troops, the administration relied heavily on
prior experience in Mexico. The initial concept of a unilateral,
mobile strike force capable of conducting a limited intervention
was taken directly from Pershing's Punitive Expedition of 1916,
as was the name of the American Expeditionary Force. Unfortunately, the imperial model was of no help whatsoever in present
circumstances. Intervention in Europe was no punitive expedition. Nor was it a marine landing, a guerilla campaign, a cavalry
raid against Indian villages, or a "splendid little war" against
the decrepit Spanish empire. Only the Civil War offered some
precedent in its mass conscript armies and industrial warfare,
but that, too, was forgotten in the current hubbub.

The first convoy of some 14,000 troops sailed out on June 14,
1917, shrouded in secrecy to minimize the danger of a German
U-boat attack. No Americans had ever made this journey into
Old World combat. Their thoughts as they glided past the Statue
of Liberty are unrecorded, but it would have been hard to miss
the symbolism of American soldiers, virtually all of European
descent in this initial detachment, carrying the torch of liberty
back to the homeland from whence their ancestors had come.[13]

American forces received a tumultuous welcome. Cheered
with great fanfare in London, Pershing went on to Paris to receive a shower of roses and cries of *"Vive l'Amérique!"* The greatest celebration occurred on July 4 when the whole of Paris
seemed to turn out to cheer the AEF as they marched on their
Independence Day from Napoleon's tomb at Les Invalides to Lafayette's grave on the outskirts of the city. Recalling the days of
Franco-American fraternity in the American and French Revolutions, the atmosphere was replete with republican symbolism.

In the crowning ceremony at Lafayette's grave, Pershing was quoted as saying, *"Lafayette, nous voilà.* Lafayette, we are here." Carried away by the rapture of the moment, one French newspaper remarked that the Atlantic Ocean had disappeared in "the fusion of Europe and America."[14]

Amid all the republican hoopla, it was possible to forget that Lafayette was an aristocrat who had turned traitor to his class and that France was home to grand cathedrals, a powerful Catholic hierarchy, a vast overseas empire, and a burdensome military establishment. Some of this old imperial France was evident when Pershing made a pilgrimage to Napoleon's tomb at Les Invalides. According to an aide, "The whole atmosphere was redolent of the great days of old France—the ancient Bourbon Church, with its memories of the Grand Monarch; the tomb of the Emperor which we knew to be at the back and which is a shrine for all the world; and the little groups of old and broken veterans who have found a home here since the days of the First Empire."[15] It is hard to square this homage to imperial, Catholic, Bourbon France with republican fraternity. From ancient Rome to Napoleonic France, republics had turned into empires. Would twentieth-century America do the same?

Whatever the fate of republicanism in the Atlantic nations, its prospects were fast growing dim in revolutionary Russia. Kerensky's Provisional Government was beset by counterrevolutionaries on the right and social revolutionaries on the left. The fact that Russia was still a mostly peasant land lacking both a broad middle class and a majority working class meant that neither moderate reform nor radical revolution could succeed through democratic means alone. Whoever would rule Russia would have to use draconian methods, which would severely test progressive sympathy for Russian revolution.

Protestant moralists were having an equally difficult time of it in Europe. From the first arrival of the AEF before any German soldier was met on the field of battle, it was clear that things were not going well on the moral front. Trouble appeared when a shocking number of red-blooded American boys made a beeline for the brothel as soon as they landed in France. American authorities had anticipated this errancy by adopting a policy of male "continence" intended to prevent all sexual contact by suppressing prostitution and fraternization in the vicinity of military encampments. Based on prior experience at the Mexican border, the policy replicated current practice at cantonments in the United States under the Commission on Training Camp Activities (CTCA), the official agency in charge of troop morale and recreation. It also won enthusiastic endorsement of the Young Men's Christian Association (YMCA), which enjoyed quasi-official status in providing wholesome entertainment for the troops.[16]

Despite differences between them, the moral reformers of the YMCA and the social engineers of the CTCA shared the same obsession with purity characteristic of the American redeemer mentality. Making American boys clean and pure in body and soul was as important as making the world safe for democracy. "If by throwing this army into France we defeat the German arms but destroy the moral health of the young men who make up that army," warned a YMCA secretary, "then most assuredly will we have done more to destroy the foundations upon which democracy rests than we can possibly do to protect them." Venereal disease came to symbolize the threat of cultural pollution, the danger that the Old World was corrupting the New.[17]

Reformers aimed at nothing less than the creation of a new kind of masculinity built around a single standard of morality. Vowing to protect the honor of European women, the CTCA promised that the new type of man would be a "red-blooded virile man who preserves his manhood" by refusing to have sex with anyone not his lawfully wedded wife. Unfortunately, the new masculinity shaded off into the old misogyny. Official publications were full of associations between women and disease. Warning against common streetwalkers, government flyers and posters declared, "A German Bullet Is Cleaner Than A Whore."[18]

Racial attitudes also came into play. American officials tried to draw the color line in France to conform to racial segregation in the United States. Referring to "the difficulty in controlling the negro," CTCA officials highlighted unconfirmed reports of colored troops being involved in rapes and went out of their way to stress the special need to enforce the policy of continence so as to prevent sex across the color line.[19]

To the dismay of American officials, France could not be policed as if it were a rural county in Georgia. As far as the French were concerned, the American obsession with purity, whether moralistic or scientific, was a bizarre Anglo-Saxon peculiarity, and the policy of continence was simply incomprehensible. When regulated brothels were declared off limits and American soldiers began roaming the streets, French Premier Clemenceau rose to the defense of French womanhood and, without batting an eyelash, offered to procure disease-free prostitutes for the randy Americans. This led Secretary of War Baker to admonish an aide, "For God's sake, Raymond, don't show this to the President or he'll stop the war."[20]

Continence was doomed to failure under any circumstances. Reformers were pushing their idea of a single standard of premarital virginity upon a quintessentially man's world still governed by the double standard. Many army and navy officers simply ignored the exhortations of the social hygienists and handed out condoms, as clear an admission of defeat as the VD epidemic among the troops. Other reports of failure came flooding in. An American medical official learned from interviews with French prostitutes of the soldiers' preference for the "French way," a euphemism for fellatio, and he worried that veterans would return home "with those new and degenerate ideas sapping their sources of self-respect and thereby lessening their powers of moral resistance." Whatever resistance American redeemers met among their own troops paled in comparison to the total failure to make a dent in French mores. The YMCA's official history of war work noted ruefully, "It was not quite possible to make over the principles of these countries as an enthusiastic American uplifter might have desired."[21]

Thus even before the frustrations of the Versailles conference, Wasp reformers were worried that in the war against vice, it seemed that vice was winning. The exhilaration of military victory was tempered by the nagging sense of moral defeat. And moral defeat overseas would bring the crusade to redeem the world crashing back upon the United States in the aftermath of the war.

Reluctant Crusaders

Even as they embarked on their world-saving mission, Americans harbored deep misgivings. Never before had an American army sailed across the invisible line running down the middle of the Atlantic drawn by the Monroe Doctrine. Nor was there any festering wrong to avenge, or territory to recapture, or Pearl Harbor to remember. In these uncertain circumstances, Americans were not entirely sure they were doing the right thing.

Indeed, the very excess of super-patriotism was a kind of backhanded testimony to the strength of peace sentiment in the spring and summer of 1917. "In nations as well as individuals," observed Max Eastman, editor of *The Masses*, "hysteria is caused by inner conflict." Toting up the list of supporters, Eastman later recalled, "We had the whole Socialist Party and the IWW with us, the pacifists, many of the humanitarian uplifters, most of the Quakers and deep-feeling Christian ministers, the Irish, the 'hyphenated Americans,' the old-fashioned patriots still faithful to George Washington's Farewell Address, and millions of plain folks."[22] Eastman's catalogue of dissenters is close to the mark. Needless to say, this mishmash of Pentecostalists, Irish nationalists, German-Americans, and anarcho-syndicalists hardly made for a cohesive antiwar movement. But it does indicate that the social base for a messianic crusade was not as wide as first appeared.

Most striking is the fact that many religious communities were reluctant crusaders. The Quakers, the Church of the Brethren, and other peace churches refused to go along, for which many of their members paid the price of ostracism, even jail. Even some fundamentalists held back until American intervention was well underway, when they began to see prophetic signs and joined in.[23] The split between pro- and antiwar fundamentalists held ironies for both sides. The premillennialists—those who believed most fervently in Armageddon and the coming Kingdom of God—were slow to enlist in the war effort. On the other hand, postmillennialists, who looked to earthly progress, pretended that the Armegeddon-like destruction of the war was part of God's design for human progress and rushed to the colors.

Outside the religious communities, doubters included lots of populist-minded plain folks from the Plains states and the upper Midwest who had given their votes to prominent opponents of intervention, such as George Norris of Nebraska and Robert La Follette of Wisconsin. In the cities, some local election results in the spring and summer of 1917 suggest the unpopularity of the war in the working class precincts of northern cities.[24]

As for Eastman's "hyphenated Americans," there was lingering sympathy for the ancestral homeland among many German-Americans, and the same was true of Irish-Americans, who wasted no love on the British ally, especially after "Bloody Sunday," when British authorities brutally suppressed the 1916 Easter Rebellion. Many eastern and southern European communities were also rife with antiwar sentiment. Among Italians, Jews, and Finns, the foreign language press routinely condemned imperialist and mercenary aspects of the war.[25]

Refusing to imitate their European comrades, the American Socialist party held true to their internationalist principles and bravely passed an antiwar resolution. Fearless as ever, Debs did not hesitate to condemn the capitalist origins of the war, and the same went for anarchist Emma Goldman. The Greenwich Village radicals were also strong dissenters. Although the very model of an avant-garde magazine, *The Masses* under Max Eastman did all it could to marshal popular traditions to stop the war. As the son of *two* Congregational ministers, Eastman had no trouble publishing Christian symbols in cartoons showing the Prince of Peace being shot as a deserter or jailed as a dissenter.[26]

In the war of inflammatory symbols, *The Masses* gave away nothing to the Creel Committee's depictions of the pornography of violence. In some of the most gripping imagery in the annals of American journalism, Henry Glitenkamp's "Conscription" showed voluptuous nudes of both sexes chained to a cannon, and R. Kempf's "Come on in, America, the Blood's Fine" depicted the grim reaper embracing three half-clad figures representing the European powers writhing in a pool of blood.[27] For all their differences in the symbolic uses of the human body, both sides played on the lust for victory as a hideous perversion of desire, and both, in their own way, perpetuated deep-seated associations between sex and violence, carnality and death.

Needless to say, only antiwar imagery was deemed unfit for publication. Determined to silence dissenting voices, Congress enacted the Espionage Act (1917), which greatly expanded the definition of treason, and the Sedition Act (1918), which prohibited even private utterances which could be deemed subversive. Under this statutory authority, Postmaster-General Burelson suppressed every antiwar publication in sight, including *The Masses* and the *International Socialist Review*. Doing his part for official intolerance, Attorney General Gregory succeeded in putting Socialist party leaders behind bars, including Debs, jailed for a speech in Canton, Ohio, condemning "capitalist war."

The most severe repression was visited on the Industrial Workers of the World. In August and September 1917, federal authorities conducted nationwide raids that led to indictments of the IWW's entire national leadership. Moving to outlaw the IWW altogether, the Justice Department charged the organization with seditious conspiracy for strikes and sabotage against war producers. With the Post Office barring Wobbly literature from the mails, the Justice Department sought to criminalize IWW's brand of radical unionism by outlawing even the motto "an injury to one is an injury to all." This was the first time since the Alien and Sedition Acts of 1798 that the federal government gave itself authority to outlaw *speech*, and it resulted in the largest group of political prisoners since the Civil War. All in all, it was the greatest campaign against free expression in the nation's history.[28]

Repression took its toll. Not only was the left rendered impotent, but more moderate critics of the war were cowed into silence. The paralysis of pacifism was personified by Jane Addams. Precisely because Addams spoke as the female guardian of the home, her criticism of the conduct of the war was taken as a presumptuous challenge to male authority. "A couple of foolish virgins" is how the *Cleveland News* characterized Addams and Jeannette Rankin, the lone woman in Congress, who had cast one of the handful of House votes against the war. Despite the fact that trench warfare was crushing heroic masculinity every day, the *New York Herald* insisted the United States had to fight, lest it become "a nation of Jane Addamses."[29]

Stung by such criticism, shaken by defections of her closest associates, and frightened of official censure, Addams refused to lend her name to peace protests. Estranged from her pacifist comrades and cut off as never before from the larger community, she felt a profound "spiritual alienation." The force of the majority was so overwhelming, she admitted, there were times when "one secretly yearned to participate in 'the folly of all mankind.' "[30]

Gradually the lifeblood of democratic debate was squeezed out. In a storm of anguish and betrayal, the American Union Against Militarism disintegrated. Former allies became enemies, and progressives in government stood by and watched as their friends and former associates who refused to support the war were denounced as traitors. The pacifists around Addams gradually ceased to state their position, and the Women's Peace Party became moribund.[31] The IWW was fast becoming a legal defense organization; the left press was silenced; La Follette and his fellow midwestern progressives were backed into a corner; Debs was in jail. For all practical purposes grassroots organizing against the war had ceased by the end of 1917.

For some progressives, wartime repression was a radicalizing experience. Frederick Howe, for example, learned to distrust the state of which he was a very disgruntled part. As wartime commissioner of Ellis Island, Howe was called upon to enforce deportation edicts of questionable legality. To overcome his guilt, on advice from a psychiatrist, he made "confessions," which turned into a political cry from the heart against the wartime "stamping out of individualism and freedom." Dismayed at the government's use of agents provocateurs and private detective agencies, Howe traced the evil of repression back to plutocracy. Speaking for other left progressives, he criticized Wilson's government for becoming a tool of business: "It became frankly an agency of employing and business interests at a time when humanity—the masses, the poor—were making the supreme sacrifice of their lives."[32]

A similar analysis issued from the pen of Randolph Bourne, the best remembered of the antiwar writers. In a set of essays written shortly before he died at an early age in the influenza epidemic of 1918, Bourne took his pro-war friends to task for their illusions about "people's war." Nonsense, Bourne replied, "War is the health of the state," not the expression of the people's will. Reformers who supported Wilson's democratic crusade were simply deluding themselves. The truth was "Democratic control of foreign policy is . . . a contradiction in terms."[33] Instead of having a higher mission, the United States was a state like any other state, the defender of class interests, the repository of "herd instincts," and the sponsor of militarism. He chided progressives for growing tired of reform crusades against the trusts and for being "only too glad to sink back to a glorification of the State ideal, to feel about them in war the old protecting arms, to return to the old primitive sense of the omnipotence of the State, its matchless virtue, honor, and beauty, driving away all the foul old doubts and dismays."[34]

In the heat of battle, even this brilliant critic of wooly-headed illusions got a bit carried away. Nonetheless, the basic truth in his critique—that a democratic state could be as repressive as an authoritarian one—led to the recognition among progressives of a need for a permanent, systematic defense of civil liberties. Quoting a liberal journal, Jane Addams recalled how that recognition came about: "Within a year after the war began the old causes were . . . abandoned like war trenches on the Western Front, and we found ourselves fighting in the last ditch for the primary bases of democratic society, the civil liberties proclaimed in the Declaration of Independence and guaranteed in the Constitution."[35] From the last ditch, progressives again returned to the founding ideals of the republic, as they had before the war. Only now their goal was to prevent a republican government run amok from violating its own founding principles.

Just as the suppression of free speech became more systematic and centralized during the war, so did its defense. Behind the guiding light of Roger Baldwin, a brave band of public defenders formed an emergency committee for civil liberties out of the fast disintegrating American Union Against Militarism. In what was to become the American Civil Liberties Union, legal eagles whose first love was the First Amendment set out to defend conscientious objectors and antiwar dissenters.

The creation of the Civil Liberties Bureau marked a proud moment in the republican tradition. With patriotic symbols flying like bullets, Baldwin advised a colleague, "We want to get a lot of good flags, talk a good deal about the Constitution and what our forefathers wanted to make of this country, and to show that we are the folks that really stand for the spirit of our institutions." Eastman, who later became a Trotskyite, intended no irony in recollecting, "I took very seriously the American ideals of freedom for all, justice and equal opportunity for all."[36]

Although divided over the war and bowed by repression, progressives were not broken. They were busy laying down the defense of free speech as a cornerstone of the new progressive politics. Out of the darkness, new stars were beginning to twinkle.

Class War/Race War

If there were a Richter scale of social disorder, the period from 1917 through 1921 would register as the biggest earthquake in twentieth-century America. Momentous class and racial conflicts rumbled through the supposedly unified nation as the growing number of strikes peaked in the middle of the period at over 20 percent of the workforce, the highest in American history, and the deadliest string of race riots began in East St. Louis, ran through Chicago after the war, and ended in Tulsa, where estimates of the dead range into the hundreds. The only events on a comparable scale were the antiwar protests and urban riots of the 1960s, but even they did not rise to the level of disorder during the First World War and its tumultuous aftermath.

The disorders arose out of the impact of world events on the class and racial divisions of American society. First of all, the war actually shifted the balance of power in industry toward wage earners. Essentially what happened was that the demand for industrial workers skyrocketed just as the usual European sources of unskilled labor dried up. In the tightest labor market of their lives, workers gained unprecedented leverage. With unemployment dropping precipitously from around 15 percent in 1915 to an astounding 2.4 percent in 1918, workers were in a position to chase after higher wages by changing jobs and going out on strike. Each year after 1914 saw a significant increase in the number of strikes, which reached 4,450 in 1917, when more than a million workers hit the bricks. No wonder Samuel Gompers quietly retracted his famous "no strike" pledge of March 1917 almost as soon as he made it.[37]

The most contentious region was the West. From the low arid arroyos of the Arizona desert to the high mountain plateau of craggy Montana, long-simmering conflicts boiled to the surface. Copper towns roiled with wildcat walkouts and large-scale strikes in the summer of 1917, and the lumber camps of the Pacific Northwest were scarcely less turbulent. In a region honeycombed with Wobblies, radical populists, and every other kind of rebel, such labor disputes were the red cape to the bull of authority.

How would the federal government react? Expectations were high for federal mediation of industrial disputes. Prewar progressives had placed high hopes in the Commission on Industrial Relations and other mediating institutions as the best way to prevent discord from getting out of hand. Now, seeking to travel the high road to labor peace, the Wilson administration hastily improvised mediation machinery, most importantly the

War Labor Board. It also beefed up the existing Newlands Commission, dispatched the newly created President's Mediation Commission to a host of trouble spots, and gave its blessing to informal efforts of state governors and private citizens.

Unfortunately, mediation failed at every turn.[38] The most spectacular episode occurred in Bisbee and Jerome, Arizona, sites of infamous deportations of striking copper workers. On July 12, 1917, officials of the Phelps Dodge copper company combined forces with the Citizens Protective League led by the local sheriff to round up over 1,000 strikers, stuff them into sealed boxcars, and send them off into the scorching desert. After the worst was over, the President's Mediation Commission finally arrived to survey the damage. Such a flagrant violation of human rights was too much for the Justice Department, which prosecuted the vigilantes, but evidently not for the U.S. Supreme Court, which acquitted them.[39]

In Butte, a similar story ended with a particularly grisly twist. Passions ran high after the incineration of 164 miners in the Speculator Mine disaster and were only further inflamed by a subsequent strike. With the collapse of Secretary of Labor Wilson's effort at mediation, control passed to the usual mix of troops and vigilantes. On August 1, vigilantes put a rope around the neck of Frank Little, a half-Indian organizer for the IWW, pinned the symbol of Old West vigilantes "3–7–77" to his shirt, mutilated his genitals, tied a rope around his neck, and flung his badly beaten body off a railroad trestle.[40]

Because the new mediation machinery was so feeble, the Wilson administration's only remaining recourse when things got out of hand was the use of force. Reflecting the spirit of nationalism and the industrial character of modern war, the War Department hastily improvised a new "public utilities" doctrine under which any private production site with even a remote connection to the war effort was defined as a public utility. That allowed any disruption of production to be deemed a threat to the national interest which could be met with federal troops.[41] Requests for troops poured into the War Department during the summer of 1917, and in short order, federal troops took possession of a string of western lumber camps, coal districts, and rail junctions. Soon soldiers were guarding West Coast lumber yards, orchards, and wheat fields against merely "threatened" strikes and the perceived "danger" of sabotage. U.S. troops did not leave copper towns from Butte to Bisbee, at opposite ends of the Rocky Mountains, until 1921.[42]

Class conflict was not confined to the West. It also played a major role in the race riots of the time. Some of the worst racial violence in the country's bloody history occurred in the context of wartime labor shortages, changing patterns of labor migration, and disruptions of existing race relations. Rising worker militancy coincided with the arrival of hundreds of thousands of African-Americans seeking opportunity in the Great Migration of rural blacks to job-rich urban centers. The result was an explosive mix of class and racial tensions.

What made the situation so volatile in northern cities was the large influx of migrants into neighborhoods formerly off limits to African-Americans. Unlike the South, where large black and white populations were deeply entwined in the hierarchical order of segregation, whites in the North attempted to enforce a pattern of racial *exclusion* from jobs, neighborhoods, schools, and political office. Thus the arrival of black workers, sometimes as strikebreakers, was sure to provoke a hostile reaction among whites.

The Great Migration crashed against the wall of white supremacy to produce a riot of major proportions in the border city of East St. Louis, Illinois. Half southern, half northern, this industrial satellite town just across the Mississippi River from St. Louis contained the worst possible combination of racial segregation *and* racial exclusion. The shortage of unskilled labor brought blacks to town in unprecedented numbers to the point where they constituted nearly a fifth of the population. Local workers were determined to take advantage of the tight labor market, and labor disputes led to strikes. Instead of bargaining with the unions, employers brought in strikebreakers, including a handful of blacks, supplied by a union-busting firm in New York, whereupon the AFL-linked Central Labor Council lodged a formal protest, and Democratic party leaders denounced the supposed "colonization" scheme of their Republican opponents to bring thousands of black voters into the city. It did not matter that there was no evidence of "colonization." It did not matter that blacks were not in direct competition with whites, or that most of the strikebreakers were, in fact, white. What counted was that blacks were taking what were deemed "white men's jobs in a white man's town." White mobs descended upon hapless blacks in a furious rampage. Self-defense was to no avail in a situation where local police and state militia often looked the other way. After flushing out its prey by setting homes afire, the mob engaged in its murderous sport, leaving at least 39 blacks and 9 whites dead.[43]

From the ashes of East St. Louis arose a cry of righteous indignation. One expression of protest was a large "silent parade" organized by the National Association for the Advancement of Colored People in New York on July 28, 1917. The parade formation imitated countless military parades of the time—a drum corps out front, precise ranks and files, and American flags held aloft. In place of regimental banners, signs read, "Mr. President, why not make America safe for democracy?"[44]

In the politics of moral outrage, the most reliable allies of African-Americans were American Jews. After watching the "silent parade," one newspaper explained, "Jews who have lived through all of these things in the Old World can well empathize with those who walked in the procession, can feel the oppression which the silent march protested." The *Vorwarts* (*Forward*), a leading Yiddish-language socialist newspaper, compared the East St. Louis riot to the infamous Kishinev pogrom of 1903: "There, in Kishinev, they ripped open peoples' bellies and stuffed them with feathers; here in St. Louis, houses were set on fire and women and children were allowed to burn alive."[45]

No attempt was made to bring the East St. Louis rioters to justice. Although the local Council of National Defence was authorized to conduct an investigation, there was a deafening silence from the White House and no acknowledgment on the part of the Wilson administration that the riot had besmirched America's reputation as the moral leader of a democratic crusade.

The class and racial conflicts of 1917 would have been unsettling under any circumstances. What made them seem doubly disruptive was the perception of a link between domestic disorder and global revolution. Against the backdrop of revolution in Mexico and China and the ongoing revolution in Russia, authorities in the United States construed social conflict as a power struggle over who should rule at home. Thus it is necessary to turn to the American responses to revolution.

People's Peace

Even as dissent was being smothered, a new internationalism was struggling to be born. In the face of battlefield stalemate and civilian suffering, a deep yearning for peace arose in the spring of 1917, coupled with renewed demands for economic justice. On these wings, a worldwide movement for a "people's peace" took flight.

The movement was buoyed upward by the continuing revolution in Russia. Although the new moderate regime under Kerensky desperately struggled to keep the war effort going, Russia was rapidly losing the will to fight. Soldiers were abandoning their posts at the front, and workers councils, or soviets, which sprang up in the major cities, were calling for an immediate end to the fighting. In the forefront of these efforts was the Petrograd Soviet, which put forth three points that would become the cornerstone of peace efforts for the remainder of the war—no forcible annexations, no punitive indemnities, and free development of nationalities.

The Petrograd formula catalyzed the international movement for a people's peace. Catching fire in European socialist and labor circles, the idea for a grassroots peace conference to be held on neutral ground in Stockholm, Sweden, gained momentum over the summer of 1917. At the risk of being arrested for treason, British laborites and French socialists agreed to meet with their German and Austrian counterparts in Stockholm.

The emergence of this impulse in Germany was of particular significance. Prewar Germany had been the homeland of the world's largest socialist party, and the SPD's support for the German war effort in 1914 had been the single most devastating betrayal of socialist internationalism. Although mainline socialists continued to support the war, breakaway leftists founded the Independent Socialist party in April 1917 and, along with other radicals, risked jail or worse to call for peace and justice.[46]

These seeds fell on fertile ground because of war weariness and class tension on both sides. German civilians had suffered through the "turnip winter," and resentment was growing against war profiteers. By the same token, the peoples of Britain and France were tired of sacrificing the flower of their youth to the generals' stalemate. Echoing these feelings, the Pope raised his voice in late summer in support of a negotiated peace. To a growing number of people, peace was becoming more appealing than victory.[47]

By the fall, hopes for peace had become thoroughly entwined with radical dreams. The idea was afoot that the popular classes—industrial workers, peasants, small trades—had both the motivation and the potential power to overthrow the ruling classes, whose greed and imperial ambition were only prolonging the war. Radical ideas gained a certain plausibility from events around the globe. Mexico, in particular, offered the vision of a red future in its 1917 constitution, which defied foreign oil and mining corporations by proclaiming all mineral resources to be the property of the nation. Meanwhile, in Russia fertile ground was being prepared for Lenin's call to turn imperialist war into class war.

These developments encouraged antiwar progressives in the United States to join their European counterparts in attempting to build a bridge across the Atlantic. The transatlantic impulse was especially strong among recent immigrants from eastern Europe who had once fought the tsar and were now electrified by revolution in Russia. In the fluid conditions before the Bolsheviks took power, Americans of many stripes—left-leaning progressives, socialists, syndicalists, and anarchists—put aside their differences to support the growing international movement for radical change.

Working feverishly through the late spring and summer of 1917, these American internationalists took up the call for a people's peace. In imitation of the Russian soviets, they set up the People's Council of America as the people's answer to the official Council of National Defence in Washington. The radicalization of the peace movement was evident in the composition of the People's Council. It drew most of its leaders from the ranks of advanced progressives, including Rabbi Judah Magnes, Florence Kelley, and the omnipresent Crystal Eastman, and it had closer ties to the Socialist party than any previous peace organization.[48]

Having kept the internationalist faith by adopting a rigorous antiwar resolution, the American Socialist party, for its part, was now ready to cooperate with other dissidents. Many party leaders occupied top positions in the People's Council, including Morris Hillquit, New York's most prominent socialist, Louis Lochner, organizer of the Ford Peace Ship, and James Maurer, head of the Pennsylvania branch of the American Federation of Labor. A good part of the organizational base around the country lay in Socialist party locals, and where there was union support, it often came from the socialist-led garment unions.

In place of Wilson's crusade for democracy through war, these progressive internationalists launched their own campaign for "democracy and peace." A throng of some 15,000 gathered in New York's Madison Square Garden at the end of May to hear a parade of speakers make a heroic effort to link up American radicalism with the international movement now afoot. In the true internationalist spirit, the People's Council embraced the Stockholm idea and endorsed the three-part formula that was fast becoming the standard radical prescription for a just peace: no forcible annexations, no punitive indemnities, and self-determination for all nationalities.

At the same time, the movement was recognizably American. The People's Council proposed peace terms that might have warmed the heart of any Wilsonian. Quoting Wilson's "peace without victory" speech at length, Morris Hillquit argued that the validity of Wilson's argument had not been diminished by U.S. entrance into the war. Throwing the president's words back in his face, Hillquit said, "Only peace between equals can last." As with the prewar peace and justice movement, the message was couched in familiar populist terms. Speakers pointed the finger of blame for the war straight at J. P. Morgan and his fellow oligarchs, and lamented the fact that it was not the rich, but the common people on both sides who were forced to do the dying.

Among the speakers at the founding convention was Scott Nearing, defrocked Wharton professor who became chairman of the People's Council's executive board. "Industrial plutocracy makes for war," Nearing told his audience, "industrial democracy for peace." Rebutting pro-war reformers, Nearing warned that war brought with it "autocratic, political control of industry in the interests of the ruling classes." The way to unseat plutocracy was not through a wartime crusade for reform, but rather by ending the war and working for economic democracy on an international scale. Calling Americans to their destiny as peacemakers and social reformers, Nearing said, "The American people, joining hands with the new democracy of Russia, must lay the basis of permanent world peace by establishing industrial democracy." In all, the People's Council was the American left's best effort to reconcile world citizenship and American citizenship at a time of war and revolution.[49]

Despite their sympathy with revolution overseas, the opponents of war used tactics that were anything but revolutionary. Neither Debs nor his comrades called for bringing the troops home *now*. Not even the rough-and-tumble IWW advised its members to resist the draft. When conscription began on June 5, there was no repetition of the Civil War draft riots, to the immense relief of the authorities.[50]

Instead, the People's Council built a mushrooming national organization that attracted overflow crowds to militant mass meetings throughout the summer of 1917. After a Second Conference in Chicago July 7–8, councils sprang up all over the country, reaching a peak of perhaps 500 local groups (if the national office can be believed). Affiliation depended on local circumstances: in Wisconsin, the movement attracted supporters of Robert La Follette; in Minnesota, the machinists union; in the Northwest, the IWW.

Although Council members were a tiny minority of the public, they gave voice to the broad doubts about the war in the country at large. That was why the Wilson administration was determined to squash them. Having cast his lot with the Allies, Wilson spared no effort to block a "premature peace," even if it bore the people's imprint. In this effort, Wilson had the support of a broad range of public figures from business conservatives like Elihu Root to labor conservative Sam Gompers, who took every opportunity to thwart the socialists in his own house. Root and Gompers were both were members of the euphemistically named League to Enforce Peace, a staunchly pro-war lobby.

As if that were not enough, urgent messages arrived in Washington from Lloyd George's government appealing for united Allied action to stamp out the Stockholm mischief. Accordingly, when delegates from the People's Council applied for passports to go to Stockholm, the request came back denied.[51] There was to be no people-to-people diplomacy on Wilson's watch.

Authorities also tried to block popular protest at home with nightsticks, arrests, and more undercover agents than American dissenters had ever seen. Under the headline "New Police Arms Awe Socialists," the *New York Times* reported on surveillance of the People's Council by a "small army" of secret service agents. Secret police were also hard on the heels of the anarchists. The sworn enemies of the state attracted 15,000 to a Manhattan meeting to protest conscription, and again the headline read, "Anarchists Awed by Police Clubs."[52]

Debate over the war reached something of a climax in September when the People's Council tried to hold a major convention in Minneapolis. This time the authorities were not to be denied. Although the mayor was favorably disposed, and the socialist police chief "is heart and soul for us," Minnesota's governor Burnquist banned the gathering on the grounds that it was likely to result in riot and bloodshed.[53]

Dissidents felt both the iron heel of repression and the softer pressures of propaganda. With support from Gompers and secret funding from the Creel Committee, officials set up the American Alliance for Labor and Democracy to counter the international drive for a people's peace. Right behind the retreating People's Council, the American Alliance made a triumphal entry into Minneapolis for its founding convention and went on to provide a megaphone to pro-war socialists. As winter came on, the People's Council and other dissident groups were reduced to paper organizations, and the lights of dissent were winking out all over America.

Organizational defeat should not obscure the significance of the new internationalism. Against crusading Americanism, it stood with the common people across national boundaries. Against the well-developed doctrine of just war, it proposed a doctrine of just peace. Each of these positions presented problems of its own—steelworkers in Chicago did not necessarily have the same interests as peasants in Ukraine. But in one version or another, this combination of peace and economic justice captured the imagination of increasing numbers of war-weary peoples and compelled their leaders not just to seek military victory but also to intensify their search for a new world order.

Just as American radicals were succumbing to the blows of the Wilson administration, Russian radicals were on the verge of overthrowing their government for the second time in a year. In the summer and fall of 1917 Russia was a cauldron of revolution and counterrevolution, as soviets of workers and soldiers fended off plots by Kornilov and his fellow generals to restore the tsar. The pot was boiling over with manifestos and proclamations from a dozen political factions ranging from moderate Mensheviks to anarchist sailors in the port of Kronstadt.

A small number of Americans were present to witness these events firsthand. Their contrasting responses reveal much about the impact of world revolution on American reformers as they wrestled every day with the central questions of internationalism. How could local struggles be linked across barriers of culture and tradition? What if the internationalist principle of solidarity came into conflict with self-determination?

One answer was to join the revolution. America's most prominent Bolshevik was John Reed. Reed's global journeys in search of history-in-the-making form one of the most remarkable odysseys in the annals of American radicalism. The very antithesis of the crusader type, Reed had been something of a playboy in his undergraduate days at Harvard. Having abandoned his hometown of Portland, Oregon, he came to Greenwich Village in search of love and revolution and found both in the spirited company of Louise Bryant, who had made a similar journey from Portland to the bohemian radicalism of the Village. There they became comrades in arms in revolt against bourgeois convention.

Initially, Reed was more a romantic than an ideologue, and he quested for adventure as much as for social change, finding both on the trail of Pancho Villa in the deserts of northern Mexico. But like so many other pilgrims of his generation, his encounters with history deepened his desire to root out the underlying causes of human suffering. After a stint in the trenches of northern France, as he thought through the causes of war, he became more convinced than ever that profit was the power behind every throne, whether the tsar, the British empire, or American plutocracy.

When revolution broke out in Russia in March 1917, Reed and Bryant decided it was something they could not miss. After long delay in receiving passports, they set sail in August to attend the people's peace conference in Stockholm. Arriving to find the conference postponed indefinitely, they moved on to Petrograd in September. Although the ancient capital of the tsars was a long way from Portland, they seemed to feel right at home. "We are in the middle of things," Reed wrote to a friend, " and believe me it's thrilling." Compared to red Russia, even insurgent Mexico had been mere rehearsal. "For color and terror and grandeur this makes Mexico look pale."[54]

They threw themselves into the Russian cauldron, heart and soul. As events moved toward a climax in early November, they rushed from one hot spot to another, going from the all-Russian Congress of Soviets to the tsars' Winter Palace, now the seat of Kerensky's Provisional Government. Their favorite place of all was the Smolny Institute, formerly a finishing school for elite young ladies, now the throbbing headquarters of the majority faction of the Bolsheviks, the "majority men" of the Russian Social Democratic party. Wherever they looked amid the din and chaos, they saw disciplined Bolsheviks taking the lead, and they were not at all surprised when, on November 7, the Bolsheviks seized the Winter Palace, toppling Kerensky's Provisional Government in a more-or-less bloodless coup. Standing at the point where history seemed to turn, they could not have been more thrilled.

Reed was fascinated with the iron-willed band of men and women who were grasping state power. Lenin, above all, captured his attention. Watching the founder of modern communism at the podium, Reed was puzzled by this short, unshaven figure dressed in shabby clothes. How strange for a popular leader to be so "colorless, humorless, uncompromising and detached." There was nothing of the swashbuckling Pancho Villa here, no man-on-horseback. Instead, Reed concluded that Lenin's commanding presence was the result of his extraordinary powers of intellect. He was "a leader purely by virtue of intellect ... with the power of explaining profound ideas in simple terms" who possessed "the greatest intellectual audacity."[55]

Interestingly enough, the same could be said of Wilson. In fact, a comparison of the Soviet leader and the American president reveals striking similarities. Both were intellectuals in politics possessed of the extraordinary ability to articulate profound truths in simple terms, whether it was making the world "safe for democracy," or "peace, land, and bread." They shared some of the same strengths of character, including personal integrity and incorruptibility, traits common among intellectuals in politics from Cromwell in the Puritan Revolution to Robespierre in the French. They also shared some of the same flaws, including absolute certainty of their own correctness. This unusual combination of virtues and flaws served these two antagonists well as they mounted the world stage to play the role history was forcing upon them, that of competing with one another for leadership of the new internationalism.

For now, it was Lenin's turn to take the lead. With Reed present on the night of November 8 to write it all down, Lenin stood before the All-Russian Congress of Soviets, looked out over the unruly crowd, and declared, "We shall now proceed to construct the Socialist order." After the roar of the crowd died down, Lenin took the first step in that direction by proclaiming the Peace Decree, which called upon the warring nations to set down their arms on the basis of the by-now familiar Petrograd formula of "no annexations, no indemnities, free determination of nationalities."

Much of what the Anglo-American left understood about the Bolshevik revolution came from Reed's red-hot account of "ten days that shook the world." Not only did it become the standard description of events, but its rhapsodies of apocalyptic transformation helped shape the myth of revolution for an entire generation. Instantly, centuries of oppression and years of terrible warfare melted away in Reed's account. Visions of peace and justice flowed forth. Tears of joy rained down. Cries and shouts melded together as the crowd at the Congress of Soviets rose as one, Reed with the rest, to sing the "Internationale." Out of the mingled voices came the universal message, "Arise ye prisoners of starvation, arise ye wretched of the earth. Justice thunders condemnation, a better world's in birth." To be sure, this was a highly exaggerated rendering of events, and soon the Bolshevik seizure of power would lead to terrors of its own. But who can deny that, at the beginning, the Bolsheviks put forward a moral vision of a better world that was far grander than the moral exaltation of war?

Some proof of good intentions came in the Soviet regime's practical lesson on the difference between the old diplomacy and the new. Making good on their stunning Peace Decree of November 8, the Bolsheviks entered into negotiations with the Germans at Brest-Litovsk for a separate peace. Others only preached peace; they practiced it. What was more, having discovered secret treaties in the tsar's archives, they exposed for all the world to see the sordid deals that defined Allied war aims: in the Sykes-Picot agreement, Britain and France had carved up the declining Ottoman Empire between them; separate agreements promised Russia the coveted warm-water port of Constantinople and Italian control of certain Austrian territories. Other agreements shared out Germany's possessions in Africa and Asia, including China's Shandong peninsula, which had the Japanese licking their chops.

By contrast, the Bolsheviks renounced the tsar's claim to Constantinople, denounced all annexations and indemnities, and urged the Muslim peoples of the East to rise up against their colonial overlords. The fact that they were shining a bright light into the dark recesses of balance-of-power diplomacy while calling for the oppressed and exhausted peoples of Europe to overthrow their masters seemed to prove their commitment to a better world. Their propaganda victory could not have been sweeter.

Unfortunately, the road to the better world ran through the Eastern Front. The negotiations with the Germans made quite clear that the new diplomacy was underwritten by Russian self-interest. Russian negotiators desperately tried to prevent German annexation of lands belonging to the tsar, refused German demands for indemnities, and insisted on self-determination for ethnic Russians in territories coveted by Germany. It was all to no avail. In the end, Russian negotiators had to concede everything, because Russian armies were no longer willing to fight. It was not the new diplomacy but the old balance of power that determined the outcome—a Christmas truce on German terms.

Whatever disappointments lay in the offing, the events of November brought about a conversion experience for Reed. Casting his lot with the international working class, he returned to the United States to spread the ideas of bolshevism and found the Communist Labor Party in 1919. Joining forces with the new communist Third International (rival to the shattered socialist Second International), Reed utterly rejected the destructive force of nationalism and threw himself completely into the tasks of building an internationalist movement. Thus began the long and troubled relationship between the American left and Russian communism.

Since communism held little appeal for American progressives, it was certain there would be other responses to the Bolshevik revolution. One that deserves close attention is what might be called progressive realism, that is, support for progressive aspects of the revolution along with acceptance of the reality of Bolshevik power. This stance was exemplified by Raymond Robins, an exemplary social citizen who believed with all his heart that a better world of economic democracy was in the offing. Robins was an unofficial part of the same Red Cross mission to Russia that included Elihu Root, and although he had no inclination to rise with the prisoners of starvation and sing the "Internationale," he was not about to sing the praises of counter-revolution, either.

Robins was a realist. Arriving in Russia in midsummer to find the new republic going to pieces, he concluded that real power lay not with the Provisional Government he had been sent to bolster, but with the local soviets. In close touch with Reed and Bryant, he was not at all surprised by the November coup d'etat. Bucking Allied military leaders and U.S. ambassador David Francis, he decided "our interest is with the Soviet" and opened back channel talks with Lenin and Trotsky. Over the next four months, he continued talking with Trotsky with the intention of bringing red Russia back into the war on the Allied side. Incredible as it seems, he even asked Wilson for funds to start a joint Russian-American propaganda bureau (to include Reed) which would undermine the enemy's war machine by promoting workers revolution in Germany! Proletarian revolt was hardly what the Red Cross, the Creel Committee, or the American embassy had in mind, but that did not distract Robins. When Washington refused to recognize the Soviet regime, he became increasingly disgruntled with Wilson and confided to Roosevelt, "our Russian policy has been a tragedy of stupid errors."[56]

Progressives had no difficulty embracing the first Russian revolution, because it brought the overthrow of autocracy and the establishment of republican government. According to Robins, the upheaval in March was a "political revolution" that after centuries "brought the framework of the Russian State up to the structural type of the progressive Western nations." Going the next step, Robins even expressed some sympathy for the turn of events in November, in so far as it represented an attempt of the dispossessed to reclaim a share in power. In that spirit, he described the November revolution as "the first fundamental economic revolution and definite, conscious attempt to create a socialist state—in history." So long as the new government fought for the people against privileged interests, it was entitled to recognition.

Of course, neither Reed nor Robins represented anything like majority opinion in the United States. Most Americans simply wanted their emissaries to hop out of the Russian cauldron before they were boiled like the proverbial frog, a cold-blooded creature which can not perceive the dangerously rising temperature until it is too late. When the futility of reviving the Russian war effort became clear, Americans began blaming Bolshevik treachery. In one of the most controversial propaganda ploys of the war, Edgar Sisson, an agent of the Creel Committee in Russia, arranged for the publication of forged documents purporting to show a "German-Bolshevik conspiracy" in which German gold had financed the Bolshevik revolution with the aim of ending the war on the Eastern Front. Falsely authenticated by some of America's leading historians, the so-called Sisson documents paved the way for the anti-German hysteria of the war to pass effortlessly into the postwar Red Scare.

Conservatives back home were only too ready to believe in this bogus conspiracy. To men like Henry Cabot Lodge and Robert Lansing, bolshevism was the very antithesis of civilization. Its message of revolution beamed to the war-weary peoples of Europe and colonial subjects all over Asia and Africa meant complete and total disorder. Compared to Lenin, even the kaiser looked good. Whereas Imperial Germany at least had "the virtue of order," according to Lansing, bolshevism sowed nothing but "disorder and anarchy."[57]

Conservative ire had been aroused on both sides of the Atlantic by Bolshevik publication of the Allied secret treaties. Revelation of the unseemly arrangements made clear that Allied war aims included all the things Wilson had repudiated. The French fought for martial glory and Alsace-Lorraine; the British for imperial expansion; and the Russians for greater control in eastern Europe and a warm-water port. It was not at all clear what these had to do with peace without victory and making the world safe for democracy.

After the bombshell of the secret treaties, cracks in the wall of pro-war sentiment among the Allied populations only grew wider. When the Stockholm idea failed, the same remnants of the labor and socialist elements in the Allied countries launched a successful move for an inter-Allied conference, inspired by the Russian example. American radicals, too, expressed sympathy with the "new democracy" in Russia, and the People's Council could say in December 1917, "A People's Peace—Coming—Now!"[58] It was a measure of the impact of the Bolshevik revolution on the American left that a besieged minority could still believe they were part of the inevitable sweep of history.

For Americans in the revolutionary world of the twentieth century, progressive realism marks an important lost alternative. In the hands of people like Robins, the principle of self-determination meant letting the Russian people, or any oppressed people or nation, work out their own destiny in their own way. If their struggle moved toward violent revolution, that did not necessarily warrant condemnation. If it brought about some kind of socialist regime, it was not for outsiders to try to undo the result.

Progressive realism is linked to a series of "what ifs." What if the Mensheviks had won their battle for control of the Russian Social Democratic party and there had been no Bolshevik coup d'etat in November? Or what if the Bolsheviks had taken power, but instead of being besieged by reactionaries at home and capitalist powers abroad, the new Soviet regime had won diplomatic recognition, as progressive realists proposed and as Wilson considered for a time? Would that have made it possible for progressives, socialists, and communists to find common ground?

The failure to find common ground played out in tragic ways over succeeding decades. Animosity between German socialists and German communists doomed the Weimar Republic. What if, instead, they had joined forces in time to block the Nazi seizure of power? Unfortunately, by the time socialists and communists came to their senses in the Popular Front of the mid-1930s, it was too late to save the Weimar Republic, or the Spanish Republic from Spanish fascists and their Nazis supporters, or the world from another war. That is why it is important to pay attention to the lost option of moderate revolution in Russia, and why progressive realism, otherwise lost to history, should not be forgotten.

❧

American intervention and the two Russian revolutions had widened the war and, at the same time, elevated it to a quest for a new world order. By the end of 1917, the leaders of the United States and Russia were in a race to shape the new world to their own design. In the United States, the force of crusading nationalism had crushed or cowed opposition, strengthening the hand of elites in their pursuit of total victory over Germany and over radicalism at home. Painting radical and labor protest as un-American disloyalty, crusading nationalists suppressed the free and open debate so essential to a healthy democracy, in war as much as in peace.

Yet the democratic impulse was by no means destroyed. To the contrary, the reluctance of large segments of the population to accept the war as a messianic crusade and the agitation of a radical minority for a "people's peace" kept such aspirations alive even through the darkest days. Indeed, national elites and democratic peoples engaged in a kind of dialectical dance in which each side called out tunes the other had to dance to. It was precisely because popular demands for reform were so strong that even as he clamped down on dissent, Wilson had to take up the message of a just and democratic peace.

That message was bolstered by events in Russia. No matter how tortured the future of communism would become, the Russian Revolution was one of the defining moments of the twentieth century. John Reed's basic judgment about the establishment of Soviet power was on target: it shook the world (though not in the way he hoped). The very sense of a world divided between capitalists and communists, "us and them," was a fundamental feature of the epoch from 1917 to 1991. Looking back on that lost world after the collapse of communism, it takes an effort of the imagination to understand a time when millions of lives—and millions of deaths—hung on the answer to the question, "Which side are you on?"

Another immediate consequence of the Bolshevik revolution was to raise the stakes in the search for peace. The Stockholm conference may have been effectively blocked, but the idea of a people's peace became ever more popular. Every passing week that the Bolsheviks remained in power increased the pressure on Wilson to raise the bid again. In order to do so, he had to transcend the narrow spirit of messianic Americanism he had done so much to foster. He could not promote self-absorbed Americanism and embrace his destiny as a world leader at the same time. He would have to embrace a more capacious internationalism.

SAVIOR OF HUMANITY: Cesare, "Let her be heard," *New York Evening Post*, ca. 1917–1919. In an expression of messianic Americanism, an erect President Wilson defends Humanity, a ravished female victim of war. At the start of the Versailles Conference, many saw the progressive American president as humanity's best hope. (Library of Congress, Prints and Photos Division)

6

World Leader

The period from the proclamation of Wilson's Fourteen Points in January 1918 to the start of the Peace Conference a year later marked an American moment in world affairs.[1] For the first time in history, an American army, backed by the most powerful economic engine in the world, was shaping the outcome of a war in Europe, and an American president was being hailed as the prophet of a new world order. Other times may have been more significant in the internal history of the United States—the Revolution, the Civil War—but this was by far America's most important moment in world history.

The emergence of American leadership marked a portentous shift in world power. As the European powers tore themselves apart, the baton of Western leadership—or hegemony—passed temporarily to the United States, just as it would pass for a much longer lap after the Second World War. It was as if, in the midst of the great conjuncture that was remaking world history, the curtains parted to reveal its deepest inner workings.

If this was an American moment, it was not because of messianic Americanism, but because of the universal message of liberty and peace enfolded in progressive internationalism. To be sure, American influence was not the result of ideas alone. Wartime changes in political economy elevated the United States to the top rank among the world's creditors, underwrote the power of U.S. banks and industrial corporations, and ushered in an administrative state that promoted efficient production and consumption. But the more Woodrow Wilson advanced the idea of a just peace enforced by a concert of nations, the more he became the first American to be recognized as a true world figure. Indeed, as he surged past Lenin in the race for world opinion and past Allied heads of state, as well, it is not too much to say that he became the first world leader of the twentieth century.

The Fourteen Points

The single most important force in winning moral authority was Wilson's formulation of Allied war aims in the famous Fourteen Points. They appeared at the beginning of 1918 against a background shrouded in gloom, because things were going badly on the battlefield. The Italian war effort had collapsed in a heap at the battle of Caporetto in October, and, far worse, the Eastern Front simply disappeared. Negotiations between the Bolsheviks and the Germans produced a Christmas truce that confirmed what generals on both sides already knew: Russian armies were no longer willing to fight. With the Eastern Front closed down, the main obstacle to German victory was gone. The fact that American troops were not yet available in large numbers only made the situation more dire.

Things were not going well on the morale front, either. Using the chaotic Italian retreat from Caporetto as backdrop, Ernest Hemingway captured the mood of rampant demoralization in *Farewell to Arms*, whose American hero makes his own "separate peace" by running away to the Swiss mountains with an English nurse. Civilian morale, already low, was dealt another blow by the Bolsheviks' publication of the Allies' secret treaties, which revealed Allied war aims to be an all-around imperialist land-grab. Against the sordid deals of the old diplomacy, the Bolshevik call for peace based on the formula of no annexations or indemnities was looking better and better.

Given this unfavorable turn of events, pressure mounted on the Allies to redefine their war aims. In Britain, radical democrats in the Union for Democratic Control called for a renunciation of territorial and punitive aims, while the Labour party embraced terms similar to Wilson's "peace without victory." Although the Stockholm idea for a "people's peace" was held in check, the fact that Germany's independent socialists were pressing their government for a negotiated settlement rekindled a spark of the old socialist internationalism.

The French government, however, would have none of it. Largely because of Clemenceau's adamant opposition to a negotiated settlement, an inter-Allied conference in late November adjourned without any formal statement of war aims. The British were only slightly less opposed to negotiations, and when Wilson sent Colonel Edward House on another diplomatic mission to the Allies, they failed to craft a joint statement. Lloyd George's tepid support for some kind of international organization to reduce armaments did not go far enough. All in all, Allied diplomacy seemed as paralyzed as the armies on the Western Front.

Amid these dangers and frustrations, Wilson moved toward a redefinition of war aims. Rejecting any "premature peace," his December 4 address to Congress seemed to echo Bolshevik peace proposals. He urged the Allies to join him in embracing the general idea of a peace without annexations or indemnities: "It ought to be brought under the patronage of its real friends," he said.[2]

When the Allies continued to temporize, Wilson took things into his own hands. On January 8, 1918, he issued the Fourteen Points. As one of the most important state papers of the twentieth century, Wilson's stunning manifesto of the new diplomacy deserves close attention. To understand why it generated so much excitement at the time, it is necessary to set it in the context of ongoing revolutionary upheavals. Far from condemning revolt in eastern Europe or rejecting Bolshevik peace proposals out of hand, the Fourteen Points expressed sympathy for the popular aspirations they represented. Calling for the evacuation of Russian territory by foreign forces, point 6 warmly welcomed Russia into the family of nations with a promise to respect "the independent determination of her own political development." In the face of conflicting reports from Americans on the scene, this promise of self-determination seemed to keep the door open for acceptance of a radical regime in Moscow. In appealing to the Russian people over the heads of their government, Wilson was playing Lenin's own game, and on his home turf, no less! By showing sympathy with the cause of Russian freedom, the president was trying to bolster moderate political forces, such as they were, and, at the same time, reinvigorate Russian resolve to fight.

It was an extraordinary gesture, one that resonated with the best in American history. Wilson's support for revolution in Europe harked back, consciously or not, to the founding generation of American revolutionaries. Playing the role of Jefferson to the hereditary princes of Europe, he echoed the Declaration of Independence with its appeal to the "opinions of mankind" in his universal call to liberty. In seeking to rally world opinion to the cause of human freedom, Wilson was, in truth, the last of the Founding Fathers.

The same message of liberation was embodied in the call for a new diplomacy. Point 1 stated the cardinal principle of "open covenants of peace, openly arrived at." The message contained implicit criticism of the Allies' no-longer-secret war aims. Since the United States had not been a party to the secret treaties, Wilson had clean hands in making this pious proposal, a fact which helped offset the damage of their publication. Freedom was also embodied in the promise of "political and economic independence" for the nations and would-be nations of Europe—occupied nations such as Belgium, suppressed nations such as Poland, and the thwarted nationalities of the Balkans.

In the end, what convinced people that Wilson really was out to create a new world order was the last of the Fourteen Points. The overarching proposal for a "concert of nations" aimed to create a kind of world parliament where conflicts could be worked out in a peaceable manner. In one of the most influential progressive ideas of the century, Wilson proposed to substitute "mutual guarantees of political independence and territorial integrity"—what later came to be called collective security—for the destructive alliances of the old balance-of-power system.

For something that seemed so incendiary at the moment, it is striking how much the Fourteen Points owed to the past. Reverting to the liberal internationalism of the prewar years, Wilson appeared in the frock coat of the Victorian gentleman to trade in the common commodities of nineteenth-century liberals. Points 2, 3, and 4 restated the basic tenets of free-trade liberalism: freedom of the seas, open markets, and reduction of armaments. There was nothing here to disturb the slumber of William Gladstone or Grover Cleveland, no battle cry of social reform, no hint of bringing big business to heel, no forecast of the social liberalism to come later in the century. There was not even a promise to make the world safe for democracy, for fear of disturbing conservative regimes.

Given all the damage being done by the warring nations, it is also striking that Wilson chose to found his new world order on the rock of the nation-state. In points 6 through 13, he went Lenin one better in spelling out terms for territorial settlements of national questions. Some of these points have all the moral eloquence of a deed to property, which, in a basic sense, is exactly what they were—promises of "territorial integrity" to both the nations and would-be nations of Europe.

Unfortunately, it was not at all clear how guarantees of nationhood to the fractions peoples of the Balkans would prevent them from replaying the bloody battles that had set the stage for the Great War itself. Nor was it clear how creating a Polish state would prevent it from preying on Jews and other enemies. Nationalism was like the proverbial wolf—anyone who got a hold of it could neither safely hold it, nor safely let it go. In embracing nationalism, Wilson blindly ignored the danger.

If nationalism was right for Europe, Wilson believed it was wrong for Europe's overseas empires. Conspicuously absent was any reference to self-determination for colonial peoples. In rather elliptical language, point 5 proposed an "impartial adjustment of all colonial claims," not between colonizer and colonized, but among colonial powers themselves. Despite a nod to the "interests of the populations concerned," the intention was clearly to sort things out within an imperial framework. References in the text to "the Imperialists" were meant to apply only to the empires of the enemies, not of the Allies. Wilson's manifesto of the new diplomacy was no charter of independence for the subject peoples of Asia, Africa, or Latin America.

Reading between the lines, it was also apparent that Wilson's new diplomacy was perfectly consistent with American self-interest. The world's biggest economy was likely to prosper in an open-door world where American business could go wherever it pleased. In the war of words against German autocracy on one side and Russian bolshevism on the other, Wilson's salvos of liberal capitalism contained a good deal of economic benefit for the United States.

Despite these limitations, evasions, and hypocrisies, Wilson's progressive internationalism captured the imagination of the world. What was historic about the proposals was not their old-fashioned liberal principles, nor the prosaic attempt to settle territorial claims. Rather, it was the vision of humanity acting for the first time in concert.

Immediately, the Fourteen Points became a kind of magic mirror in which different segments of humanity saw their best face reflected.[3] To the European left, Wilson's message was the call for a just peace they had long been waiting for. British progressives in the Union of Democratic Control abandoned the Bolsheviks and went over to Wilson, while their French counterparts were also drawn to Wilson's transatlantic republicanism. Delegates from both countries arrived at the second Inter-Allied Labor and Socialist Conference in late February 1918 ready to support the Fourteen Points as the best chance for a people's peace, despite the fact that the Wilson administration was nervous about unauthorized peacemaking and had refused to issue a passport to a would-be American delegate.

Wilson's star rose even higher after Russian humiliation in the Treaty of Brest-Litovsk signed at the end of March. Despite the

Christmas truce with the Germans, Russian foreign minister Leon Trotsky, hoping to get agreement for a general peace conference, continued to conduct back channel negotiations with Allied emissaries. Unable to win support for this proposal and beset by counterrevolutionaries at home, the Bolsheviks finally concluded a separate peace with the Germans. Trotsky's double-game and the Carthaginian terms of the Treaty of Brest-Litovsk looked a lot more like the old diplomacy than the new. The treaty transferred a huge chunk of Russian territory—upwards of one-third—to German hands, while freeing Germany's eastern divisions for service on the Western Front. Within two months Germany began the last great offensive of the war.

With Russia out of the fighting, the American contribution loomed much larger. The Fourteen Points had a vital impact on Allied morale. The *Times* of London saw nothing less than "the reign of righteousness" in Wilson's message, and Lloyd George extended his appreciation.[4] Across the Channel, the French press and public were also very enthusiastic. Clemenceau, however, was predictably frosty. "Wilson has his Fourteen Points," he sneered, "God needed only Ten Commandments. We shall see." But elsewhere in conquered Belgium and disheartened Italy, Wilsonism became a popular phenomenon.

Even in Germany, Wilson's message was well received. In another speech in September, Wilson appealed directly to the German people over the head of their government, extending the promise of self-determination to them, provided they overthrew the kaiser. Needing little prodding, they replaced the centuries-old Hohenzollern dynasty with a new republican regime. And when German authorities finally decided to sue for peace in November, it was not the Allies they contacted, but Woodrow Wilson.[5]

As he received the thanks of a grateful world, Wilson stood at the very pinnacle of world leadership, higher than any previous American, save perhaps George Washington. As with other world leaders who came after him—Winston Churchill and Mikhail Gorbachev are two examples—the moment on Olympus would quickly end, and, like the others, Wilson would suffer rejection by his own people. But for now, he seemed to please everyone.

When American conservatives looked into the magic mirror of the Fourteen Points, they, too, saw much to their liking in the prospect of great power status for the United States. Far from accepting American isolation, some conservatives had taken the lead in promoting overseas expansion ever since the Spanish-American War. They had backed the preparedness movement, supported the president's war message, and joined the League to Enforce Peace. Led by such luminaries as former president Taft, League members were in agreement with Wilson on the goal of a decisive military victory over the Central Powers and the need to squelch any moves toward a "premature peace." Standing next to Wilson on a high peak overlooking the future, they envisioned a role for the United States as Britain's successor as world hegemon.

That does not mean they saw eye to eye with Wilson on everything. To these diplomatic realists, the aim of statecraft was to enhance American power, not redeem the world. Although they could give after dinner speeches about the glories of American principles, their days were filled with the hard work of power politics. No one better represented the realist viewpoint than Elihu Root. Schooled in "dollar diplomacy" as Taft's secretary of war, Root wanted no part of any redemptive crusade. He had supported U.S. intervention on the grounds of American national interests, pure and simple. While ardent Wilsonians were turning logical somersaults to somehow make the Monroe Doctrine into "the doctrine of the world," Root kept his eye fixed on the defense of U.S. hemispheric interests against the German threat.

Conservatives also pushed their own agendas. Arch-nationalists, such as Henry Cabot Lodge, collaborated with the champions of 100 percent Americanism in the National Security League and other patriotic societies to preserve maximum freedom of action for U.S. diplomacy. Although Lodge was a thoroughgoing Anglophile, he opposed any wartime "entangling alliance" and, instead, insisted on fighting not as an "ally" but as an "associated power." The fact that Lodge was a militant nationalist did not mean he was an isolationist. Far from supporting a stay-at-home foreign policy, Lodge rubbed his hands with glee over the projection of U.S. power overseas, so long as it came on U.S. terms. He was, instead, a unilateralist who wanted nothing to do with collective security. Unilateralists would soon join forces with isolationists to oppose collective security provision of the Versailles Treaty. But for the time being, Wilson's enemies had to bide their time.

Reformers of all stripes were predictably enthusiastic. Christian idealists were taken by the illusion that the foreign policy of the United States could be made the instrument of a higher power. Many Christians who had opposed U.S. intervention now clambered up the hill to stand with Wilson on the moral high ground, including the prewar secretary of the pacifist Church Peace Union, who endorsed Wilson's program as the embodiment of Christian idealism.[6]

Secular progressives, for their part, saw in Wilson's magic mirror a vision of democratic internationalism. In the new world to come, the main actors on the world stage would be nations and peoples, not nation-states and diplomats. Their idea of a league of nations was a democratic legislature writ large, comprised of *peoples'* representatives from around the world, not a league of nations, strictly speaking. The democratic message effectively silenced Wilson's progressive critics in Congress.

In the enthusiasm of the moment, many American reformers followed Wilson's lead in reaching out to the Russian people as a "fit partner" in the proposed league. Suddenly, they caught a glimpse of America's own revolutionary heritage in Russia's upheaval. According to *The Survey*, "America is herself a child of revolution and her history shows that she has always viewed with sympathy the efforts of a people to make themselves free."[7]

Even radicals saw what they wanted. Wilson's call for a concert of nations seemed to be just what radicals had been demanding since the previous April, that is, a statement of war aims consistent with the Petrograd-Stockholm-Bolshevik formula. Although the People's Council was reduced to little more than a paper organization, it could say, in hailing the Fourteen Points, "Again the program of the People's Council stands vindicated." Persuading herself that a "democratic peace" and an "American peace" might be the same thing, the ever-resilient Crystal Eastman helped fashion the American Union for a Democratic Peace out of the wreckage of earlier peace and justice organizations. Echoing Wilson almost word for word, she took a leaf from the book of messianic Americanism to proclaim that democracy and America were synonymous in the sense in which "America has stood for the hope and freedom of all peoples."[8]

What a predicament for the radicals to be in! World history was heading their way, the president was talking their language, and all they could do was cheer from the sidelines. What was worse, the leader they were cheering was throwing a lot of them in jail. Shortly before being arrested under the Sedition Act, Eugene Debs was heard to give "unqualified approval" to the Fourteen Points. Max Eastman wrote in private, "I was still regretting we had entered the war, but I felt that Wilson might find a fruitful way out of it."[9] Unfortunately, he could not write this in his own magazine, because *The Masses* had been shut down by Wilson's government. The People's Council embraced Wilsonian internationalism, even though Wilson thwarted their efforts to promote international solidarity at every turn. In the spring of 1918 the State Department again summarily rejected requests for passports to attend the second Inter-Allied Socialist and Labor Conference in London.

Despite these blows, a parade of leftists repented their former antiwar views. The *Appeal to Reason*, the largest circulation socialist paper in the country, urged its readers to support the League of Nations idea. Mother Jones, "the Miner's angel" with impeccable radical credentials, endorsed Liberty Bonds. By the spring of 1918, conservatives, progressives, and radicals alike had been co-opted by Wilsonian internationalism.[10]

By raising impossible hopes, Wilson's efforts to win over reluctant crusaders succeeded too well. In retrospect, it is easy to spot the illusion. Nation-states tend to be the pursuers of self-interest conservatives said they were. They rarely put high moral principle first, the way progressive internationalists hoped. Progressives might have done a better job guarding against the illusion that the United States was an exceptional nation, the only nation that could transcend self-interest to be a beacon of redemption for a warring world.

Yet posterity should not judge them too harshly. All those who ever set out to change the world have tried to make their country behave ethically. Who can blame progressives for trying to turn national traditions in internationalist directions? Reconciling national and international impulses was exactly what Walter Weyl, a leading progressive writer, was trying to do. In a book on "the end of the war," the Philadelphia-born son of German-Jewish immigrants called upon his fellow citizens to turn U.S. intervention into a new American mission: "We leave behind our old Americanism to find abroad a new and broader Americanism; an Internationalism." Just as Americans ought to adopt a new spirit of internationalism, so American influence might make the new international order more democratic. Weyl insisted that the new Americanism was a form of "democratic internationalism."[11]

Weyl's credibility on the point of democratic internationalism was enhanced by his willingness to criticize imperialist impulses in his own country. Knowing that Debs had landed in jail for just such a statement, Weyl nonetheless warned that in the pursuit of post-war spoils the United States "is as likely to become imperialistic as are the other nations." Noting that the United States had acquired a string of colonies and protectorates in the Western Hemisphere, he predicted that "small economic groups possessing vast influence" would seek to expand American power, just as the emergence of America as the world's biggest creditor pointed toward full-scale "financial imperialism."[12]

The specter of American capital haunting the world's less developed peoples became manifest in American participation in the Allied intervention in Russia. Refusing to accept the Bolshevik separate peace at Brest-Litovsk, the Allies sent troops into Russia in the spring of 1918 with the ostensible purpose of reopening the Eastern Front. Although reluctant at first, Wilson actually supplied more troops than the Allies in a futile effort fatally flawed by association with tsarist counterrevolutionaries. The Russian imbroglio drew fire from some progressives, including Senator Hiram Johnson, who growled, "the real thing behind the scenes in this Russian situation is the international banker."[13] Somehow Wilson escaped the blame for the Russian intervention. It was put down to the French, or international bankers, or monarchists.

In fact, nothing seemed to diminish the luster of his ideas. For a fleeting moment all of humanity looked into Wilson's magic mirror and saw themselves not as they were, but as they hoped to be. In Europe, the vision of a just peace lifted demoralized spirits. In the United States, it illuminated a shining moment of common purpose. In colonial regions, it carried the promise of self-determination, despite itself. After the collapse of the socialist Second International and before the Communist International gained purchase, the lines between reform and revolution blurred, and progressive internationalism seemed capable of becoming the vehicle of popular hopes for radical change everywhere.

Was that enthusiasm misplaced? In some ways, yes, since it rested on a good deal of smoke and mirrors. Yet, at a time when the old balance-of-power politics stood disgraced; when rebels had overthrown autocrats in Mexico, China, and Russia; when aged dynasties—the German *Kaiserreich*, the mighty Habsburgs, the Ottoman Turks—were about to tumble; under these circumstances, enthusiasm was understandable. As the weight of centuries lifted, it seemed possible that the "war to end all wars" might just bring about a better world.

Industrial Killing

The contrast between lofty idealism and brutality on the ground could not have been more extreme. Visions of peace had no place in the grotesque landscape of northeastern France where gentle rolling hills had been blasted into a barren moonscape of water-filled craters by countless artillery shells. Over the preceding two and a half years, the features of industrial warfare— barely visible at the beginning—had emerged in all their ghastly detail: the pulverizing artillery barrage, the tangled web of barbed wire, the relentless fusillade of the machine gun, and the searing pain of poison gas.

What made it so horrific was the Frankenstein combination of scientific rationality and impassioned irrationality. Never before had the wonders of modern civilization—science, mass production, mass communication, bureaucratic organization—been so deeply imbued with a crusading spirit against an enemy seen to be evil incarnate. Modern war combined the worst of both worlds.

By the spring of 1918 the face of industrial warfare was all too familiar. The worst aspects of the war of position at Verdun and the Somme in 1916 were repeated at the Chemin des Dames and Passchendaele in 1917. Despite the lesson of these battles that the broad offensive could not achieve a breakthrough, German generals were determined to try again. Bringing up troops from the now-quiet Eastern Front, Ludendorff kicked off the last great offensive of the war in March 1918. Having supped full well with horrors, it seemed the powers somehow could not stop gorging themselves.

It was during this offensive that the American Expeditionary Force entered the fighting in large numbers. One of the doughboys was Private Larry Duren of Company K, a salesman and amateur actor from upstate New York. Duren encountered industrial killing at Chateau-Thierry, where American soldiers were rushed into forward positions in the summer of 1918 to hold the line just 80 kilometers from Paris against the German offensive. Like so many hundreds of thousands of soldiers before him, he saw firsthand the hideous landscape of tree stumps and shell craters where rational, mechanized warfare drove people into fits of madness. In a memoir titled "An Experience," written a few years after the war, Duren described the mad rage that welled up in the face of the enemy's "grim death machines" as one after another of his buddies was gunned down: "I think I must have been quite mad, as the other were, screaming with rage, longing to reach those dirty swine who were annihilating our Company."[14]

A similar recollection was offered by Clarence Mahan, a 23-year-old auto mechanic in Terre Haute, Indiana. In a somber memoir, this Hoosier doughboy recalled, "we had to develop a numbness and an unfeeling attitude toward it all. Otherwise, we would have lost our minds." The numbness of one moment, however, could turn into rage the next. Mahan continued, "To see blood and carnage everywhere as men, horses, and mules are blown to bits developed in us a certain savagry [sic] and hate that pushed us on toward a terrible enemy with a willingness to see him destroyed."[15]

Not everyone remembered the war in these terms. To many, the stint in France was the most exciting time of their young lives, a rite of passage full of eye-opening adventures. Perhaps the prevailing mood among the troops was neither horror nor adventure but a kind of grim struggle for survival. As reflected in journalistic accounts at the time and oral testimony from veterans years later, many soldiers approached their task with stoic resignation to the rule of Murphy's law. The assumption that things will go wrong pervaded Charlie Chaplin's film *Shoulder Arms*, which appeared four weeks before the Armistice, loaded with gallows humor poking fun in typical Chaplin fashion at the absurdities of military life.[16]

For soldiers with a background in industry, the stoic attitude was carried over from work. Industrial workers contributed more than their share to the armed forces. The biggest contingent of men on the battle line probably came from lower ranks on the production line. Using estimates made by General Enoch Crowder, head of the Selective Service System, it is clear that industrial workers had a participation rate that was higher—as much as five times higher—than agricultural workers.[17]

Unlike the Civil War draft—where anyone could hire a substitute—selective service was supposed to be fair and efficient. Getting underway in June of 1917, the draft developed into an ostensibly scientific mechanism for balancing the labor needs of military and industry under a five-class system intended to enlist only common laborers, unskilled workers, and other expendables, while essential personnel—managers, assistant managers, administrative experts, and skilled laborers—were put in protected categories. That is precisely what was meant by "selective." In emphasizing the scientific nature of the system, General Crowder proudly proclaimed there would be no repeat of the Civil War scandal of rich men hiring substitutes to do their dying for them, but in its own bureaucratic way, selective service produced the same result.[18]

Experience in industry stood young conscripts in good stead. Hailing miners in uniform, the president of the United Mine Workers wrote, "Our hearts go with them across the sea, and we know that these heroes of ours, who have faced the perils of the mines year in and year out, risking their lives in the production of coal, will not be found wanting when they face the foreign foe."[19] Industrial workers were no strangers to danger. The landmark investigation of work accidents conducted by Crystal Eastman for the Pittsburgh Survey painted a picture of mechanized killing that made the shop floor seem like a battle zone. Causes of death included blast furnace explosions, asphyxiation by furnace gas, being crushed under a 3-ton bucket, and being hit by flying shrapnel from a huge device to break apart slag know as a "skull cracker."[20] The comparison to warfare was obvious.

Constant danger bred a certain fatalism. Railroad brakemen normally boarded a train by standing in front of the moving engine, knowing that one slip meant certain death. Said one, "There is a kind of fascination about it. You win or you lose. It's a gamble." Calling this attitude the "soldier spirit," Eastman observed, "This spirit stands by the men in danger and makes them meet death bravely. It stands often a harder test; you will not break the spirit of a railroader by cutting off his arm or giving him a wooden leg."[21] Having defied death at the hands of industrial machinery may have made it easier to go into the teeth of enemy fire, especially to prove one's manhood. "C'mon you sonsabitches," yelled Sergeant Dan Daly at his flagging troops at the battle of Belleau Wood, "do you want to live forever?"[22]

Certainly, industrial workers went into battle with fewer illusions than the civilians who were fighting a war without tears. Until American casualties became numerous in the late spring of 1918, American civilians had it easy. Measured on any scale of human suffering, they were eating more, living better, and losing far fewer loved ones than any of the exhausted and grieving peoples of Europe. And unlike civilians during their own Civil War, they did not experience the ravages of war on their own soil.

Even after the American death toll began to mount, moral redeemers cried tears without salt. Sentimental moralism was especially strong in the YMCA. One Y secretary who had been a Presbyterian pastor described coming upon his first soldier dead on the field of battle. With honest blue eyes wide open, the dead soldier gazed into the westward sky where the sun was slipping below the crests of the hills. The secretary imagined the soldier sending this message to the dear ones at home: "I have fought the good fight. I have finished my course, I have kept the faith."[23]

This sugar-coating of death with the syrup of sentimentality was a common practice among Protestant visitors to the battle zone. Edward Bok, longtime editor of the *Ladies' Home Journal* and chair of a Philadelphia YMCA commission, became convinced on a battlefield tour in October 1918 that the experience of war was not as bad as it seemed; after all, it had taught a generation given to materialism and pleasure-seeking that there was a Divine plan that accounts for "the marvelous rotation and order which prevail in the world."[24]

Converting chaos and brutality into God-given order was the stock in trade of high-toned Anglo-American writers. For example, Conningsby Dawson, a British-American publicist for Anglo-Saxon unity, wrote that death on the battlefield was redeemed by "the glory of the trenches." Redemption by death was also a central theme in Willa Cather's *One of Ours*, whose American hero dies believing "Ideals were not archaic things, beautiful and impotent; they were the real sources of power among men." Cather's sentiments were crowned with the Pulitzer Prize in 1922.[25]

The battlefields of France were the staging ground for some of the most important literary battles of the century. Thoroughly disgusted by such sentimentality, literary realists turned their backs on the nineteenth-century genteel tradition. In his "farewell to arms," Ernest Hemingway penned an oft-quoted expression of disillusionment: "I had seen nothing sacred, and the things that were glorious had no glory and the sacrifices were like the stockyards at Chicago if nothing was done with the meat except to bury it."[26] Literary realists tried to strip death down to the physical essentials. In "Squad" by James B. Wharton, a soldier has been disemboweled by a shell fragment and is carried to an underground dugout: "Already the pallor of death is over his face. His features stiffen. His lungs are soaked. He drowns in his own blood." By the end, plenty of American tears—real tears—were being shed by loved ones of the dead and wounded.[27]

Out of the experience of war, irony and cynicism emerged for the first time in American letters. They were present in the mocking title of Mary Lee's *It's a Great War*, in the hard-boiled detectives of Dashiell Hammett's mystery novels, and in John Dos Passos's 1921 story *Three Soldiers*, a tale of manhood crushed by the war machine. In his mammoth trilogy *U.S.A*, Dos Passos affected a tough, working-class stance and created a cast of hardened cynics to convey his own deep disillusionment. Instead of hailing heroic manhood, realists picked up a theme once confined to pacifists that modern warfare had no room for heroism.

As for progressives, nothing in their optimistic outlook prepared them for the combination of cold, scientific calculation with hot, uncontrolled rage that produced the rational madness of the battlefield. Once this beast was unleashed, there was nothing war managers could do to keep it under control, nor anything progressives could do to humanize it. The beast might be compared to Dr. Frankenstein's monster, a symbol of hyper-rationality turning on its creator; or it might be the dark side of human nature rising up against reason; to fundamentalists, it was the Beast of the Apocalypse. Whatever it was, industrial warfare was definitely *not* redemptive. It was not what would save humanity, but what humanity needed to be saved from. Sad to say, it would rise again on the sands of Iwo Jima and the beaches of Anzio, during the death march at Bataan, in the firebombing of Tokyo and Dresden, and in the mushroom cloud over Hiroshima.

Total War

Industrial killing was the gruesome consequence of what later came to be called total war. When the mass conscript armies of western Europe got on trains and trucks and drove out to face one another's machine guns, everyone discovered to their surprise that war between great powers would not end quickly but would turn into a protracted struggle between the war machines of whole societies. Grosvenor Clarkson, one of the technocrats in charge of American mobilization, summed up the connections: "War today is a contest of all the powers of the antagonists—intellectual, moral, and industrial. To the romance of armed men moving upon the stage of history has been joined the drama of industry militant, of titanic economic forces loosed and then governed to the need of the nation in arms."[28]

Having pioneered industrial warfare in their own Civil War, Americans now cranked up a war machine bigger than anything Lincoln's generation could have imagined. Behind endless sloganeering about "the man behind the man behind the gun," American industry achieved titanic feats of production. The Allies had been buying vast quantities of food and supplies before U.S. intervention, and now came the added need to equip the AEF with 17,000,000 pairs of woolen trousers, 33,000,000 tons of steel for shells and ships, and upwards of 6 *billion* feet of lumber to build cantonments and landing docks.[29]

Only the United States could have supplied so many different commodities in such enormous quantities in so short a time. Allied leaders paid homage to the heroes of production in their own homelands and singled out the millions of tons of food and materiel sent over by American industry for special praise. "If this help had not been forthcoming, our army could not have held," recalled Georges Clemenceau, "the army of the United States could not have fought."[30]

Even the Germans agreed. Their generals were well aware that America's economic might was tipping the scales heavily against them. Comparing the two sides, the Allies (U.S./France/U.K.) produced two and a half times as many manufactures as the Central Powers (Germany/Austria-Hungary).[31] What finally convinced General von Hindenburg that Germany could not win was the seemingly inexhaustible supply of American resources.

Keeping the war machine humming was a set of emergency agencies that comprised what is called an "administrative state." Stopping short of public ownership, the administrative state merged business and government, private and public authority, Wall Street and Washington. According to Walter Weyl, "The Brigadier-Generals in their resplendent uniforms are supplanted by manufacturers, merchants, bankers and advertising men, for the war has proved that war is business, and that military efficiency is useless without economic efficiency."[32] Although the merger did not go nearly as far as in Germany, it showed how far liberal America had moved away from open markets toward managed ones.

The premier example of the administrative state was the War Industries Board. In selecting Bernard Baruch to run the board, Wilson chose wisely. Baruch was a Wall Street insider close enough to the House of Morgan to reassure big money, but he was also seen as an outsider, both as a Jew and as something of a political maverick. Leaving day-to-day operations to business executives themselves, Baruch worked hand in glove with trade associations and other industry leaders to map out production targets, allocate resources, and set prices using the controversial "cost-plus" formula, under which businesses were guaranteed a nice round profit. With money in their pockets, most businessmen were quite happy to do their patriotic duty.

Progressive opinion was divided about the War Industries Board. To those at the top, including the president himself, the board embodied a long-sought progressive goal of government regulation of the trusts. To the defenders of small businesses, on the other hand, the board set aside antitrust statutes, effectively authorizing what amounted to government-sponsored cartels. Even the board's official historian admitted it was "a tremendous invigorator of big business and hard on small business."[33]

In another blow to small business, the Webb Pomerene Act (1918) exempted American exporters from antitrust statutes. Senator Robert La Follette denounced the act as a plan to facilitate an international combination that would bring together "our exploiters" with "foreign exploiters," after which a bigger navy would be needed to protect foreign trade, and from there, La Follette warned, "it is but a short step to absolute imperialism."[34] However, beyond fuming about unconscionable war profiteering, there was little that critics could do.

Progressive opinion also divided over the regulation of consumption. Among urban progressives with working-class constituents, the arrival of prohibition was a major irritant, as was the failure to reign in inflation for essential foodstuffs. Middle-class Protestants, on the other hand, cheered the closing of the saloon and accepted voluntary conservation of food.

Under the Lever Act of August 10, 1917, Congress authorized the creation of the Food and Fuel Administration and, again, Wilson choose wisely in appointing Herbert Hoover to run it. Hoover's Depression-era reputation as a sour old curmudgeon whose "trickle-down" economics hurt the poor has obscured the fact that no public figure was held in higher regard during the Great War. Admired by progressives and conservatives alike for his direction of food relief for starving Belgians, Hoover was seen to possess that rare combination of humanitarian instinct and administrative ability.

Under the slogan "Food Will Win the War," the Food Administration was obsessed with conservation. Hardly a poster or pamphlet left the office without some reference to it. Flyers showed patriotic families bowing their heads at the evening meal with the sign "Do Not Waste Food" stuck on the wall. Speakers were instructed to stress that conservation would help prevent "strikes, riots and disorders which would destroy our economic and financial efficiency in this war." Nothing was to be wasted, not even garbage, which was to be recycled on instructions from the Garbage Utilization Division; and even shutting down the breweries was touted as a means of conserving grain.[35]

Progressive attitudes toward war finance were generally favorable. War expenditure rose to the rate of $2 million an hour and eventually reached a total of $35.5 billion (including $9.5 billion in loans to the Allies), an amount three times the total of federal expenditures during the first hundred years of the nation's existence.[36] To fund these billions, the Wilson administration relied on three sources of revenue. First and foremost were Liberty Bonds. According to Secretary of the Treasury William McAdoo, modern war was as much a matter of the "financial front" as the battle front. "A man who could not serve in the trenches in France might nevertheless serve in the financial trenches at home."[37] Second, Congress dramatically increased taxes. Although the left called for "the conscription of wealth" in the form of confiscatory taxes on excess war profits, most progressives were content to settle for increased income and estate taxes on the well-to-do in the progressive Tax Act of 1916. The third source of revenue was harder to pin down. The hidden hand of runaway inflation rapidly increased the amount of cheap money available to the government, but with the unfortunate consequence of also increasing the cost of living for ordinary Americans. Thus the invisible hand of the market took back from ordinary taxpayers at least a portion of what the visible policy of progressive taxation had given.

Progressives cheered the temporary nationalization of the railroads and telegraphs. Under Secretary of the Treasury McAdoo, the Railroad Administration took command of the main lines, granted wage increases to workers, and mollified management with the cost-plus formula, plus the promise of a prompt return to private hands after the emergency. Along with the U.S.

Shipping Corporation, where the government actually built transport ships, the Railroad Administration marked the furthest extent of state intervention to that point in American history. That a public official actually got to boss big business around was a progressive dream come true.

What can be said about the overall impact of total war on progressivism? Far from originating in progressive demands—or in military doctrine, for that matter—total war was an outgrowth of modern society itself, the result of the growing integration of the capitalist economy and civil society with the institutions of the state. As part of that process, it hastened the transition from laissez-faire to a new form of liberalism built around government regulation of the market. Did that further progressive aims? Although no one was around to conduct a poll, clearly, opinion was divided. To some progressives and to many on the left, the close partnership between big business and government was a dangerous consolidation of corporate power that would be hard to reverse. To others, it was a step in the right direction. Even some socialists believed that "war collectivism" would hasten the evolution of capitalism into a more collective system. In the end what can be said is that the war helped consolidate corporate capitalism, even as it promoted a greater role for wage earners and consumers within it.

The Dance of Democracy

What made progressive hearts beat fastest were wartime gains for social and economic justice. To fight total war, it was not enough for the Wilson administration to manage the economy and suppress dissent; in a democratic society, it was also necessary to win the consent of the governed. Wilson had to promise a better world, one that would address the needs of women, industrial workers, and ethnic minorities, to bring disaffected groups into the fold. That set in motion what might be called a dance of democracy, a process in which the people and their leaders, the ruled and the rulers, were each forced to dance to each other's tunes.

Looking first at everyday life, we see an extraordinary degree of state intervention. A chorus of billboards exhorted citizens to plant Victory Gardens, observe "meatless Tuesdays," and report "slackers" to the nearest branch of the American Protective League, the semi-official amateur spy agency. Social scientists at federal agencies charged with maintaining war production poked their noses into family kitchens to prepare detailed studies of family budgets as a basis for setting wage and hour guidelines. The fact that ordinary housewives and consumers were rendering service to the state took off the cloak of privacy from family life to reveal its essentially political nature.[38]

The politicization of everyday life threw gender relations into question. In some respects, total war reinforced conservative values. That was true, for example, of the belief that woman's place was in the home. A barrage of traditional images reminded everyone of wives patiently waiting like Penelope for Odysseus to come home from the Trojan wars. Mothers dutifully served their country in patriotic homes, while fathers protected the home from foreign foes. What was perhaps most significant, the campaign for efficient consumption linked housewives to the emerging realm of mass consumption. Government propaganda of all sorts reinforced the assumption that consumption was women's domain, and that domain was in the home.

The link between women and consumption was not necessarily conservative. In fact, before the war, consumer consciousness was most often associated with feminism and other progressive causes. In *Drift and Mastery*, Walter Lippmann expressed a commonly held opinion that consumers were closer to the public interest than either labor or capital. "With the consumer awake," Lippmann wrote, "neither the workers nor the employer can use politics for his special interest." And who were the most wide-awake consumers? The mass of women who went to market and had to make ends meet in the face of the high cost of living. Many readers no doubt agreed that "their influence will make the consumer the real master of the political situation."[39]

Master or mistress, progressive women were well represented in Florence Kelley's National Consumers League, which promoted socially responsible shopping to combat factory abuses. Epitomizing the cross-class strategy of social reform embraced by most progressives, these organizations were examples to later generations of how the better-off could promote higher living standards for the poor to the benefit of all.

It must be added that progressives were of two minds on the question of women's place. Most reformers, including most women in the reform camp, believed in the primacy of maternity and took the division of roles between wife/homemaker and husband/breadwinner to be a fact of nature. Thus the call for a "living wage" for men—normally defined as income sufficient to support a wife and children—usually took precedence over equal pay.

The tendency of wartime regulation of consumption was to reinforce the more conservative view of gender roles. First of all, government regulators assumed that women's place was in the home. In its *War Cook Book*, the Food Administration offered suggestions for patriotic service: "The Government cannot save food: it must be done by the people, by each woman in her home." In a massive pledge campaign, schoolchildren brought home pledge cards for their mothers to sign, vowing efficiency in food preparation.[40]

Second, women were asked to stop demanding the regulation of business and take it upon themselves to make the necessary sacrifices. Business was only too happy to cooperate. Taking their cue from Hoover, advertisers tailored their messages to the theme of the hour—efficiency. According to Holeproof Hosiery, "efficiency in living is the spirit of the times," and what better way to be efficient than by buying supposedly "holeproof" stockings? Fashion-conscious women were asked to sacrifice, but not to the point of giving up fashion. *The Ladies' Home Journal* observed, "War in Europe has made it both fashionable and patriotic to practice thrift," and dress manufacturers responded by promising their customers both "style and economy."[41]

At the same time, total war pushed in the opposite direction toward gender equality. In order for women to give the patriotic service their country demanded, the public sphere had to change in ways that undermined the old republican distinction between a male public sphere and a female domestic one. To a large extent, the campaign for efficient consumption was conducted *by* women. In addition, a number of high-profile ladies were present in the upper echelons of Washington bureaucracies, including Anna Howard Shaw at the Women's Advisory Committee of the Council of National Defence. At the level of junior officers and among the legions of foot soldiers, the ranks were overwhelmingly female. Society dames were put in charge of the Women's Land Army, which organized city girls to go into the country to dig potatoes. College women were enlisted by the thousands to spread the word about "meatless Tuesdays," and the like.[42]

The support of a grateful nation for women's public service hastened the coming of equal suffrage. With the National Women's party keeping an eye on the administration by burning "watchfires" near the White House, the president finally came out for suffrage. Before the armistice was signed in November 1918, the House passed the Susan B. Anthony Amendment; the Senate followed suit a year later, and three-quarters of the states ratified just in time for women everywhere to vote alongside men for the first time in 1920.

In addition, the social agenda of the women's reform organizations advanced a few steps. Spurred by such indomitable leaders as Julia Lathrop at the Children's Bureau, Congress passed another bill outlawing child labor, in the ultimately vain hope it could sidestep a hostile Supreme Court. Responding to the great influx of women workers into war industry, advocates for working women succeeded in getting Congress to set up the Women in Industry Service (later the Women's Bureau). Raising the banner of "equal pay for equal work," Mary Anderson, the first director, set out on the daunting task of narrowing the enormous gap between men's and women's wages.

The fact that total war politicized daily life gave certain advantages to subordinate groups fighting a protracted war of position against those above. That was especially true of industrial workers. The reason was simple: labor was essential to the war effort and working people knew it. "Our ships cannot sail, our railroads cannot operate, our munitions plants must close down," said the president of the UMW, "if the coal miner fails to play his part." With patriotic bunting decorating their workplaces, the knowledge that they were indispensable kindled a powerful sense that now was the time for wrongs to be redressed.[43]

Officials got the message. From the Creel committee came a torrent of praise for "the man behind the man behind the gun." Every industrial worker was hailed as if he were the equal of Sergeant York, the sharpshooter hero from Tennessee who single-handedly took out an entire German regiment. "If he slacks or fails," said no less than President Wilson, "armies and statesmen are helpless."[44] When Wilson journeyed to Buffalo in November 1917 to become the first president in history to address an AFL convention, the visit carried enormous symbolic significance.

Seizing the moment, progressives strove to turn Wilson's war for democracy into a campaign for industrial democracy. Walter Lippmann's vow was typical of the increasingly labor-oriented progressives: "We shall turn with fresh interest to our own tyrannies—to our Colorado mines, our autocratic steel industries, our sweatshops and our slums."[45] Under the banner of industrial democracy, reformers pressed forward on every front of social reform from short hours to collective bargaining.

They had to settle for a good deal less than they wanted. The most important wartime labor agency was the National War Labor Board, a tripartite commission of business, labor, and the public to mediate labor disputes. It arose out of a political compromise between business and labor. The idea for a national board actually originated in business circles. As war clouds gathered, the National Industrial Conference Board, a newly minted business lobby, recommended the creation of a tripartite agency to adjust industrial disputes. Seeking to thwart any move to upset the nonunion status quo in 90 percent of American industry, the board's goal was to maintain existing standards as defined by the *employer*—that is, the open shop, management determination of wages, and managerial control of production. From the opposite side of the fence, Samuel Gompers saw a completely different opportunity. After decades of waiting, here was a chance to meet employers on an equal footing. He seized upon the idea of a tripartite agency as a way of promoting standards as defined, not by business, but by *organized labor*—the union shop, union wage scales, and collective bargaining.[46]

Exhibiting his best political skills, Wilson resolved these opposing aims in typical progressive fashion. He authorized the creation of the tripartite War Labor Board and allowed the opposing camps to nominate cochairs. The choice of William Howard Taft was a brilliant stroke, because it mollified conservative Republicans (Taft had a well-deserved reputation as an antilabor judge), while shunting the former president off on a side rail, where he had neither influence in the administration nor opportunity to criticize it.

The selection of Frank Walsh was no less astute. A feisty labor lawyer and Missouri Democrat, Walsh was the former head of the Commission on Industrial Relations, set up under Taft to investigate industrial violence. Combining the moderate philosophy of institutional economists with a willingness to work with labor radicals, Walsh had endeared himself to working people in his unsparing exposure of industrial atrocities, such as the Ludlow Massacre. Possessed of the tenacity of an Irish republican, a talent for showmanship, and a knack for expanding the boundaries of political possibility, he personified the wartime reconstruction of progressivism along worker lines.

With the zeal of the true believer, Walsh made the War Labor Board a command post in the crusade for industrial democracy. "The country, I promise you, is beginning to understand that we may have 100 per cent democracy in the form of our political government and yet autocracy of the most despotic type in industry."[47] Walsh was determined to change that. Typically what happened was that the board intervened only after a strike or lockout threatened to interrupt war production. At that point, a mediator (Henry Ford in one case) would arrive to take testimony from both parties and then render what was supposed to be an impartial verdict that would start the wheels of industry turning again.

Although the board never required any company to recognize a union, the very fact that the government was listening to independent representatives chosen by workers themselves was a significant boost to labor. In the same vein, the defense of workers' right to organize and bargain collectively implicitly rejected the "yellow-dog" contract, which prohibited employees from joining a union, and the Supreme Court's 1917 *Hitchman* decision, which upheld it. Although workers were often frustrated with the failure to implement board decisions, business was the more disgruntled party, deeming the board an impermissible infringement on property rights and managerial authority.[48]

Through the War Labor Board and related state interventions, progressives and organized labor moved closer to one another. In tilting toward government mediation, progressives took a step away from the voluntarism of civil society toward state intervention in the market. Their approach to changing the world combined realistic recognition of the need to make incremental changes with visionary aims of a just society.

For their part, working people were moving closer to the progressive outlook at the same time. From its inception, the whole thrust of the labor movement ran against the legal doctrine of "liberty of contract," and labor progressives often worked closely with socialists and other radicals. Despite the wartime arrest of their most prominent leaders, socialists accounted for about a third of AFL members, led the state federation in Pennsylvania and elsewhere, and took the helm at the machinists, the garment workers, and several other unions. Although they had to muffle their radical views for fear of arrest, such leaders as John Fitzpatrick in the Chicago Federation of Labor and his counterparts in a host of state federations pressed every advantage to win industrial democracy. They were rewarded in 1918 with a landmark decision by Judge Julius Altschuler in favor of the "basic" eight-hour day. Everyone who has ever received premium pay for overtime owes the judge a debt of gratitude.

Coal miners exemplified the progressive turn. In Illinois and Ohio, many locals called themselves "Progressive" and worked comfortably with progressives in state legislatures. John White, president of the union, was a prominent opponent of U.S. intervention in the war who worked with the American Union Against Militarism, and he was also a vociferous critic of Samuel Gompers's "no-strike" pledge. Deeply involved in politics, miners rejected any notion of "voluntarism" and pursued a wide array of political strategies that ranged from the Republicanism of the young John L. Lewis to the socialism of Mother Jones. William B. Wilson had left his union office in 1913 to become Secretary of Labor, where he earned a reputation as a leading progressive in the Cabinet.

As other unions picked up the reform agenda, the progressive idea of steady improvement increasingly took hold. Hitherto, American optimism had seemed altogether foreign to many Jewish socialists, who were sometimes given to extreme views of catastrophe or perfection, nihilistic destruction or socialist paradise. But now, the Amalgamated Clothing Workers and other "new unions" with large Jewish membership were coming on board. East European Catholics were also edging closer to the progressive faith in gradual improvement, as urban Democratic machines and even staid craft unions cooperated with progressive reformers on such issues as child labor, short hours, and women's protections. In a number of states, labor-progressive coalitions had won laws to regulate hazardous occupations, such as coal and metal mining, and now these laws were passing muster in court decisions that invoked the state's "police power" to protect citizens against danger. In the notable *Bunting* decision of 1917, for example, the Supreme Court even upheld Oregon's blanket 8-hour statute, checking the *Lochner* ruling of 1905.

Every step toward labor reform increased the pace of the dance with political elites. Working people were increasingly infused with a vision of a just peace based on self-determination abroad and industrial democracy at home. Indeed, these hopes helped fuel the strike wave which was already rolling and which would burst the dams of wartime controls in 1919 to become the largest in American history. In the mutual embrace of the moment, few foresaw that the dance would spin out of control, setting industrial workers and their government—including progressives in the government—on a collision course.

A similar movement unfolded in ethnic relations. To persuade varieties of ethnic Americans to support the war effort, it was necessary to open the door to hitherto unwelcome Slavs and Italians. Anticipating the ethnic pluralism that would come to prevail in American culture by mid-century, leaders of the three major faiths ended sectarian sparring and agreed to work together. In an unprecedented example of ecumenical cooperation, the YMCA, the National Catholic War Council (with the Knights of Columbus in tow), and the Jewish Welfare Board joined forces in the United War Work Campaign to raise money for social services. By the time the war ended, the united campaign had exceeded its goal and raised over $200 million. Americanization of immigrants took a step forward. For example, Irving Berlin, a Russian-Jewish immigrant, composed a patriotic hymn to his adopted homeland. Although at the time he put it away in his trunk, twenty years later, "God Bless America" would become a World War II anthem.[49]

For Jewish-Americans, the war was an ethical trial. Prior to U.S. entrance into the European conflict, most American Jews had opposed the war on the grounds that the slaughter in the trenches was evil, and American Jews had nothing to gain by participating in it. Whereas none of the leading advocates of preparedness was Jewish, there were any number of Jewish leaders among the pacifists, including Lillian Wald, director of the Henry Street Settlement in New York who headed the American Union Against Militarism, and Rabbi Stephen Wise, who was active in its ranks.

After U.S. intervention, however, the moral choices got more complicated. Many Jewish radicals stuck to their guns and blasted the war's immorality. Morris Hillquit and Rabbi Judah Magnes, for examples, aligned themselves with the People's

Council and agitated against Wall Street's war. From the same labor-socialist milieu, Paole Zionists asked how a bad war could possibly be good for the Jews.

As circumstances changed, however, a majority of Jews came around to support the war. To well-assimilated German Jews, support for American policy was a simple matter of patriotic duty, and to those keeping watch on eastern Europe, the Russia revolution of March 1917 gave a reason to support the Allied cause. With the embarrassment of the tsar out of the way, Rabbi Steven Wise was typical in shifting around to an ardent pro-war stance and later resigning, along with Wald, from the American Union Against Militarism. Zionists were added to the pro-war column in the fall when the British issued the Balfour Declaration on November 2, 1917. Even though Wilson temporized—it was not until the summer of 1918 that he expressed his public support in a letter to Wise—the fact that the Allies now seemed to be fighting for a Jewish homeland in Palestine was enough to keep Zionists in the fold.[50]

In the enthusiasm for a homeland in the Holy Land, other complications were brushed aside. Never mind that Palestine was already home to thousands of Muslims, and that strict adherence to the Wilsonian principle of self-determination, therefore, might not lead to a Jewish homeland at all. And never mind that what the British had in mind was not an independent Jewish state but a protectorate in furtherance of their own imperial interests in the Middle East. Events had changed the character of the war enough to convince most American Jews that the Allies were now fighting simultaneously for a good cause and for the good of the Jews.

Nothing better illustrates the dance of democracy than the case of African-Americans. In every war since the American Revolution, African-Americans had turned dominant myths to their own ends, and the Great War was no exception. After the bloody rampage of white mobs in East St. Louis, Illinois, in July 1917, a mass meeting in Los Angeles fired off resolutions to the White House which stated that if America meant to preserve civilization and democracy against German barbarism and militarism, then it ought to protect Negroes back home against mob violence, lynching, and Jim Crow. A black officer returning from France sounded a note of optimism. He told a cheering crowd in Chicago's black belt that black troops believed "the democracy for which they are fighting will include the American Negro when peace is signed in Berlin."[51] When in history had a people so abused retained such faith in the same ideals as their abusers?

Although most African-American leaders supported the war, collaboration came in different degrees. Looking past the Wilson administration's sorry record on segregation and lynching, Emmett Scott brought key black leaders to Washington in June 1918. Among them was W. E. B. Du Bois, who had visions of silver linings in the clouds of war. Having just accepted an offer from Joel Spingarn, chairman of the NAACP, to join him at U.S. Military Intelligence, Du Bois penned his controversial *Crisis* editorial of July 1918 entitled "Close Ranks," in which he urged his readers to "forget our special grievances and close our ranks shoulder to shoulder with our white fellow citizens and the allied nations that are fighting for democracy."[52]

That was too much for some of his colleagues. Controversy erupted within the NAACP, whose leaders included white pacifists such as Mary White Ovington and Oswald Garrison Villard. Moreover, few black people were ready to forget their grievances, war or no war. Among Du Bois's longtime critics, William Monroe Trotter, editor of the Boston *Guardian*, taunted the Wilson administration for its lack of "clean hands" and gathered his forces to counter Scott's influence. In addition, black socialists, such as the young A. Philip Randolph, heaped ridicule on the idea that black grievances should be forgotten during the war.[53]

In the end, most African-Americans stood ready to support the war effort, provided its high ideals could be turned against the racial status quo. Mindful of the idealism of the Fourteen Points, Du Bois projected the possibilities for emancipation hidden in the ideas of democracy and self-determination. Speaking in his best prophetic voice, he wrote in the June 1918 issue of *The Crisis*,

This war is an end and also a beginning. Never again will darker people of the world occupy just the place they had before. Out of this will rise, soon or late, an independent China, a self-governing India, an Egypt with representative institutions, an Africa for the Africans, and not merely for business exploitation. Out of this war will rise, too, an American Negro with the right to vote and the right to work and the right to live without insult.[54]

Neither colonial independence nor racial equality was included in the Fourteen Points. But it is a measure of the impact of Wilson's manifesto of progressive internationalism that observers as shrewd as Du Bois could invest so much hope in it. Or rather, that American progressives were still optimistic enough to believe that the dialectical force of history itself would somehow hew progress out of a mountain of suffering.

As Du Bois's prophecy suggests, popular expectations for a just peace were, if anything, higher at war's end than at the beginning. As if dancing to a Joplin rag, elites and popular movements had moved in syncopated rhythm responding to one another's lead over the past four years. Beginning in the neutrality period, reformers had led off by linking ideas of a just society to a just peace. That, in turn, made it politic, perhaps even necessary, for Wilson to couch American intervention in terms of a democratic crusade. The result was to quicken hopes for a democratic peace, even as the grassroots organizations that best embodied them were crippled. Thus when the war ended, hopes for a democratic peace were even higher than when Wilson had launched his crusade eighteen months earlier. That is exactly what would make the immediate postwar years among the most explosive in American history and would cause Wilson's magic mirror to shatter into a thousand pieces.

The End of the War

By the fall of 1918, the meaning of "progressive" had undergone important changes. It was still linked, above all, to the kind of social reform that Jane Addams had personified in 1914, including women's suffrage. But the war had made its impact. First of all, the state loomed much larger in the progressive outlook, both positively and negatively. On the positive side, the wartime administrative state set the example that future president Franklin D. Roosevelt would come back to again and again searching for techniques to combat the emergency of the Great Depression. On the negative side, progressives learned the lesson of government repression the hard way and dedicated themselves to the defense of civil liberties.

Second, progressives were drawing closer than ever to labor. Having worked together to pass the reforms of 1916 and elect Wilson, reformers and unions went on to collaborate in the national War Labor Board and in grassroots alliances that set a precedent for postwar politics. Third, internationalism became more urgent, not the easy internationalism of the prewar years, but a new battle-tested internationalism that was alive to the extraordinary events of the period. With the blows of world war and revolution falling everywhere, the question was not whether to be internationalist, but whether to support nationalist, republican, or communist forces of global change.

The new internationalism points to an extraordinary change in the global role of the United States. As the country loosed its hemispheric moorings and sailed out to assume ideological leadership among the Allies, the last year of the war blossomed into an American moment in world history. Wilson even attempted to extend American influence across hostile borders into the Central Powers and, most remarkably, into Bolshevik Russia. Coupled with the emergence of the United States as the world's biggest creditor, this moment prefigured American hegemony later in the century. Hegemony involves both force and consent, and American leadership in 1918 forecast the situation after the Second World War when the United States, with its monopoly of the atom bomb, emerged militarily supreme, but also relied on extensive regulation of the market at home and abroad (the Marshall Plan) to win leadership of the Western alliance.

Not all Americans were ready to make this leap. Opposition appeared in the November elections, held just a few days before the Armistice. Republicans had kept up a steady criticism of Wilson's conduct of the war, and in the case of Henry Cabot Lodge, Republican leader in the Senate, animosity toward Wilson knew no bounds. Fed up with Republican complaints, Wilson went out on the hustings and asked the voters to give him a friendly Congress. In the first major mistake of his presidency, he forgot that the United States did not operate under a British parliamentary system, where the prime minister is the leader of the majority party in the House of Commons, but under a much looser system, where the president could be of a different party than the majority in Congress. And so it turned out. The election was a disaster. Wilson Democrats fell like spruce to a bucksaw.

The election result, however, was completely overshadowed by the end of the fighting in Europe. When the last of their "final" offensives bogged down over the summer, the German general staff finally concluded that the balance of forces arrayed against them, above all the economic and military resources of the United States, made the war unwinnable. They had gambled on a knockout blow and lost. Ironically, when they decided to sue for peace, it was their nemesis that they contacted. Taking the Fourteen Points at face value, they believed Wilson would be more magnanimous than the other Allies, especially if they got rid of the kaiser. Accordingly, in defeat and disgrace, they overthrew the centuries-old Hohenzollern dynasty in early November and presented themselves to Wilson as fellow republicans.

The republican revolution in Germany cleared the way for the signing of the Armistice in a railcar at Compiègne just north of Paris on November 11, 1918. Once it was clear that this was the real thing (there had been false reports of a truce a few days earlier), the end of the war released a flood of emotion comparable to the outburst of 1914. At least among the victors, euphoria burst forth in spontaneous celebrations from the humblest hamlets to the greatest capital cities, as civilians took off from work, sounded fire sirens, danced in the streets, and got rip-roaring drunk. For a day or two, the authorities smiled benignly on the pandemonium, allowing the celebrations to balloon into a worldwide carnival of peace, a wild escape from everyday restraints. Like the village carnival that temporarily turned the world upside down, these celebrations posed no threat to authority, because everyone knew they would be over by morning.[55]

The greatest war in human history was over. For those who survived Armageddon, the question was, what would come next?

FOR PEACE AND FREEDOM: Delegates to the Fourth Congress of the Women's International League for Peace and Freedom, Washington, 1924, including Jane Addams, president (third from right), and others from France, Germany, Britain, and the Netherlands. In the aftermath of the war, progressives commonly linked the quest for world peace to struggles for social justice. (Swarthmore College Peace Collection)

7

The Millennial Moment

After Armageddon came the Millennium. Emerging from the death and destruction all about, survivors came forth to redeem wartime pledges of a peaceable and democratic world. Casting aside princes and potentates of the old order, they looked to new messiahs—Woodrow Wilson, progressive prophet of a new world order, and V. I. Lenin, communist savior of the toiling masses—to begin history anew. In terms reminiscent of the great French Revolution, a character in John Dos Passos's *Nineteen Nineteen* captured the feeling of a new cycle of history beginning on "the first morning of the first day of the first year."[1]

Given all the suffering, were not the survivors entitled to a new era? Great changes *were*, in fact, taking place. Antiquated pillars of the old regime were snapping like matchsticks, bringing down the rotted empires of the Romanovs, the Hohenzollerns, and the Habsburgs, taking down centuries of oppression along with them. With the spread of democratic ideas, the old balance-of-power diplomacy was discredited and patriarchal authority was weakening. Nor were the younger industrial and commercial classes able to rest easily in the saddle in the yet-to-be-defined postwar international system.

In this highly fluid situation, all the movements for change that had been diverted by the war came flooding back onto the scene to mingle with the currents of social revolution and the first stirrings of colonial independence. As rulers and ruled began the next round of the dance of democracy, there was new music in the air—African rhythms, Indian ragas, Chinese folk tunes, and the communist "Internationale."

The concurrence of these varied movements made it seem as if they were all melded together in one great revolt against the old predatory civilization. "It is a world-wide movement," wrote *The Nation* on October 25, 1919. "In Russia it has dethroned the Czar and for two years maintained Lenin in his stead. In Korea and India and Egypt and Ireland it keeps up an unyielding resistance to political tyranny." The movement even spread to the United States: "In Seattle and San Francisco it has resulted in the stevedores' recent refusal to handle arms or supplies destined for the overthrow of the Soviet Government."[2]

If one did not look too carefully, it was possible to believe that the world was actually splitting in two between the forces of change and the forces of order. On one side, the great bulk of suffering humanity, on the other, a diminishing circle of oppressive elites, and it seemed as if the two had entered an apocalyptic struggle that might result in the final triumph of one or the other. The thrill of the moment was evoked in a retrospective view by American journalist George Soule: "I suppose that from 1919 to 1921 the world seemed more in flux, more ready for fundamental changes, than it ever has since."[3]

For sheer intensity, none of the secular views could match the apocalyptic visions drawn from the biblical book of Revelations. Having at first opposed U.S. intervention, Protestant fundamentalists increasingly saw American swords as the instruments of their Lord's vengeance and began to decipher prophetic signs in the internecine warfare among Christians and the promise of a Jewish homeland in Palestine. Most telling of all was the triumph of godless bolshevism in Russia, perhaps marking the beginning of the time of Tribulation, the seven-year reign of the Antichrist, which would end gloriously with the victory of the saints at the battle of Armageddon. After that came the Millennium, the thousand-year reign of Christ.[4]

Social Movements

Leaving religious prophesy aside, nothing contributed more to the sense of a new day than the belief that women and men could never go back to the old ways. Veteran campaigners for women's suffrage knew that nothing could stop them now, and equal suffrage soon came to Bolshevik Russia, Weimar Germany, and Great Britain (with limitations). In the United States, the ratification of the Anthony Amendment in August of 1920 marked a giant step on the road to equal citizenship.

It was widely assumed that women's votes would lead straight to another round of social reform. The women's suffrage association christened itself the League of Women Voters, proudly renamed its journal *The Woman Citizen*, and immediately set about promoting social legislation, including a new child labor law, federal funds for maternal and infant health, and working women's protections. In keeping with its upper-class base of support, the league also called for educational restrictions on the franchise.

Even the new women's fashions conveyed a feeling of freedom. Out went whalebone corsets, up went hemlines, and off went heavy woolen brocade. On went loose-fitting chemise dresses and more practical, active garb. The transition had been hastened by occasional cross-dressing during the war, when women had appeared in men's clothes in men's jobs in formerly all-male settings of machine shops, streetcars, and shipyards. All this undermined Victorian notions of separate spheres, and for once, a change in fashion marked deeper social changes.

Nor were sexual mores ever the same. Although social hygienists boasted of "the American Plan" to promote premarital chastity for men by shutting down the brothels, popular tastes were opening up new avenues for sexual expression. All the contemporary surveys of sexual behavior showed increasing rates of sexual intercourse before marriage and more erotic delights in marital bedrooms.[5] Bathtub gin, college petting parties, and the Jazz Age were just around the corner.

Along with this new behavior, a "new morality" was emerging. Resuming the revolt against Victorianism that had been suppressed during the war, brave souls of the birth control movement, such as Mary Dennett, picked up where Margaret Sanger had left off. Seeking to enhance "the very greatest physical pleasure to be had in all human experience," Dennett would later be jailed for publishing "obscene" material. But in the heady days after the war, she spoke for a significant number of feminists who were seeking to cut sex loose from procreation, as well as from bourgeois marriage, commercial exchange, and all its other moorings in the property-obsessed civilization of the nineteenth century. Let sex be bound up with love or desire, but, please, not with mortgage payments.[6]

The allure of sexual freedom was part of the excitement of being an American in Paris after the war. "How you gonna keep 'em down on the farm / After they've seen Paree?" asked Tin Pan Alley. Inspired by French mores, a few American writers set out to erase the double standard by creating female characters as earthy as the men, such as Catherine, the sexually adventurous English nurse in Ernest Hemingway's *A Farewell to Arms*. Likewise, John Dos Passos rendered sensitive portraits of volunteer relief workers, Red Cross nurses, and secretaries in *Nineteen Nineteen*, nearly all of whom had gone to bed with a man before their tour of duty was out. The exception was a lone lesbian who "kept all the men away," but presumably, not the women. One free-spirited Texan explained, "I guess it's the war and continental standards and everything loosens up people's morals."[7]

Sexual freedom, however, shaded over into salaciousness, especially in the movies. The good girl/bad girl dichotomy was replicated in the contrast between fresh-faced Mary Pickford— "America's sweetheart," epitome of the prevailing white, Anglo-Saxon image of feminine innocence—and sultry Theda Bara, personification of female sensuality. Bara, the Cincinnati-born daughter of an immigrant Jewish tailor, introduced the "vamp" to audiences entranced with the power of female sexuality, and soon even high school girls in God-fearing Lutheran villages of the upper Midwest were collecting yearbook testaments to their "vamping" powers, even as they were dressing to look like "America's sweetheart."

Bara's male counterpart was Rudolph Valentino, Italian immigrant heartthrob, whose romantic allure won legions of admirers. In *The Sheik* (1921), Valentino played an English aristocrat posing as an Arab sheik who wins the heart of an English woman in the Middle Eastern desert and only then throws off the class and racial masquerade to reveal his true identity. Soon even Baptist farm boys in rural hamlets of the southern Bible Belt were playing Valentino to their sweethearts in porch-swing romances.

Because American culture in this period was torn between the opposite poles of Victorian self-denial and modern self-indulgence, Hollywood had to perform a delicate balancing act between them. Early movies had earned a reputation worthy of Sodom and Gomorrah, leading straightlaced moralists to decry "the sins of Hollywood," in the title of one exposé.[8] Attempting to placate traditional morality, Cecil DeMille, a legendary producer, hit upon a brilliant compromise. He shifted his lens to place scenes of wanton debauchery within a frame of pious virtue. The formula of virtue-triumphs-over-vice proved enormously successful in *The Ten Commandments* (1923), a morality tale in two parts. The first is a retelling of the ancient story of Exodus in which God's wrath falls on Pharaoh's army in the Red Sea, depicted with pioneering special effects. The second is a modern tale of the wages of sin in which the bad brother breaks all the Commandments on the road to temporary pleasure and ultimate destruction, while the good brother, an honest, Christlike carpenter, keeps the true faith and triumphs in the end. Along the way the audience is treated to a saturnalia of debauchery that includes Egyptian dancing girls, golden idols, wild orgies, bribery, corruption, murder, and, to top it all off, an adulterous rendezvous with a voluptuous Franco-Chinese leper. The beauty of the DeMille formula was that the audience could eat of the forbidden fruit, and yet leave the theater with the sweet taste of virtue in their mouths. All in all, the new hedonism confirmed the sense that everything was in flux.

At the same moment, industrial capitalism was shaken to the core by the workers of the world. To keen observers such as George Soule, national differences did not obscure the worldwide revolt: "There had been the Communist revolution in Russia, the Socialist revolution in Germany, and the tremendous growth of the British Labor party, with its ambitious Nottingham program."[9] Even in countries that had won the war, ruling classes worried that things were getting out of hand. While Italian workers were occupying factories in Turin and Milan, and industrial workers in the Ruhr were in revolt, British mining, rail, and transport unions joined together in the Triple Alliance, whose threat of a general strike prompted Prime Minister Lloyd George to call the bluff of union leaders by asking if it was their intention to run the country. As he expected, they backed down.

The most gripping drama was played out in central and eastern Europe. Amid hunger and deprivation, the specter of bolshevism came alive in one leftist uprising after another against the untested moderate regimes that had replaced the Hohenzollern and Habsburg empires. In January 1919, Germany was shaken by the Spartacist revolt in Berlin and shortly thereafter by Kurt Eisner's short-lived people's republic in Munich. In a similar revolt, Hungary came under the rule of communist leader Béla Kun.

The handful of Americans on hand to witness these events were carried away by a sense of impending revolution. Even U.S. diplomats stationed in Hungary and Czechoslovakia soberly reported that some kind of socialism was inevitable in the states emerging from the Austro-Hungarian empire. A minor American official fictionalized in Dos Passos's *Nineteen Nineteen* "had it on good authority the syndicates were going to seize the factories in Italy the first of May. Hungary had gone red and Bavaria, next it would be Austria, then Italy, then Prussia and France: the American troops sent against the Russians in Archangel had mutinied: 'It's the world revolution, a goddam swell time to be alive, and we'll be goddam lucky if we come out of it with whole skins.' "[10]

Desperate for information about the spreading revolt, Herbert Hoover asked Mary Heaton Vorse, New-England-bred rebel journalist, and Abraham Cahan, socialist editor of the Jewish *Forward*, to go on a mission to Budapest for the American Relief Association. Having caught the radical fever, Vorse had all she could do to contain her excitement upon meeting Red Guards at the Hungarian frontier; but even her enthusiasm paled in comparison to that of Cahan, who "was in a state bordering on ecstasy."[11]

Equally fervid, Crystal Eastman traveled through eastern Europe for the *Liberator* to learn all she could about revolution. She studied how radical regimes nationalized banks and industry, confiscated the estates of the wealthy, and set minimum wages, whether or not there was any money to pay them when so few factories were in production. Believing it was necessary to choose sides, she put aside qualms over proletarian dictatorship. When the "Internationale" was played in the movie theaters of Budapest, she felt just like John Reed and Louise Bryant had in Petrograd two years earlier: "you have to stand up."[12]

The "Internationale" was being sung in cities all over Europe, with its promise to the prisoners of starvation that a better world was in birth. Filled with apocalyptic imagery of "the final conflict," the anthem of the exploited looked beyond the Communist Third International and the new Union of Soviet Socialist Republics toward the day when "the international working class will be the human race." Even the supposedly sober scientific socialists of the newly founded American Communist party were carried away by the apocalyptic mood: "The world is on the verge of a new era. Europe is in revolt. The masses of Asia are stirring uneasily. Capitalism is in collapse. The workers of the world are seeing a new life and securing new courage. Out of the night of the war is coming a new day."[13]

Under normal circumstances, predictions of workers revolution in capitalist America were sheer fantasy. But in view of the volcanic eruptions that rumbled through American industry all through 1919, that notion was less outlandish than usual. The disruptions started with a bang in the Seattle General Strike, where even the local AFL labor council was caught up in the exhilarating adventure of shutting down an entire city, if only for a few days. Eruptions spread in the summer through the sweltering packing houses of the Midwest to the teeming garment districts of New York and the textile factories of New England. In each of the biggest strikes, hundreds of thousands poured forth like masses of human lava, some five million in all.

Emblematic of the upheaval was the great steel strike. It was an outpouring of new immigrants emboldened by wartime conditions. Slovaks, Hungarians, Sicilians, and members of a dozen other groups toiled in an environment that conjured up visions of hell—fiery furnaces flaming out from the eerie darkness in vast, tomb-like buildings filled with sulphur-choked smoke. With the mill running full tilt, common laborers were obliged to risk life and limb twelve hours a day, extended to twenty-four hours when the shifts rotated from day to night. The setting conjured up images of Dante's inferno.

Escape from inferno had not seemed possible until wartime conditions raised hopes for a measure of democracy in industry. Interviews of steelworkers conducted for the Carnegie Endowment and the Interchurch World Movement revealed a new-found sense of entitlement among European ethnics to the much-touted American standard of living, and bitterness over being told "the good jobs are not for hunkies."[14] The same interviews turned up little millennialism among these stoical Catholics and Orthodox Christians, but there was plenty of dogged determination to wrest a degree of freedom from the steelmasters. Everyone saw the eight-hour day (plus time-and-a-half for overtime) as the key to improvements in wages, health, work pace, and leisure time for the family. In promising "American" conditions, the wartime Americanization movement apparently had done its work too well.

Seeking to shape these inchoate impulses into a disciplined organization, labor progressives in Chicago hastily assembled an ad hoc committee behind feisty Irish-American John Fitzpatrick and set out to bring together bedraggled craft unions and the hitherto unorganized semiskilled and unskilled laborers.

The goal was to substitute the good order of "industrial democracy" for the hellish conditions in the mills. Knowing he was helpless to stop this irresistible strike force, Samuel Gompers threw up his hands in the face of a last minute appeal from President Wilson for a postponement, and the greatest industrial battle the country had ever seen got under way on September 22.

Among the 365,000 steel strikers were some of the most downtrodden members of American society, "Hunkies" and "Guineas," despised for their ignorance and poverty, hired like cattle to do the dirtiest, backbreaking jobs. Now, all of a sudden, the wretched of the earth were commanding the attention of the press and forcing high and mighty industrialists and diplomats to respond to *their* agenda. Following the lead of Elbert Gary, commander of the flagship United States Steel Corporation, corporate executives dug in their heels against union recognition, with the result that localized industrial conflict turned into class war.

The analogy of war imbued everything. William Zebulon Foster, New England–born syndicalist, was the field commander of the organizing drives in meatpacking and steel. He saw the postwar upheaval as the first general assault on capital and ran his campaign like a military strategist, with frontal assaults, flanking attacks, clever feints, and strategic retreats. Journalists routinely described the strikers as industrial armies and compared them to the trench fighters on the Western Front.[15]

On the wings of such conflicts, the hopes of American radicals soared. George Soule recalled, "The labor movement in the United States was strong, aggressive and fermenting with ideas. We had genuine samples of class conflict on an arresting scale—great strikes in basic industries such as coal, steel, and railroads."[16] It was true that the strikers were as likely to be under conservative leadership of the sort represented by John L. Lewis, Republican field general of the coal strike who voted for Warren G. Harding in 1920, as under radicals such as A. J. Muste, young minister of the Fellowship of Reconciliation who found himself leading the textile strike in Lawrence, Massachusetts. It was also true that much of the top leadership of the IWW and the Socialist party had been put out of commission by jail sentences.

Nonetheless, the movement gave rise to the most significant labor party activity in American history. Radiating out from its midwestern core, a farmer-labor drive was launched in 1919 that continued to agitate the electoral scene for the next five years. (A fuller discussion will follow in chapter 9.) In addition, following a path that started in the war, an increasing number of progressives came over to the camp of labor. Members of the fractious Committee of 48, heirs of the New Nationalists, joined the farmer-labor effort and later combined forces with the union-backed Conference for Progressive Political Action. Moreover, residence in an Atlanta prison did not prevent Eugene Debs from winning almost a million votes in his hoosegow campaign for president in 1920.

Meanwhile, a militant minority "went bolshi." Having returned from witnessing the historic events in Russia, John Reed became locked in a sectarian struggle over the formation of an American communist party, with the result that two parties vied for affiliation with the new Communist International formed in March of 1919. Reed's Communist Labor party was smaller and more "American" in membership than its rival Communist party, which came mostly out of the foreign-language federations of the badly splintered Socialist party. Factionalism aside, both communist parties plotted the imminent overthrow of capitalism.

Like the war itself, labor discontent spread to the farthest reaches of the globe, bringing organized protest to places that had never before seen a trade union. There was labor trouble from southeast Asian rubber plantations to South African gold mines and wherever the tendrils of the capitalist market had spread. Coupled with the exceptional level of activism in developed countries, the labor movement appeared to Lloyd George as the greatest force in the world, a view echoed by President Wilson, who repeatedly expressed the opinion that the issue of labor was "all through the world the one central question of civilization."[17]

Internationalists of various stripes labored to bring some cohesion to this sprawling global movement. Seeking to live down the betrayal of 1914, European socialists made fitful attempts to reconstitute the Second International before its upstart communist rival could gain the upper hand. Meanwhile, moderate European trade unionists looked to negotiators assembling in Paris for the peace conference to build what became the International Labor Organization. At the same time, American and European reformers were laying plans for a series of international conferences of working women.

Efforts to unite the workers of the world ran up against a host of obstacles, none more potent than racial division. In Chicago, for example, union attempts at biracial organizing had to contend with white-hot hatreds that erupted in the summer of 1919 in a bloody race riot. Steeped in the invidious racial consciousness of the day, Irish social and political clubs spearheaded white mobs in grisly attacks on African-American newcomers to the city's industrial districts. Ugly street battles went on for days, leaving 39 dead, most of whom were black, before the National Guard came in to restore order.[18]

Even so, international organizing sometimes spanned the racial divide. In Panama, for example, years of festering resentment against the pernicious gold-silver system, with its blatant discrimination against West Indians and Panamanians, finally came to a head with the organization of unions among the silver workers, leading to large-scale strikes in 1919 and 1920 that interrupted canal shipping. In a sign of these extraordinary times, the AFL temporarily broke with tradition to welcome West Indians into the ranks, and even the otherwise lily-white railroad brotherhoods sent in paid organizers and, for a time, accepted affiliation from the mostly black union in Panama.[19]

African-Americans participated in many of the postwar union organizing drives, and the brief experience left a lasting imprint. Asa Philip Randolph, for example, African-American editor of the socialist newspaper *The Messenger*, developed a lifelong commitment to interracial unionism. The son of an itinerant African Methodist Episcopal preacher, Randolph spoke for the "New Crowd" of young Negro radicals who hailed the revolutionary arrival of a New World and looked toward an alliance with white radicals among the IWW, the Socialists, and the Non-

Partisan League. Like so many on the left who had replaced religious heaven with an earthly utopia, Randolph hoped "to build a new society—a society of equals, without class, race, caste or religious distinctions."[20]

In these days of deliverance, nothing was ruled out, not even the coming of the people's Messiah. Even a seasoned trade unionist like Sidney Hillman, leader of the Amalgamated Clothing Workers, could not help being caught up in the excitement of a labor movement which had doubled union membership during the war and now surged forward in mass strikes. Drawing on the story of Exodus and prophesies of the Messiah, Hillman preached a message of deliverance, telling the wage "slaves" of Montreal that their day was at hand. Looking out at the throng of expectant faces opened his heart, and he experienced a kind of revelation. Hillman told his eager listeners that an awakened people were their own Messiah: "He may be with us any minute—one can hear the footsteps of the Deliverer—if only he listens intently. Labor will rule and the World will be free."[21]

If wage earners dared to believe their deliverance lay in their own collective organization, not in crusading Americanism, Rockefeller's benevolence, or religious salvation, then, surely, a new day *was* at hand.

Promised Lands

In an atmosphere thick with prophesies of deliverance, millennial hopes arose, too, among oppressed peoples and nations. The defeat of Germany and Austria made it all but certain that new nations would sprout up in their former imperial territories throughout eastern Europe and the Balkans. In addition, the movement for Irish independence had quickened with the Easter Rebellion during the war, and Zionist hopes for a Palestinian homeland had been raised by the Balfour Declaration. Even among colonial peoples, shattering the mystique of European superiority made it possible to envision free and independent nations delivered from colonial bondage all over Africa and Asia.

Each of these movements had its own origin and dynamic, each was rooted in its own unique setting, and the differences among them were considerable. Take the Garvey movement. Under the banner of "Africa for the Africans," Marcus Garvey preached an undiluted message of black nationalism. A prophet for prophetic times, the Jamaican-born stevedore had been raised from obscurity to become the era's greatest messenger of Negro liberation. Having emigrated to New York in 1916, Garvey immediately set about rallying the children of the African diaspora to the red, black, and green colors of the Universal Negro Improvement Association (UNIA). Growing by leaps and bounds in the immediate aftermath of the war, the UNIA quickly became the most popular Pan-African movement ever launched, eclipsing all its rivals, including a postwar series of Pan-African congresses spearheaded by the NAACP.

Garvey's core message was black nationalism—the solidarity of peoples of African descent across national and imperial boundaries. In an era of Jim Crow in the American South, bloody race riots in the North, and rampant colonialism in Africa and the Caribbean, the nationalist message was bound to resonate all the way from Liberia through the West Indies to the rapidly expanding ghettos of North America. "Up, you mighty race," Garvey exhorted, "you can accomplish what you will." Drawing together many cultural threads in the tapestry of Pan-Africanism, he brought to the diverse peoples of the African diaspora the sense of common African identity.

Garvey believed that Pan-Africanism would encompass both black capital and black labor. On the business side, he was a relentless—some said reckless—promoter of the Black Star Line, the UNIA's financially and legally troubled shipping company. On labor's side, the Garvey movement was a leaven in the great postwar rising of colonial and working people. Where West Indian labor was on the move, as in the Panama Canal Zone, the UNIA sent funds and sought affiliation with local trade unions.

Garvey's message held special appeal to uprooted West Indians like himself. It also appealed strongly to the hundreds of thousands who trekked out of the American South in the Great

Migration. Their Exodus from the segregated South to northern ghettos had led not into Canaan but into another Egypt. If the journey for freedom had to start over again, then, maybe the place to look for Canaan was not in America but in Africa.

Of all African lands, Liberia was best positioned to link up with the UNIA. Nominally independent, Liberia had been an informal U.S. protectorate since the 1820s, when it had become the point of contact for efforts to solve the problem of slavery by exporting freed slaves to Africa. Transatlantic contacts persisted in the intervening decades, and the UNIA chose Liberia as the core of a future Pan-African empire. As the Black Star Line laid plans for regular shipping runs, Garvey received several plenipotentiaries from Monrovia, accorded them honored positions at UNIA conventions, and appointed one "secretary of state" in his provisional government. For a time, the Liberian government reciprocated, promising "every facility legally possible" to help in acquiring large tracts of land for future settlement. Unfortunately, the Firestone Tire and Rubber Company had its own plans for Liberian real estate. To win favor with the Liberian government for its expanding rubber plantations, Firestone arranged for Monrovia to receive a badly needed loan from the United States. That was all the Liberian government needed to reverse itself and repudiate Garvey's land acquisition and settlement plans as an "incendiary policy."[22]

At the height of the movement, the UNIA held a mammoth conference in New York City in August 1920. Sessions at the organization's own Liberty Hall and at Madison Square Garden were staged with theatrical pomp to showcase transnational racial solidarity. Places on the platform of dignitaries were reserved for delegates from Monrovia, Montreal, and the British West Indies, and international delegates also received places of honor in the great Silent Parade of the New Negro that wended its way through Harlem, the largest such march to that point in American history.[23]

Despite his wide appeal, Garvey had many critics, not all of them white. The black community was, and has never been, a monolith. Many black Christians who accepted the mainstream image of Africa as the dark continent in need of missionary up-lift disdained Garvey as a dangerous impostor. W. E. B. Du Bois saw him as a West Indian demagogue preaching world revolu-tion to his deluded followers, in alliance with dangerous bolshe-viks and Sinn Feiners. Socialist A. Philip Randolph saw him as a false prophet who would lead the masses out of the frying pan of white capitalism into the fire of black capitalism. The critics pointed out that his dreams of power and riches merely repli-cated prevailing mentalities, and the same went for his intense race consciousness. The myth of a unified African identity among millions of diaspora Africans was less an alternative to the reigning ideology of white supremacy than an imitation of it. Much of Garvey's appeal rested on his ability to fashion a mirror image of the white world led by black potentates and black businessmen.

At the same time, it is necessary to recognize that Garvey had a hold of something deeper. The yearning for freedom is one of the taproots of Western culture and a universal human desire, if ever there was one. Garvey attracted supporters because of his audacious prophecy that someday the oppressed will escape their bondage, justice will rain down, the first shall be last, and the last shall be first. Wherever struggles were underway against European colonialism, even in the Irish and Jewish diasporas, they could count on Garvey's support.

> Four millions of Irishmen and women are struggling for the inde-pendence of Ireland. Twelve millions of Jews are clamoring for the restoration of Palestine. The Egyptians are determined to get Egypt as an independent country. Three hundred millions of Indians are determined to have India. Four hundred million Negroes realize that the time has come to restore Africa to the Africans.[24]

In this extraordinary conjuncture, what is striking is the degree of reciprocal influence among liberation movements. It was one of the few points of mutual support, for example, among the otherwise hostile Irish and black communities in American cities.

A similar yearning for freedom underlay the Jewish search for a promised land. Palestine appealed to Zionists in the same way that "Africa for the Africans" appealed to many American blacks, as a sanctuary of freedom. Although Zionists represented a relatively small part of the Jewish community, the millennial atmosphere of 1919 tightened the already strong bonds felt by the two peoples most likely to be the targets of race hate in the United States. Although kept apart by many things, including Jewish racism and black anti-Semitism, they had much in common. As peoples of the Book, African-American preachers and Jewish rabbis outdid each other in embracing Moses and in claiming spiritual descent from the Hebrews of the Old Testament. Garvey did all he could to cultivate his image as "the Black Moses" and encouraged his followers to see his movement as "black Zionism." From the other shore, the Zionist press was overwhelmingly favorable to Garvey. It appeared to many contemporaries that Zionism and black nationalism were ideological twins.[25]

There were differences, however. For one, Zionism was much more acceptable to progressives than Garveyism. In fact, the preeminent American Zionist also happened to be one of the most prominent progressives in the country. Louis Brandeis was many things: the very model of a successful professional, a brilliant Boston lawyer, author of Woodrow Wilson's campaign philosophy of the New Freedom. Beginning in 1914, he was also the leader of the American branch of world Zionism. To Brandeis, Zionism was "a freedom movement" in the sense that by finding a homeland in Palestine, Jews would gain what Americans and other peoples already enjoyed . . . a nation they could call their own. His appointment to the U.S. Supreme Court in 1916 was more a sign of the arrival of progressivism than of Judaism in the highest circles of power, but it also suggested there was no necessary conflict between the two.[26]

To those who complained that Zionism posed a conflict of loyalty for American Jews, Brandeis had a briefcase full of answers. In his brand of Zionism, there could be no division between

America and Palestine because "It is Democracy that Zionism represents. It is Social Justice which Zionism represents, and every bit of that is the American ideal of the twentieth century." In one breath, he compared settlers in Palestine to pioneers going to California; in another they were modern-day Puritans: "Zionism is the Pilgrim inspiration and impulse over again." Surely these were miraculous times when it was possible to have not one, but two promised lands.[27]

Of all the contemporary quests for a homeland, the most venerable was the cause of Irish freedom. Three and a half centuries of Irish resistance to British rule going back to Oliver Cromwell made it the oldest of the anticolonial struggles of the day. In the United States, the Irish cause dated back to large-scale immigration in the 1840s and was associated with ill-fated Fenian attempts to attack the British in Canada. The bloody suppression of the Easter Rebellion had marked a new phase of hostilities, and now, in the spirit of the times, Sinn Fein proclaimed an Irish Republic in November 1919.

Not all Irish themselves were convinced the time for independence had arrived, nor was Britain willing to let Ireland go quietly. Nonetheless, there was a feeling in the air that independence was only a matter of time. Using Wilsonian rhetoric for its own purposes, the Irish Race Convention, held in the United States in March 1919, declared its aim was "to settle the Irish question on the basis of self-determination." Large numbers of Irish-Americans rushed to join the Friends of Irish Freedom and the American Association for Recognition of the Irish Republic, pushing membership in the two organizations above a million. The cause of Irish independence was a model for fledgling independence struggles from West Africa to South Asia and, as such, was a bridge over the troubled racial divide.[28]

The role of the Irish cause in the development of progressivism has gone almost unnoticed. That is strange, given the large Irish segment of the working class, Irish prominence in the labor movement and the Democratic party, and, finally, the impact of Irish progressives themselves. Frank Walsh, for example, a Dem-

ocratic labor lawyer from Missouri, was not only an ardent
champion of Irish independence, but also cochair of two quintessentially progressive institutions—the prewar Commission on
Industrial Relations and the War Labor Board. For every conservative Irish labor leader there was also an Irish progressive or
radical, such as Tom Mooney, whose false imprisonment for the
bombing of a 1916 preparedness parade in San Francisco became
an international *cause célèbre*.

Furthermore, the key figure in every labor-progressive political initiative from 1919 to 1921 was another Irish-American. John
Fitzpatrick's intense support for the newly declared Irish Republic helped strengthen the anti-imperial current among American
trade unions. Fitzpatrick's anticolonial views, no doubt, contributed to his ability to break the mold of racial exclusion in the
labor movement. Against considerable opposition from his own
rank and file, he insisted on bringing African-American workers
into the postwar organizing drive.

Africans, Jews, and the Irish were peoples without a nation
and nations without a state. Under the prevailing ideology, unless a people had a nation-state to call their own, they might be
located squarely in time, but they were lost in space, not knowing where they were. Having a homeland with its own flag, fron-
tiers, statesmen, and generals was seen to be essential to one's
very identity.

In retrospect, these quests for a homeland appear to have all
the negative characteristics of what would later be called "identity politics." Parochial, self-serving, and exclusive, they called
for Africa for the Africans, Palestine for the Jews, Ireland for the
Irish . . . and nobody else. In their narrow focus on winning a
state for their own people, they posed a threat to civic and pluralist conceptions of how a state should be organized to avoid
oppressing ethnic minorities within it.

And yet, in the context of their own time, they should not be
judged too harshly. African independence, Zionism, and Irish
independence all had the potential to lessen oppression. Imagine
a world in which black Africans controlled the continent south
of the Sahara, Jews controlled Palestine, and Ireland was a free

state. At the very least, if things got too bad in Kingston or Chicago, there would always be a place of refuge. Nor were these quests entirely self-serving. Mutual support for anticolonial struggles helped break down barriers between them, adding an important element of ethnic pluralism to progressive internationalism. Pluralism was also a powerful antidote to the social Darwinist ideology of racial inequality. Clearly, a sense of international citizenship was having a healthy impact on citizenship at home.

People's Peace

Released from the confinements of war, social movements immediately rushed toward Paris to get in on the peace conference which began in January 1919. "Paris was the capital of the world that spring of the Peace Conference," wrote young John Dos Passos, who was there basking in the excitement.[29] Actually, there were two very different gatherings: the official meeting of diplomats at the old Bourbon Palace of Versailles, to be discussed shortly, and the unofficial gatherings of people's representatives, most of whom were not welcome in Paris and had to find someplace else to meet.

The idea of a "people's peace"—even Wilson used the phrase—rose like a phoenix from the ashes of war. Social movements from the Western countries sought entry to the gates of Paris to press their demands for labor legislation, women's rights, and the Stockholm idea for a people's peace conference. Brandishing Wilson's Fourteen Points, American progressives came to support a "league of free peoples." Even Walter Lippmann and other members of The Inquiry, the official team of policy experts brought along to advise the American peace commissioners, were warm to the notion of a people's peace.

Also drawn into the vortex of Paris were colonial peoples, most of whom came knocking on President Wilson's door. According to George Seldes, an American correspondent on the scene, "All the oppressed nations sent kings, princes, premiers and delegations to Mr. Wilson and called him the sole arbiter of the New World."[30] Among the supplicants was a young Vietnamese student named Ho Chi Minh, who, like all the other colonials from Asia or Africa, went away disappointed.

Despite disappointments, Paris was a focal point of the first worldwide wave of anticolonialism. Although freedom for Asian and African peoples was not yet in the cards, Du Bois's optimistic prophesy was coming true in its broadest sense— "never again will darker people of the world occupy just the place they had before." With Du Bois's help, a handful of Africans and Caribbeans managed to launch the Pan-African Congress, first in a series of postwar gatherings that crystallized demands for equal treatment.

In the flux of the moment, the line between a people's peace and a peace among nations grew indistinct. In pressing their claims for self-determination against imperial rulers, nationalist leaders in the cause of Irish, Polish, or Arab freedom were seen to be on the side of democracy, and in many respects, they were. In some cases—Masaryk of Czechoslovakia, Sinn Fein in Ireland—they were aligned with social reform or even social revolution. Moreover, the very fact that Asians and Africans were claiming the right of self-government, never mind the character of the government they would set up, ran contrary to European colonialism.

So it was with the controversial Japanese proposal to insert a clause proclaiming "racial equality" in the treaty. Even as Japan was grabbing a piece of imperial spoils in China's Shandong peninsula, the Japanese proposal for equality electrified the subjects of European rule. Especially among educated Asians, ideas of equality were taking hold just as the terrible slaughter in Europe battlefields was shattering the mystique of Western superiority. In some places elites were linking up with mass movements for self-government, as in India under the Congress party, and in the Dutch East Indies. The strengthening of such movements was an unintended consequence of colonial participation in the war.

Like the supplicants from the colonies, social activists from Western countries discovered that Versailles was not very hospitable. Socialists trying to reconstitute the Second International were thwarted when Allied governments denied citizens of the Central powers access to Paris, just as the Stockholm conference had been thwarted during the war. That forced the socialists to move to Bern, Switzerland, where delegates from the battered socialist parties of the former warring countries tried with little success to overcome the nationalist hatreds that had divided them since 1914. Mary Heaton Vorse, an American radical on the scene in Bern, found the timidity and bickering pathetic. Clearly, socialism had not recovered its prewar momentum, and it never would.[31]

Other eyes were on communism. Although red Russia was excluded from official Paris, the influence of communist internationalism was felt everywhere. Partly because so many radicals in the West were hitching their wagons to the Soviet star, the manifestos coming from Petrograd fluttered like red flags over Western capitals. Built on the iron will of Lenin and his followers, the communist Third International, founded in March of 1919, managed to achieve the organizational discipline its rivals lacked. From that day forth, all efforts to rebuild internationalism from below had to reckon with this new force.

Recognizing the challenge from the left, Wilson picked up the pace in what he saw as a race between reform and revolution. On his way to the Peace Conference, he told his advisors that "liberalism must be more liberal than ever before, it must even be radical, if civilization is to escape the typhoon."[32] Badly needing something to counter the bolshevik menace, Allied statesmen authorized the creation of an international labor commission to promote stable relations between labor and capital. The idea was to co-opt the international labor movement into any future league of nations in the same way that trade unions had been incorporated so effectively into the state machinery of the warring nations.

To chair the commission, Wilson selected the supremely loyal Sam Gompers. Relishing his status as Wilson's "labor ambassador," Gompers gratefully accepted the appointment, moved into the sumptuous Hotel Crillon, headquarters of the U.S. delegation, and immediately began sparring with his British and French colleagues over the design of what became the International Labor Organization. In a foretaste of the battle brewing in the U.S. Senate over the League of Nations, Gompers opposed European proposals for an international agency with quasi-legislative powers to mandate worldwide labor standards. Threatened by the prospect of international interference in collective bargaining, the AFL abandoned the ILO, which was partly its own creation, before the year was out.

Women reformers had always been more sympathetic to international labor legislation than the men of the AFL. Together with their European counterparts, American women dared to believe they might serve in some kind of advisory role in the peace conference. But it was not to be. Disappointed to find all doors closed in Paris—even the International Labor Organization was closed off—they sailed off to Washington. Refusing to allow exclusion from official circles to keep them out of the public square, the National Women's Trade Union League, led by Margaret Drier Robins (wife of Wilson's unofficial emissary to Russia, Raymond Robins), offered to host the first International Congress of Working Women in October 1919.

Meeting at the same time as the first ILO convention, women reformers from the Allied countries gathered to establish what they hoped would become a permanent body. Over the next four years, the Congress (later Federation) of Working Women agitated for industrial and social legislation of special interest to women around the world. But like many international efforts, it, too, foundered on national differences, with European women choosing to affiliate with the International Federation of Trade Unions, while their American sisters acceded to the wishes of the AFL and bowed out.[33]

The spirit of 1919 lived longest in the quest for peace and justice. Women reformers reforged international links that had been broken during the war. Veterans of the wartime Hague Conference kept their vow to reunite once the shooting stopped.

When German and Austrian sister delegates were barred from Paris, the intrepid organizers chose a neutral Swiss city, Zurich, as the location for the founding in May 1919 of the Women's International League for Peace and Freedom. Believing that the root causes of war lay in structures of inequality—social, economic, and political—they issued Cassandra-like warnings that the seeds of future war were being sown in the unequal terms of the Versailles Treaty. Great power domination of the proposed League of Nations, they believed, would reinforce imperialism, underwrite poverty, and deny oppressed peoples access to power.[34]

The Women's International League brought moral realism into the swelling pacifist movement. Picking up the thread where it had been dropped upon U.S. entrance into the war, Jane Addams, Emily Green Balch, and other leaders worked to temper power politics with the universal ethics of peace and justice. As such, they represented the best in the new postwar progressivism, sadder and wiser, but with ideals intact.

Other pacifists, however, swung back toward a more sentimental kind of idealism. Grassroots pacifists came out of hiding to join with international disarmament leaders to create the National Council for Prevention of War, a leading force for pacifism in the 1920s. Unlike their power-wise female counterparts, many of these pacifists of the 1920s and 1930s were idealists, pure and simple. As if to escape the horrors of industrial killing, they took refuge in the movement to "outlaw" war and other emotionally satisfying but impractical proposals for world peace.

The chief focus of idealism was Wilson himself. In the winter of 1918–19, the author of the Fourteen Points became a vessel into which all the hopes and dreams of the moment were poured. When he made his procession from the Brittany seacoast to the French capital on his way to the peace conference, Catholic villagers along the rail route were said to have stood in the December cold and prayed for his success. Upon arrival in Paris, he was welcomed with a tumultuous celebration that even exceeded the reception given arriving American soldiers two years earlier. When he made a triumphal procession to Rome, he was received as "the King of Humanity." His call for self-determination made him the champion of oppressed peoples from eastern Europe to East Asia.

It is not too much to say that between the end of the war and the beginning of the peace conference, Wilson was the leader of the world. "For a brief interval," wrote H. G. Wells, "Wilson stood alone for mankind."[35] In that moment, he was to the world what Napoleon was to republican Europe at the dawn of the nineteenth century or Mikhail Gorbachev was at the end of the Cold War: not just one world leader among many, but, truly, the leader of the world.

To Wilson's more exuberant supporters, even that was not enough. They insisted he be raised to the level of a messiah, as if he were the Second Coming of Christ. Although the Anglo-American journalists who covered Wilson in Europe harbored no deep religious convictions themselves, they could not help but couch their stories in messianic terms. Lincoln Steffens, the dean of American muckrakers, for example, claimed that "all the common peoples were putting their hope in the American president whose advent was Messianic." In the same vein, Frederick Howe claimed "all England bowed to the Messianic Wilson." English writers, too, drew on the same rich storehouse of Christian allegory. H. G. Wells wrote, "He was transfigured in the eyes of men. He ceased to be a common statesman; he became a Messiah."[36]

The legend of Wilsonian idealism was born out of this moment. Harboring no territorial ambitions or imperial claims of his own, so the story went, the president of the New World republic was the only one to arrive in Paris with clean hands. Compared to the sordid self-seeking of Old World diplomats, Wilson seemed to stand for the universal principles of peace without victors, freedom of the seas, and self-determination. "Wilson the Just," as Clemenceau mockingly called him, carried the hopes of the dispossessed from the streets of Paris into the very den of the possessing classes at Versailles. There in gilded chambers resplendent with the plunder of kings and emperors, the humble champion of the common man preached a new world order.

Wilsonian idealism attracted support at the time and in the decades to come for reasons not entirely idealistic. In the Allied countries, ruling interests that had welcomed U.S. intervention in 1917 for reasons both military and moral, now hoped Wilson's presence would legitimate their war aims. From the time of his 1917 "Peace Without Victory" speech, British journalists and reform politicians had been hailing the New World leader for showing the way "out of the wilderness." Even as they prepared to ignore his principles, the English press "sanctioned his idealism as the idealism of English peoples," according to one observer. French elites, too, performed a delicate balancing act, on the one hand embracing Wilson as a symbol of moral legitimacy for their cause, and on the other, doing everything in their power to squash the popular aspirations he represented. Wilson's American supporters had their own reasons for fostering the legend: if things turned out badly in Paris, it would not be their fault.[37]

In the end, Wilson the man was less important than Wilson the symbol. Just as the Fourteen Points had been a magic mirror in which all manner of reformers beheld their own image, so Wilson on the road to the peace conference became a many-faceted symbol of hope to millions around the world. Agnes Nestor, an American labor activist, recalled, "We were living in a time of great dreams—dreams of co-operation between the working peoples of the world, dreams of dignity and plenty for all, dreams of lasting international peace."[38] After the hell of war, dreams of heaven on earth—what could be more logical?

The advent of Wilsonian idealism marked another round in the dance of democracy that had begun during the war. The return of social movements at war's end, singing the ancient song of deliverance with new stanzas about democracy or communism, heightened popular expectations for a new day. That, in turn, forced statesmen and business leaders to listen and to act in ways they would not otherwise have done. No matter what the outcome, the fact was that ordinary people forced elites to dance to their tune. In the process, they split apart wartime consensus and put popular movements on a collision course with ruling elites.

Versailles

Amid great expectations, the official gathering got underway in January 1919 in the baroque palace of the Bourbon kings at Versailles just outside Paris. Meeting in the Hall of Mirrors surrounded by the gilded trappings of the *ancien régime*, the victorious statesmen hammered out peace terms to be presented to the vanquished Germans and Austrians. The irony of meeting in a prime symbol of the old regime while attempting to forge a new world order was not lost on contemporaries. The Versailles conference was often compared to the 1815 Congress of Vienna, which had attempted to reestablish the old order in the aftermath of the French Revolution and the Napoleonic Wars.

The comparison, however, was misleading. The Allied statesmen were not hidebound reactionaries. They had not come to Versailles to restore plumed aristocrats and hereditary princes to the throne. Except for a few diehards, everyone acknowledged that the old aristocratic order was gone forever. Rather, they came to recast the modern bourgeois order. Flickering newsreel images showed the diplomats in their formal morning coats and top hats looking like Victorian gentlemen on their way to redraw the map of the world in a way that would foster prosperity and political stability.

A better architectural symbol of their intentions was the Hotel Crillon. Architecture reveals much about a society's beliefs and values, and the Crillon was no exception. Located on the Place de la Concorde at the foot of the elegant Champs-Elysées, the Crillon had come to be a marker of the reestablishment of order after the French Revolution on the foundations of property, nationalism, and empire. The main feature of the Greek revival edifice was a massive colonnade of Corinthian columns surmounted by simple pediments, all of which were designed to convey the sense of strength and stability. In contrast to the style of baroque monarchy at Versailles, the neoclassical Crillon reflected the French imperial republic.

Another reason the Crillon was a fitting symbol of republican order is that it served as headquarters for the American delegation. Setting up shop in the elegant marble building, none of the Americans, least of all the trade unionists among them, harbored the slightest sympathy for the old regime. The United States had nothing to compare with the palace at Versailles, not even the most ornate mansion at Newport. There was, however, an exact replica of the Crillon under construction in Philadelphia. The city's new public library was situated along the just-completed Benjamin Franklin Parkway, which itself had been modeled on the Champs-Elysées. Disturbed by the notorious political corruption and physical squalor of their city, Philadelphia civic leaders believed they could elevate the tenor of public life by creating beautiful public spaces. Influenced by the prewar City Beautiful movement, they had decided to create a grand boulevard along the lines of the most elegant street in Paris. In place of the dirt and congestion of city streets, there would be a resplendent swath of open space to replace the grimy tracks of the Pennsylvania Railroad. The boulevard would be anchored at one end by the ornate Italian Renaissance City Hall (dating from the Gilded Age, it was the largest municipal building in the United States), and at the other by an edifying art museum in the form of a massive Grecian temple, not yet completed, on a "faire mount" overlooking the Schuylkill River.

In between was a cluster of public buildings at Logan Circle done in neoclassical style, one of which was the public library. As a monument to republican principles, the "free" library was intended to promote civic engagement by opening its doors to the general public. The idea for a replica of the Hotel Crillon was brought back from Paris by Julian Abele, the first African-American graduate of the University of Pennsylvania's school of architecture and the chief designer for the main architectural firm hired to design the library. At a time when modernism was taking over commercial buildings and making inroads on residential design, the preference for Greek revival in public buildings reflected the belief that neoclassical design would somehow impress the viewer with republican stability and imperial power, along the lines of the great railway stations in Washington and New York.

Republican men of affairs would no doubt have given their right arms to be in Paris at the Crillon. However, in a fateful decision that would have dire consequences in the fight over ratification, not a single Republican of stature had been invited. Bypassing the grand old men of the Grand Old party—ex-President Taft, former presidential candidate Charles Evans Hughes, and senior statesman Elihu Root—Wilson chose only one low-profile member of the opposition. The mistake was in not joining forces with those outward-looking Republicans who relished America's new great power status and eagerly anticipated a leading role for the United States in the proposed League of Nations. Instead, they were left behind to choke on their anger.

The reason has to do with Wilson's desire to take all the glory for himself. Convinced of his own unsurpassed virtue, Wilson succumbed to his own megalomania. He took along only the most trusted advisors, above all, Colonel Edward House. The suave Texas Democrat was a promoter of Mexican investment schemes, a thoroughgoing Anglophile, and the first American to become an influential member of the elite club of world-class diplomats. Another member of the team was Robert Lansing, Wilson's son-in-law. Lansing had come to the War Department from Wall Street, and he was an arch-Presbyterian obsessed with the bolshevik threat.

Like a medieval court, a significant chunk of the executive branch also accompanied Wilson to Paris, though there was nothing medieval about the telephones and typewriters going full tilt at headquarters. In John Dos Passos's vivid description, "The corridors of the Crillon were lively as an anthill with scuttling khaki uniforms, marine yeomen, messenger boys, civilians; a gust of typewriter clicking came out from every open door. At every landing groups of civilian experts stood talking in low voices, exchanging glances with passersby, scribbling notes on scratchpads." Asked what this hive of activity meant, someone replied, "Not peace."[39]

Americans rubbed elbows with leaders of the Atlantic nations. The key figures were Lloyd George, the wily Welshman who was Liberal prime minister, and Georges Clemenceau, the tenacious French premier known as "the Tiger." Together with Wilson, they were seen to personify the new regime of commoners and self-made men. Certainly, in comparison to the deposed Kaiser Wilhelm II and the Habsburg emperor, they were elected leaders of constitutional regimes (unwritten, in Britain's case) and, in some sense, heirs of the great republican revolutions of the eighteenth century.

Yet they were by no means revolutionaries themselves. Despite Wilson's rhetoric about the need for radical change, the more they got down to the business of constructing a new world order, the more the emphasis shifted from "new world" to "order." Against what Wilson had called the "typhoon" of revolutionary threats to family and property, they set out to reconstruct an order where contracts were sacrosanct, debts repaid, marriages revered, and authority respected. Wartime promises had to be set aside. The revolt against the old civilization had gone far enough.

The first to go was the new diplomacy. Never mind what the Fourteen Points had said about open covenants openly arrived at. The peacemakers were not about to conduct their solemn business under the pressure of a mob. At first, the representatives of popular movements were allowed to stand outside the Hall of Mirrors with their noses pressed against the glass, so to speak, looking in on the official proceedings. Early on, however, plenary sessions became unwieldy, and what had begun as open discussions were increasingly closed to the press and public. Key decisions were referred to the Supreme Council of Ten, then the Council of Four, and when the Italian premier Orlando went home in a huff over the disputed city of Fiume, it was reduced to the Big Three.

The most fateful decision was made even before the conference opened. Without even a hint of protest from the one-time spokesman for "peace without victory," Germany and Austria were excluded from the deliberations. In a decision fraught with danger for the future, the victors undertook to make peace without any representation from the most powerful single country on the continent. The absence of Germany permitted the victors to write the soon-to-be-infamous "war guilt" clause, saddling Germany with full blame for the war, and with responsibility for paying damages in the form of reparations. Whether or not reparations were justified, they fostered resentment that would soon come back to haunt the world.

An equally weighty matter was international political economy. Some of the wiser heads at Versailles urged reestablishment of the more or less open borders that had characterized the prewar world, but four years of intense nationalism ruled that out. Instead, both at Versailles and after, each nation pursued its own narrow economic interests without regard to the stability of the international system as a whole. In addition to millions in reparations demanded of the Germans, Americans also demanded repayment of wartime loans extended to the British, instead of regarding them as a sound investment in Allied victory. With each nation jealously looking out for its own industries, there were no agreements on reducing tariffs. To the contrary, import duties rose sky high.

In the face of bolshevik repudiation of tsarist debts, a prime goal in recasting the bourgeois world was ensuring that everyone pay their debts. What was new in the international equation was that the biggest share of world debt was now owned in the United States. Thanks to its wartime credits to British and other European borrowers, the United States had emerged as the world's biggest creditor, with some $10 billion in private and public debt outstanding. With Wall Street making ready to challenge the City of London as the headquarters of world lending, Americans such as Thomas Lamont, associated with the House of Morgan, became key players in international finance.

The Big Three also confronted a shambles in international relations. Seeking to consolidate a new system, they chose to rebuild international relations around a much-expanded system of nation-states, large and small. Thus a whole new tier of nation-states came into being in eastern Europe all the way from the Baltic republics on the north through Poland, Austria, Hungary, and Czechoslovakia down to the Balkan states on the south. Some of the new states were top-down creations of the great powers, but they also embodied widespread popular demands for national self-determination.

Even so, the complete ascendancy of nationalism is something of a puzzle. Nationalism had much to do with conflict between the great powers and everything to do with the wars in the Balkans which had been the tinderbox of the Great War itself. If national rivalries had helped start the war and nationalist hatreds had kept it going, why add fuel to this fire?

In explanation, the first thing that stands out is the place of nation-states in the prevailing ideology of the day. As representatives of their respective nation-states, the statesmen simply could not conceive of an alternative. Since the bourgeois societies of the West took the form of national markets, most everything else took national form, as well—currencies, armed forces, flags, ruling interests, and ruling ideas. It was not just rulers who thought in terms of national interest, but ordinary people, too, who imagined themselves to be nations. Once the system of national states was in place, no nation could afford to be left out, with the result that nations without states, like the Poles, demanded that a state be created for them.

Efforts to create viable nation-states were immensely complicated by eastern Europe's complex cultural diversity. In the arc stretching from the Baltic Sea in the north to the Balkan peninsula in the south, the architects of the new world order confronted a bewildering array of languages, religions, and ethnic identities. In this too-rich soil, a multitude of nationalisms had taken root among the educated middle classes, well watered by patriotic poets and journalists, and had grown into a luxuriant tangle of conflicting political claims.

No matter how many times they retraced the maps of the region, members of The Inquiry, the special team of American academic advisors, were unable to carve uniform nations out of this jungle. As everyone recognized at the time, the new states confounded the link between state and cultural nation. Poland had Jewish and German minorities; Czechoslovakia was made up of two different nationalities; and Yugoslavia topped them all, a wholly artificial conglomeration of cultural minorities—Serbs, Croats, Montenegrans, Albanians—sure to be restive under any central government.

The best hope was that, once in place, the new states would somehow generate the kind of civic nationalism of the sort pioneered by the American and French republics. In his eloquent public addresses, Wilson, the last of the Founding Fathers, never failed to link peacemaking to the civic ideals of liberty and self-determination, hoping these would bring a measure of cohesion to a potentially chaotic situation.

The nation-state found its apotheosis in the League of Nations. Heedless of national rivalries, such as that between Germany and France over Alsace-Lorraine, that had done so much to bring on the Great War, the commissioners proposed an international forum for working out national disputes, and if that failed, a "concert of nations" under which member states would join together against an aggressor nation, of which Germany was taken as the arch-example. No matter how much Wilson declaimed about a "league of peoples," it was neither that, nor even a true league of nations, but, in fact, a league of nation-states.

In the view from the top at Versailles, nation-states were a safe answer to peoples movements, unless they happened to be colonial peoples. For anyone living under Western rule, Versailles was the graveyard of national liberation. None of the Big Three, not even Wilson, had any intention of extending the principle of self-determination outside Europe. The colonial world would have to remain a giant chessboard in the game of imperial power.

So it was in the Middle East. Anticipating the defeat of the Ottoman Empire, British and French diplomats began making promises during the war for the future of the region. Palestine, in particular, was promised to the Jews (Balfour Declaration), to the Arabs (to induce the Saudis to join the Allies), and to the British (in the Sykes-Picot agreement, one of the infamous secret treaties). In a quip that made the rounds at Versailles, Palestine became a "much-promised land."

There was little in the way of democracy or progressive politics among any of the would-be nations. Certainly Emir Faisal of the Arabian peninsula could present no liberal credentials whatsoever. Accompanied by General Nouri Pasha and Colonel T. E. Lawrence ("Lawrence of Arabia"), Faisal and his fellow potentates may have been "the most resplendent figures that had ever entered the Quai d'Orsay,"[40] but no one could have mistaken the elegant robes of the patriarchal, monarchical, theocratic son of the Sherif of Mecca for the trappings of democracy. Meanwhile, Zionists conveniently forgot that Palestine was no more unoccupied territory than was New England before the arrival of the Puritans.

In the end, neither Arabs nor Jews were able to play the Big Three against one another; instead, European imperial control was preserved behind the fig leaf of League of Nations "mandates." Japan got into the mandate game by taking control of Shandong, the former German territory in China. The Japanese proposal to insert a "racial equality" clause into the treaty threatened to upset the imperial applecart, but in return for backing away from the incendiary proposal, the Big Three accepted the Japanese landgrab in China. For his part, Wilson pretended ignorance of the secret treaties and refused to have anything to do with the mandate system (Armenia had been suggested for U.S. oversight), but he made sure to protect American protectorates, colonies, and spheres of influence in Latin America by winning explicit recognition for the Monroe Doctrine in the treaty.

What added special urgency to the deliberations were the fires of social revolution burning on the horizon. Everyday, the Big Three could look outside the windows of the Hall of Mirrors and imagine these fires getting closer. Having already consumed Russia, they were flaring up in central and eastern Europe, feeding on the highly combustible fuel of starvation and economic dislocation. For this reason, no one wanted to allow Lenin's Russia a place at the table. In western Europe, too, hunger and hardship were a threat, and even in America, so rich and secure, elites were gripped by a fear of disorder. With events between Moscow and Paris spinning out of control, a bewildering set of social changes—women's suffrage, ethnic revolt, race riots, industrial discord—looked more threatening to otherwise secure rulers than they actually were.

That was why bolshevism seemed such a menace. To western elites, bolshevism began and ended in chaos. It was a product of economic dislocation and moral decay, and once in power, it set about creating chaos through tyrannical methods of proletarian dictatorship that destroyed the good order of civilization. In their perception of the bolshevik threat, western elites were, in effect, bourgeois Marxists. They had come to believe in a nightmare version of *Communist Manifesto* where their own destruction took place at the hands of proletarian gravediggers.

At the time, what seemed the worst thing about bolshevism was not heavy-handed authoritarianism of the sort Joseph Stalin would later come to personify, but rather the opposite—total disorder. The infamous Madame Aleksandra Kollontai, a commissar for family issues, was pilloried in the West almost as much as Lenin and Trotsky for her condemnation of bourgeois marriage as a mercenary exchange of sex for financial support and for her defense of state nurseries and free love. It was not so much the seizure of state power that aroused opposition in the West, as the seizure of banks, mines, and Orthodox churches under an ideology of collectivism that seemed to strike at the propertied family, the very foundation of the social order.

Every major decision at Versailles was made with one eye on the revolutionary fires. To deal with the Bolsheviks themselves, the Big Three sent troops into Russia. The ill-fated Allied intervention had begun a year earlier with the purpose of reopening the Eastern Front. Troops were sent to Arkhangel'sk and Murmansk in northern Russia and to Vladivostok in Siberia, where they remained without a clear mission when the war ended. The Big Three considered a proposal brought back by a special mission under William Bullitt for a peace conference to be held at the island of Prinkipo in the Black Sea. When that idea was vetoed by Clemenceau, the most ardent anticommunist of the

three, Lloyd George and Wilson swallowed their disappoint-
ment and agreed to change the mission of the intervention and
come to the aid of Russian counterrevolutionaries in an effort to
overthrow or at least cripple the Bolshevik regime. In their last
formal act at Versailles in June 1919, they agreed to support Ad-
miral Kolchak in his increasingly desperate campaign to restore
the old ruling classes to power.

The American contribution to the Allied misadventure in Siberia consisted of a detachment of 5,000 troops to prevent mines,
oil fields, and the sprawling Trans-Siberian Railway from falling
into the wrong hands. In addition, the American Red Cross and
other private organizations acted as supply agents for Kolchak,
while the State Department piously attested that these aristocratic holdovers and Cossack warlords were really democrats at
heart. Confronted with reports of atrocities committed by Kolchak's generals—massacres of civilians, wholesale executions,
Jewish pogroms—the response in Washington was to say, never
mind, the Bolsheviks were worse. Anyone who questioned support for Kolchak, such as General William Graves, the stubborn
Yankee commander of the Siberian expedition, was tarred with
the brush of harboring Bolshevik sympathies.[41]

Erecting a firewall against the westward spread of bolshevism
was a main reason the Big Three had set up the tier of new nation-states in eastern Europe in the first place. Called a *"cordon
sanitaire,"* it was intended to get new states up and running as
quickly as possible to fill the vacuum of authority left by the
collapse of the defeated empires, just as the mandate system was
supposed to seal off colonial regions from bolshevik ideas.

There is no doubt that the situation in eastern and central Europe was fraught with peril. Journalists and diplomats on the
scene from the Baltic to the Balkans regaled their respective contacts at Versailles with terrifying tales of bloated bellies swelling
the ranks of street demonstrators. Tracing communist insurrec-
tions in Germany to hunger and privation, Lloyd George called
for an immediate lifting of the blockade so that food could be
sent in. "As long as order was maintained in Germany, a break-
water would exist between the countries of the Allies and the

waters of Revolution beyond." The Americans were even more convinced that food was the answer to revolution. Putting it crudely, Lansing said, "Empty stomachs mean bolsheviks. Full stomachs mean no bolsheviks."[42]

What made leaders doubly nervous was the unsettled situation in their own backyards. France, with its ruined villages and broken economy, and Britain, suffering economic dislocation and high inflation, were home to restive workers demanding the redemption of wartime pledges of "a land fit for heroes." In a typical rhetorical flourish, Lloyd George warned that unless the peacemakers acted quickly to stabilize Germany, "he could not speak for France but trembled for his own country." He was worried because a "state of revolution among the working classes of all countries would ensue with which it would be impossible to cope."[43]

Did the fires of revolt threaten the United States? Opinion was divided. With a whiff of smoke in their nostrils, some Americans at Versailles worried that somehow the flames might leap across the Atlantic. Lansing, for example, believed the peril to America was "very great" because of the high level of disorders in American streets. Despite the fact that America was unscathed by the fighting, he urged quick delivery of food to restore order in Europe because "we stand to further the forces of disorder in the United States if we stand idle."[44]

Others agreed with Hoover that the United States was immune to revolution. Believing the Atlantic Ocean was a deep firebreak between two vastly different ways of life, he was sure "the irreconcilable conflicts between Old and New World concepts of government and of social and economic life" would keep America safe. The essential difference, in his view, had to do with class. The Old World was imperiled because "the gulf between the middle classes and the lower classes is large, and where the lower classes have been kept in ignorance and distress, this propaganda will be fatal and do violence to normal democratic development." Fortunately, the New World had been spared deep class division and was, therefore, immune to bolshevism. "For these reasons," he said, "I have no fear of it in the United States."[45]

Seeking to recast the bourgeois order, the peacemakers did their best to bury the remains of aristocratic and autocratic Europe and replace it with an order based on modern property, the middle-class family, and self-governing nation-states under the "covenant" of the League of Nations. Although Germany was excluded from the League, adding punishment to defeat, everyone assumed that after a period of probation it, too, would join the community of nations. Meanwhile, acceptance of the United States as a great power was a sign of European willingness to augment European global hegemony of the past with a broader reign of the West.

With Germany excluded and Russia sidelined, most of the political battles had taken place among the Big Three themselves. Given all the wrangling, they came to be seen in many quarters not as peacemakers but as deal makers. John Dos Passos spoke for a disillusioned generation in portraying them as three old cynics playing a diplomat's game of cards, dealing out decisions on one issue after another—the Rhineland, the Polish corridor, Fiume, Shandong. In this high-stakes poker game, Dos Passos added with some cynicism of his own, "Oil was trumps."[46]

Ever the optimist, Wilson hailed the Versailles Treaty as the fulfillment of the Fourteen Points. His supporters went along, portraying it as a triumph of Wilsonian idealism. In reality, it was anything but. Instead of making a place for common people at the table of wealth and power, the Big Three rejected social reform, spurned power-sharing in the colonies, and gave only weak support to international labor standards. Far from embracing radicalism, as Wilson had once proposed, they sent an army to Russia to crush it. By the end, Wilson's magic mirror lay shattered. When many progressives looked into the treaty, they beheld not their hopes for a better world, but the ghastly face of reaction. Characterizing it as the work of "reactionaries," *The Nation* declaimed, "In the whole history of diplomacy there is no treaty more properly to be regarded as an international crime than the amazing document which the German representatives are now asked to sign."[47]

By the time the peace conference concluded in June, the Big Three had forfeited their hold on the imagination of the world. Feeling betrayed by world leaders, the forces of change lost their enthusiasm for "Wilson the Just" and his new world order. The millennial moment had been brief. What Dos Passos had called "the first year" ended a few short months after it began. At the same time, conflicts between the forces of change and the forces of order continued to rage, making the ensuing years among the most tumultuous of the century and forcing Americans to rethink what they meant by "progressive."

COUNTER-REVOLUTION: Untitled cartoon by W. A. Rogers, ca. 1919. The machine guns of the U.S. Army defend American streets against a violent rabble of Industrial Workers of the World and others bent on installing a Soviet government in America. In part a reflection of anticommunist hysteria, the cartoon is also a perfect illustration of the more calculating mentality behind War Plans White, top-secret plans drawn up by the Army War College instructing military commanders on how to suppress revolution in the United States. (Library of Congress, Prints and Photos Division)

8

Retreat from Reform

When President Wilson sailed for home at the end of June 1919 with the Treaty of Versailles in his satchel, the future of the United States in world affairs was yet to be decided. Although Americans had played a leading part in the war and the peace conference, it was not clear whether they would try to extend their leadership into the postwar era, even though the opportunity seemed to be there for the taking. With Germany defeated, France consumed by vengefulness, Russia in the throes of civil war, and Britain staggering under its imperial load, European dominance in world affairs had reached the beginning of the end. If there was to be a new preeminent power, it could only be the United States.

To be sure, the path to preeminence was strewn with many obstacles, above all, the tradition of isolation from European affairs. Still, the United States stood at the very pinnacle of economic strength. Its army had grown in size and sophistication, and its navy rivaled the British. It had earned what President Wilson called "moral leadership" by raising the universal banner of democracy. In short, it possessed many of the requisite qualifications for hegemony. For over a century, Britain had played the role of hegemon—economic engine, military policeman, guiding diplomat, and paragon of civilization. Now, when British energies were flagging, it seemed the United States might step in to become what Colonel House called "the gyroscope of world order."[1]

So the fact that it did not is something of a puzzle. Having played the role of world leader to the hilt during the American moment at the end of the war, why did Americans reject membership in the very League of Nations they had done so much to create? If they had no desire to take over the leading role from Britain, why not at least an equal one?

Certainly, their refusal was the source of much lamentation later on from architects of Cold War foreign policy. Even critics of that policy fostered such a strong impression of the inevitability of U.S. expansion that rejection of the League appeared almost as a breach with destiny. Explanation has focused on elites—their diplomatic inexperience, isolationism, and preference for "informal" empire, rather than active political management of world affairs.[2]

Although these views contain much truth, they give insufficient attention to the impact of discontent from below on the higher circles of power. For debate over the Versailles Treaty was affected at every turn by the turmoil wracking the country—and the world—from the summer of 1919 through the end of 1921. Widespread unrest caused American leaders to wonder if they had won the war and lost the peace. The messianic crusade, long directed toward redeeming the Old World, was now turned back onto American shores, and came crashing down like a tidal wave. Unable to change the world according to plan, beset by explosive class and racial conflicts, elites abandoned both progressive internationalism and reform at home.

Transatlantic Discontent

The proposition that high politics were affected by the grass roots can be tested in a comparison of British and American responses to popular discontent. Certainly, authorities in both countries had to wade through waves of unrest washing up all around the Atlantic basin—massive industrial strikes, race riots, suffrage demonstrations, revolutionary agitation, anticolonial rumblings in the West Indies, and revolt in Ireland. Rulers on both sides of the Atlantic were compelled to respond.

In some ways, unrest drove the two countries together. That was true, for example, of colonial discontent. Ever since Kipling had urged his American cousins to "take up the white man's burden," Anglo-Saxon elites on both sides of the Atlantic had been united by the shared ideology of social Darwinism. Now they cooperated to thwart independence for African and Asian subjects, rejecting any notion that self-determination applied to nonwhites. So long as Anglo-American elites were united in support of colonialism and segregation, neither colonial peoples nor African-Americans were able to exploit divisions among the powerful for their own gain. Everyone from Wilson to Garvey was right in linking the fate of the American Negro to the future of Asia and Africa.

At the same time, different imperial histories had created quite different problems. While the British had exported the "race problem" to the colonies, Americans had imported it generations earlier by bringing African slaves to America's shores, whose descendants now amounted to something like 10 percent of the population. Certainly, the British did not have to cope with anything like the series of convulsive race riots that began in East St. Louis in 1917, ravaged Chicago two years later, and ended in Tulsa in 1921, leaving hundreds dead, millions in property destroyed, and hatred smouldering in the ruins.

Although the scale of conflict owed something to the fighting spirit of the New Negro, most of the damage was done by rampaging mobs of white men, and in that sense, the "race problem" was, at bottom, a problem of white racism. When authorities finally decided to take action, their idea of restoring order was to send in the National Guard to separate the races. Although the Civil War division between North and South had made possible the emancipation of the slaves and the civil rights amendments to the Constitution, Yankee and Dixie elites had long since united around segregation. In the face of calls from the interracial Chicago Commission on Race Relations for civil rights reforms, northern leaders of every political stripe from progressive to conservative preferred to join with their southern counterparts to keep African-Americans in their segregated place.

Another difference between Britain and the United States lay in the treatment of class conflict. In Britain, the liberal tradition had been modified over the years to accommodate the working classes. Capital had learned to accept a degree of labor's power, and a modicum of social welfare had found its way into government policy, with the result that Britain had left industrial violence behind. Additional social compromises arrived under "war collectivism," which subjected the free market to extensive government regulations, and Prime Minister Lloyd George's promise of a "land fit for heroes" raised expectations for even more benefits at war's end. Heightened expectations collided with postwar inflation to produce intense discontent among industrial wage earners, whose power was growing through the Labour party, which had overtaken the Liberals, and through quantum leaps in the level of organization exemplified by the formation of the Triple Alliance of coal, rail, and transport workers.

Faced with a potentially explosive situation, British authorities continued to pursue labor peace through compromise. To promote negotiation, the government set up Whitley Councils, labor-management teams in several industries charged with settling disputes before they got out of hand. In the same vein, when the Triple Alliance threatened a paralyzing strike in March 1919, Lloyd George chose to sit down with union leaders and hammer out an agreement acceptable to both sides that ended the threat of disruption without the need to call out the military.

The United States also faced massive discontent. As in Britain, working-class militancy collided with postwar inflation to throw millions of strikers into the streets in what contemporaries regarded as an international movement. Speaking for business opinion, John J. Raskob, an executive at General Motors, took note of "a very disturbed labor situation existing throughout the world, which is manifesting itself quite strongly in this country."[3]

The difference was that American industrialists were unwilling to accommodate organized labor. Faced with business intransigence, political leaders backed off from social compromise. Upon war's end, the Wilson administration quickly dismantled the War Labor Board and other machinery that might have forced corporate executives to accept mediation. Even after a decade of reform and two years of wartime mediation, laissez-faire was a powerful force in the United States. While in Britain liberals accepted a greater role for the state, American liberals still kowtowed to the oligarchs of the marketplace.

Working themselves free of government controls, corporate executives returned to their preferred path of managerial control, but now with an added measure of inter-industry cooperation. A prime example of the new coordination in business was the semi-secret Special Conference Committee, comprised of a small circle of top-flight executives loosely associated with the Rockefeller interests, including Standard Oil, DuPont, General Motors, and General Electric. Their task was to plan postwar strategy for handling major issues of the day, including the labor problem.

At a power dinner at New York's Metropolitan Club on April 2, 1919, the exalted executives listened to an emissary from Secretary of State Lansing breathlessly outline the dimensions of the problem: "It is not chiefly wages the workmen want, but a new order of social and economic relations." To make matters worse, Washington could not be trusted. Lansing's man stated his fear "that President Wilson and his advisors might come back to the United States imbued with the idea that the safety of America from Bolshevism lay in a much more complete unionization of industry." To forestall any pressure to recognize AFL unions, the corporate heavy hitters put down their dessert spoons and drew up a list of reasons, to be relayed to the president, why trade unions in general, and Whitley Councils in particular, were wrong for America.[4]

This resolve to go it alone without trade union or government interference was dubbed "the American Plan," otherwise known as the open shop. The battle cry of "the American Plan" was heard on every front of industrial conflict in 1919, resulting in violent battles between strikers on one side and "scabs," police, vigilantes, and, ultimately, federal troops on the other. In the absence of private collective bargaining or public mediation, all the familiar features of the wartime campaign against the IWW and other labor radicals now reappeared in the use of troops to protect strikebreakers, military spying on civilians, deportation of alien radicals, and the coordination of vigilantes, local police, and federal troops.

The pivotal battle took place in the steel industry, fulcrum of the modern economy, source of immense profits, and employer of hundreds of thousands of overworked employees. The industry revolved around the U.S. Steel Corporation, which was under the resolute command of Elbert "Judge" Gary. Seemingly unperturbed by the fact that 365,000 steelworkers had walked off the job on September 22, shutting down the world's largest corporation and the rest of the industry along with it, Gary calmly turned a deaf ear to all appeals for a "conference" with his employees. To an imperious executive like Gary, it would have been a derogation of status, even a loss of manhood, to bow to the will of an unruly bunch of immigrant laborers.

After holding the fort for a week, Gary decided to take the offensive. Relying on the large number of "American" skilled workers who had remained loyal, he reopened the plants, imported strikebreakers under company guard, redoubled anti-union espionage, branded the strikers bolsheviks, and otherwise mobilized his considerable resources on behalf of the open shop.

As on countless other occasions in America's long-running labor wars, the introduction of strikebreakers precipitated a violent reaction. The sight of "scabs" forcing their way into the mill to take away jobs brought anger to the boil, resulting in skirmishes in several steel towns. One of the main flash points was Gary, Indiana, western stronghold of U.S. Steel, where the atmosphere was charged by the presence of a large number of African-American newcomers from the South. When black strikebreakers were attacked by white strikers, nervous authorities in Gary, remembering the racial conflagration that had gripped nearby Chicago two months earlier, had the pretext they needed to call in the army.

The habit of using the army and the National Guard in industrial disturbances had a long history. Starting with the railroad strikes of 1877, the federal government had repeatedly called upon the military to do their constitutional duty of suppressing "domestic insurrection," and during the war, federal troops had been called out in dozens of disputes. Now, as a growing sense of urgency gripped the administration, progressives in the Cabinet (Baker and Palmer) joined with dyed-in-the-wool conservatives (Lansing) to sponsor a crackdown on industrial discontent and political radicalism. On September 29, 1919, three days after President Wilson collapsed on a national speaking tour, Baker issued instructions to department commanders to furnish troops to suppress disorder directly upon the request of civil authorities, without even so much as a formal notification to the president. Despite the dubious constitutionality of this order overriding civilian supremacy, troops were used some twenty times in the twelve months after the summer of 1919, a level of military intervention about as high as during the war itself.[5]

The crisis found General Leonard Wood, commander of the Army Sixth Area Corps, itching to act. The former military governor of Cuba and protagonist of preparedness had been preparing for months for action on the home front, and when the phone call came in the dead of night on October 5, it took a mere twelve minutes to start his troops moving toward Gary. Upon arrival in the wee hours of the morning, Wood proclaimed martial law and explained to his superiors, "The strikers, mainly aliens, many not speaking English, paraded the public streets and declared their intention to continue to parade in defiance of the mayor's order. Worst influence comes from certain red agitators who desire to ferment trouble."[6]

Over the next few days, Wood's men swept the streets clean of crowds, prohibited union picketing, raided strike support organizations, and issued a steady stream of press releases condemning bolshevik and other foreign influences. Indifferent to protests over raw violations of civil liberties, Wood found time to take in a World Series game between the Cincinnati Reds and the Chicago White Sox (who would later become infamous for throwing the series) and to discuss over an elegant dinner the progress of his candidacy for the Republican presidential nomination (things were going well). Having restored order to the complete satisfaction of steel executives, he looked forward to business support in his upcoming race for the nomination.[7]

Chances of a compromise settlement of the strike, slim to begin with, were reduced to none by the collapse of the national Industrial Conference, which had convened in Washington the day General Wood marched into Gary. A typical progressive response to industrial discord, the Industrial Conference was intended to be a supreme industrial council bringing together the three great social interests—business, labor, and the public—in a belated attempt to fill the breach left by the dismantling of wartime mediation machinery. However, it proved impossible to stage a peace conference in the midst of class war, particularly when it was announced that the "public" representatives included John D. Rockefeller, Jr., still stained with the blood of Ludlow coal miners, and none other than Elbert Gary himself! On October 14 when these presumptive representatives of the public vetoed Gompers's proposal for a panel to adjudicate the steel strike, the conference collapsed. Eventually, so did the strike. Denounced as disloyal foreigners, suppressed by the Army, and abandoned by Wilsonian progressives, the steelworkers went down to defeat.

A similar drama was being played out in the nation's coal fields. At a time when coal was the basic energy source for the entire economy, everyone recognized the stakes could not have been higher when 400,000 miners responded to the same postwar squeeze and walked off the job in October. While British miners were able to parlay their strategic position into a settlement negotiated by no less than the prime minister, American miners were slapped with an injunction issued by Attorney General A. Mitchell Palmer ordering them back to work. Gompers denounced it as "so autocratic as to stagger the human mind."[8] Behind-the-scenes maneuvering by other cabinet officials was to no avail, and the largest strike in American history was eventually ended at the point of a bayonet.

The contrast between British mediation and American coercion was also evident in the respective responses to international labor standards. With British delegates carrying the ball, the International Labor Organization (ILO) held its founding conference in Washington in late October. As a part of the Versailles settlement, the ILO was immediately suspect in the eyes of the treaty's Republican opponents, but Wilsonians were not very enthusiastic, either. Even Gompers, who had presided over its creation in Paris, turned against what he now regarded as a dangerous European device.

By the time European delegates to the ILO left for home at the end of November, hostility was mutual, causing great embarrassment to Raymond Fosdick, the cosmopolitan associate of the Rockefeller Foundation and lonely American delegate to the convention. In a letter to his British counterpart, Fosdick vented his anger and embarrassment over his government's role in the steel and coal strikes: "The drastic methods to which the Government resorted to break these strikes have made a most unfavorable impression upon the Conference. The novel use of the injunction as a weapon of industrial warfare, the employment of the State constabulary in Pennsylvania—dubbed Cossacks— to break up meetings of strikers, and the general hostile attitude of the press toward the attempts of the unions to obtain recognition, have given the delegates from Europe the impression that America is the center of industrial Bourbonism."[9]

Anxiety among America's industrial Bourbons was heightened by the collapse of the commander in chief on September 26 during his national speaking tour in support of the League of Nations. Unable to continue, Wilson was rushed home only to suffer a crippling stoke a few days later. Gaunt, half-paralyzed, and barely able to speak, the once robust world leader was reduced to a bedridden invalid, like so many other wounded veterans of the war. Word of the president's incapacity reached the Cabinet on October 3, where it "fell like a pall on all hearts."[10]

The stroke led to a kind of interregnum where it was not clear who was in charge. Was it the president's inner circle—his

strong-willed wife Edith Galt and his personal secretary Joe Tu-
multy—standing guard outside the White House bedroom? Or
was it the Cabinet, where several members, including A. Mitchell Palmer and William McAdoo, harbored presidential ambitions of their own? In this situation worthy of Shakespearean
tragedy, issues of the utmost gravity came to the fore—the first
Senate vote on the League of Nations; food aid to starving Europe; the ongoing intervention in Russia; the steel and coal
strikes. The timing of the stroke could not have been worse.

The collapse of the nation's preeminent progressive was an
apt symbol of the collapse of progressivism. From the end of
November 1919 onward, the nation's top business and political
leaders abandoned reform at home and progressive internationalism abroad. Wilson's infirmity hastened this retreat, but even
if he had been the picture of health, it is doubtful his administration would have behaved much differently. That was because, at
heart, Wilson remained a Victorian liberal. He had grafted social
justice and state intervention onto the free market philosophy of
the New Freedom, but when postwar circumstances brought the
contradictions of capitalist society to a head, he, too, sided with
property and order. Moreover, as a southern gentleman, he had
no sympathy for the demands of the New Negro, and as a high
Presbyterian, he had no defense against the spirit of intolerance
his wartime crusade had unleashed. Finally, he had already
compromised so much at Versailles that internationalism lay in
tatters. If there was a single moment when elites abandoned
progressivism, this was it.

Red Scare, White Plan

By the late fall, the country was in the grip of a full-fledged Red
Scare. Extending the wartime campaign against radicalism to
new heights, Attorney General Palmer resurrected the amateur
G-men of the American Protective League, combined forces with
anti-red squads in police departments around the country, and
trained his sights on immigrant radicals in a series of November

raids. Imitating Justice Department raids on the IWW two years earlier, Palmer rounded up an assortment of leftists, including anarchists Emma Goldman and Alexander Berkman, packed 249 of them aboard the *Buford*, and shipped them off to Russia.

Palmer's November raids were only a rehearsal for the massive nationally coordinated roundup of radicals that took place on the night of January 2, 1920. Ignoring a mountain of legal tradition—freedom of association, innocent until proven guilty, no arrest without cause, *habeas corpus*—Palmer's agents, under the zealous direction of young J. Edgar Hoover, caught some 4,000 hapless people in the dragnet, mostly immigrants. It was the greatest single assault on constitutional rights that had ever taken place in the United States.

Palmer's excess was the result, in part, of a personal vendetta, understandable for someone who was the target of one bomb intercepted by a postal inspector and another that blew apart the front porch of his Washington residence. All the same, there was more of the political than the personal in his crusade against the "red menace." Playing to the same crowd as Leonard Wood on the Republican side, Palmer was hoping to ride the Red Scare all the way to the White House on the wild horses of super-patriotism.

Like a long line of demagogues who came after, Palmer was careless about whom he harmed and reckless with the truth, firing off a constant barrage of false pronouncements intended to win headlines like "Terror Reign by Radicals, says Palmer." Antiradical mobs, often in cahoots with local police, were active in many places. The House of Representatives refused to seat Victor Berger, a duly-elected socialist from Wisconsin, and the Senate took time off from its high-profile investigations of bolshevik influence in the United States to adopt a unanimous resolution urging the deportation of alien revolutionaries. Fomented by power-hungry men like Palmer and Wood, anti-red hysteria in 1919 and 1920 seemed to be on the way toward crushing all opposition.

There was nothing to compare with the Red Scare in postwar Britain. Britain did not lack for superpatriots eager to inflame the electorate against a foreign menace, as proved in the "khaki" election in the fall of 1919, which produced a thumping Conservative majority in Parliament. However, the foreign devil in this case was Germany, not the Soviet Union. Despite the fact that the British Labour party had surpassed the Liberals and had come out for nationalization of big property, the level of anxiety about socialism was nowhere near as high as it was in the United States, where the combined forces of the left were much smaller.

Why was the Red Scare so much more potent in the United States? Explanations of American anticommunism often focus on ideology. As we have seen, bolshevism was a useful enemy for embattled industrialists and aspiring politicians, all the more so because, in the United States, bolshevism was less a real enemy than a demon conjured up by their own ideology. From within the world view of the free market, bolshevism was a threat because it seemed to stand for the overthrow of all authority in family and property. Associated with the radical movements of the day for worker control, public ownership, racial equality, and sexual freedom, bolshevism represented the chaos that would engulf civilization if radical movements had their way. (It is interesting to note that during the Cold War, communism came to symbolize the opposite: not chaos, but the rigid order of totalitarianism.)

Gender ideology also played a role. To straightlaced Americans, radical calls for a new morality of free love and birth control looked like a recipe for sexual anarchy. Even women's suffrage caused some consternation in this regard. In the heated imagination of American superpatriots, male and female alike, the supposed fact that Russian Bolsheviks had "nationalized" women was but the natural accompaniment of the nationalization of property, just as Russian feminist Aleksandra Kollontai seemed almost as dangerous as Lenin himself.

Sensationalized stories of communal living became grist for the publicity mills of superpatriotic organizations. The Sentinels of the Republic, for example, proclaimed from the masthead of its anti-suffragist, anti-reform newspaper *The Woman Patriot*: "Dedicated to the Defense of the Family and the State against

Feminism and Socialism." Likewise, the president of the National Security League, counterposed bolshevism to American manhood: "Manhood means ambition, self-denial, thrift. These ideals can spring only from the right of property—the right of individual possession of property as guaranteed by the Constitution. He who does not believe this cannot be an American."[11]

And yet the ideological explanation lacks one important element—timing. It does not explain the waxing and waning of anticommunism, which rose to a frenzy in the early 1920s, fell in the 1930s, turned into friendship during the Second World War, and then erupted again in McCarthyism after the war. As this pattern suggests, the impact of anticommunism was bound up with America's changing role in the world. Whatever underlying beliefs were involved, the outbreak of panic was the result of specific historical circumstances in which Americans experienced the rude awakening that events overseas were beyond their control.

Beginning with U.S. intervention at Veracruz in 1914, Americans had come to believe that overseas expansion and participation in the Great War had so entangled the United States in the web of world events that strikes and disorders in American cities were bound up with revolutions overseas. Daily reports in American newspapers reinforced by dispatches to leading officials brought home the impact of events in revolutionary Russia and Mexico.[12] By the time Wilson arrived at Versailles to proclaim his New World Order of open markets and democratic values, disorder anywhere was seen as a threat to bourgeois order everywhere.

The sense of a world spinning out of control was especially strong among Anglo-Saxon Protestants up and down the social scale, conservatives and liberals alike, whose crusade to remake the world in their own image had run into brick walls everywhere from Vladivostok to Versailles. Frustrated overseas and now venting their frustration upon everything at home that seemed to be foreign, Protestant redeemers set out to purify the homeland by purging the country of immigrants, bolsheviks, and "un-American" ideas.

One clear indication of the link in the minds of authorities between domestic disorder and world revolution was the preparation of top-secret war plans to put down revolution in the United States. Now buried deep in the National Archives in Washington, D.C., War Plans White reveal the steps the federal government was taking to meet what was seen as a revolutionary threat to the Constitution. Unearthing these secret contingency plans, the historian feels a certain disquiet in contemplating the ways a government prepares to make war on its own people. Somewhere the full story of the White Plan deserves to be told.

For now, it is enough to examine these remarkable documents to see what they reveal about the mind-set of American elites. In that regard, it is illuminating to compare the White Plan with its British counterpart, the Supply and Transport Committee. These two sets of master plans for implementing nationwide states of emergency codified what authorities in both countries were already doing to suppress domestic strikes and riots, while also combating revolution overseas. Although military planners shared ideas across the Atlantic, they pursued significantly different approaches.

In the absence of a Red Scare, British authorities defined the problem not as revolution, but as industrial unrest. Emergency planning developed in a dramatic series of escalating responses to industrial unrest focused around the Triple Alliance, the unity pact among miners, railway workers, and transport workers. Working feverishly in February 1919, the Cabinet set up an Industrial Unrest Committee to head off the threat of a paralyzing strike by the Triple Alliance, and eight months later, still under the gun, it created a more elaborate system for coordinating military and civil authorities under the Supply and Transport Committee, whose euphemistic title barely disguised the strikebreaking purpose involved in coordinating "volunteer" workers, otherwise know as "blacklegs."[13]

Military commanders were reluctant to engage in domestic peacekeeping, not out of any squeamishness about strikebreaking, but over concern that British military force was already overextended overseas. As far as the Imperial General Staff was concerned, the empire came before all else. In a candid admission of imperial overextension, the chief of staff bluntly told the Cabinet in November 1919 that the army would be unable to meet any large-scale demand for troops on the home front and that the military should only be used as a last resort in future industrial disturbances so that it might "be allowed to prepare itself for its legitimate duties in the defence of the Empire."[14]

What this evidence suggests is that Britain's international situation—especially the increasing burden of empire—had a major impact on the domestic balance of power. Even as Britain's imperial commitments bolstered the civil service and state institutions in general, overextension encouraged the government to mediate industrial disputes at home. Lloyd George became a master at cutting deals for labor peace by quietly leaning on employers, while cajoling and bribing unions to settle. He put these skills to good use during a major coal strike in early October 1920, when his mediation narrowly averted another crisis. This time, Parliament felt the need to enact special emergency powers. The trend toward state intervention in the market culminated in April 1921, when yet another threat of a paralyzing strike prompted the Cabinet, after ordering home infantry units from Ireland, Malta, and the Rhine, to proclaim a full-scale State of Emergency.

Although no state of emergency was ever declared in the United States, Americans were, characteristically, a good deal more trigger-happy. With the collapse of government mediation machinery at the end of the war, the velvet glove came off the iron fist, and federal authorities reverted to the tried-and-true method of sending in the troops to quell industrial disturbances. As in Britain, War Plans White grew out of actual government responses to the disorders of 1919. Planning took place in the Army War College under the auspices of military intelligence, which had gone into the business of domestic espionage in addition to its regular work overseas. At the juncture of domestic and foreign affairs stood the head of military intelligence, Marlborough Churchill, whose very name points to the close connection between American and British intelligence services. Doing double duty, Churchill tracked the fight against bolshevism from the frozen tundra of Siberia, where General William Graves kept 5,000 U.S. forces on alert, to Gary, Indiana, where General Leonard Wood was sweeping the streets clear of striking steelworkers.

Planning got under way in October in the wake of Wood's march into Gary, continued in November during the Palmer raids and the injunction against the coal strike, and developed further against the backdrop of troop alerts around racial disturbances and the ongoing military occupation of the copper fields. About the time Palmer overreached himself to predict a full-scale red rebellion slated for—what else?—May Day, the plans were nearing completion. Soon secret memos were going out from military intelligence warning department commanders about incendiary events in the offing: "Suppose the whole industrial area from Pittsburgh to the Mississippi River suddenly flares up with outlaw strikes, and you have that mass on your hands, with radical uprisings, labor and everything stewed up in flame in that section."[15]

In contrast to the British, American authorities defined the problem in terms of a revolutionary threat to the Constitution. It is striking to see how seriously Washington elites took the threat of revolution in the one country where, in retrospect, it seems least likely to have happened. They contemplated nothing less than full-scale civil war between forces loyal to the Constitution—everyone from the Rotary Club to the Daughters of the American Revolution—on one side, and revolutionary forces on the other, including, predictably, such radical organizations as the Socialist party, the Machinists Union, and the IWW.

Even more striking, however, is the way the White Plan construed the enemy in much broader terms: not only the predictable political opponents, but also whole segments of society defined by class and ethnicity. Presumed enemies included the entire population of immigrant Italians, Austrians, Hungarians, Poles, other east European "racial groups," and, indeed, the bulk of the population beyond the pale of white, Anglo-Saxon Protestants. Recent immigrants were never "entirely recasted in the American 'Melting Pot,' " and were, therefore, presumed to be "susceptible to hostile leadership against Anglo-Saxon Institutions." When we see whole swaths of ethnic America defined as potential enemies of the Constitution, we begin to understand why the upper-class authors of the White Plan believed they faced a fundamental challenge to their authority.[16]

Further understanding comes when we discover that "Negroes," not just black radicals, but the entire body of African-Americans were on the enemies list. According to the plan for the Mid-Atlantic region, Negroes were not to be trusted because "Their class consciousness, racial instincts, poverty, instinctive hostility to the white race and susceptibility to propaganda, makes [sic] this group a fruitful recruiting field for radical agitation." In a revealing combination of Negrophobia and Bolshiphobia that would characterize the Federal Bureau of Investigation at least until the death of J. Edgar Hoover decades later, Negroes were said to be lured to "the communistic cause under assured promises of the realization of that Utopian dream of social equality."[17]

However irrational at one level, the White Plan reveals a sober, calculating assessment of the balance of social and political forces. The drafters relied not only on the often dubious reports of undercover agents, but also on sophisticated analysis of census data taken straight from Progressive Era social science to produce careful tallies of the precise numbers of illiterate Italians in Illinois coal mining towns. Why illiterate? Because those unable to read government propaganda were deemed least likely to become loyal Americans.[18]

The difference between British mediation and American coercion revealed important differences between the two countries—the more intense anticommunism of the American Red Scare, the greater American use of coercion, and the deeper gulf between America's upper and lower classes. In most standard views, classless, democratic America is counterposed to class-ridden, hierarchical Britain. Yet when the full range of social traits is taken into account, the gap between top and bottom in the United States was actually deeper. Although Britain was far from homogeneous, its diversity was nothing compared to patchwork America, where a mostly white Protestant establishment of north European descent looked down on an impoverished working-class population that included Catholics, Jews, Slavs, Italians, and African-Americans. All told, American workers were more isolated by class, religion, ethnicity, and culture than their British counterparts, a fact represented in the enactment of a string of harsh measures—prohibition, eugenic sterilization, and immigration restriction—inimical to America's laboring population.

In summary, engagement with war and revolution since 1914 had the effect of turning domestic disorder into what was perceived as a mortal threat to the Republic. For Anglo Saxon elites in the national establishment, the way to meet it was not by compromising with industrial workers, promoting racial justice, or furthering social reform, but by cracking down on discontent. Since the turn to coercion violated the principle of social compromise that was the very foundation of progressive politics, it appeared to many at the time and in retrospect that progressivism had been stabbed in the back by its own leaders. In the same motion, having lost confidence in their ability to handle disorder at home, American elites began to turn away from participation in the League of Nations.

The League Fight

When President Wilson arrived home with the trophy of the Versailles Treaty at the beginning of July 1919, the country strongly favored U.S. participation in the League of Nations. Still basking in the afterglow of victory, most Americans were confident that in joining the League and subscribing to Article X, which called upon member states to enforce "collective security," they could enhance their position in world affairs without giving up their freedom of action. American concern about retaining U.S. preeminence in the Western Hemisphere had been addressed by attaching a clause specifically recognizing the Monroe Doctrine.

For these reasons, most were ready to respond when Wilson called America to a noble destiny in his address to the Senate on July 10. "There can be no question of our ceasing to be a world power," he intoned, "The only question is whether we can refuse the moral leadership that is offered us."[19] To his more adoring supporters, Wilson's call for moral leadership confirmed his status as the idealistic New World hero who had wrested the promise of world peace from the bloody hands of the Old World. With most newspapers giving their endorsement, even Wilson's archenemy Henry Cabot Lodge, Republican chair of the Senate Foreign Relations Committee, took pains to appear favorable.

Over the next several months, however, debate over the treaty turned increasingly partisan as doubts about American leadership overseas became thoroughly entangled with the tumultuous conflicts being played out on social and economic battlefields. Contrary to the once-prevailing view of a battle between "internationalists" and "isolationists," it is clear that only a few of Wilson's enemies were genuine isolationists, in the sense of opposing U.S. engagement overseas.

Instead, the leading Republican critics are better characterized as nationalists. Men like Lodge had been actively promoting U.S. expansion overseas since the days of the Spanish-American War, and when Teddy Roosevelt died at the start of the year, Lodge picked up his fallen mentor's "big stick" and proposed a set of strong reservations to Article X aimed at blocking any infringement of U.S. sovereignty. A key reservation, for example, renounced any obligation to use economic sanctions or military force "to preserve the territorial integrity or political independence of any other country."[20] While opposing the principle of collective security, Lodge was quite happy to throw U.S. weight into the scales of world power and endorsed a proposal for a mutual assistance pact among the former Allies.

The "mild reservationists" were no less outward-looking. Led by former president Taft, the group included such eminent figures as Root and Hughes, along with popular younger men such as Herbert Hoover, all of whom regarded the League as, in some sense, the fruit of their own work in the wartime League to Enforce Peace.

Domestically, Lodge and his peers were equally ardent nationalists. Upper-class conservatives had led the fight for preparedness in 1915–16 in the belief that patriotism and military discipline would overcome social divisions and bring dissidents into line, and they had supported intervention in 1917, believing it would have the same effect. In a way, it did. By the end of the war, most left-wing dissidents were either in jail or in cowed agreement with official war aims, while most urban workers and small farmers were doing their part for the war effort.

Unfortunately, the outcome of the war upset everyone's plans. Instead of unity, the country was engulfed in strife and dissension, while the fires of revolution burned overseas. To make matters worse, nationalism itself was a source of division, as the multitude of ethnic nationalities in the United States with ties to ancestral homelands came to blows over the Versailles settlement. While Polish nationalists cheered the creation of a greater Poland, Jewish-Americans, all too familiar with Polish anti-Semitism, warned, "there can be no greater menace than a greater Poland."[21] Croatian immigrants may have gloated over the fact that Fiume (Rijeka) was not awarded to Italy, but that only made Little Italy seethe with resentment. "Anyone who votes the Democratic ticket," warned Republican Fiorello La Guardia, "is an Austrian bastard." Irish-Americans were up in arms over the failure to grant a hearing to supporters of the Irish republic, which allowed Senator William Borah to make political hay by condemning the provision that augmented the power of the Empire by giving several British dominions voting rights in the League. And African-Americans were deeply disappointed by the treaty's acceptance of colonialism.

Historians have paid too little attention to the impact of social upheavals that wracked the country while the Senate debated the treaty's fate. Worry about losing control to striking workers and "hyphenates" dovetailed with concern that Article X would cede control of U.S. foreign policy to foreigners. It was bad enough to have to deal with the cacophony of immigrant voices; how much worse if the United States were obligated under the treaty to intervene on one side or the other in European quarrels. Root unburdened himself of his concern in a revealing letter to his close friend Lodge. "How can we prevent dissension and hatred among our own inhabitants of foreign origin," Root asked, "when this country interferes on foreign grounds between the races from which they spring?" Surely the unhappy result of intervention abroad would be "bitterness and disloyalty towards our own government."[22]

The same statesmen who were happy to support new nations in the Balkans were alarmed at the balkanizing impact of European nationalities on their own country, and Wilson unintentionally abetted their concern. During his ill-fated national speaking tour, the president held up the treaty as "the redemption of weak nations," prompting his listeners to wonder if they would be asked to die in a future war to defend the boundaries of the new Slavic states. At another stop on the same tour, Wilson tried to present the League as an antidote to the bolshevik poison that was spreading across the Atlantic, warning against "the poison of disorder, the poison of revolt, the poison of chaos." But he opened a Pandora's box in asking, "And do you honestly think, my fellow citizens, that none of that poison has got into the veins of this free people?"[23] Gripped by the same fear, a growing number of Wilson's opponents drew back, fearing that participation in the League would only open American veins to still more poison.

Gender entered the debate at many points. Editorial cartoonists seemed to agree that Peace was feminine and War masculine, so the only question seemed to be, which men were the better protectors of Peace, the Lodge nationalists or the Wilsonian internationalists. Strong male egos on both sides widened the polarization. Disturbed about forfeiting manly independence to effete foreigners, Lodge accused Wilson of cowardice and dishonor. From the other side, the usually unflappable Raymond Fosdick still had his masculine dander up in a retrospective view 20 years later: the Lodge reservations were "emasculating," defeat of the Treaty was "humiliating," and rejecting membership in the League broke paternal faith with "those boys coughing out their lungs."[24]

Idealism and realism were there, too, though it was not a simple conflict between Wilsonian idealists on one side and Republican realists on the other. On his cross-country tour, Wilson traveled both the idealist and realist roads. While calling the treaty "the only hope for mankind," he also touted it as the political foundation for the prosperity that would come with expanding world markets. Like the Victorian liberal he remained after all the years of progressive ferment, he saw growing markets as the key to both world and American prosperity: "If we are to save our own markets and rehabilitate our own industries, we must save the financial situation of the world and rehabilitate the markets of the world." There was no need to worry about whether the United States would come out on top; "let me predict we will be the senior partner. The financial leadership will be ours. The industrial primacy will be ours. The commercial advantage will be ours."[25] What Wilson could not explain was why League membership was necessary for America to obtain the economic preeminence it already enjoyed.

As in domestic policy, progressives found themselves divided. Many supporters of the president clung to the belief that the covenant carried forward the principles of the Fourteen Points. At the same time, a sizable contingent regarded it as a betrayal of progressive internationalism. Noting the failure to make room for "popular representation," Walter Lippmann, former staff advisor on The Inquiry, described the League as "a somewhat vague alliance of the Great Powers against the influence and the liberty of the people who live between the Rhine and the Pacific Ocean." As proof that the League was a reincarnation of the Holy Alliance set up after the Congress of Vienna to contain the French Revolution, Lippmann pointed to the Allied intervention in Russia. Although he wasted no love on the Bolsheviks, Lippmann condemned the Russian intervention in the strongest terms as "the bloody and immoral policy of counter-revolution in Russia."[26]

Current intervention foretold an oppressive future for the League of Nations, and when a Senate vote early in the year came within a whisker of cutting off funds for the Russian adventure, it predicted trouble ahead for the treaty.

Most of the senators who strongly identified as progressives went over to the "irreconcilables," the group of some sixteen senators led by William Borah of Idaho who opposed the treaty in any form. That does not mean all of the "irreconcilables" were progressives. Mellon banking interests funded some of the opposition publicity, and the group included arch-conservative Senator Knox of Pennsylvania and border-state conservative Senator Reed of Missouri.[27] Although later tagged as isolationists, many of the progressive critics—Borah, La Follette, Norris—were internationalist in spirit. Far from burying their heads in the soil of the midwestern prairie, they kept in close touch with world affairs, called for recognition of Russia, and paid close attention to everything from the Nottingham program of the British Labour party to the Indian National Congress. They objected not to foreign involvement per se, but to America becoming the world "policeman" for the House of Morgan. Picking up where they had left off in 1917, they lambasted the treaty as a charter of privilege that betrayed popular hopes into the unclean hands of imperialists, moneylenders, and munitions makers.

Many factors worked against passage of the proposed treaty. Much has been made of the personal animosity between the two main protagonists, Wilson and Lodge, which was compounded by Wilson's political blunder of not taking any prominent Republican with him to Versailles, and further exacerbated by Wilson's debilitating stroke, which brought out his most stubborn side. Political arithmetic also worked against passage. Facing the constitutional requirement of a two-thirds majority for ratification, the generals on both sides ordered their troops to reject any compromise, with the result that the treaty failed twice. In the first vote on November 19, 1919, with the Lodge reservations attached, Wilsonians joined "irreconcilables" to defeat the bill by a vote of 39-55; and in the second vote, with the reservations removed, Republicans joined "irreconcilables" to defeat Wilson's treaty as originally drawn by a similar tally of 38–53.[28]

In explaining the outcome, however, too little has been made of the surrounding social upheaval. For supporters of the Covenant, the timing could not have been worse. The debate proceeded against the backdrop of mounting class conflict and intensifying Red Scare. U.S. troops entered steel towns October 5, the first Palmer raids occurred on the night of November 7, and the first Senate vote came only twelve days later. The Senate again considered the issue four months later on March 19, 1920. In the interim, the Red Scare had peaked, nativism had intensified, and anxiety about overseas entanglements had only grown, with the result that Wilson's position lost ground.

Senate rejection of membership in the League did not end public debate. As victory over Germany turned sour, Americans asked a question they would pose after every other war in the twentieth century except World War II: what went wrong? And they gave contrasting answers. To the Wilsonians of the League of Nations Association, the mistake came with the Senate vote against membership. Adding a tragic twist to the legend of Wilsonian idealism, they portrayed their New World hero besting the lions of Old World diplomacy, only to be stabbed in the back by his own countrymen in what one author called "the great betrayal."[29] The story of peace betrayed by the Senate took on added significance after U.S. entrance into World War II, on the dubious assumption that U.S. participation in the League might have provided the backbone needed to resist fascist aggression in the 1930s.

To others, however, what betrayed the world's hopes for a just peace was the Versailles Treaty itself. If Wilson was a tragic figure, it was because he had already compromised all of the high principles embodied in the Fourteen Points in order to get a fatally flawed agreement, leaving him, in the end, like King Lear, a stubborn old man blindly clinging to a lie.

Progressives continued to argue among themselves in the interwar years about whether the League was the best hope of peace or the source of discord. For many who continued to call themselves "progressive," however, the argument was second-ary to the issue of the war itself. To many postwar progressives, it was the Great War that had been the great mistake. U.S. inter-vention under a combination of messianic and mercenary mo-tives had done nothing to rectify it, nor had the League of Na-tions redeemed it. That is why, as we will see in the next chapter, progressives gave so much of their energy to the postwar peace movement.

The Wasp Republic

The abandonment of social compromise at home and interna-tionalism abroad marked the collapse of progressivism in the major parties. With the dismantling of the wartime boards for labor and industry, talk of "reconstruction" along lines laid out by the British Labour party all but ceased. Visions of a demo-cratic league of peoples had evaporated at Versailles, and social welfare proposals languished for lack of support. As Democratic and Republican leaders alike sought to return to what Warren G. Harding called "normalcy," it appeared that the republican revival of the past two decades had run its course. Instead of a voluntary republic of engaged citizens seeking the public good, what seized the imagination of national leaders after 1920 was the idea of a 100 percent pure America, a biological republic dominated by white, Anglo-Saxon Protestants.

The flight of elites from progressivism was illustrated by the fate of the Plumb Plan. Named after labor lawyer Glenn Plumb, the plan proposed to continue the government's wartime take-over of the railroads, effectively nationalizing them. The plan re-ceived enthusiastic support from the normally conservative rail-way brotherhoods, which had made great gains in membership and pay under the Railway Administration, but not from Wil-liam McAdoo, the one-time tsar of the railroads. Wanting noth-ing to do with something that smacked of socialism, McAdoo arranged for the immediate return of the lines to their former owners.

To compound labor's defeat, Congress passed the Transportation Act in March 1920, whose Senate sponsor Albert Cummins, a mild Iowa progressive, saw to it that owners were entitled to a "fair return" and that the unions would have to submit to an arbitration board.[30] The board promptly ordered wage cuts, and when a second round of cuts in 1922 provoked a massive strike by railway machinists and other shopmen, the attorney general procured an injunction even more sweeping than Palmer's in the coal strike, sent in thousands of federal troops, and bludgeoned the unions into submission.

The presidential nominations of 1920 also demonstrated the retreat from reform. Indeed, in an effort to lower the political temperature, party leaders passed over the more extreme figures—erstwhile progressive Palmer and one-time New Nationalist Wood—correctly gauging that the public was fed up with crusading Men on Horseback. Instead, they chose two lackluster Ohioans, the middle-of-the-road Democratic governor James Cox and the amiable, corrupt emblem of the old politics in the Senate, Warren G. Harding. Going out of their way to blur the issues, Harding refrained from attacking the League, while Cox was anything but ardent in its defense. Support for the League came from Franklin D. Roosevelt, Democratic vice-presidential nominee, who, unfortunately, committed the campaign's greatest gaffe by giving out the imperialist boast that he had drafted the Haitian constitution.

Harding's landslide victory swelled the Republican trend begun in 1918 and amounted to a repudiation of all the enthusiasms of the past several years—the war for democracy, social reform, the League, even anti-red hysteria—and of the high-minded leader who had asked so much of his fellow citizens. As future presidents Herbert Hoover and Lyndon Johnson would discover, the creation and destruction of idols would become a familiar cycle in twentieth-century politics. And as future progressives would discover, attempting to combine good citizenship with being good citizens of the world was no sure route to electoral success.

One of the most noteworthy aspects of the 1920 election was the advent of women voters under the just-ratified Nineteenth Amendment. The appearance of women in polling places throughout the country for the first time was, in itself, a major shift in the gender boundaries of the public sphere. To everyone's surprise, however, women's votes did not make possible a new round of reform. To the contrary, a series of decisions by the laissez-faire-minded Supreme Court erased previous gains, as in the case of the *Bailey* decision of 1922, which squashed federal restrictions on child labor, and the *Adkins* decision of 1923, which threw out minimum wages for women on Fifth Amendment grounds of due process.

At least the New Woman got to celebrate her first-class citizenship. That was not the case with the New Negro. As seams of class and race ripped open, the civil rights and women's rights movements parted company. From the 1830s onward, the two had often moved in the same direction, though not always hand in hand, but now civil rights for African-Americans took a step backward. In the face of horrific outrages of white mobs, North and South, and despite wartime service and militant defense of civil rights by the NAACP and other progressive organizations, the New Negro, if anything, faced even worse prospects than before the war.

Something similar could be said of European ethnics. Although the black/white divide was the major fault line of American racism, a variety of European "races" also came in for degradation at the hands of Anglo-Saxons, Nordics, and other self-appointed superior "races." As an analytical category, "race" leaves much to be desired, obscuring more social variation than it reveals. And yet, as a deep-seated ideology, race was a potent part of reality. Race may be a mask—a false face that covers over complex social practices—but if the beholder believes the face has magical power, then it has the same effect as if it were real.

In the intense race consciousness of the day, people wore many masks, not always voluntarily. These included the familiar ones of black and white, plus a whole range from Nordic to Jewish. In fact, among Americans of European descent, "white" may not have been the most prominent. It was not as whites alone, but as white, Anglo-Saxon Protestants—as Wasps—that the Knights of the Ku Klux Klan, for example, rode to power in the early 1920s. Although the term "Wasp" only came into wide use later, it is a convenient shorthand to convey the presumptuous effort to equate being a "true" American with British, and more narrowly, Anglo Saxon descent.

Americans of British descent were fighting to retain cultural leadership against their inexorable demographic decline, as recorded in the 1920 census, when they fell below 50 percent for the first time. Still, their demographic base remained huge. As many as 45 million people counted in the census of 1920 (42 percent of the total of 106 million) could claim British descent, and the bulk of those were English rather than Scottish or Welsh. Their social networks ran outward from the large Protestant denominations—Methodist, Presbyterian, Congregational, Episcopalian—to encompass the immense web of women's clubs, exclusive summer resorts, YMCA centers, church circles, Mayflower Societies, and Daughters of the American Revolution.

It should be noted that many enmeshed in these networks wanted nothing to do with the militant assertion of a Wasp identity. Many progressives, for example, from Jane Addams to John Dewey who fit the ethnic profile went out of their way, all the same, to embrace a cosmopolitan kind of American identity. But others, including other progressives, somehow linked "true" Americanism to all things English—Alfred Lord Tennyson and Sir Walter Scott, the Magna Carta and Agincourt, and King Edward VII.

Although some aspects of ethnic pride were innocent enough, most of the Wasp revival was shot through with the guilty stain of Anglo-Saxon racism. Among the upper crust, reaction against European ethnics heightened the racial element in their version of Americanism. Madison Grant's notions of Nordic superiority became the staple of dinner table conversation at Harvard and Yale. Women's associations of the Episcopal and Presbyterian churches sponsored lectures on the hereditary causes of crime and poverty.

To the Mayflower set and others who spent hours poring over their pedigrees, the specious science of eugenics proved irresistible. Under the generous patronage of Mrs. E. H. Harriman, heiress of the great railroad fortune, the Eugenics Record Office served as a publicity bureau for scientific racism. Seeking to give a scientific aura to theories of racial inequality, the chief spokesman Charles Edward Davenport saw to the publication of scholarly papers in the *Journal of Heredity* purporting to show the hopeless inferiority of the "dysgenic classes." Eugenicists did not shrink from compulsory sterilization of the feebleminded, because, in the blunt opinion of Supreme Court Justice Oliver Wendell Holmes, "Three generation of imbeciles are enough."[31]

The infamous army intelligence tests administered to 1.7 million recruits became grist for the mills of eugenics. For literate doughboys, the Alpha test asked questions that reflected the everyday knowledge of Anglo-Saxon Protestants living in the northeast. What is the most prominent industry of Gloucester? Where is Cornell University? Who is Alfred Noyes? In language reflecting racial assumptions, the Alpha test also inquired as to the number of legs on a kaffir (the South African equivalent of "nigger").[32] The Beta test administered to illiterates contained similar biases, for example, in asking questions about tennis courts and telephones of people who had neither.

Oblivious to these cultural biases, defenders of the tests, including Robert Yerkes, chief army psychologist, pretended they were measures of innate intelligence, and when the so-called races of southern and eastern Europe, as well as Asians and Negroes, all turned in subnormal scores, it was said to be proof positive of their inborn mental inferiority. Settling into their overstuffed leather chairs in the mahogany-paneled reading room of the Union League or the Metropolitan Club, the brandy-and-cigar set could pick up genteel journals such as *The Atlantic Monthly* to read the shocking fact that almost half the white men tested were "morons" (defined as having a mental age between seven and twelve) and that whopping majorities of Poles, Italians, and Russians were "inferior-minded," suitable, perhaps, to perform unskilled labor, but the source of crime, indigence, prostitution, and corruption that were undermining the Republic.[33]

Inside the biological republic of Wasp Americans, democracy was reserved for the racially elect. Rejecting the egalitarian doctrines of the reformers, cultural conservatives embraced literacy tests for African-Americans and unlettered European immigrants alike, compulsory sterilization of the feebleminded, "positive eugenics" to encourage the propagation of superior breeds, and quotas on racially undesirable immigrants from southern and eastern Europe. Efforts to improve society through minimum hours, mothers' pensions, and civil rights laws were worse than useless because they only rewarded the unfit. Proposals for the endowment of motherhood—state stipends to mothers of young children—would only give support to the dysgenic classes, according to William McDougall, Harvard professor of psychology and author of *Is America Safe for Democracy?* (1922). Democracy was best restricted to the races, above all the Anglo-Saxons, that had proved themselves capable of self-government. "Such a democracy can, in the last analysis, spring only from good blood."[34]

Although the belief in "good blood" says a lot about the racial ideology of the day, it does not explain why a belief that had been around for some time had such a great impact on public policy now. To understand the advent of the Wasp republic, again, it is helpful to set domestic events in the context of world affairs. Here the critical factor was the reverse flow of messianic Americanism. Having made no headway in getting Europeans to abolish prostitution or drink, moral crusaders cast their censorious eye upon their own country, already beginning to cut loose in the running party known as the Jazz Age.

The impact of the messianic wave was evident, for example, in the nationalist language adopted by social purists in their renewed campaign against obscenity and sexual license. Social engineers of the American Social Hygiene Association believed they were clearing away the debris of prejudice and ignorance to put sexuality on a sound scientific footing. Yet their ardent support for a continuation of their wartime campaign against prostitution, now dubbed the "American Plan," betrays the underlying cultural nationalism in their thinking.

The same was true of the Eighteenth Amendment. Prohibition of the manufacture and sale of alcoholic beverages was advancing toward final victory behind a coalition that included southern elites who had pioneered prohibition in their home states, managerial elites seeking to impose efficiency in the factory and undermine immigrant political machines in the North, and small-town Yankee Protestants seeking to impose their evangelical values on sinful cities.[35] One man's wine was another's poison, and evangelical impulses were reinforced by class and nativist prejudices against German brewers, Italian wine makers, and the city saloon, favorite haunt of foreign workingmen. At last, the Prohibition Amendment was ratified in the fall of 1919, to take effect the next year; and just to make sure no one got tipsy in the meantime, Congress passed the Volstead Act over Wilson's veto.

Was Prohibition also a triumph for the women's movement? Many thought so at the time. From the Federation of Women's Clubs to the League of Women Voters, the whole range of respectable women joined with the Women's Christian Temperance Union to claim credit for getting the whole country off the beer truck and onto the water wagon. No doubt, women reformers were delighted when the Prohibition party accepted nearly every plank in the League of Women Voters program of mild social reform.

Yet the impulse was less a reflection of feminism than of the class and ethnic makeup of the leading women's organizations. Their opposition to the saloon reflected the attitudes and values of the overwhelmingly white, middle-class, Protestant social milieu from which most of them came. In other social contexts, Prohibition simply did not resonate with women. Although drunkenness was an issue among Catholic women, total abstinence was out of the question in a culture where wine and beer watered the cycle of life from christenings and weddings to funerals. In truth, one woman's poison was another's wine.

These divisions of class and culture were glaringly apparent in the ongoing campaign to Americanize the immigrant, which took on added force in the nativist reaction against everything foreign. Deprived of a foreign military foe, "100 percent Americanism" now turned its full fury against foreigners within the gates. Often imposed with haughty presumptions of Anglo-Saxon superiority, Americanization became a dirty word in districts where foreign languages were spoken at home and at school. Nativism oozed from articles in the *Ladies' Home Journal* advising Women's Clubbers to set up English classes for the ignorant foreigners in their towns, and it inspired several proposals of the League of Women Voters: to raise qualifications for naturalization, to impose an educational qualification for the vote, and, most sweeping of all, to make English the "national language" and instruction in English "compulsory in all public and *private* schools."[36]

The reverse flow of messianic Americanism had a major impact on the battle over immigration. Like the Red Scare and the League fight, the campaign for immigration restriction illustrated the interconnection between foreign and domestic policy. Immigration policy, after all, *was* foreign policy, in so far as it was about foreigners, and it certainly raised the hackles of several foreign governments. Worried that the League of Nations might attempt to impose international standards regarding migration, restrictionists lent their weight to the fight against the League, and it was no accident that the Senate leader of the League fight, Henry Cabot Lodge, was also president of the Immigration Restriction League.

The upper crust had long been of two minds on the subject of immigration. On the one hand, big employers, the National Association of Manufacturers, and readers of *The Commercial and Financial Chronicle* wanted the flow of cheap labor to continue and opposed any severe curbs. On the other hand, urban patricians, the Immigration Restriction League, and readers of articles about mongrel Europe by Kenneth Roberts in *The Saturday*

Evening Post were anxious about losing cultural leadership and stepped up their efforts to staunch the influx.

What tipped the balance in favor of closing the gates was the returning tide of messianic Americanism. Just as they had given up on remaking Europe according to American design, so the would-be redeemers now lost confidence in Americanizing the immigrants and pushed, instead, for their exclusion as "undesirables." According to Dr. Henry Fairfield Osborn, president of the American Museum of Natural History, in his welcoming address to the Second International Congress of Eugenics held in 1921, the only way to save the American republic was "through barring the entrance of those who are unfit to share the duties and responsibilities of our well-founded government."[37] Ever since the Dillingham Commission of 1911 had defined "undesirable" in a way that favored northern and western European against the "new immigrants" from southern and eastern Europe, the restrictionists had aimed to reduce the number of Slavs, Jews, and peoples from the Mediterranean.

Victory came in 1921 along those lines with the first law in American history that imposed national quotas on immigration. The idea for a quota system came, appropriately enough, from a Christian missionary named Sidney Gulick, whose testimony in Senate hearings convinced the Immigration Committee to set a ceiling of 3 percent of the number foreign-born counted in the 1910 census, and then apportion spaces according to the relative numbers of foreign nationals present at that time. Since much of the "new" immigration had taken place after 1910, this had the effect of shifting the balance back toward British, Irish, and other supposedly desirable immigrants.

Even so, it was not enough. Congress listened to more testimony from H. H. Laughlin and other eugenics experts to the effect that "race," not nationality, was the determining factor in desirability. Members of Congress extolled "the Aryan race." In a message to Congress, President Coolidge propounded his racial theory of American institutions—"They were created by people who had a background of self-government"—and demanded, "America must be kept American." In response, Congress adopted the National Origins Act in 1924. Going several steps further, the act lowered the ceiling, temporarily shifted the base to the 1890 census, and, for the long term, apportioned quotas according to the supposed "national origins" of the American population in the expectation that the newcomers from southern and eastern Europe would be reduced to a trickle. And so it was between the late 1920s, when the act became fully effective, and 1965, when it was effectively repealed. The irony was that instead of promoting homogeneity, restriction had the unintended consequence of stimulating a massive influx of Mexicans and other Latin Americans, who were exempt from the quotas.[38]

The reverse flow of messianic Americanism was exemplified in perverse form by the Ku Klux Klan. Somehow the Klan gathered together all the seething currents of the postwar reaction—nativism, isolationism, anti-radicalism, white supremacy, male dominance, and Protestant moralism. For that unholy reason, the second Klan had a much broader appeal than the old cross-burning terrorists of southern Reconstruction. It spread like a prairie fire through the small towns and hamlets of the South and Midwest, driven by gusts of moral panic among the forgotten men who hung around the courthouse and women who attended the hardshell Baptist church. With their small worlds reeling from wartime contacts with the wider world, these lower-middle-class men and women responded to every new shock of postwar disorder with ever-greater resolve to suppress foreign influences and all the other stereotypical evils that beset them—international Jewish bankers, the tyrant of Rome, the red menace, foreign devils in general, and the uppity Negro.

Although it was an extremist hate group, the Klan was able to dominate many communities because it also tapped into mainstream Americanism. Led by run-of-the-mill Protestant ministers, small businessmen, Masons, and the Junior Order of American Mechanics, it achieved a certain respectability among the broad run of the not-quite-successful by giving vent to prejudices buried deep in American culture—Protestant bigotry, nativist intolerance, anti-radicalism. In calling upon husbands to rule their wives according to the strictures of St. Paul, reject sexual freedom, shun birth control, and practice chivalry, it expressed a deep anxiety about the threat of the New Woman to male prerogatives. And in linking sexual license to "social equality" between the races, its Negrophobia tapped into the prevailing myth of white supremacy.[39]

Like the Creel Committee, the Klan made use of the most up-to-date methods of advertising to fan the flames of patriotic fear. Elizabeth Tyler and Edward Clark of the Southern Publicity Association created a network of Klan publications, including *The Searchlight*, and turned old vigilante traditions of the secret society—hooded robes, night riding, secret passwords, lynch mobs—into the stuff of a mass movement. In using modernist methods of mass communication to protest the trends of modernity, it was caught up in the same contradiction as the more respectable Rotarians and Women's Clubs.

At its peak, the Klan boasted hundreds of chapters, millions of members, a stranglehold on many localities in the South, effective control of the state of Indiana, and enough influence in the Democratic party to beat back an attempted censure at the national convention in 1924. The fact that it stood on the winning side in battles over Prohibition, the League of Nations, and immigration restriction, lent a specious credence to its claim of representing the majority of "true Americans." Yet, in the end, its triumph was temporary. In rejecting the huge numbers of Catholics, Jews, Slavs, African-Americans, and others who could not possibly conform to the Wasp standard, the Klan vividly demonstrated why, in the long run, Wasp Americanism was incapable of winning consent from the emerging majority of the American people.

❧

By the end of 1921, with conservatism riding high, it was clear that the national establishment had abandoned progressivism. With business back in the saddle in Washington, the long struggle to regulate the market had ground to a halt, as existing regulations were either enfeebled by indifferent enforcement or overridden in laissez-faire courtrooms. Meanwhile, the labor movement reeled from a string of defeats, social reform hit a brick wall, and large sectors of the population—industrial workers, urban ethnics, African-Americans—were pushed to the margins, squashing dreams for a cosmopolitan America. As society seemed to break down into warring tribes and competing economic interests, or still further into atomized individuals, the social ethos withered, and even the notion that there was anything like "the public interest" came into question. In foreign policy, too, decision makers backpedaled on their recent commitment to progressive internationalism, refused to accept even the watered-down Covenant of the League of Nations, and started closing the gates to immigrants.

The turn to "100 percent Americanism" at home and unilateralism abroad amounted to a rejection of the "moral leadership" that Wilson had embraced in the American moment at the end of the war. Hegemony can be defined as "rule by consent," with equal emphasis on both "rule" and "consent," and America's rulers had given up on winning consent at home from large parts of the population and no longer cared about moral leadership abroad.

To many disheartened crusaders, elite abandonment of progressive aims seemed like the death of progressivism itself. Others, however, kept the faith. Disenchanted with the consequences of the peace, wary of moral uplift, and chastened by defeat, progressives set out to make the best of a bad situation in the early 1920s and, in the process, reconstructed progressivism in ways that gave it a new lease on life.

THE OLD PARTY WAY

THE PROGRESSIVE WAY

THE PROGRESSIVE CAMPAIGN OF 1924: John Baer, "The Old Party Way / The Progressive Way," ca. 1924, People's Legislative Service. Probably used as a flyer in Robert La Follette's disappointing run for the presidency, the cartoon pits the grafting politician against hardworking people, the former enriched by Wall Street and the oil companies, the latter personified by a sturdy housewife sweeping politics clean of corruption and an independent carpenter building an honest party organization. The homage to working people in the La Follette campaign contrasts with sympathy for the oppressed consumer in the Bull Moose party, evident in the illustration for chapter 2. (Library of Congress, Manuscripts Division)

9

Progressive Rebirth

As progressivism died out in the higher circles of power, it was reborn in social movements down below. It came to life in the vital postwar peace movement, in the hard-fought struggles of organized labor, in the protests of small farmers, and in the spirited defense of civil liberties. Although most of these influences had been present in the big tent of prewar progressivism, they now had a much smaller tent to themselves. And instead of being at the center of American politics, progressivism moved to the left, where it more or less remained for the rest of the twentieth century.

World Consciousness

Contrary to former characterizations of the United States as "isolationist" in the 1920s, historians now recognize a strong American hand in world affairs. Despite absence from the League of Nations, Americans played a leading role in everything from pacifist conferences to international financial agreements, and they set the example to the world of a freewheeling business civilization. Although the architects of a unilateralist foreign policy who came to power with the Harding administration had lost interest in idealistic reforms, they would have agreed with Jane

Addams, perennial bellwether of progressive opinion, that the period was marked by "a growing world consciousness."

In a 1929 sequel to her famous account of *Twenty Years at Hull House*, Addams concluded that "the modern world is developing an almost mystic consciousness of the continuity and interdependence of mankind." Addams had first learned about interdependence in the multiethnic neighborhoods of Chicago, and now she applied the lesson to the world at large. "There is a lively sense of the unexpected and yet inevitable action and reaction between ourselves and all the others who happen to be living upon the planet at the same moment."[1]

This sense of interdependence was the key to progressive internationalism, and it helped fuel the strongest peace movement of the twentieth century. With growing impact, peace activists trotted out numerous schemes to prevent any recurrence of the horrific violence of the Great War. Latter-day Wilsonians of the League of Nations Non-Partisan Association exhumed ideals buried at Versailles and campaigned for disarmament and collective security. Others agitated on behalf of arbitration, the World Court, and similar international machinery. Pacifists at the National Council for the Prevention of War attracted widespread support for a variety of plans for permanent peace. One of the most popular was the scheme to "outlaw" war. If nations forswore violence in foreign policy, then their neighbors would not have to resort to war in self-defense. The idea grew so popular that scores of governments eventually signed onto the 1928 Kellogg-Briand pact renouncing the use of force as an instrument of foreign policy.

Critics were not impressed. Accusing the pacifist movement of wooly-headed idealism, they showered contempt on the idea that war could somehow be prevented by making it illegal. The critics had a point. The pacifist movement did contain a strong strain of sentimental moralism, and much of its rhetoric seemed to rest on the assumption that condemning evil would be enough to make it go away. The point was painfully sharpened at the end of the 1930s by the outbreak of World War II.

At the same time, the movement also contained an equally strong strain of moral realism. Having given up illusions of idealism at the top, reformers such as Jane Addams and Frederick Howe adopted a more realistic view of American diplomacy. Instead of "the chosen nation," they saw the United States as a nation like other nations, without any messianic mission. Instead of having a special moral dispensation from God, it was an orphan of providence.

Moral realism underlay the newly created Women's International League for Peace and Freedom. Founded in Zurich in 1919 with Jane Addams as its first president, the Women's International League brandished a small arsenal of high ideals in its very name. It campaigned against militarism and imperialism on the belief that there could be no peace without social justice, and vice versa: the path to a just society ran through a peaceable world. Its ideals were grounded in realistic analysis and tough-minded activism. Rejecting the Christian piety that infused a number of other groups, it welcomed advocates of armed resistance into its ranks, while at the same time supporting the militant nonviolence of Gandhi's crusade against the British raj. It cheered, as well, the "passive resistance" of German civilians against French occupation of the Ruhr in 1923.

To the moral realists of the Women's International League, the Versailles Treaty was an obstacle to true peace. Almost before the ink was dry, they were busy drawing up a list of revisions, at the top of which stood disarmament. Seeing a recipe for future war written into the provisions that disarmed the vanquished but left the victors armed to the teeth, they called for real disarmament on all sides. They saw the League of Nations as a false start on the road to collective security and joined with a number of other pacifist and reform organizations to press European and American governments to forge new agreements that would revise Versailles.

As a *women's* organization, the Women's International League took a special interest in war's brutal treatment of women. Though it rejected illusions of innate feminine moral superiority, it often couched its appeals to the mothers of humanity. The same was true of the fledgling League of Women Voters. Swelled with the responsibilities of their expanded citizenship, readers of *The Woman Citizen*, organ of the League of Women Voters, kept tabs on the spate of international conferences devoted to working women, social reform, and world peace.

Nobody loved an international conference more than Crystal Eastman. Having been at the Hague peace conference in 1915 and at several postwar gatherings, Eastman remarked, "Not long ago foreign affairs were considered the preserve of highly placed men." But not any more. With considerable pride, she noted, "Not only domestic problems, of food, housing, old age, and maternity, are now recognized on the agendas of women's conferences, but foreign affairs are boldly discussed."[2] No one in her generation better personified women's wider horizons than Eastman. Starting as a lawyer and social investigator, she became a transatlantic pilgrim for peace and justice during and after the war.

Thanks to a vibrant generation of New Women, women's voices commanded unprecedented attention in foreign policy debates. In their own organizations and through shared leadership in other pacifist groups, women peace activists could claim some credit for pushing diplomats to take seriously questions of disarmament, arbitration, and the outlawing of war. It would be too much to say that American foreign policy was thoroughly feminized, but women activists and feminine ideals of caring enjoyed greater influence than ever before in the councils of power.

Testimony to that fact came in the Washington Naval Conference of 1921–22, the major U.S. diplomatic initiative of the early 1920s. Initial pressure for the conference came from the Women's International League and other arms of the international pacifist movement, which found an advocate in Senator William Borah of Idaho, a vocal progressive and persistent critic of the Russian intervention and the League of Nations. Borah won unanimous passage of a Senate resolution that called upon Secretary of State Charles Evans Hughes to invite the powers to Washington for a discussion of disarmament. A cautious realist, Hughes saw an opportunity to advance U.S. interests by breaking the diplomatic entente between Britain and Japan and stabilizing great power competition.

The outcome of the conference was not the agreement on disarmament that pacifists had pushed for, but a series of treaties aimed at establishing the ground rules for imperial competition in the Pacific. In the Five Power agreement, the world's greatest naval powers, Britain, the United States, and Japan, agreed to maintain their fleets at a ratio of 5:5:3, which led to the sinking of a lot of obsolete British ships and the construction of some new American and Japanese ones. With an eye toward reducing imperial friction, the Four Power treaty gave mutual guarantees to the great powers in Asia. In the Nine Power agreement, the powers promised to share equally the fruits of Chinese markets, in effect, endorsing the U.S. Open Door policy, though nobody ever bothered to consult the Chinese on the matter.

In this environment, postwar progressives were compelled to take greater account of imperialism than their prewar counterparts. What was most noteworthy was that American progressives did not quail from attacking the imperialism of their own country. In the teeth of Red Scare attacks, Jane Addams was not afraid to condemn U.S. occupations in Central America and the Caribbean, and she warned that militarism was growing because of American "imperialism," a term she would have been reluctant to direct at her own country before the war. Similarly, the Farmer Labor party compared the United States in Latin America to the British in Ireland and called for the abolition of imperialism from all quarters.[3]

Acting on the anti-imperialist impulse, progressive internationalists mounted vigorous campaigns against ongoing U.S. occupations in Latin America. Using Wilsonian rhetoric, critics insisted that Nicaraguans and Dominicans had as much right to self-determination as Poles and Czechs. In a widely read series of *Nation* articles on "Self-Determining Haiti," James Weldon Johnson of the NAACP attacked the domination of the black republic by American marines and National City Bank. When a

Senate inquiry failed to ease the Haitian occupation, African-Americans in the International Council of Women of the Darker Races joined forces with the Women's International League to sponsor an interracial delegation to the troubled island. Their widely read report on "occupied Haiti," written by Emily Greene Balch, leveled the charge that "there has been for some time a drift towards imperialism" and that "our actions in Haiti are perhaps most flagrant."[4]

The contrast with prewar progressivism is quite striking. Before the war and the interventions in Mexico and Russia, the progressive tent had been big enough to include both ardent interventionists—Roosevelt and Wilson—and their critics—La Follette and the American Union Against Militarism. With the exit of establishment progressives, however, only opponents of overseas adventures were left inside. As a result, progressivism itself shifted position in the early 1920s. Where it had once sprawled across the political spectrum from left to center, it now occupied a much narrower band on the left.

Part of that leftward shift involved a turn to political economy. In the case of Haiti, James Weldon Johnson laid heavy emphasis on the role of National City Bank in explaining "the loss of their political and economic freedom." Picking up old populist arguments, progressive Senators George Norris and Robert La Follette identified capital investment as the spring in the mechanism of intervention, whether in the Caribbean to collect debts for New York banks or Siberia to repossess mines from the Bolsheviks. The same applied to Mexico, where Wall Street investors wanted to overturn Article 27 in the Mexican constitution authorizing seizure of oil reserves. According to a progressive journal, Yankee investors "fattened by plunder extorted from the American people have been despoiling Mexico of her natural wealth."[5]

The larger imperialism loomed, the more progressives were convinced that it was a structural component of American political economy, not an aberrant policy. Perhaps it was only natural in the age of business to see imperialism in terms of money-making, but sophisticated critics picked up arguments of J. A. Hobson and others that had been around since the 1890s that explained empire as the search for overseas outlets for surplus capital. Parker Moon, for example, wrote that "imperialism seeks to relieve the pressure of surplus goods and surplus capital on a temporarily saturated market." In this environment, writers close to the Communist party gained influence beyond their numbers, as in the case of Joseph Freeman and Scott Nearing, whose book *Dollar Diplomacy: A Study of American Imperialism* became something of a classic.[6]

Unfortunately, economic analysis could easily degenerate into crude economic determinism. Men like Frederick Howe and Lincoln Steffens, embarrassed at having followed a false messiah in the war, now affected the tough stance of hard-headed materialists. Seeing only craven motives in U.S. policy, Howe put everything down to economic interests, pure and simple: "Our State Department was thinking in terms of oil in Mesopotamia, of oil in Mexico, of gold and railroads in Haiti and Santo Domingo."[7]

In their eagerness to expose economic underpinnings, such progressives tended to overlook other aspects of international relations. Racial and ethnic factors, for example, were also important in both imperialism and its opposition. Racial ideologies—Anglo-Saxon, European, or white—not only survived the war but redoubled in intensity as Atlantic elites united to maintain some form of control over what they regarded as "backward" peoples. By the same token, anticolonial movements were often couched in racial terms. That was especially true in the Atlantic world, where racial myths were extremely potent. In upside-down fashion, they inspired the black nationalism of Marcus Garvey, with his call to supplant the white master with an all-black power structure.

A more subtle approach that combined class and racial aspects came from W. E. B. Du Bois. Like many of his fellow progressives, Du Bois entered the battle against laissez-faire as a reform Darwinist, believing in the upward striving of races as the vehicle for human progress. It was not long, however, before he came to regard racialized classes as the prime movers of history.

Having joined the New York City branch of the Socialist party, he came to identify "the problem of the color line" with the labor problem. In the midst of World War I, he wrote, "the world today consists, not of races, but of the imperial commercial group of master capitalists, international and predominantly white: the national middle classes of the several nations, white, yellow, and brown, with strong blood bonds, common languages, and common history; the international laboring class of all colors: the backward, oppressed groups of nature-folk, predominantly yellow, brown, and black."[8] For this reason, Du Bois's brand of Pan-Africanism targeted both the myth of white supremacy and the economic predominance of Western business interests in Africa. Inspired by Gandhi's attack on British rule in India, Du Bois and his colleagues joined forces with Western-educated Africans at a series of Pan-African conferences in 1919, 1921, and 1927 aiming at both political and economic independence of Africa.

Turning to the "labor problem" itself, everyone recognized its international dimensions. Despite being abused and abandoned by the Wilson administration, Sam Gompers continued to see himself as America's labor ambassador to the world and behaved as if the highly beneficial wartime pact with the government was still in effect. Continuing to collaborate with U.S. authorities against communists and Wobblies, he also sponsored the Pan-American Federation of Labor to woo Latin American workers away from radical unions and lure them onto the American path of "free trade unionism."[9]

Looking to build their own international ties, progressives in the labor movement steered clear of the U.S. government. The Chicago Federation of Labor and the International Association of Machinists, for examples, rode the fast-moving currents of labor radicalism and ethnic revolt toward the far-off promises of a world parliament of working people and a League of Oppressed Nations. In addition, the National Women's Trade Union League embarked on its own international venture at the juncture of labor feminism and social reform by helping to establish the International Federation of Working Women, whose congresses from 1919 through 1923 promoted international labor standards. By the mid-twenties, the tides turned against them, but even then, the impulse they represented survived in a number of localities.

Labor radicals carved their own path to international solidarity. One practical project was the curious Russian venture of the Amalgamated Clothing Workers. Responding to an urgent request from Lenin for help in building socialism, the union of mostly Jewish and Italian garment workers sponsored the construction of half a dozen garment factories in the Soviet Union. In a remarkable twist to the story, American workers were sent to show Soviet managers how to implement the latest methods to increase worker productivity, despite widespread discomfort with efficiency schemes among American workers.

The trophy for the most rigorous example of internationalism belonged to the Communist International. With the dream of insurrection fading fast, the Communist International, or Comintern, settled down to the hard work of forging a disciplined body that could advance working-class interests around the world, or at least uphold the "workers state" in Russia. From the time of John Reed's pilgrimage to St. Petersburg in 1917, American radicals had latched onto the Soviet Union as the substance of things hoped for and the evidence of things unseen in their own country. Now, as American communists came out of hiding to form a legal political party in 1921, the mostly immigrant members bound themselves tightly to the Comintern, believing Moscow was the headquarters of a genuinely international movement, not of a narrow nationalist tyranny.

In their different ways, the social movements of the early 1920s picked up the threads of internationalism where their prewar predecessors had dropped them. Although they operated in a more hostile environment, the various movements dedicated to world peace, women's rights, labor reform, and workers' revolution demonstrated the truth in Addams's claim for a growing world consciousness at the grass roots.

The American Model

A very different version of "world consciousness" was evident in efforts of Western elites to build a stable international order in the wake of Versailles. In Europe, the early 1920s were still a time of hardship and turmoil. The most destructive war in history had left transportation networks a shambles; banks could barely open their doors; manufactures did not recover prewar levels until 1925. In these circumstances, disillusionment with progress went deep. According to one observer, the war proved that progress "turns upon itself like a serpent. It pursues a splendid path, and then suddenly swings round, and we are worse than our fathers."[10]

Bad enough as the war had been, the peace settlement made things worse. The ink was barely dry on the Versailles Treaty when John Maynard Keynes, a dissenting member of the British delegation, warned that the cost of reparations would impose an intolerable burden on the German economy and impede recovery everywhere else. Even Keynes did not foresee the hyperinflation that turned German marks into pieces of paper so worthless they had to be trundled to market in wheelbarrows, but he was right that reparations made for the continuation of war between France and Germany by economic means. When Germany threatened to default, the French invoked the terms of the treaty and invaded the Ruhr in 1923. Russia was in the worst shape of all, a cauldron of war, civil war, revolution, and outside intervention. It did not recover its prewar manufacturing level until the end of the decade, when Stalin's harsh, forced-draft industrialization got under way.[11]

The contrast with the United States could hardly have been more dramatic. First of all, the U.S. economy, having long since vaulted to the top of the world's industrial nations, now increased its lead, as production levels rose nearly 50 percent above prewar levels by 1925, putting national output on a par with the combined output of all of Europe. What was even more striking was how catastrophe had been so kind to American finance. Although the City of London continued to be the fulcrum of the world economy in many ways, the United States emerged from the war as the world's leading creditor, and the Wall Street–Washington nexus played an increasingly central role in world affairs. Having been shaken by postwar disorder, American optimism now returned in full force to stimulate a flood of overseas investments. Atop billions in wartime loans from the likes of J. P. Morgan, foreign investments surged as book value doubled from $3.8 billion in 1919 to $7.5 billion ten years later.[12] Truly, the United States was a New World economic colossus.

Spurning calls for isolation, American leaders joined in diplomatic efforts to stabilize the postwar world. At the Washington Naval Conference of 1921–22, as we have seen, the United States and Britain joined forces to stabilize the Pacific. Meanwhile, in a series of diplomatic conferences, the unfinished business of Versailles was addressed, first at Rapallo on the Italian Riviera, where Germany and Russia—the twin pariahs at Versailles—buried the hatchet in 1922, and then three years later at the Swiss mountain resort of Locarno, where French and German diplomats settled their boundary disputes, leading to much hopeful talk about "the spirit of Locarno" bringing peace to the continent.

In contrast to their absence from Rapallo and Locarno, Americans were central to economic readjustment. Despite a short depression in 1921–22, the United States was the only country with sufficient resources to lead in this effort. A network of international bankers and corporate leaders came together to stabilize exchange rates and otherwise knit together the international economy. The transatlantic link was personified by the close friendship between Montague Norman, secretive head of the Bank of England who exuded both sophistication and anti-Semitism, and Benjamin Strong, head of the New York branch of the Federal Reserve.[13] They joined with their German counterparts Walter Rathenau and Gustav Stresseman in seeking to bring order to world financial markets. Out of this transatlantic financial network came a succession of agreements to reschedule German reparations payments: first, the Dawes Plan of 1924, which stretched out the payments; then the Young Plan of 1929, which reduced them; and finally, the 1931 moratorium on debt payments proposed by President Hoover.

In the short run, the Dawes Plan was widely credited with greatly improving the situation in central Europe by easing payments and giving reparations a lower priority than interest payments on other investments. The improved climate for foreign investment attracted a flood of capital into Germany, some of it in the form of branch factories of Ford, General Motors, and other fledgling multinational corporations. Much of it, however, came in the form of speculative investments in bonds and securities, causing an American commercial attaché to wonder how long U.S. bankers would keep fighting over "the privilege of floating doubtful German municipal loans."[14]

In the window of stability between the Dawes Plan and the Crash of '29, America stood forth to the world as the very model of a modern business civilization. Whether the world liked what they saw or not, everyone seemed to think that the combination of high productivity and high consumption with a minimum of state intervention and limited social welfare was the image of the future. "Everyone interested in the future of mankind" should look to the New World, wrote novelist Mary Borden, "for the scaffolding of the world of the future is reared against the sky of America."[15]

Germans were especially dazzled by *das amerikanische Wirtschaftswunder*. A constant stream of German pilgrims made the hajj to the Mecca of Detroit to see the American economic wonder firsthand. They came for different reasons: industrialists to learn more about high productivity and rationalized production; trade unionists and Social Democrats to see firsthand the fruits of Ford's famous five-dollar day. But whatever their differences, they never failed to come away impressed by America's dynamism. One of the pilgrims was Alice Salomon, Germany's pioneer social worker, who said the visitor "dates a new period of his life from his trip to America. He expands his European experiences to a 'world view.' " In America, she wrote, the traveler "glimpses the future of humanity."[16]

What made the biggest impression was the high standard of living. Per capita income in the United States was more than twice that of Germany and France, and 50 percent higher than in Britain.[17] Germans were not alone in their envy of American riches. To Henry Nevinson, a London novelist, the United States seemed a veritable cornucopia of material goods. On leaving New York, he wrote, "Good-bye to central heating and radiators, fit symbols of the hearts they warm! Good-bye to frequent and well-appointed bathrooms, glory to the plumber's art! . . . Good-bye to the long stream of motors—the 'limousines' or 'flivvers'!"[18] Even the Soviets were interested in some aspects of the American model. Desperate to rebuild Russian manufacturing as quickly as possible after the war, Lenin recommended Frederick W. Taylor's scientific management to Soviet factories as part of the New Economic Policy of 1921, which opened the door for market pricing, foreign technology, and other capitalist techniques.

In some quarters, American popular culture, even in its commercialized form, was received as a democratic battering ram against the staid, elite culture of the Old World. Europe's cultural avant-garde found a breath of fresh air in New World jazz, Negro spirituals, Hollywood movies, and Madison Avenue salesmanship. While Paris nightclubs toasted the exotic dancing of Josephine Baker, Igor Stravinsky composed a work entitled *Ragtime*, and even young leftist Bertolt Brecht, bored by the stale atmosphere of German high culture, celebrated the energy of America.

Everybody loved Hollywood movies. There was something very American about the freewheeling individualism of the Wild West hero battling the bad guys in black hats, but there was also a universal appeal in the devil-may-care Charlie Chaplin and the impish Mickey Mouse making their own way in an unpredictable world. That universal appeal helps explain why Hollywood became the movie capital of the world. In the 1920s American movies accounted for 70 percent of films shown in France, 80 percent in South America, and fully 95 percent in Canada and Britain.[19] In the same way, Charles "Lone Eagle"

Lindbergh was taken to European hearts after making the first solo flight across the Atlantic in 1927, a symbol of the common man rising above titled princes and bourgeois titans alike.

All the same, many Europeans refused to bow down to the American idol. In *Brave New World* (1929), Aldous Huxley penned a scathing indictment of business civilization. In his dystopian vision, "Ford" was worshiped as God, and everything was controlled from above. Intellectual ability was controlled through test-tube breeding of Alphas and Betas (based on the infamous I.Q. tests of World War I), and feelings were controlled through the mind-numbing drug "soma" and moving pictures, dubbed "feelies."

From the right, Catholic and conservative critics lambasted the godless materialism of the United States and worried that the richness of their own national cultures would be crushed under the crass commercialism and robot standardization of American modernity. Johan Huizinga, the great Dutch historian of the spiritual life of the late Middle Ages, came away from a visit to the United States alarmed at the debasement of the American dream by the quest for material possessions.

From the left, communists unleashed scathing criticism. Antonio Gramsci, leading light of Italian communism, depicted America's high-productivity-high-wage form of capitalism—which he labeled "Fordism"—as a modern managerial tyranny, complete with repressive regimentation, adamant anti-union-ism, Puritanical prohibitions on smoking and drinking, and sur-veillance of employees' moral behavior. He saw all these as the ingredients of capitalist "hegemony" in the United States, [20] although in later decades union recognition turned out to be a good deal more effective in that regard than union-busting.

Some leftists saw an alternative model in the Soviet Union. As one traveler concluded after visiting both countries, American-style capitalism and Soviet communism were "the two poles of the contemporary era."[21] Although the moment of revolutionary hope between 1917 and 1919 had quickly passed, western Europeans had not completely given up their fascination with the Soviet model of a command economy.

Whatever their viewpoint, everyone agreed that America had a major impact. Indeed, when Europeans modernized their own economies, they referred to the process as "Americanization." According to a writer for the *National Geographic*, Americanization advanced rapidly in the 1920s: "Travel where you will you can't escape American customs and fashions. Berlin flocks to its first elaborate soda fountain for nut sundaes, served by snappy soda 'jerkers.' American movies, automobiles, dental schools, typewriters, phonographs, and even its prize fights lead in spreading American fashions and customs throughout the world."[22]

Such incorporation of the American economic model in the growing "world consciousness" opened the way for broad American influence. Although America-as-symbol retained its association with democracy, the prevailing image that came across the Atlantic in the mid-1920s was not based on the ideals of liberty that Europeans had beheld in Wilson's Fourteen Points, nor was it the image of Jane Addams questing after social justice. Instead, what European admirers dreamed about were Model Ts and flush toilets. Materialistic or not, Americanization widened the opportunity for U.S. leaders to convert economic power to cultural leadership, a requisite for the hegemony they would later come to exercise after the Second World War.

At this stage, however, American leaders were unwilling to go that far. Although isolationism played a part, the main factor in the spurning of world leadership was the insistence on going it alone in world affairs. For the most part, the Republicans who came to power in the 1920s were not isolationists, but nationalists who anchored foreign relations on the rock of national interest. That was obvious in their opposition to Article X of the Versailles Treaty as an infringement on national sovereignty, and it was equally apparent in their pursuit of overseas markets for U.S. business and even in efforts to stabilize international credit. In fact, successive Republican administrations embraced a narrow definition of national interest keyed to the interests of American business. With regard to Allied war debts, they adopted the stance of a petty accountant in refusing to forgive the loans. "They hired the money," Coolidge said, as if Allied victory was not in itself the best repayment of the debt.

What was more, Congress threw reason to the wind in erecting the highest tariff barriers in a high-tariff history. At a time when Europe desperately needed foreign markets, Republican majorities in Congress struck repeated blows against imports—and, not incidentally, against the principle of free trade embodied in Wilson's Fourteen Points. First the Fordney-McCumber tariff of 1922 and then the Smoot-Hawley tariff of 1931 raised rates to their historic peak at a time of collapsing international trade, no doubt making a bad situation worse. Along with self-interested efforts at global stabilization, the trend toward nationalist controls that had gripped the world economy during the war continued in peacetime and would deteriorate further into the ruinous economic nationalism of the 1930s.

Given the strong nationalist stance of American policy in the 1920s, it is confusing to characterize it in "internationalist" terms, as some scholars have done.[23] The fact that Republicans were not isolationists does not make them internationalists, at least not in any sense that would have been comprehensible to either die-hard Wilsonians or other postwar progressives. Rather, the choice was between two strategies of world engagement. The prevailing strategy was unilateralist. Putting national interests first, Republican policy makers sought to advance, unilaterally, the economic and strategic interests of their own country, even if that meant forgoing the opportunity for a grander role as world leader. The other strategy was keyed to interdependence. Putting multilateral cooperation first, progressive critics of U.S. policy argued that collective security was the necessary requirement for peace and prosperity in a shrinking world of increasingly interdependent peoples.

From the postwar years onward, the United States was torn between nationalism and internationalism. Before the United States could ever again become the world leader, its rulers would first have to learn the lesson that a hegemon must sometimes put the interests of the world system as a whole above the narrow self-interests of one country. Even after that lesson was driven home in the Second World War, the nationalist impulse would return time and time again, and the United States would go it alone, producing many strange instances where the leader of the world had no followers.

Producers and the Public Interest

On the domestic side, a new progressivism was born. Disenchanted with moral crusades and chastened by defeat, keepers of the faith took a turn toward economics, threw in their lot with the producing classes, and set out to win economic justice for farmers and workers. In taking the economic turn, postwar reformers edged closer to the left and set progressivism on a path it would follow for the next three decades.

Before examining the change in progressivism itself, it is necessary to look at the context in which it developed. The era of Harding and Coolidge was the most pro-business that Washington had seen in a generation. After a quarter century of inroads on laissez-faire, the national establishment embraced the market with a vengeance. Announcing that "the business of America is business," President Coolidge took over upon Harding's death in 1923 and continued the pro-business foreign policy of "the diplomacy of the dollar." With business back in favor, private interests feasted on public resources. After passing a bribe to Secretary of the Interior Albert Fall, oil industry executives received permission to begin drilling on public lands at Teapot Dome. At regulatory agencies such as the Federal Trade Commission, foxes were standing guard over the chicken coop. Moreover, in a dramatic reversal of progressive tax policy, Secretary of the Treasury Andrew Mellon shamelessly handed out billions in tax rebates, including a sizable donation to his own companies. Not since the Gilded Age had private interests had their snouts so deep in the public trough.

At a deeper level, corporate capitalism was gaining the legitimacy it had long been denied. Proclaiming the advent of "people's capitalism," corporate leaders identified "the American way of life" with high consumption, posed as public benefactors, and went so far as to anoint the market itself as a public sphere. Herbert Hoover, regarded by some as the Prime Minister of the Coolidge administration, pointed to the dominance of business organization: "The dominating fact of this last century has been economic development. And it continues today as the force which dominates the whole spiritual, social and political life of our country and the world."[24] It is an overstatement to say, as one critic did, "The early twenties brought the American people to their knees in worship at the shrine of private business and industry." But at the very least, big business was emerging from the shadow of suspicion that had hung over it since the days of the Robber Barons.[25]

The legitimation of business was furthered by the culture of consumption. During the era that Republicans loved to call "Coolidge prosperity," consumers took off in a seemingly unending race for Victrolas and Model Ts, worshiped movie idols Mary Pickford and Douglas Fairbanks, Jr., and followed every move of sports heroes such as Babe Ruth. Behind the commercialization of popular pastimes, a new consumer ethos was spreading in which people increasingly found personal gratification and self-esteem in the buying of things.

So long as prosperity continued, the consumer ethos continued to spread. Thanks, in part, to the rise in consumer spending after the depression of 1921–22, most of the indices of economic well-being rose over the next seven years. Convinced that the exceptional economic boom would last forever, business boosters proclaimed that progress had taken a new turn. Using the accumulation of consumer goods as the measure of improvement, one adman boasted, "We advertising writers are privileged to compose a new chapter of civilization."[26]

The turn toward private life hurt the cause of social reform. To Jazz Age flappers of the younger generation, the once-sainted Jane Addams seemed out of place among the new movie stars. Where young rebels had once intended to build a just society from the bottom up, the Flapper just wanted to have fun. Unlike the prewar New Woman, who occupied a pivotal position in a broad range of reforms, feminists of the 1920s re-treated to the narrow ledge of the Equal Rights Amendment, worthy in its own right, but cut off from any larger project of social change.

Having accomplished the passage of American women through the gateway to first-class citizenship, the old suffrage and reform lobbies regrouped into new organizations, such as the Women's Joint Congressional Committee, and set to work on a modest reform agenda. They were successful in converting the wartime agency for women workers into a permanent Women's Bureau, and their greatest achievement was passage of the Sheppard-Towner Act in 1921. Aimed at improving maternal and child health through prenatal education and nutrition pro-grams, the spanking new clinics that appeared mostly in the rural South and several northern cities were a landmark in fed-eral funding for public health.

Unfortunately, Sheppard-Towner was the exception that proved the rule. There was no other significant addition to the stock of social legislation at the federal level in the entire decade. Even after lowering their sights, reformers were stymied at every turn. Child labor is a typical example. Reformers threw their all into one last crusade for an amendment to the Constitu-tion prohibiting child labor. Despite a valiant effort, the amend-ment met its doom in Massachusetts at the hands of an alliance between the manufacturers association and the Catholic Church.

Meanwhile, consumption became so thoroughly identified with the American way of life that it was seen as a kind of pain-less substitute for civic engagement. As private satisfactions ate away at public life, growing numbers of Americans turned away from politics altogether. Voter participation in presidential elec-tions declined to (then) historic lows of less than 50 percent turn-out of the eligible electorate.

Confronted with these developments, intellectuals began to question the very notion of a public interest. In a series of books and newspaper articles attacking "the phantom public," Walter Lippmann, for example, bid farewell to the engaged citizen. He saluted, instead, "the private man" whose highest aspiration was to be left alone: "You cannot move him then with a good straight talk about service and civic duty, nor by waving a flag in his face, nor by sending a boy scout after him to make him vote. He is a man back home from a crusade to make the world something or other it did not become."[27] Lippmann went so far as to deny that there even was such a thing as an overarching public interest. Instead, in a view that echoed James Madison's argument for a republic of competing interests held together by checks and balances, Lippmann argued there were only competing publics, each with its own interest, bound together by their cross-purposes, which ought to be refereed by "responsible administrators." Having traded in the notion of the common good for the "anarchy" of private goods, in effect, Lippmann was proposing a broker-state as the appropriate administrative machinery for a society built around the marketplace.[28] As one of the most articulate of the founders of progressivism, Lippmann's repudiation was all the more significant.

Given all these discouraging developments, progressives might have been expected to fold their tents. Many did. But most significantly, a hardy band that kept the faith refashioned progressivism as a cry of protest in a conservative era. One of them was John Dewey, the country's most prominent public intellectual. Goaded by Lippmann's farewell to reform, Dewey restated the progressive case for "the public and its problems." Unwilling to give up the notion of the common good, Dewey embraced what he called the Great Community. Despite his seemingly Platonic idealism, Dewey grounded his concept in social reality, portraying the Great Community as the conscious expression of the webs of interdependence that made up modern society. The key to maintaining the common good, Dewey contended, lay in vigorous communication free of state coercion and open to all regardless of wealth. Instead of control by advertisers and other merchants of desire, the channels of mass communication should overflow with ongoing public conversation "so that genuinely shared interest in the consequences of interdependent activities may inform desire and effort and thereby direct action."

Somehow, behind his plodding prose, the essence of civic engagement shone through.[29]

Progressives also took an economic turn in the 1920s. Disenchanted with idealistic crusades, disgusted with 100 percent Americanism, and defeated on cultural battlefields, they decided that the best hope for progress lay in the unfolding of impersonal economic forces. According to journalist George Soule, his generation gave up their faith in messiahs and manifestos and, instead, "We felt the power of great historical tides; we were forced to recognize economic determinism and the strength of social habit."[30]

As part of this turn, progressives drew the connection between the public interest and the economic interests of the producing classes. Until now, they had wanted nothing to do with "special interests," fearing that too close an association with either labor or capital would undermine their efforts to balance the two sides. No longer posing as neutral citizens, they now proudly championed the interests of the producing many against the propertied few. Working with the Peoples Legislative Service, a Washington lobby for progressive causes, veteran reformer Frederick Howe reported, "My ideals were still undimmed: I had found a class whose interests ran hand in hand with the things I desired."[31]

For middle-class reformers like Howe, the embrace of economic forces came, ironically, as a kind of conversion experience. The old Howe was a self-described "moralist" who divided the world into good people and bad and saw politics as a melodrama of virtue versus corruption. Doubts crept in, however, that do-gooders could clean up the cities or pay a living wage, and by the end of the war, Howe had lost any illusion about upper-class messiahs bringing about a new world order. Finally, the new Howe was reborn as a self-described "realist," who believed that "the morals men held were in some way shaped by the things they wanted, by their economic interest, by the class in which they worked and lived." That led Howe straight to the cause of labor. Having discovered that "in America, as in Europe, there was conquest, plunder," Howe chose to cast his lot with the working classes, because he believed their interests were most directly opposed to plunder and closest to the common good.[32]

In siding with the producers, progressives rightly worried that the consumer ethos was eclipsing the social ethos. If people believed the good life could be obtained through shopping, why would they be concerned about social responsibility? The self-absorbed materialism of the day caught the eye of progressive author Sinclair Lewis, who took a satirical swipe at the hapless hero of *Babbitt* (1922), hopelessly enamored of household gadgets and motorcars. Progressive complaints about consumption sometimes took on a high-and-mighty tone, as in the plea of *The People's Business* for the American people to "turn aside from their present absorption in money, movies, radio, automobiles, and sports and respond wholeheartedly to a magnetic leader who will call them to the service of high ideals."[33] The demand that people give up their Model Ts and movie stars for the second coming of Woodrow Wilson was a sure loser. It also forfeited the chance to expose the subtle psychological and cultural alienations built into the commodification of desire.

Keeping faith with the producers, progressives reaffirmed the work ethic. Calling upon women to reject the manipulation of feminine identity by the hawkers of household appliances, feminist Anne Martin took a swipe at advertising images of homemakers "with sweet, seraphic smiles on their faces" working hard at electric stoves, furnaces, carpet sweepers, washing machines, and all the other wares of the advertisers.[34] Feminists who had read their Charlotte Perkins Gilman were galled by the advertisers' portrayal of work without sweat. Housework, after all, was *work*, and it was performed almost exclusively by women, either in their own homes, or as servants in someone else's.

Respect for work was central to the team of anthropologists headed by Helen Lynd and Robert Lynd who set out to examine in microscopic detail everyday life in Muncie, Indiana. Their book *Middletown* contained an exhaustive exploration of the decline of workmanship and its replacement by the treadmill search for satisfaction in leisure-time activities. Such criticism, however, had a hard time beating against the tide of consumerism with its illusion of freedom. What was an academic critique of the sexual sell compared to the charms of Theda Bara?

The progressive journey to the producers went down two paths. One headed out into the countryside. Rural reformers had a special aversion to the consumer ethos. Welling up from the deepest currents of American Protestantism, the feeling that consumption was the devil's pastime drove preachers and editors in the small towns of middle America to rail against the self-indulgent sensuality of the Jazz Age. Deeply suspicious of the wizards of flim-flam, plain folk saw fast-talking salesmen as con men who used the deceptive enticements of advertising to entrap the unwary. Against the images of slick-haired gents and flouncing flappers in the rotogravure section of the Sunday paper, progressive political cartoons pictured broad-shouldered carpenters hammering in the planks of the prosperous future alongside stocky housewives in aprons baking bread.[35]

Picking up where populists had left off a generation earlier, small farmers hurt by the collapse of the wartime boom and the closing of European markets banded together to fight high-interest banks, corporate agribusiness, and rate-gouging railroads. In an effort to reduce the power of parasitic middlemen, farmers seeded the Midwest with thousands of marketing co-ops, held up as an alternative to the corporate-dominated economy by the movement's most effective proselytizer, James Warbasse.

Farmers also called for national legislation to bring "parity" between agricultural and industrial prices. Hog and wheat growers, in particular, rallied to the banner of McNary-Haugenism, named for its Congressional sponsors, which proposed a complex set of taxes, price supports, and foreign dumping to boost farm income. Harking back to the mercantilism of the eighteenth century, McNary-Haugenism revived republican practices of public regulation of the market. Although it suffered the first of several defeats in Congress in June of 1923, and later a presidential veto, it remained very much on the agenda.

Going a step further, backers of public power called for government ownership of dams and fertilizer plants in the Tennessee River valley. From farming regions around the country came strong support for a proposed series of dams in the Tennessee valley to control floodwaters and generate electricity at the same time. In addition, there was the enticing prospect of cheap nitrate fertilizer from Muscle Shoals, originally built during the war as a government munitions plant. The question was whether development would go forward under public or private auspices, with none other than Henry Ford seeking to lease Muscle Shoals for his own purposes.

Supporters of public control were led by the indomitable Senator George Norris, "fighting liberal" from Nebraska. From his early days on a hardscrabble Ohio farm, Norris had been enchanted by a vision of rural development with electric lamps lighting up the farmstead surrounded by lush, well-fertilized crops, and he was not about to let the "trusts" take over the project. Vowing to take "the unconscionable profit out of the handling and development of property which belongs truly to the American people," Norris launched what became a ten-year crusade to put the Tennessee River project under "public control, public operation, and public ownership."[36]

The second path of the new progressivism led into the working-class districts of industrial cities. Nothing symbolized the difference between the old progressives and the new better than attitudes toward booze. Whereas the older generation often supported prohibition, the newer group were reborn as "wets," which enabled them to join with large numbers of Catholic voters in Al Smith's "wet" campaign for president in 1928.

Even more important in reconstructing progressivism was the growing weight of urban labor. Despite defeat in postwar strikes and declining membership in trade unions, working-class constituents had to be taken into account by a new generation of political leaders. In New York, for example, so-called "new unions," such as the Amalgamated Clothing Workers under the brilliant leadership of Russian immigrant Sidney Hillman, were close to the organizations of soon-to-be Senator Robert Wagner and Fiorello La Guardia, feisty member of Congress. The fact that all of these leaders were based in New York points to the shift in the center of gravity of progressivism from La Follette's midwestern laboratory of "the Wisconsin idea" to the sidewalks of Manhattan and legislative halls of Albany, where reforms were being incubated that would become key parts of the New Deal.

No one was more important in bringing progressive social movements into Democratic party politics than Eleanor Roosevelt. Her role in this regard, was, to say the least, unexpected. As a pedigreed daughter of the patriciate, she was raised among upper-class kin who were so "old money" they even looked down on the Vanderbilts as vulgar upstarts. Taken around Washington by her Uncle Henry Adams, she was given away by "Uncle Teddy" (the former president) at her society marriage to cousin Franklin. As a young woman, she volunteered at settlement houses and joined the National Consumers League out of a sense of *noblesse oblige* toward the poor.

Not until after the war did she acquire the commitment to progressive ideas that would animate the rest of her reform-filled life. While attending the 1919 international women's congress she experienced a new awakening to the problems and strengths of working women and converted to the kind of cross-class reform exemplified by women labor reformers. Joining the New York circle that included future Secretary of Labor Francis Perkins, she linked these women labor reformers to her husband's 1920 vice-presidential campaign.

Unlike many who found it impossible to make the transition from suffrage campaigner to political organizer, Roosevelt worked hard to mold idealistic reformers into political realists. Having acquired her political savvy in association with one of the consummate politicians of all time, she rapidly developed her own understanding of power. "Against the men bosses," she insisted, "there must be women bosses who can talk as equals, with the backing of a coherent organization of women voters behind them." Although frustrated for now, her circle of women reformers would become influential in her husband's term as governor of New York and then in the New Deal.[37]

Another aspect of the rebirth of progressivism was the ardent defense of civil liberties against the greatest suppression of free speech in American history. The catalogue of shame between 1917 and 1921 was thick with incidents: hundreds of antiwar dissidents in jail; Wobblies imprisoned under "criminal syndicalism" statutes; immigrant radicals held for deportation; five duly-elected socialists denied their seats in the New York state legislature; teachers fired for radical ideas from the public schools to Columbia University; homosexuals stalked by undercover police agents and arrested for consensual sex; and free-thinking sex radicals tried for speaking and writing what social purists deemed "obscenity." Undoubtedly, the most extensive violations took place in industry, where surveillance was constant, and countless thousands of labor activists were fired and blacklisted.

In response, dissident movements turned the defense of civil liberties into a shining light of progressive politics. In the thick of official persecution during the war, the American Civil Liberties Union had been conceived with radical sympathizer Roger Baldwin at the helm. Meanwhile, labor organizers who had lots of wartime experience dodging both company spies and the tin-star G-men of the American Protective League formed defense committees and enlisted the services of such heroes of free speech as flamboyant defense attorney Clarence Darrow. The defense of free speech and assembly was given top priority by the Farmer-Labor party, whose 1920 platform included as its very first plank "restoration of civil liberties," coupled with the freeing of political prisoners and the repeal of espionage, sedition, and "criminal syndicalism" statutes. For good measure, the party also called for an end to the anti-union injunction.[38]

It was in these years that the close links between liberty and labor were forged. The most famous international *causes célèbres* of the day were all linked to the labor movement. The list of causes included campaigns to liberate the aging Eugene Debs from an Atlanta penitentiary and to win freedom for Tom Mooney and Warren Billings, falsely imprisoned for bombing a preparedness parade in San Francisco. The most celebrated of all was the worldwide defense of Nicola Sacco and Bartolomeo Vanzetti, Italian working-class anarchists sentenced to death for a Massachusetts robbery and murder in a trial widely condemned as a travesty of justice, even by future Supreme Court justice Felix Frankfurter.

The systematic defense of civil liberties for labor organizers was evidence of the turn of the new progressivism toward working-class issues. In the repressive conditions of the 1920s, there was little that progressives could do besides issue furious protests, but the link between labor and liberty established then would hold fast into the 1930s, when the altered political climate permitted the passage of laws outlawing labor injunctions and supporting the right to organize. As with economic justice, the foundations were laid for a future in which the needs of the poor and working people would once again be linked to the public interest.

The New Progressive Politics

Although forgotten in years to come, the early 1920s was an exceptionally fertile period for progressive politics. Expulsion from the temples of power did not mean the end of progressivism, but rather the beginning of a new politics keyed to the producing classes, devoted to economic justice and world peace, and located on the left. Typically, it was associated once again, as in 1912, with insurgencies and third parties.

Third-party activity began in 1919 and continued the following year when a handful of labor progressives hastily assembled a Farmer-Labor party and made a quixotic run for the presidency with the backing of such local organizations as the Chicago Federation of Labor, the New York garment unions, and the Non-Partisan League. Meanwhile, the rapidly disintegrating Socialist party garnered almost a million votes for their imprisoned leader Eugene Debs. Despite resounding defeat, these efforts were the first round in what became the most vital period for progressive third parties in the entire century.

The origins of this remarkable foray into independent politics lay in the setbacks suffered by the labor movement since the end of the war. In addition to business-backed class legislation, union organizing had been stymied by the open shop drive in such basic industries as steel and meatpacking. Even where unions survived, their power was curbed, as demonstrated by the use of thousands of federal troops to suppress the mammoth 1922 strike of 250,000 railway shopmen. The shopmen's strike proved to be the last of the great volcanic eruptions of the era.

Defeat on political and industrial battlegrounds convinced even conservative trade unionists that the time had come for independent political action. Smarting from the rejection of the Plumb Plan for government ownership of the railroads, the otherwise conservative railway brotherhoods joined with machinists and clothing workers, among others, in the spring of 1922 at the Conference for Progressive Political Action. Despite discouraging vote totals for previous Farmer-Labor efforts, the progressive conference attracted a broad coalition of reformers and radicals to the cause of the producers. Stalwarts included the agrarian radicals of the Non-Partisan League, the National Catholic Welfare Council, and the Committee of '48, heirs of the first Progressive party who helped make the Conference for Progressive Political Action the pivotal progressive organization of the day.

Instead of the cross-class alliance of prewar years, more and more middle-class progressives were drawn into the orbit of the producing classes, where they attempted to refashion the Jeffersonian antimonopoly tradition for modern times. Echoing the populists of old, the progressive conference called for the election of candidates "pledged to the interests of the producing classes and the principles of genuine democracy in agriculture, industry and government." Hammering away at the producer theme, Frederick Howe, secretary of the conference, appealed to "the class that produces . . . to vote together, and leave the exploiters to vote together."[39] Fueled by union funds, the new progressive bandwagon picked up speed over the next several months and rolled to victory over conservatives in a good many congressional districts in the fall 1922 elections.

Meanwhile, a more radical force had come upon the scene. In a special case of the economic turn, the emergence of the communist movement in the United States represented in its own fashion the growing attention to political economy and third parties. Instead of appealing to middle-class conscience against the products of sweatshop labor, communists urged class-conscious workers to resist their own exploitation. At the same time, they rejected the syndicalist idea that workers could do it on their own. Instead of the idea of the Industrial Workers of the World (IWW) that "one big union" should take control of the means of production, they called for the "dictatorship of the proletariat" through the "worker's state."

Developments in Russia reinforced these shifts, particularly in respect to state power. Under "war communism," the Bolsheviks had seized the "commanding heights" of the economy—finance, international trade, and heavy industry—transferring capitalist property to the control of the worker's state. Having survived civil war and war with Poland, the Soviet Union emerged as the only successful radical regime in the world. Overlooking the terrible cost in blood, communists everywhere joined the Communist International, convinced that the Soviets must be doing something right.

By 1921, however, there was a sense all around that the revolutionary crisis had passed without either overthrowing capitalism or destroying communism. It was clear that everyone was in for the long haul. Lenin took advantage of the relaxation to decree the New Economic Policy, which reduced state controls in favor of market incentives accompanied by a range of openings to the West, including expanded trade, famine relief organized by none other than Herbert Hoover, and, eventually, accommodation with Germany at the 1925 Locarno conference.

The same slight relaxation was evident in the advice from the Communist International to the three separate American communist factions to emerge from underground in 1921 and form a single, legal organization. Unlike other parties, however, the Workers party, as it was then called, was a centrally organized, tightly disciplined organization. The hypocrisy of fighting for liberation while accepting the iron discipline of a party which called for proletarian "dictatorship" was explained away in terms of the historical necessity of defending communism against its many powerful enemies.

Ever since the Bolshevik revolution, communism had been an extremely contentious issue among American progressives, far more so than socialism. A good many progressives had passed through socialist territory on their journey of reform, stopping often to refresh themselves at the well of socialist ideas. Progressives and socialists had been adversaries but not, for the most part, mortal enemies. A handful of progressives who had moved left after the war found communist waters refreshing, too. The most famous was Lincoln Steffens, who returned from a trip to study economic planning in Lenin's Russia to say, "I have been over into the future, and it works." But by and large communism was a source of rancorous division. To Sam Gompers, any collaboration with communists was tantamount to treason, both to the labor movement and to the United States. Extending his running battle against the left, Gompers wielded the same kind of virulent anticommunism as the most rabid fomenters of the Red Scare. For their part, communists gave as good as they got, denouncing the aging autocrat of the AFL and his fellow misleaders of labor as capitalist lackeys.

Despite this animosity, communists had staked a claim to a prominent role in the labor movement on the strength of proletarian ideology, steely discipline, and proven courage under fire. Enthralled by the triumph of Soviet power, they believed as fervently as any crusading nationalist in the myth of their own historical destiny to bring about the ideal future. They were certain, too, that they and *only* they could provide correct leadership. Having rejected "dual unionism," the adversarial stance of the IWW, in favor of "boring from within" existing AFL unions, they engaged their adversaries in legendary battles for control of many trade unions. After emerging from underground, they also fought for control of third parties. The factional fights that ensued disrupted one progressive gathering after another, turning one-time allies into bitter enemies. For example, dismayed that his former comrade-in-arms William Z. Foster helped engineer the communist takeover of the 1923 Farmer-Labor convention, John Fitzpatrick vowed never again to cooperate with communists. Given all the sectarian bloodletting, about the only positive aspect to these factional battles was that control of third parties was actually something worth fighting for.

Under other circumstances, the farmer-labor movement might have bid for control of a major party, as the populists had done with Bryan's takeover of the Democrats in 1896. But as the 1924 election approached, progressives faced exclusion from the inner councils of the major parties. On the Republican side, the presidential nomination was sewn up by Calvin Coolidge, an incumbent riding a wave of prosperity. The contest on the Democratic side was much more heated, both for the nomination, which eventually went to lackluster John Davis, an Ohio governor with links to the Rockefellers, and for the soul of the party. Torn between urban Catholics and small-town Protestants, the convention could not even summon the courage to pass a resolution condemning the Ku Klux Klan.

In this dismal atmosphere, many progressives decided they had nowhere else to go but a third party. Fortunately, the progressive bandwagon had enough momentum to make a run for the presidency seem feasible. Built on the scaffolding of the Conference for Progressive Political Action, the new Progressive party presented itself as an organization of, by, and for the producers. In selecting "Fighting Bob" La Follette as their nominee, the delegates to the July 4 convention in Cleveland chose someone who had been fighting for social and economic justice for more than two decades. Unable to find another progressive of national stature, the campaign selected the relatively unknown Senator Burton K. Wheeler of Montana as the vice-presidential running mate.[40]

Like all protest movements, the La Follette campaign was no ordinary run for office but a righteous crusade. Campaign literature lionized hardworking men and women who had the taste of sawdust or flour dust in their mouths and whose blood boiled at the thought of grasping middlemen and rich society dames stealing the fruits of honest toil. In pitting honest working people against corrupt moneyed interests, the campaign reenacted the familiar populist division between "the people" and Wall Street.

Whenever there was a need to summon a righteous host to battle against the forces of evil, someone was sure to put new words to the "Battle Hymn of the Republic," and the La Follette campaign was no exception. Echoing labor's anthem "Solidarity Forever," another variation on the same theme, a campaign song rallied the workers of the cities, farmers of the valleys, and miners of the mountains to join the struggle of "Fighting Bob."

> They may beat us with their money, but they'll know they've
>   had a fight;
> The masses of the people now begin to see the light;
> Raise the flag of freedom for La Follette and the right,
> While we go marching on.[41]

Revving up the rhetorical assault on plutocracy, the Progressive party called for public control of railroads, mines, utilities, and the like, although, in deference to conservative trade unions and middle-class reformers, it stopped well short of any demand for full-scale nationalization of big business. In the same fashion, it called for modest regulations of the labor market—the living wage, equal pay for women and men, women's protective laws—but stopped short of socialist proposals for public employment. Likewise, it supported moderate social welfare, such as the Sheppard-Towner program. Overall, the Progressive party combined the agrarian radicalism of the populists with the reform goals of urban labor and social reformers, toned down for a conservative era. In comparison to previous third parties, it stood somewhere between the heated populist calls for nationalization in the 1890s and the tepid proposals of the New Nationalists of 1912. In comparison to the major parties in 1924, it was clearly on the left.

Party organizers did their best to unify agrarian and urban discontent. While the party's major voting base lay in the countryside, the core of party organization and nearly all its budget came from the trade unions—notably, the railway brotherhoods, the Machinists, and the Mine Workers. Furious at being excluded from the higher circles of power, even the AFL with the aging Gompers at the helm made an exception to its nonpartisan rule and supported the party. To please the anticommunist ideologues including those at the AFL, La Follette publically rejected any cooperation with communists, whom he deemed "mortal enemies."[42] Additional support came from social reformers of the League of Women Voters and feminists of the National Women's party, who organized a Women's Committee for Political Action that was folded into the campaign organization. Although exclusion from the voter rolls meant African-American voters were too few in number to be a significant force, the party's social justice credentials were enhanced by endorsement from several NAACP officials, including the persistently progressive W. E. B. Du Bois.

Analysis of voting patterns reveals the outlines of the progressive coalition.[43] In the upper Midwest and the plains states (Minnesota, Iowa, the Dakotas), German and Scandinavian farmers and skilled workers rallied to La Follette's banner, and he also drew support from the bastions of reform in California and Washington. In all of these states, he came in second. He also did well in Chicago and a few other cities where the nexus of left-wing unions, socialists, and farmer-laborites gave progressivism a toehold among urban ethnics.

Nonetheless, when the votes were tallied, the Progressive party was thoroughly trounced. While Coolidge ran away with the victory, La Follette came in a distant third. His 4.8 million votes were some 17 percent of the total, more than the People's party of 1892, but a good deal less than Teddy Roosevelt's 27 percent for the Progressive party of 1912. The party had many weaknesses. For example, it made a poor showing among women voters, which came as a surprise to women's rights activists who believed, with Eleanor Roosevelt, that "women are by nature progressive."[44] Equally disappointing was the failure to attract other progressives, such as George Norris of Nebraska. The absence of breakaway segments of the major party organizations was fatal. Votes have to be rounded up at the local level on election day, and the only place where a local machine went to work for La Follette was his native Wisconsin, which gave him the only electoral votes he received.

Still, the Progressive party would have done much better were it not for a total blank in the South. Given his stands on lynching, women's rights, and imperialism, there was no point even in campaigning in the segregated South, and La Follette actually finished *behind* the hated Republicans in *all* deep south states from Virginia to Arkansas, in several border states, and in the southwest. Before the war the progressive tent had been big enough to include improvement-minded southerners, including President Wilson himself, but when elite Wilsonians abandoned reform in 1919, that left the field to left-leaning movements that were anathema in Dixie.

La Follette's defeat ended the postwar flurry of third-party activity, but it did not wipe out progressivism. Reconstructed around the peace movement and the producing classes, progressivism was born anew in the early 1920s. Although obscured behind a cloud of discouragement, the new lease on life quite unexpectedly prepared progressives well for the very different political climate that arrived with the Great Depression.

INTERNATIONALISM AND SOCIAL REFORM: The Women's Peace Party promotes international cooperation against war and imperialism. Progressive internationalists such as Crystal Eastman (far right) typically fought for world peace and social justice (including gender equality) as parts of the same quest for a better world. (Courtesy of the Swarthmore College Peace Collection)

Conclusion

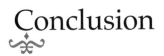

The string of defeats on all fronts could easily have made the 1920s the graveyard of progressivism. In the tumultuous aftermath of the war, the national establishment drew back from reform, fearing that ideas they had embraced only yesterday had somehow morphed into mortal threats to civilization. Although grassroots reformers were not without influence in foreign policy, their idea of international cooperation was a far cry from the unilateralism of U.S. diplomacy, just as hopes for social welfare and labor reform were dead letters in the succession of business-oriented Republican administrations.

Instead of the forecasted "new day" of people's power, the United States entered what was called a New Era dominated by giant corporations and international finance. Beginning in 1924 with the advent of European recovery and "Coolidge prosperity," the American economic model, supplemented by international financial agreements funded by American capital, seemed to have overcome the dislocations of war and the mistakes of the peace. In this climate, it was not the kind of dialectical materialism associated with the Soviet Union that seemed to point to the future of humanity, but the capitalist materialism of prosperous America.

Anyone who objected to the notion of a brilliant New Era had their noses rubbed in the skyrocketing prices on the New York

Stock Exchange. Prosperity fostered the belief that the last chapter was being written in the book of human progress. After seven fat years, Herbert Hoover dared to prophesy in 1928 that a utopia of universal abundance was at hand. "We in America today are nearer to the final triumph over poverty," he boasted, "than ever before in the history of any land."[1]

No wonder the mood among reformers was grim. Gone was the fresh-faced optimism of the prewar years. Gone were the illusions of the war for democracy. Gone were the visionary hopes of the early days of peace. Instead, there was discouragement all around. Looking back on the earlier excitement, Walter Lippmann decided, after all, "It was only Berlin, Moscow, Versailles in 1914 to 1919, not Armageddon, as we rhetorically said."[2] A pall of cynicism spread over the land, as exemplified in Dashiell Hammett's somber crime novel *Red Harvest*, which is set in a corrupt and violent town, no doubt intended to stand for the country as a whole, presided over by a malign mayor named Elihu Willsson, a grotesque hybrid of President Wilson and his political opposite Elihu Root.[3]

In this bruising environment, many remaining progressives acquired a hard edge. Adopting "hardman" as a kind of *nom de guerre*, J. B. S. Hardman, a seasoned labor organizer, bid farewell to the millennial hopes of the immediate postwar period: "The emotions that overwhelmed people in those momentous days fail to excite us today."[4] Another veteran of the protests agreed. Tracking what had become of his comrades, George Soule noted that some had become "tired radicals" while others had become prophets of Hoover's New Era. The few who retained their radical convictions became "hard-boiled" and turned their attention to the economic interests of the producers.[5]

The economic turn was a mixed blessing for the progressive tradition. In some respects, it marked a retreat from the fulsome era of reform before the war. Prewar progressivism had been a vast, protean effort aimed at many things—regulating the trusts, curbing corruption, protecting workers, promoting the New Woman, and supporting internationalism. Although imbued with color prejudice, it had welcomed many ethnic groups into the American family, while seeking to raise the educational and moral level of the population. It had sprawled across the entire political landscape from the grass roots to the high peaks, from the Republican Roosevelt to the Democrat Wilson, from mild socialists to enlightened conservatives, and from the moral reformers of the Women's Christian Temperance Union to the social engineers of the American Social Hygiene Association. It had encompassed both spread-eagle imperialists and little-America critics of overseas expansion.

By comparison, postwar progressivism was a more compressed affair, resting primarily on the quests for world peace and economic justice, vital in their own right, but with much less political weight. The break came in 1919, and in chronicling the change, we have found it necessary to examine the ways social conflicts at home were entangled with world war and world revolution. As many sensed at the time, the 1910s saw the beginning of an epoch-making conjuncture in world history involving deep economic and social disturbances in industrial countries, a wave of revolution in the agrarian belt from China to Mexico to Russia, and the beginning of the end of European hegemony.

In responding to these events, progressives from Wilson on down were torn between two impulses, one messianic, the other cosmopolitan. Sometimes they aimed to change the world according to American design—to redeem corrupt Europe, control the Mexican Revolution, and rescue Russia from bolshevism. At other times, they sought to cooperate with other peoples in improving social and economic conditions and crafting a "peace without victory." They pursued divided impulses in domestic policy, as well. While promoting labor peace with the War Labor Board, the Wilson administration also suppressed dissent with the Espionage Act. While imposing public control of the railroads, it consolidated corporate power with the War Industries Board. And while promising self-determination for oppressed nations, it fomented intolerance with the Creel Committee.

These inconsistencies did not prevent the United States and Woodrow Wilson, in particular, from enjoying a spectacular moment of world leadership at the end of the war. From all quarters, war-weary and oppressed peoples looked to Wilson and his Fourteen Points to lead them our of the horrors of war into a new day. In the United States, social movements burst forth in dreams of industrial democracy and social justice, along with visions of international cooperation for world peace. It takes a considerable effort of the imagination to recapture this moment of millennial hope when everything seemed possible.

But it could not last. There were too many contradictions—nationalism and internationalism, capital and labor, revolution and counterrevolution, white supremacy and black rebellion—for radical change to sweep them away, or for Wilson's "new world order" to override them all. Faced with unprecedented class and racial disorder at home, the Wilson administration turned its back on progressivism's highest ideals—social and economic justice, civic engagement, internationalism—and ordered the suppression of popular discontent.

When the national establishment turned its back on reform and world leadership at the same time, many believed progressivism was doomed to die. The founding generation was, in fact, dying off. All through the 1920s, obituaries were being written for its leading lights, starting in 1919 with Teddy Roosevelt and followed over the next several years by Woodrow Wilson, who never fully recovered from his paralyzing stroke, and Robert La Follette, who would not have lived out his term had he been elected president in 1924. Eugene Debs and Sam Gompers joined the parade to the grave, as well, remembered afterward as very different kinds of heroes. Sadly, some were cut down too early. When Crystal Eastman died in 1927 at 46 of chronic nephritis, her colleagues paid her glowing tributes: Claude McKay, poet of the Harlem Renaissance, praised her "daring freedom of thought and action" and Freda Kirchwey, future editor of *The Nation*, remembered how Eastman threw herself "with reckless vigor into every cause that promised a finer life to the world. She spent herself wholly, and died—too young."[6]

But to paraphrase Mark Twain, reports of the death of progressivism were greatly exaggerated. In fact, it was alive and kicking. Taking inspiration from old-timers like the indomitable

Jane Addams, an emerging generation that included reformers like Eleanor Roosevelt and unionists like Sidney Hillman were heading off in new directions. The broadest movement was toward world peace, where a deeper realism about the behavior of nation-states was accompanied by intensified criticism of U.S. imperialism. Another was the much-expanded struggle for civil liberties. Yet another was economic justice, where the new progressives picked up old populist themes to place a new emphasis on economic reforms of direct benefit to the producers, including labor's right to organize, rural development, production for use instead of profit, national planning, redistribution of wealth, and social welfare. What is most significant is that the whole range of proposals carved out in the harsh conditions of the early 1920s would become basic building blocks of progressive politics for decades to come, returning to the center of American politics in the 1930s when they had a significant impact on Franklin Roosevelt's New Deal.

The new progressivism, then, was in some ways an advance. In addition to expanding the search for world peace and economic justice, it was more inclusive of the broad range of the American population. Even as it abandoned cultural issues dear to Anglo-Saxon Protestants, it drew closer to the diverse ethnic and religious mix on the sidewalks of New York and other cities. Having lost its crusading zeal, it gained a healthy spirit of toleration that went into making the repeal of Prohibition so popular.

As these points suggest, the future of progressivism belonged to third parties—La Follette's progressive machine in Wisconsin, Farmer-Laborites in Minnesota, the Wallace movement in 1948. It also had a bright future among Democrats. Having begun as a Republican insurgency led by the likes of Robert La Follette and Teddy Roosevelt, progressivism had shifted toward the Democrats under Wilson, only to be shut out of both parties in 1924. But the Democratic shift continued, in part, because of deepening links to urban working people, who were also moving into the Democratic column on election day. Much of the entourage around the La Follette campaign of 1924 showed up as the Progressive League for Al Smith in the losing Democratic effort four years later, and progressives opened new initiatives on the borders between liberalism and the left, including the Conference for Progressive Labor Action and the League for Independent Political Action, with John Dewey as chair.[7] In addition, the conservative capture of the Republican party had the unintended consequence of creating lots of future supporters of the New Deal, including one-time New Nationalist Harold Ickes and ardent agrarian Henry Wallace, both of whom wound up as prominent members of Franklin Roosevelt's cabinet.

For all these reasons, posterity would owe a debt of gratitude to those who trekked through the political desert of the Coolidge years. Their creativity and endurance in the face of adversity preserved the vision of a better future until its time could come round again. Having lost faith in revolution, George Soule nonetheless urged his fellow "progressives"—his choice of label—to work for "the disappearance of traditional capitalism or its change into something radically different, just as feudalism disappeared and changed in its day."[8]

Soule's challenge points to the key to progressive strength. The reason it survived adversity was the same reason it had emerged in the first place: because of the need to address the wrongs of the capitalist market and the failures of the international state system. American progressives were not the only ones to do so, but their example—both positive and negative—deserves to be remembered by anyone interested in changing the world.

WHICH WAY FOR PROGRESSIVE INTERNATIONALISM?: "Uncle Sam at the Cross Roads," The National Forum, ca. 1929–1930. Typical of the moral realism in postwar progressivism, Uncle Sam faces only hard roads ahead, but it is clear that the best choice is "international co-operation." (Swarthmore College Peace Collection)

Legacy

> And thus the whirligig of time
> brings in his revenges.
> —Shakespeare, *Twelfth Night*

It remains to inquire into the legacy of the founding generation of progressives. To become a tradition, especially in an ever-changing society like the United States, a legacy has to change if it is going to persist, and so it was with progressivism. From the late 1920s onward, progressives had to adapt to a succession of circumstances that were in some ways more daunting than the ones they had already faced, leading to unexpected changes in the quarrel with liberalism that had launched progressivism in the first place.

In watching progressives adapt to new circumstances, we would do well to consider the wisdom of the great French historian Marc Bloch. Musing on the nature of history before being killed by the Nazis, Bloch wrote, "Now, this real time is in essence a continuum. It is also perpetual change. The great problems of historical inquiry derive from the antitheses of these two attributes."[1] As we will see, the interplay of continuity and change governed the handing down of progressivism, as well.

In tracking the tradition from the aftermath of the Great War to the early twenty-first century, three periods can be marked out. In the first, from 1919 to 1948, progressives threw out the moralism of Prohibition and adapted ideas of economic justice and cooperative internationalism to a world that went awry in the Depression and World War II. In the second, which more or less coincides with the Cold War, progressivism seemed to disappear, pushed to the margins of a narrowing field of acceptable ideas in an era dominated first by liberalism and then after 1968 by conservatism. As we will see, the disappearance of a once vital practice raises the question of historical memory, or, in this case, historical forgetting. Not until the end of the century did the memory of progressive vitality show signs of returning during an uncertain period that began in the late 1990s. Explaining these changing fortunes is the goal of what follows.

To pick up the story at the outset of the Great Depression, progressive prospects took a turn for the better. Ideas only recently seen as ugly ducklings came swimming like a flock of swans back into the mainstream. With the revival of the labor movement, links between producers and progressive politics that had been broken with the defeat of third parties were forged again under depression conditions. The La Follette machine in Wisconsin, the Minnesota Farmer-Labor party, and other organizations in the upper Midwest pushed the Democrats to the left. Nothing was more important to the progressive revival than the 1935 formation of the socially minded Congress of Industrial Organizations, which provided regular Democrats with a large labor constituency eager for reform.

Again, as in the prewar heyday of socialism, the left was an essential part of the story of reform, only now the left was increasingly communist. In demanding radical change, the left's unemployed councils, hunger marches, and leadership of several CIO strikes widened the margins of political debate and put economic justice on the national agenda. Another goad to reforming the capitalist economy was the example of Soviet success in averting depression. Just as Wilson and the first Roosevelt had seen progressivism as an answer to the left, so the reforms adopted under the second Roosevelt were responses to more radical alternatives.

Once again, doors at the top were opened to progressives. The list of key players in the Roosevelt administration who had been schooled in progressive social movements is a long one. It included Frances Perkins, Felix Frankfurter, Harold Ickes, Harry Hopkins, and Henry Wallace, not to mention Eleanor Roosevelt herself. For the first time, the labor movement had one of its own in a president's inner circle, in the person of Sidney Hillman, president of the Amalgamated Clothing Workers. As in the past, such access to power was vital to progressive policy making.

In this altered climate, the "whirligig of time" brought progressives a lot of revenge. After more than a decade of frustration, the Tennessee Valley Authority, brainchild of Senator George Norris, finally became reality. Embodying the principle of "production for use," TVA exemplified the most advanced progressivism of the day. So did the Works Progress Administration, which put everyone from common laborers to mural painters to work constructing and decorating public buildings. As much as the great railroad stations of the early 1900s represented the triumph of private money, the post offices and museums of the 1930s represented the public alternative.

Some of the New Deal's fiscal policies bore a progressive imprint. Reversing the Mellon policy of rebating taxes to the rich, the New Deal reverted to the progressive principle embodied in the first income tax, leading to an increase in rates for those with the most ability to pay. Meanwhile, the imposition of a new "wealth tax" on top of the old estate tax led to howls of protest against "soaking the rich." Although little money was actually skimmed off the top, the wealth tax was a symbolic victory for redistribution, the principle that the state has a duty to redress inequality generated in the market. No previous administration had ever gone this far.

Another case of Depression-era revenge was the string of victories for the labor movement. In the 1932 Norris-La Guardia Act, for example, named for progressive warhorse George Norris and New York's feisty Fiorello La Guardia, trade unions won exemption from debilitating injunctions. By the time of Roosevelt's First Hundred Days, labor had shaken off its lethargy to win a clause in the National Recovery Act guaranteeing the right of workers "to join organizations of their own choosing," a right significantly expanded in the Wagner Act of 1935, the most significant piece of labor legislation ever passed in the United States. The poor were also enjoying a modest redress in New Deal social legislation. In dealing with the increasing numbers of have-nots in their midst, New Dealers drew on progressive practices to create the Public Works Administration, emergency relief, the Social Security Act of 1935, and the Fair Labor Standards Act of 1938.

Looking only at the boatload of reforms from TVA to fair labor standards, one might conclude that progressivism had, at last, won the quarrel with liberalism. Neither Teddy Roosevelt nor Woodrow Wilson had ever dreamed of bringing the federal government so deeply into everyday life with the purpose of redressing the inequities of class. Although some of the progressives who had come of age in the earlier period were unhappy with that degree of state intervention, it is fair to say that this social and economic legislation represented the progressive side of the New Deal.

But before awarding a victory in the quarrel, other aspects of the New Deal must be considered. As in the past, progressive goals were checked by the prevailing liberal solicitude for the market. Groping blindly toward a Keynesian approach, New Deal legislators tried to rebuild consumer markets by raising "purchasing power." The Wagner Act, for example, sought to boost consumption by encouraging workers to win higher wages through union organizing. Likewise, in providing income to the unemployed, the elderly, and the disabled, Social Security sought to rebuild consumer markets. Social Security also incorporated market determination of living standards by pegging benefits to prior earnings in the labor market.

The New Deal accommodated other kinds of inequality, as well. Despite pressure from the NAACP, the Communist party, and the circle around Eleanor Roosevelt, the New Deal refrained from challenging the racism built into American society, and, instead, supported racial segregation in housing and racial disparities in program benefits. By the same token, under the belief that women's place was in the home, it did little to disturb gender inequalities in the market and, in fact, replicated them in its own social welfare programs. Compared to the pioneering of the founding generation, the New Deal was timid about gender.

Disparities of race and gender were structural features of American capitalism, and in other ways, too, the New Deal went further in accommodating corporate capitalism than most 1930s progressives would have wanted. The Bank Holiday, the National Recovery Administration, and the Agricultural Adjustment Administration were intended to stabilize competition, improve efficiency, and otherwise rebuild producer and financial markets. The main precedent for these alphabet agencies was the so-called administrative state of the First World War, remembered with great fondness by many in the Roosevelt administration, including the president himself, who had been a minor official in the War Industries Board.

After temporary forays into state planning, the New Deal settled into the pattern established in the Wilson years of government regulation of a market system that, unlike nineteenth-century markets, was planned and managed by private corporations with the regulatory assistance of the state. Whether or not this new system is called "corporate liberalism," the fact was that the New Deal made peace with big business, just as the Wilson administration had, especially in the administrative state during the First World War.

The Second World War played a similar role in consolidating corporate capitalism. Even before Pearl Harbor, as the economy geared up for war production, the emphasis shifted away from changing the inner workings of the capitalist system to making the system work efficiently. The tendency to accommodate the market was evident in the increasingly Keynesian approach. For all the temporary expansion in government bureaucracy, the prevailing view at the end of the war was that the state's role in economic management should not rest on national planning, let alone a government takeover of giant corporations, but on rebuilding consumer markets through counter-cyclical fiscal policies aimed at maintaining consumer demand.

When all is said and done, the most reasonable conclusion is that the New Deal co-opted progressive demands in fashioning what was rightly called "New Deal liberalism." This new brand of liberalism *contained* progressivism in both senses of the term. That is, it incorporated progressive elements within it to create a new kind of social liberalism based on a social compact between business and labor; in the process, it stunted further progressive growth. At this stage of the quarrel, each side was forced to concede key ground to the other.

Turning to world affairs, progressive internationalism had its ups and downs in the interwar years. The rise of fascist dictatorships bent on military conquest posed an enormous problem, and, for the first time, at least some progressives joined with communists to oppose the common enemy. For their part, communists set aside years of castigating "bourgeois" reformers and socialist alike to forge a Popular Front with their erstwhile adversaries. This led to the mobilization of antifascist International Brigades in defense of the Spanish Republican government, one of the finest hours for both communist and progressive internationalism. Unfortunately, it was too late to stop Hitler and Mussolini, or to save the Spanish Republic.

As in the years before U.S. entrance into the First World War, American progressives were divided on how to deal with the renewed threat of world war. While some called for action against the dictators, many progressives joined with isolationists and pacifists to oppose it. Nonetheless, even before war finally came at Pearl Harbor, the trend among progressives was toward intervention, and their brand of internationalism had much to contribute to the ideological combat of World War II. Echoing the idealism of Wilson's Fourteen Points, the Roosevelt administration sought out the moral high ground by defining war aims in a series of idealistic proclamations beginning in early 1941 with Roosevelt's proclamation of Four Freedoms, followed by the Atlantic Charter and later by Vice President Henry Wallace's declaration of "The Age of the Common Man."

The once scorned progressive idea of collective security returned stronger than ever. Putting aside qualms about cooperating with communists, progressives joined other Americans in support of the Grand Alliance, the best example of collective security against aggression that had yet come along. Although the alliance between capitalist America, imperialist Britain, and Stalin's Soviet Union was primarily a marriage of convenience, the Allies swore allegiance to democracy, while the Axis powers vowed to destroy it. Progressive internationalism had its Second Coming at the founding conference of the United Nations in 1945. The UN seemed at the time to fulfill the old progressive dream of a concert of nations united in pursuit of world peace and social justice, and this time the United States would be a full participant. As the UN started to function, progressives had reason to expect something like the wartime Grand Alliance to continue into the postwar period.

Expectations were upended, however. Within three years of the end of the war, reform had ground to a halt, the Grand Alliance had split into Cold War camps, and progressives were being treated as ideological outlaws. Truman's ascension to the White House was followed by increasing antagonism with the Soviet Union, signaled by the adoption of "containment" in the 1947 Truman Doctrine, which was accompanied by a program of domestic anticommunism exemplified in the loyalty oaths required of government employees. The Cold War division of the world into seemingly symmetrical Western and Eastern blocs erected a wall between "us" and "them" that progressives, with their continued adherence to internationalism, found it impossible to breach.

Indeed, "internationalism" was taking on a whole new meaning in the Cold War. Instead of global interdependence of the sort Jane Addams would have embraced, the Truman Doctrine redefined internationalism to mean, in the polemical terms of the day, U.S. leadership of the "free world" against Soviet "totalitarianism." Cold War liberals counterposed internationalism to isolationism, which, in their view, had led to the blunder of Senate rejection of the League of Nations in 1919 and to the still worse American complicity in the appeasement of Hitler at Munich. Dismissing the likes of Addams as wooly-headed innocents, Cold War liberals, such as George Kennan, lambasted the peace movement of the 1920s for its sentimental pacifism, exemplified in its silly feminine campaign to "outlaw" war. They pilloried the Neutrality Laws of the 1930s as foolhardy isolationism. Such ideas, they argued, were totally unacceptable in the dangerous environment of the Cold War, where the Soviet threat required a tougher, realistic attitude. In making the case for a Cold War version of internationalism, President Truman asked rhetorically, "Which is better for the country, to spend twenty or thirty billion dollars to keep the peace, or to do as we did in 1920 and then have to spend 100 billion dollars for four years to fight a war?"[2]

Obscured beneath the seeming symmetry of Cold War antagonism was a deeper development, the ascension of the United States to hegemony in the international system. Beginning with the Bretton Woods agreements of 1944, which established the framework of the postwar global economy, the United States finally stepped into the role that Britain had played in the nineteenth century, supplying investment capital, stabilizing currencies, opening its doors to imports, and acting as world policeman. In addition, just as Britain had anointed itself the paragon of civilization, so American leaders took a leaf from the book of Wilsonian idealism and presented the United States as the model of freedom.

The precondition for world hegemony was internal stability, and progressives also had a hand here. New Deal and wartime economic reforms had forged a social compact between business and labor in which high-wage production, supplemented by the welfare state, stimulated mass consumption and provided the internal balance necessary for American leadership of the "free world."

What would the founding generation have thought of America's new role? If the ghosts of the founders could speak, what would they have said? It seems likely they would have given out different opinions. Both Wilson and Roosevelt would probably have been proud of American world leadership and the social compact at home and would have supported the Truman Doctrine and other Cold War policies. But others would have been Cold War dissidents. Looking down on the string of CIA-sponsored *coups d'état*, the spiraling arms race, and the Vietnam War, the ghosts of Addams and La Follette would have cried out against the overseas buildup of American power in a seeming quest for world dominance.

The dissident side of the progressive legacy had its last hurrah in the 1948 presidential campaign of Henry Wallace, the third time the Progressive banner was raised in American politics. With the New Deal in retreat and anticommunism on the rise, the Progressive Citizens of America, formed by associates of Sidney Hillman and Harold Ickes, decided to mount a third-party run for the presidency as a way of slowing the rightward slide. As the most prominent leader of progressive Democrats, Wallace was their obvious choice. Having been Roosevelt's secretary of agriculture and vice president until 1944, he had returned as Truman's secretary of commerce. Equally committed to economic justice and progressive internationalism, Wallace looked forward to the expansion of New Deal reforms and a continuation of wartime cooperation with the Soviets. That put him out of step with the administration, however, and when he spoke out in March of 1947 against the drift toward hostility, Truman promptly kicked him out of the cabinet.

Not one to go quietly, Wallace continued to speak out. Like La Follette, for whom he had voted in 1924, Wallace called for expanded economic justice, objected to the infringement of civil liberties in the loyalty oaths, and was not timid about criticizing U.S. policy toward the Soviets. In one crucial matter, however, Wallace departed from La Follette. He kept the door open to communists. The Progressive Citizens refused to exclude them from their ranks, with the result that communists, who had learned to call themselves progressives in the CIO and the Popular Front, became mainstays of the Wallace effort.

The presence of communists helped guarantee a strong stand against racism, exemplified in the defense of Paul Robeson's right to speak at a campaign rally in Peekskill, New York, against vigilantes of the American Legion. Militant support for one of the country's most prominent spokesmen for racial equality marked a new stage in progressive politics. Although La Follette had won the support of African-American civil rights leaders, he had not made civil rights an issue in his campaign. Wallace did.

However, so did Truman. In crafting his Fair Deal, Truman stole a lot of Progressive thunder on domestic issues, including support for full employment, national health insurance, and a civil rights plank in the Democratic platform that drove the so-called Dixiecrats to mount their own third-party campaign behind conservative firebrand Strom Thurmond (whose political career would last into the next century). Using support for civil rights to bolster their own moral credentials, Truman Democrats opened fire on the Progressive party for its communist associations. Arthur Schlesinger, Jr., impetuous member of the liberal Americans for Democratic Action, mocked Wallace progressives as deceitful "doughfaces" who resembled the despicable northern defenders of southern slavery before the Civil War.[3]

The criticism was unfair. The Progressive Citizens of America were not communist "fellow travelers" and did not support anything like workers revolution, democratic centralism, or proletarian dictatorship. Attempting to remove all doubt on the matter, Wallace, now editor of *The New Republic*, still a bible of progressive thought, declared himself a "progressive capitalist." But to no avail. In the increasingly rabid climate of the time, mere association was enough to make him guilty.[4]

At first, it seemed as if the split between progressive internationalists and Cold War liberals would also divide the labor movement, with much of the CIO going for Wallace, while the AFL went for Truman or the Republican Tom Dewey. In the end, however, it was no contest. Discovering great benefits in the Marshall Plan's reconstruction of western Europe and in Truman's Fair Deal, the CIO rejected the third-party option and went on to expel a number of left-led unions, most of which had supported the Progressive party, for refusing to sign non-communist affidavits required under the 1947 Taft-Hartley Act.

Wallace's resounding defeat ended almost a half century of progressive ferment. Whipped at the polls and unable to slow the juggernaut of anticommunism, progressivism all but disappeared, except as a not-very-effective camouflage for leftists. With organized labor growing increasingly complacent at home and militantly anticommunist abroad, progressivism lost what had been a central component of progressive politics from 1919 until 1948—its base among working people.

Part of the explanation for the precipitous decline of progressive fortunes lies, in part, in the success of New Deal liberalism in co-opting progressive ideas. To labor reformers, civil rights activists, and women's political action committees, there seemed to be little need for a progressive alternative so long as the liberal wing of the Democratic party was committed to maintaining social programs. Many whose hearts were with Wallace could not get around the familiar question in a two-party system: why squander your vote on a sure loser if you can defeat the right by electing a liberal?

A more important part of the explanation, however, was the chilling impact of the Cold War. Progressivism had flourished best when the border was open to the left—to socialists in the 1910s and early 1920s, to communists in the Popular Front and World War II. When these borders closed during the Cold War, progressivism lost both a source of inspiration and a spur to reform. Because everything from socialized medicine to racial equality was subjected to red-baiting, the margins of political debate narrowed significantly in the 1950s. It was true that social movements were sometimes able to use Cold War ideology as a lever of reform; the civil rights movement, for example, was brilliant in demanding that the United States, as the leader of the free world, grant freedom to African-Americans within its borders. But if, as Robert Kennedy liked to say, "politics is the art of the possible," then much less was possible in America after 1948.

The Cold War also hurt progressive prospects by blotting out the kind of historical memory necessary to maintain a living tradition. Historical memory is essential to a reform tradition in two rather different ways that evoke Bloch's paradox of change and continuity. First, remembering a past that is different from the present makes it possible to imagine a future that is also different from the present. Without historical memory, the status quo seems unalterable; with historical memory, change seems possible. On the other side of the paradox, remembering the past also provides a sense of continuity with those who came before. Memory knits together past and present in an overarching narrative that gives contemporaries a sense of purpose and direction. In blotting out the memory of the once rigorous progressive politics of the first half of the twentieth century, the Cold War nearly killed the progressive tradition.

For these reasons, it is not surprising that liberalism was seen in the 1950s by triumphant liberals and disappointed leftists alike as the *only* viable political tradition in America. In the quarrel with progressivism, it seemed that liberalism had silenced its adversary for good. While academics harkened to the message of Louis Hartz, progressive trade unionists such as Walter Reuther and economists such as John Kenneth Galbraith, who would have been social democrats in Europe, joined the ranks of America's liberal luminaries in support of Adlai Stevenson and John Kennedy. When it finally came time for another round of reform in the mid-1960s, the achievements of Lyndon Johnson's Great Society, including Medicare and the war on poverty, were seen as extensions of New Deal liberalism. And so they were. But they were only credited to the account of liberalism because the memory had been obliterated that these reforms had originally sprung from the progressive imagination early in the twentieth century at a time when it was borrowing from the left.

So thorough was the triumph of Cold War liberalism that the reform movements of the period were almost always identified with liberalism, not progressivism. The 1960s were brimming with vibrant social movements and illustrious reformers, but they, too, were recorded in the liberal column. The civil rights activists around Martin Luther King and the polite dissenters of the early antiwar movement were seen, and saw themselves, as liberal reformers. Likewise, Betty Friedan and her sister feminists of the National Organization for Women were avowedly liberal, forgetting that Friedan had once worked for a progressive union that had been expelled from the CIO and that, still

earlier, women's suffrage had been one of progressivism's greatest achievements. Historians contributed their share to the denigration of progressive reformers by painting them as Wasp elites
bent on social control of immigrant workers. Despite its kernel
of truth, this portrait did not do justice to the founding generation of progressives, the most cosmopolitan group of American
reforms yet to come along.[5]

Even when reform veered left in the late 1960s in militant protest against the Vietnam War, activists still shunned progressivism, associating it with imperialists like Roosevelt, while forgetting the bold anti-imperialist stands of Addams, La Follette, and
the Women's International League for Peace and Freedom. Likewise, when radical feminists went back to the Progressive Era
for inspiration, they looked to radicals such as Emma Goldman,
forgetting that the sex radicals were one wing of a larger movement of progressive New Women. All in all, the founding generation of progressives were showered with a condescension they
did not deserve.

Except in the area of racial justice. In a kind of delayed revenge upon the bulk of white progressives who, at the very
least, acquiesced in segregation, the increasingly militant movement of the late 1960s sought inspiration in black nationalists,
such as Marcus Garvey, and remembered Du Bois largely for his
race leadership, despite the fact that he was a thoroughgoing
progressive. The fact that the African-American freedom movement was the catalyst for the revival of other social movements
of the day helps explain why antiwar activists and feminists did
not want to be associated with a tainted progressivism.

The 1970s and 1980s did little to rescue progressivism from
exile. As "the Movement" shattered into a dozen fragments with
little sense of common purpose, there was a turn to culture and
to the identity politics of multiculturalism. Among intellectuals,
a vogue for "postmodernity" took "difference" as its yardstick
and refused to "privilege" any single struggle—certainly not
class—above others. The embrace of difference cast a shadow
over the whole idea of history as a single narrative, let alone a
narrative of progress. Replaying the economic turn of the 1920s

in reverse, the cultural turn was associated with the postindustrial decline of blue collar workers and the rise of information-age office workers who lived in a consumer economy that ran on imagery and symbols. Few on the cultural left thought of themselves as descendants of such resolute partisans of maternalism as Jane Addams or such tribunes of the producers as Robert La Follette. The lack of connection to a progressive past did not seem to matter, because difference and diversity seemed to be winning out over authority and cohesion anyway.

Victory in the culture wars, however, was overshadowed by resounding defeat in political economy. After a long wait, conservatives finally had *their* revenge. Modern conservatism had been born in the mid-1930s when old-style free-market liberals were forced to define themselves as conservatives in opposition to New Deal liberalism. Conservatives went on to suffer repeated political defeats, notably, in Barry Goldwater's disastrous 1964 presidential campaign. Although Richard Nixon won the presidency twice with conservative support, he was more of a political opportunist than a true believer, and, in any case, betrayed his supporters in the Watergate affair and left office in disgrace. Likewise, racial conservatives had been in retreat since the Dixiecrat bolt of 1948, while moral conservatives had been overwhelmed by the permissiveness of the 'Sixties and came out on the losing side in subsequent culture wars.

At long last, conservatives tasted victory in 1980 with the election of Ronald Reagan, a triumph reinforced overseas by Margaret Thatcher in Britain and Helmut Kohl in Germany. Wielding a slash-and-burn free-market philosophy, they proceeded to put the torch to progressive taxation, social welfare programs, and detente with the Soviets. The irony was that these free-market neo-liberals succeeded in turning "liberal"—that is, the social liberalism coming out of the New Deal—into a swear word.

Would a strong progressive presence have made a difference? It is hard to say. The years of conservative ascendancy did not lack for protest. Social movements staged some of the biggest protest marches in the nation's history. Solidarity Day in 1981, the largest labor rally ever mounted in the United States, recalled the days from 1919 to 1948 when progressive politics were sustained, first and foremost, by the labor movement. The ghost of progressive internationalism also hovered over the 1982 anti-nuke march in New York, the biggest peace demonstration in America history, which harked back to the vigorous peace movement of the 1920s. And the same ghost hovered over numerous rallies against intervention in Central America, which recalled the early days of progressive opposition to U.S. imperialism. Might these protests have become the basis for a new round of progressive politics?

For a brief moment, that seemed possible in Jesse Jackson's electrifying 1988 run for president. To anyone with a long historical memory, Jackson's insurgency resembled earlier Progressive party campaigns. Sounding a call to move "from the racial battleground to the economic common ground," Jackson's themes of anti-imperialism and economic justice resonated perfectly with the Wallace and La Follette campaigns, a fact overlooked by commentators who insisted on identifying him as a populist. On economic and foreign policy issues, Jackson was squarely in the tradition of dissident progressives going back to the early 1920s. Most significant, the campaign made racial justice an issue, while also showing that many strands of rainbow colors could be woven together in a more or less cohesive politics of reform, a point driven home by the fact that Jackson was African-American. Unfortunately, the suppression of historical memory took its toll. Cut off from the memory of a progressive tradition, the strands unraveled almost as soon as the campaign was over.

What's in a name? Did not a reform like Medicare smell as sweet, whether it was called progressive or liberal? Did not the high tides of reform under Wilson, Roosevelt, and Johnson contain both liberal and progressive currents? For that matter, were not the labels "liberal" and "progressive" often used interchangeably?

It is not a question of labels, but of what interests the political system is responsive to. And on that score, it *does* matter which tradition is in play. As the dominant tradition, liberalism is so bound up with the established order at any given time that it is often blind to suffering caused by the market and unable to imagine alternatives, let alone strive toward them. Victorian liberalism degenerated into a rigid orthodoxy. New Deal liberalism made peace with big business and failed to address inequalities of race and gender. Cold War liberalism shrank the limits of the possible.

So, too, with what was called neo-liberalism in the 1990s. The election of Bill Clinton, a nominally liberal Democrat, in no way marked the resurgence of the New Deal. Although Clinton's style and appointments acknowledged the cultural victory of 'Sixties permissiveness over 'Fifties conformity, his economic policies were cut from the same neo-liberal cloth as his nominally conservative opponents. Especially after the defeat of health care reform in his first term, he became a cheerleader for what was known as the "Washington consensus" around support of free markets. He pushed hard for the North American Free Trade Agreement and the World Trade Organization, and he got down on his knees next to Alan Greenspan, head of the Federal Reserve Board, at the alter of balanced budgets. When he proclaimed that the era of big government was over and fulfilled his pledge to "end welfare as we know it," it also seemed to be the end of liberalism as it had been known since the New Deal. Bad enough as it was for New Deal liberals, it looked even worse for progressives. They were thought to be a dying breed. To one author, they had been "left for dead"; to another, in what passed for optimism, "they only look dead."[6]

So many obituaries had been written for progressivism that everyone was surprised to see a stirring in the casket. Nonetheless, in the late 1990s, eyes fluttered open, and the long hand of the past reached out to put its bony finger on the present. Intellectuals rediscovered the virtues of civic engagement, Ted Kennedy, dean of the New Deal liberals, called for "a new progressive era," and the Democratic Leadership Council christened one of their favorite think tanks the Progressive Policy Institute.[7] Since the Democratic Leadership Council was a nest of neo-liberals, it is hard to avoid the suspicion that they were donning "progressive" as a kind of protective camouflage in an era when "liberal" had become a dirty word. Stranger still, from the ranks of conservative Republicans came John McCain to embrace one part of the progressive legacy in championing campaign finance reform. Appropriately enough, his hero was Teddy Roosevelt, like McCain, a conservative in progressive clothing.

But all was not masquerade. To the contrary, the progressive tradition of Addams, La Follette, Hillman, and Wallace really did show signs of life at the end of the twentieth century. The new-found Progressive Caucus in Congress sought new ways to counter neo-liberal orthodoxy and defend Social Security, Medicare, and other bedrock programs in the New Deal mold. The fact that these measures are commonly labeled liberal, not progressive, only underscores the distortions of memory. In addition, the new progressives marked the transformation of progressivism by fighting to preserve 'Sixties civil rights and affirmative action. At the same time, the new regime that took over the AFL-CIO in 1995 turned what had been a stuck-in-the-mud defender of the status quo into a vital force in favor of "fair trade," as against "free trade." Nowhere was that clearer than in the streets of Seattle in 1999, when the AFL-CIO joined environmentalists and other activists to protest the World Trade Organization's slavish devotion to the Washington consensus.

From Washington, D.C., to Genoa, Italy, demonstrations against globalization marked the first widespread, transnational protest against the ruling institutions of the global political economy. Just as progressivism first emerged at the end of the nineteenth century in a rejection of the laissez-faire orthodoxy of the day, so it seemed possible at the beginning of the twenty-first century that progressivism could become a vehicle for combating neo-liberal orthodoxy. Ideas of civic engagement and social justice made something of a comeback against the idea that the market automatically produces the best of all possible societies. Progressive internationalism seemed to be reborn in calls for "globalization from below." Just as an earlier generation discovered that to be a good citizen requires being a citizen of the wider world, so recent reformers rediscovered the connections between the local and the global.

That connection was driven home in perverse fashion by the terrorist attacks on the World Trade Center and the Pentagon on September 11, 2001. Whatever the long-term impact, it was clear that in the short term the progressive revival was dealt a serious setback, as the Bush administration's ensuing "war on terrorism" quieted many critics of U.S. foreign policy. Partly for that reason, the prospects of contemporary progressivism are filled with uncertainty. On the one hand, the end of the Cold War and the collapse of communism have invited progressivism to come out of the shadows and back into the sunshine where it had been before the days of red-baiting. On the other hand, the absence of a strong left—socialist, communist, or otherwise—removes a major stimulus to reform and a vital source of progressive ideas at a time when southwestern conservatives, not liberals, are in the saddle.

Will the reaction against the unwanted consequences of the global market lead to a new round of social reform? Will the outcry over private corruption inspire a renewed commitment to the public interest? Will protests over globalization lead to a new internationalism? Having left behind the most violent and destructive century in history, is it possible to restore faith in progress? Who knows? But wherever such questions are asked, the legacy of progressivism will be there to help address them.

Notes

Introduction

1. Anne Wiltsher, *Most Dangerous Women: Feminist Peace Campaigners of the Great War* (London, 1985), 211, 210.

2. Lippmann, *Drift and Mastery: An Attempt to Diagnose the Current Unrest* (Englewood Cliffs, NJ, 1961; orig. 1914), 16.

3. The growing literature on international reform includes Daniel Rodgers, *Atlantic Crossings: Social Politics in a Progressive Age* (Cambridge, MA, 1998); Ian Tyrrell, *Woman's World/Woman's Empire: The Women's Christian Temperance Union in International Perspective, 1880–1930* (Chapel Hill, NC, 1991); Leila Rupp, *Worlds of Women: The Making of an International Women's Movement* (Princeton, 1997).

4. James Kloppenberg, *Uncertain Victory: Social Democracy and Progressivism in European and American Thought 1870–1920* (New York, 1986). On the other hand, comparison of welfare states emphasizes the differences between America and Europe; Peter Flora and Arnold Heidenheimer, eds., *The Development of Welfare States in Europe and America* (New Brunswick, NJ, 1981); Theda Skocpol, *Protecting Soldiers and Mothers: The Political Origins of Social Policy in the United States* (Cambridge, MA, 1992).

5. Louis Hartz, *The Liberal Tradition in America* (New York, 1955); Richard Hofstadter, *The American Political Tradition and the Men Who Made It* (New York, 1948).

6. Lippmann, *Drift and Mastery.*

7. A key work for understanding the progressive response to war and revolution is Lloyd Gardner, *Safe for Democracy: The Anglo-American Response to Revolution, 1913–1923* (New York, 1987). The link between progressives and American expansion was first established by William Leuchtenberg, "Progressivism and Imperialism: The Progressive Movement and American Foreign Policy, 1898–1916," *The Mississippi Valley Historical Review*, vol. 39, no. 3 (Dec., 1952),

483–504. For a comparison of the two leading figures, see John Milton Cooper, *The Warrior and the Priest: Woodrow Wilson and Theodore Roosevelt* (Cambridge, MA, 1983). For a discussion of "missionary diplomacy," see Arthur Link, *Woodrow Wilson and the Progressive Era, 1910–1917* (New York, 1954); Link was updated by, among others, Emily Rosenberg, *Spreading the American Dream: American Economic and Cultural Expansion, 1890–1945* (New York, 1982).

8. Jane Addams, *The Second Twenty Years at Hull House: A Growing World Consciousness* (New York, 1930), 115; Addams, *Newer Ideals of Peace* (New York, 1907).

9. The first to develop the term "progressive internationalism" was Thomas Knock, *To End All Wars: Woodrow Wilson and the Quest for a New World Order* (New York, 1992), in which he shows the influence of social reformers and radicals on what is more narrowly called "Wilsonian internationalism." See also, Robert Johnson, *The Peace Progressives and American Foreign Relations* (Cambridge, MA, 1995). Knock and Johnson build on such earlier studies as C. Roland Marchand, *The American Peace Movement and Social Reform, 1898–1918* (Princeton, 1972).

10. The first to use the term was Arthur Walworth, *America's Moment, 1918: American Diplomacy at the End of World War I* (New York, 1977).

11. Michael Sandel, *Democracy's Discontent: America in Search of a Public Philosophy* (Cambridge, MA, 1996); Robert Putnam, *Bowling Alone: The Collapse and Revival of American Community* (London, 2001 ed.). See also Robert Bellah, et al., *The Good Society* (New York, 1991); E. J. Dionne, *They Only Look Dead: Why Progressives Will Dominate the Next Political Era* (New York, 1996); Alan Wolfe, *Whose Keeper? Social Science and Moral Obligation* (Berkeley, 1989); Michael Schudson, *The Good Citizen: A History of American Civic Life* (Cambridge, MA, 1998).

12. For a recent example of interpretive controversies among historians, see Glenda Gilmore, ed., *Who Were the Progressives?* (Boston, 2002). Variations of the top-down view can be found in James Weinstein, *The Corporate Ideal in the Liberal State* (Boston, 1968); John McClymer, *War and Welfare: Social Engineering in America, 1890–1925* (Westport, CT, 1980); Christopher Lasch, *The True and Only Heaven: Progress and Its Critics* (New York, 1991). Examples of more favorable views include Kevin Mattson, *Creating a Democratic Public: The Struggle for Urban Participatory Democracy during the Progressive Era* (University Park, PA, 1998); Leon Fink, *Progressive Intellectuals and the Dilemmas of Democratic Commitment* (Cambridge, MA, 1997); Alan Dawley, *Struggles for Justice: Social Responsibility and the Liberal State* (Cambridge, MA, 1991); Elizabeth Sanders, *Roots of Reform: Farmers, Workers, and the American State, 1877–1917* (Chicago, 1999); Robert Westbrook, *John Dewey and American Democracy* (Ithaca, 1991).

Chapter 1. The New Internationalism

1. Quoted in Thomas Peyser, *Utopia and Cosmopolis: Globalization in the Era of American Literary Realism* (Durham, NC, 1998), vii–viii.

2. The literature on international reform is growing rapidly. Recent works include Daniel Rodgers, *Atlantic Crossings: Social Politics in a Progressive Age* (Cambridge, MA, 1998); Ian Tyrrell, *Woman's World/Woman's Empire: The Women's Christian Temperance Union in International Perspective, 1880–1930* (Chapel Hill, NC, 1991); Leila Rupp, *Worlds of Women: The Making of an International Women's Movement* (Princeton, 1997).

3. Jane Addams, *Newer Ideals of Peace* (New York, 1907), 237, 145. On p.18 in the same volume, she wrote, "It is not that they are shouting for peace—on the contrary, if they shout at all, they will continue to shout for war—but that they are really attaining cosmopolitan relations through daily experience." Jane Addams, *The Second Twenty Years at Hull House: A Growing World Consciousness* (New York, 1930), 115.

4. Randolph Bourne, "Trans-national America," *The Radical Will: Selected Writings, 1911–1918* (New York, 1977), 248–64.

5. Addams, *Second Twenty Years*, 115.

6. Balch address of Feb. 22, 1916, in Emily Greene Balch, *Beyond Nationalism: The Social Thought of Emily Greene Balch*, ed. Mercedes Randall (New York, 1972), 39.

7. Defenders of the "new" immigrants often made their case for admission on the grounds of shared culture and color with European-descended native whites. See Gary Gerstle, *American Crucible: Race and Nation in the Twentieth Century* (Princeton, 2001), 120–21.

8. *The Atlantic Monthly* (April 1992), 50.

9. Quoted in Arthur Schlesinger, Jr., *The Cycles of American History* (Boston, 1986), 19.

10. William James, "The Moral Equivalent of War," *The Writings of William James*, ed. John McDermott (Chicago, 1977), 660–70.

11. Norman Angell, *The Great Illusion* (New York, 1910); the quote is from the 4th ed. (New York, 1913), xii.

12. On the role of gender in shaping foreign policy, see Gail Bederman, *Manliness and Civilization: A Cultural History of Gender and Race in the United States, 1880–1917* (Chicago, 1995); Kristin Hoganson, *Fighting for American Manhood: How Gender Politics Provoked the Spanish-American and Philippine-American Wars* (New Haven, 1998).

13. This and following two paragraphs are based on Carol Highsmith and Ted Landphair, *Union Station* (Washington, DC, 1988), 24–29; Works Progress Administration, *Washington, D.C.: A Guide to the Nation's Capital* (Washington, DC, 1976 ed.); Kenneth T. Jackson, ed., *The Encyclopedia of New York City* (New Haven, 1995), 890–92; Lorraine B. Diehl, *The Late, Great Pennsylvania Station* (New York, 1985); in addition, for Grand Central Station, opened in 1913, see William D. Middleton, *Grand Central: The World's Greatest Railway Terminal* (San Marino, CA, 1977).

14. Highsmith and Landphair, *Union Station*, 28.

15. Material on Wright in this and the next paragraph is from Meryle Secrest, *Frank Lloyd Wright: A Biography* (Chicago, 1992), chs. 5, 7, 8.

16. Sources for this and succeeding paragraphs on the Ludlow Massacre are Graham Adams, *The Age of Industrial Violence, 1910–1915* (New York, 1966),

146–75, George McGovern and Leonard Guttridge, *The Great Coalfield War* (Boston, 1972), the book developed from the Ph.D. thesis by one-time presidential candidate McGovern.

17. Primary source material can be found in the Rockefeller Archives, Rockefeller Family Papers, RG 2 "Business Interests," pertaining to the Colorado Fuel and Iron Company.

18. For Walsh's interrogation, see Adams, *Age of Industrial Violence*, 161–68.

19. Goldman quoted in Christine Stansell, *American Moderns: Bohemian New York and the Creation of a New Century* (New York, 2000), 117.

20. Lloyd Gardner, Walter LaFeber, and Richard McCormick, *The Creation of the American Empire: United States Diplomatic History* (Chicago, 1973), 305.

21. The account of the Mexican Revolution is based largely on John Hart, *Revolutionary Mexico: The Coming and Process of the Mexican Revolution* (Berkeley, CA, 1987); Robert F. Smith, *The United States and Revolutionary Nationalism in Mexico, 1916–1932* (Chicago, 1972).

22. "Mexico," *The Outlook*, May 2, 1914, p.14.

23. Hart, *Revolutionary Mexico*, 285, 289, 295.

24. Arthur Link, *Woodrow Wilson and the Progressive Era*, 119.

25. McGovern and Guttridge, *Great Coalfield War*, 269–71.

26. "Mexico," *The Outlook*, May 2, 1914, p.14.

27. Quoted in David Thelan, *Robert M. La Follette and the Insurgent Spirit* (Boston, 1976), 126.

28. "Resolutions" of April 26, 1914 in Justice Department File 168733; see also National Archives RG 94, Attorney General File 2154620–1,2,3.

29. Alfredo Varela, preface, *Insurgent Mexico* (New York, 1969; orig. 1914), 19.

30. Norman Angell, *Prussianism and Its Destruction* (London, 1914), 3.

31. Quotes taken from Ronald Stromberg, *Redemption by War: The Intellectuals and 1914* (Lawrence, KA, 1982), 3, 42, 1; see also, Robert Wohl, *The Generation of 1914* (Cambridge, MA, 1979); the key work for France is Annette Becker, *La guerre et la foi: De la mort à la memoire* (Paris, 1994).

32. Stromberg, *Redemption by War*, 43; Arlie Hoover, *God, Germany, and Britain in the Great War: A Study in Clerical Nationalism* (New York, 1989), 11.

33. *The Milwaukee Leader*, July 30, August 4, August 10, 1914.

34. *New York Times*, January 1, 1915, 1, 10.

Chapter 2. The Social Republic

1. Lippmann, *Drift and Mastery: An Attempt to Diagnose the Current Unrest* (Englewood Cliffs, NJ, 1961; orig. 1914), 16–17.

2. For a thought-provoking effort to encompass the entire Western attempt to subject the market to social control, see Karl Polanyi, *The Great Transformation: The Political and Economic Origins of Our Time* (Boston, 1944).

3. E. A. Ross, *Social Control: A Survey of the Foundations of Order* (New York, 1901); Theodore Roosevelt, introduction to E. A. Ross, *Sin and Society: An Analysis of Latter-Day Iniquity* (Boston, 1907).

4. Jane Addams, *Democracy and Social Ethics* (New York, 1902), 166, and passim.

5. Jane Addams, *Twenty Years at Hull House* (New York, 1910); Allan Davis, *Spearheads of Reform: The Social Settlements and the Progressive Movement, 1890–1914* (New York, 1967).

6. Jane Addams, *The Second Twenty Years at Hull House* (New York, 1930), 98.

7. Gompers was reported to have included some version of this in his speeches and he offered it as Congressional testimony; it was finally written down by *Labor*, August 4, 1956 (in George Seldes, ed., *The Great Thoughts* [New York, 1985], 166).

8. See Kathryn Sklar, *Florence Kelley and the Nation's Work: The Rise of Women's Political Culture, 1830–1900* (New Haven, 1995).

9. Addams, *Second Twenty Years at Hull House*, 159.

10. Frederic C. Howe, *The Confessions of a Reformer* (Kent, OH, 1988; orig. 1925), 252.

11. Max Eastman, *Love and Revolution: My Journey through an Epoch* (New York, 1964).

12. Margaret Sanger, *The Woman Rebel*, vol. 1 (March 1914), 8.

13. Emma Goldman, "The Traffic in Women," in Alix Shulman, ed., *Red Emma Speaks* (New York, 1972), 145.

14. Addams, *A New Conscience and an Ancient Evil* (New York, 1912), 206. Scientific studies showed that sometime around 1900 women's premarital sexual activity took off, so that by the generation that came of age in the 1930s, two-thirds had lost their virginity before marriage. Studies by Lewis Terman and the famous Kinsey report are summarized in Susan Kellogg and Steven Mintz, *Domestic Revolutions: A Social History of American Family Life* (New York, 1988), 112.

15. Floyd Dell, "Feminism for Men"; Wright quoted in Meryle Secrest, *Frank Lloyd Wright: A Biography* (Chicago, 1992), 213. Sex radicalism is discussed in Ellen Kay Trimberger, "Feminism, Men, and Modern Love: Greenwich Village, 1900–1925," Ann Snitow, et al., eds., *Powers of Desire: The Politics of Sexuality* (New York, 1983).

16. Jonathan Ned Katz, *The Invention of Heterosexuality* (New York, 1995), 1–32, persuasively argues that the couplet heterosexual/homosexual acquired its contemporary meaning in the early twentieth century. Trimberger, "Feminism, Men, and Modern Love," in Snitow, et al., eds., *Powers of Desire*, 131–52.

17. Du Bois quoted in Gail Bederman, *Manliness and Civilization: A Cultural History of Gender and Race in the United States, 1880–1917* (Chicago, 1995), 27.

18. For accounts of southern progressivism, see C. Vann Woodward, *Origins of the New South: 1877–1913* (Baton Rouge, LA, 1951; Dewey Grantham, *Southern Progressivism: The Reconciliation of Progress and Tradition* (Knoxville, TN, 1983); Glenda Gilmore, *Gender and Jim Crow: Women and the Politics of White Supremacy in North Carolina* (Chapel Hill, NC, 1996).

19. Belle Kearney quoted in Anne F. Scott, *The Southern Lady From Pedestal to Politics* (Chicago, 1970 ed.), 182.

20. George Tindall, *The Emergence of the New South, 1913–1945* (n.p., 1967), 13–17, 321–22.

21. Robert La Follette, *La Follette's Autobiography* (Madison, 1913), 760, italics in original; Amos Pinchot, *History of the Progressive Party, 1912–1916*, ed. Helene Hooker (New York, 1958), 127.

22. John Dos Passos, *The 42nd Parallel* (New York, 1969; orig. 1930), 371.

23. Whether the emphasis is on the persistence of free competition, as in Philip Scranton, *Figured Tapestry: Production, Markets, and Power in Philadelphia Textiles, 1885–1941* (Cambridge, Eng., 1989), or on managed competition, as in Alfred Chandler, *The Visible Hand: The Managerial Revolution in American Business* (Cambridge, MA, 1977), depends on whether the focus is on run-of-the-mill firms or on industry leaders.

24. Paul Kennedy, *The Rise and Fall of the Great Powers* (New York, 1987), 244, 271, manufacturing ratio calculated with 1913 figures.

25. Clarice Stasz, *The Rockefeller Women: Dynasty of Piety, Privacy, and Service* (New York, 1995), 137.

26. *New York Times*, January 1, 1914, 1.

27. John M. Glenn, et al., *Russell Sage Foundation, 1907–1946* (New York, 1946), 12.

28. Donald K. Gorrell, *Age of Social Responsibility: The Social Gospel in the Progressive Era* (Macon, GA, 1988), 174–75; see also Walter Rauschenbusch, *A Theology for the Social Gospel* (New York, 1917).

29. Quoted in Christopher Lasch, *The True and Only Heaven: Progress and Its Critics* (New York, 1991), 298.

30. Herbert Croly, *The Promise of American Life* (New York, 1963, orig., 1909), 25, 22.

Chapter 3. Empire and Reform

1. Herbert Croly, *The Promise of American Life* (New York, 1963, orig., 1909), 305, 304.

2. U.S. State Department, quoted in Paul Drake, "From Good Men to Good Neighbors," in A. Lowenthal, ed., *Exporting Democracy: The United States and Latin America* (Baltimore, 1991).

3. Roy Acheson, *Wycliffe Rose of the Rockefeller Foundation: 1862–1914* (Cambridge, Eng., 1992), 74, 75–80; Catherine Lewerth, *et al.*, *Source Book for a History of the Rockefeller Foundation*, 21 vols. (unpublished collection in the Rockefeller Foundation Archives, Rockefeller Archive Center, North Tarrytown, NY), II:294, 280, 439; Raymond Fosdick, *Chronicle of a Generation: An Autobiography* (New York, 1958), 257–59.

4. Jack C. Lane, *Armed Progressive: General Leonard Wood* (San Rafael, CA, 1978), 86–101. In other respects, Wood's attempts to impose American-style "good government" and the Anglo-Saxon jury system made little headway against traditional political practices and the existing Roman-Spanish, judge-centered legal system.

5. Quoted in Robert F. Smith, *The United States and Revolutionary Nationalism in Mexico, 1916–1932* (Chicago, 1972), 56.

6. Emily Rosenberg, *Financial Missionaries to the World: The Politics and Culture of Dollar Diplomacy, 1900–1930* (Cambridge, MA, 1999), 82–84.

7. Mary Renda, *Taking Haiti: Military Occupation and the Culture of U.S. Imperialism, 1915–1940* (Chapel Hill, 2001), 10, 301–3; John Johnson, *Latin America in Caricature* (Austin, TX, 1980), 161. Gail Bederman, *Manliness and Civilization*, 31–41. See also, Michael Hunt, *Ideology and U.S. Foreign Policy* (New Haven, CT, 1987).

8. Quoted in Hunt, *Ideology and U.S. Foreign Policy*, 127.

9. Quotes from ibid., 80, 129.

10. Quoted in Anders Stephanson, *Manifest Destiny: American Expansion and the Empire of Right* (New York, 1995), 90.

11. W. E. B. Du Bois, *Souls of Black Folk* (New York, 1990 ed.; orig. 1903), 10.

12. French Strother, quoted in Kevin Starr, *Americans and the California Dream, 1850–1915* (New York, 1973), 304–5.

13. Frank Morton Todd, *The Story of the Exposition* (New York, 1921), III:96.

14. Quoted in ibid., III:36.

15. Michael Kazin, *Barons of Labor* (Urbana, IL, 1987), 217.

16. Quoted in Robert Rydell, *All the World's a Fair* (Chicago, 1984), 211.

17. Ibid., 224.

18. Todd, *Story of the Exposition*, III:62–64.

19. The main sources for my discussion of the building of the canal are David McCullough, *The Path between the Seas: The Creation of the Panama Canal, 1870–1914* (New York, 1977), and Michael Conniff, *Black Labor on a White Canal: Panama, 1904–1981* (Pittsburgh, 1985).

20. McCullough, *Path between the Seas*, 576.

21. John Butcher, quoted in McCullough, *Path between the Seas*, 577; thanks to Stuart McCook for the lyrics to "West Indian Man."

22. John H. Clarke, *Marcus Garvey and the Vision of Africa* (New York, 1974), 8.

23. Marie Louise Degen, *The History of the Woman's Peace Party* (Baltimore, 1939), 30–37; Schwimmer was no stranger to the Americans, having been instrumental in organizing the International Woman Suffrage Alliance, of which Carrie Chapman Catt was now president. Catt arranged an audience with President Wilson, to whom Schwimmer presented a million signatures on a women's petition beseeching America to take the lead in mediating the conflict.

24. Harriet Hyman Alonso, *Peace as a Women's Issue: A History of the U.S. Movement for World Peace and Women's Rights* (Syracuse, NY, 1993), 56–66.

25. Woman's Peace Party, *Addresses at the Organization Conference* (n.p., 1915), 2–5; Degen, *Women's Peace Party*, 36.

26. Eastman quoted in Blanche Wiesen Cook, ed., *Toward the Great Change: Crystal and Max Eastman on Feminism, Antimilitarism, and Revolution* (New York, 1975), 23; Anne Wiltsher, *Most Dangerous Women: Feminist Peace Campaigners of the Great War* (London, 1985); Jane Addams, *Peace and Bread in Time of War* (New York, 1922).

27. C. Roland Marchand, *The American Peace Movement and Social Reform, 1898–1918* (Princeton, 1973), 240–43.

28. Marchand, *American Peace Movement*, 240–43; Blanche Wiesen Cook, ed., *Crystal Eastman on Women and Revolution*, (New York, 1978); Cook, *Toward the Great Change*.

29. Barbara Kraft, *The Peace Ship* (New York, 1978), 50, 94, and *passim*.

30. Quoted in *The Atlantic Monthly* (April, 1992), 50.

31. Following Peter Skerry, *Mexican Americans: The Ambivalent Minority* (New York, 1993), 25, "Mexican" will be used as a kind of shorthand for people of Mexican descent on both sides of the border; and "American" will be used for non-Mexican U.S. nationals, recognizing that in the larger sense Americans are a hybrid population that includes many Mexicans.

Mexican author-diplomat Carlos Fuentes forecasts "the problem of the other" as the defining problem of the twenty-first century: "California and especially Los Angeles, a gateway to both Asia and Latin America, poses the universal question of the coming century: How do we deal with the Other? North Africans in France; Turks in Germany; Vietnamese in Czechoslovakia; Pakistanis in Britain; black Africans in Italy; Japanese, Koreans, Chinese and Latin Americans in the United States." Carlos Fuentes, "The Mirror of the Other," *The Nation*, 12, March 30, 1992, 410.

32. David Healy, *Drive to Hegemony: The United States in the Caribbean, 1898–1917* (Madison, WI, 1988), 268–71, 263–66, which also reports that the U.S. absorbed nearly 80 percent of all Caribbean exports, including the products of the remaining British colonies; Lloyd Gardner, Walter LaFeber, and Richard McCormick, *The Creation of the American Empire: United States Diplomatic History* (Chicago, 1973), 305.

33. Information drawn from D. W. Meinig, *Southwest: Three Peoples in Geographical Change* (New York, 1971); R. E. Ruiz, *The People of Sonora and Yankee Capitalists* (Tucson, AZ, 1988); Harvey O'Conner, *The Guggenheims* (New York, 1937), 360; Carey McWilliams, *North from Mexico* (Philadelphia, 1949), 168, 179, 163; Eric Wolf, *Peasant Wars of the Twentieth Century* (New York, 1969).

34. Martin Luis Guzman, *The Eagle and the Serpent*, trans. Harriet de Onis (Gloucester, MA, 1969; orig. 1928), 38, 142.

35. Oscar Martinez, *Border Boom Town: Ciudad Juarez since 1848* (Austin, TX, 1975), 57.

36. Raymond Fosdick, confidential memo to Newton Baker, August 10, 1916, Fosdick Papers, box 2, Mudd Library, Princeton University; Bascom Johnson, "What Some Communities Have Done," reprinted from *Social Hygiene* (October 1917).

37. On the opposing side, restrictionists obsessed with race purity dredged up the theory of racial degeneration through hybridization to warn against the onslaught of the Mexican peon: "This blend of low-grade Spaniard, peonized Indian, and negro slave mixe[d] with negroes, mulattoes, and other mongrels, and some sorry whites already here." Quotes from David Gutierrez, *Walls and Mirrors: Mexican Americans, Mexican Immigrants, and the Politics of Ethnicity* (Berkeley, CA, 1995), 48–54; for additional evidence, see John Britton, *Revolu-*

tion and Ideology: Images of the Mexican Revolution in the United States (Lexington, KY, 1995), 27–30.

38. In the same vein, a report of the House Committee on Immigration warned against "the creation of a race problem that will dwarf the negro problem of the South; and the practical destruction, at least for centuries, of all that is worthwhile in our white civilization." Quotes from Gutierrez, *Walls and Mirrors*, 54, 55.

39. The account of the Mexican Revolution is based largely on the following: Wolf, *Peasant Wars of the Twentieth Century*; Lester D. Langley, *The Banana Wars: An Inner History of American Empire, 1900–1934* (Lexington, KY, 1983); John Hart, *Revolutionary Mexico: The Coming and Process of the Mexican Revolution* (Berkeley, CA, 1987); Robert F. Smith, *The United States and Revolutionary Nationalism in Mexico, 1916–1932* (Chicago, 1972).

40. Smith, *The United States and Revolutionary Nationalism in Mexico*, chs. 3–5.

41. Lloyd Gardner, *Safe for Democracy: The Anglo-American Response to Revolution, 1913–1923* (New York, 1987), 69.

42. Britton, *Revolution and Ideology*, 35.

43. Eastman quoted in Marchand, *American Peace Movement*, 243–44; Smith, *United States and Revolutionary Nationalism*, 53–54.

Chapter 4. Messianic America

1. Beginning with George Kennan, realist historians have torn away the mask of self-righteousness to expose the underlying strategic and economic interests in American foreign policy. Examples of realist works include George Kennan, *American Diplomacy, 1900–1950* (Chicago, 1951); Ernest May, *The World War and American Isolation, 1914–1917* (Cambridge, MA, 1959); Robert Dallek, *The American Style of Foreign Policy: Cultural Politics and Foreign Affairs* (New York, 1983). From another quarter, (anti)imperial historians following William Appleman Williams have stressed a relentlessly expanding economy: William Appleman Williams, *The Tragedy of American Diplomacy* (New York, 1959); Emily Rosenberg, *Spreading the American Dream* (New York, 1982); Lloyd Gardner, *Safe for Democracy: The Anglo-American Response to Revolution, 1913–1923* (New York, 1987). An ideological explanation is found in N. Gordon Levin, *Woodrow Wilson and World Politics: America's Response to War and Revolution* (London, 1968).

2. "1914—The End of an Era?" *The New Republic*, January 2, 1915, 12–13.

3. For insightful commentary on nationalism, see Eric Hobsbawm, *Nations and Nationalism since 1780: Programme, Myth, Reality* (New York, 1990); Benedict Anderson, *Imagined Communities: Reflections on the Origin and Spread of Nationalism* (London, 1983); Gary Gerstle, *American Crucible: Race and Nation in the Twentieth Century* (Princeton, 2001).

4. For insight on myth as the narrative form of ideology, see Richard Slotkin, *Gunfighter Nation: The Myth of the Frontier in Twentieth-Century America* (New York, 1992).

5. In the absence of a full-scale study of messianic Americanism, the following provide insight on specific aspects: Anders Stephanson, *Manifest Destiny: American Expansion and the Empire of Right* (New York, 1995); Ernest Tuveson, *Redeemer Nation: The Idea of America's Millennial Role* (Chicago, 1968); H. Richard Niebuhr, *The Kingdom of God in America* (New York, 1937); Albert K. Weinberg, *Manifest Destiny: A Study of Nationalist Expansion in American History* (Baltimore, 1935); Frederick Merk, *Manifest Destiny and Mission in American History* (New York, 1963).

6. For discussions of conservative nationalism, see John Finnegan, *Against the Specter of a Dragon: The Campaign for American Military Preparedness, 1914–1917* (Westport, CT, 1974); Jack C. Lane, *Armed Progressive: General Leonard Wood* (San Rafael, CA, 1978); John Carver Edwards, *Patriots in Pinstripes: Men of the National Security League* (Washington, DC, 1982); Gerd Korman, *Industrialization, Immigrants, Americanizers* (Madison, WI, 1967); Frances Kellor, *Straight America: A Call to National Service* (New York, 1916); John Higham, *Strangers in the Land: Patterns of American Nativism, 1860–1925* (New Brunswick, NJ, 1955).

7. Roosevelt quoted in John Milton Cooper, *The Warrior and the Priest* (Cambridge, MA, 1983), 84, 41, 85, 326. See also, Theodore Roosevelt, *Fear God and Take Your Own Part* (New York, 1916), 18.

8. Barbara Steinson, *American Women's Activism in World War I* (New York, 1987), 174–81.

9. Richard Leopold, *Elihu Root and the Conservative Tradition* (Boston, 1954), 114–15.

10. Kellor quoted in Gerd Korman, *Industrialization, Immigrants, Americanizers* (Madison, WI, 1967), 153; Kellor, *Straight America*; Higham, *Strangers in the Land*, remains the best account of 100 percent Americanism.

11. See Werner Sollars, *Beyond Ethnicity: Consent and Descent in American Culture* (New York, 1986); Gerstle, *American Crucible*.

12. Dewey, "America in the World" (1918), quoted in Robert Westbrook, *John Dewey and American Democracy* (Ithaca, NY, 1991), 203, 205.

13. Balch address of Feb. 22, 1916, in Emily Greene Balch, *Beyond Nationalism: The Social Thought of Emily Greene Balch*, ed. Mercedes Randall (New York, 1972), 39.

14. Kallen wrote, "in society each ethnic group is the natural instrument, its spirit and culture are its theme and melody, and the harmony and dissonances and discords of them all make the symphony of civilization." Kallen quoted in Westbrook, *John Dewey and American Democracy*, 213. Addams quoted in Marie Louise Degen, *The History of the Woman's Peace Party* (Baltimore, 1939), 17. Dewey embraced the orchestra idea, too, provided "we get a symphony and not a lot of different instruments playing simultaneously"; in Westbrook, *John Dewey*, 213.

15. Working closely with the Woman's Peace Party, she helped stage parades featuring horse-drawn floats with great billboards that condemned military training in the public schools. Harriet Alonso, *Peace as a Women's Issue: A History of the U.S. Movement for World Peace and Women's Rights* (Syracuse, NY, 1993), 71.

16. Grace Isabel Colbron, "The Ballad of Bethlehem Steel," in an AUAM pamphlet, *Seven Congressmen on Preparedness*, Swarthmore College Peace Collection. Another verse read: "A whisper, a rumor, one knows not where; / A sign, a prayer from a torn heart rent; / A murmur of Peace on the death-laden air, / But Bethlehem Steel drops thirty per cent."

17. Quoted in Arthur Link, *Woodrow Wilson and the Progressive Era* (New York, 1954), 274.

18. "The Titanic Struggle in Picardy," *Current History* (October 1916), 16; Romeo Houle, "The Horrors of Trench Fighting," *Current History* (July, 1916), 748; "Human Losses in the First Two Years of the War," *Current History* (November 1916), 450.

19. Irony is the hallmark of Paul Fussell, *The Great War and Modern Memory* (New York, 1975); a direct assault on Fussell's position is mounted by Jay Winter, *Sites of Memory, Sites of Mourning: The Great War in European Cultural History* (Cambridge, Eng., 1995); romanticism is emphasized in Charles V. Genthe, *American War Narratives, 1917–1918* (New York, 1969), which supplies a wealth of not always reliable annotations in an otherwise useful bibliography. A rich literary analysis is available in Stanley Cooperman, *World War I and the American Novel* (Baltimore, 1967), which stresses disillusionment with the war machine.

20. Arthur Empey, *"Over the Top," by an American Who Went* (New York, 1917); Frederick Palmer, *My Second Year of the War* (New York, 1917), 89; Mary Borden, *The Forbidden Zone* (Garden City, NY, 1930), 124.

21. Wilson quoted in Thomas Knock, *To End All Wars: Woodrow Wilson and the Quest for a New World Order* (New York, 1992), 107.

22. Samuel Gompers, *American Labor and the War* (New York, 1919), 175. See also, Melvyn Urofsky, *American Zionism from Herzl to the Holocaust* (Garden City, NY, 1975), 130–31.

23. *The New Republic*, June 26, 1915, 189; March 20, 1915, 166–68.

24. See Eric Foner, *The Story of American Freedom* (New York, 1998).

25. In Urofsky, *American Zionism*, 82, 79.

26. Mary Antin, *The Promised Land* (New York, 1980; orig. 1912).

27. Leonard Dinnerstein, *The Leo Frank Case* (New York, 1968); Hasia Diner, *In the Almost Promised Land: American Jews and Blacks, 1915–1935* (Westport, CT, 1977), 19–23.

28. George A. Devlin, *South Carolina and Black Migration, 1865–1940: In Search of the Promised Land* (New York, 1989), 184; W. E. B. Du Bois, "The Migration of Negroes," *The Crisis* (June 1917), 64–66; William Tuttle, *Race Riot: Chicago in the Red Summer of 1919* (New York, 1982), 90, 95.

29. President Wilson, the first southern Democrat elected to the office since the Civil War, hallowed the Civil War in the same terms used by Lincoln at Gettysburg, that is, an awful travail necessary for a new birth of freedom: Wilson, speeches to the Grand Army of the Republic, Sept. 28, 1915, *The Papers of Woodrow Wilson*, ed. Arthur Link, et al. (Princeton, 1982), 34:146; Feb. 10, 1916, 36:361.

30. For contemporary views, see W. T. Stead, *The Americanization of the World: Or the Trend of the Twentieth Century* (New York, 1902); H. G. Wells, *The*

Future in America (London, 1906). True, the America model was often a negative one. To European conservatives, the prudish moralism and crass commercialism of the United States were a clear warning against democracy and social
equality. To European socialists, on the other hand, America was a capitalist
hell-hole whose conversion to the socialist promised land seemed increasingly
unlikely. See David Strauss, *Menace in the West: The Rise of French Anti-Americanism in Modern Times* (Westport, CT, 1978); R. Laurence Moore, *European Socialists and the American Promised Land* (New York, 1970).

31. On the links between Protestantism and the Enlightenment, see Tuve-
son, *Redeemer Nation*; Reinhold Niebuhr, *Faith and History: A Comparison of
Christian and Modern Views of History* (New York, 1949); H. Richard Niebuhr,
Kingdom of God in America; Richard Miller, "The Grammar of Exceptionalism,"
Interpretations of Conflict (Chicago, 1991). On the relationship between reli-
gious/mythical thinking and historical consciousness, see Peter Munz, *The
Shapes of Time: A New Look at the Philosophy of History* (Middletown, CT, 1977);
John C. Gunnell, *The Political Philosophy of Time* (Middletown, CT, 1968). On
time and history, see David Carr, *Time, Narrative, and History* (Bloomington, IN,
1986); Paul Ricoeur, *Time and Narrative*, trans. Kathleen McLaughlin and David
Pellauer, 2 vols. (Chicago, 1984; orig. 1983).

32. Frederic C. Howe, *The Confessions of a Reformer* (Kent, OH, 1988; orig.
1925), 17. For discussion of context, see John Whiteclay Chambers, *The Tyranny
of Change: America in the Progressive Era, 1890–1920* (New Brunswick, NJ, 2000).

33. Paul Boyer, *When Time Shall Be No More: Prophecy Belief in Modern American Culture* (Cambridge, MA, 1992), 96–100; Robert Westbrook, "The End of
History," *Reviews in American History*, 21 (Dec. 1993), 628–33; George M. Marsden, *Fundamentalism and American Culture: The Shaping of Twentieth Century
Evangelism, 1870–1925* (New York, 1980), 149–51, capitals in original; to the
question of whether a Christian should go to war, *Our Hope* answered an un-
equivocal "No," even after the U.S. declaration of war. Spurning the postmil-
lennial Covenant of Works—the idea that human betterment was a sign of
God's favor—fundamentalists affirmed, instead, the Covenant of Faith—the
idea of the unencumbered power of God's grace to shape human destiny.
Scorning profane history, they embraced premillennialism, according to which
historical time followed a sacred calendar through three stages or "dispensa-
tions" that led ultimately to the raising of the dead at the Last Judgment.

34. Wilson, Address to the Senate, January 22, 1917, *The Papers of Woodrow
Wilson*, ed. Arthur Link, et al. (Princeton, NJ, 1982), 40:533–39.

35. French and British officials quoted in *The North American*, April 20, 1917,
in *The War from This Side*, vol. 3 (Philadelphia, 1917), 386, 387; A. G. Gardiner,
journalist, quoted in Knock, *To End All Wars*, 71. The French Ambassador argued for U.S. intervention, Jules Jusserand, *With Americans of Past and Present
Days* (1916).

36. U.S. Bureau of the Census, *Religious Bodies* (Washington, DC, 1919), part
I, p. 33. This is the source for all figures on church membership. An exact count
is impossible, owing to different definitions of membership; Jews, for example,
were seriously undercounted.

37. Woodrow Wilson, Address to Joint Session, April 2, 1917, *The Papers of Woodrow Wilson*, 41:519–27.

38. Senator George Norris, speech April 4, 1917, *Congressional Record*, 1st sess., 65th Cong. (Washington, DC, 1917), vol. 55, part I, 213.

39. Senator Myers, Senate speech April 4, 1917, *Congressional Record*, 1st sess., 65th Cong. (Washington, DC, 1917), vol. 55, part I, 223; Senator Ashurst, ibid., 222.

40. Senator Lodge, ibid., 208.

41. Robert La Follette, ibid., 225–34.

42. George Norris, Senator Williams, Senate speeches April 4, 1917, ibid., 214.

43. Senator Swanson, ibid., 205.

44. Ray H. Abrams, *Preachers Present Arms* (Scottdale, PA, 1969; orig. 1933), 86; *The North American*, April 9, 1917, reprinted in *The War from This Side* (Philadelphia, 1917), 3:373.

45. Walter Lippmann, *Drift and Mastery* (New York, 1914), 16, 17.

46. E. P. Marsh, *United Mine Workers Journal*, July 13, 1916, 7.

Chapter 5. World War and Revolution

1. Adler quoted in John F. McClymer, *War and Welfare: Social Engineering in America, 1890–1925* (Greenwood, CT, 1980), 173; William G. McAdoo, *Crowded Years* (Boston, 1931), 374; Ray Abrams, *Preachers Present Arms* (Scottdale, PA, rev. ed., 1969), 57, 58, 117; Joanne Karetzky, *The Mustering of Support for World War I by the "Ladies' Home Journal"* (Lewiston, NY, 1997), 39. The mainstream Protestant churches, YMCA, YWCA, and most institutions connected with the social gospel, such as the Federal Council of Churches of Christ, were conspicuous in avoiding criticism of the war. See Donald K. Gorrell, *The Age of Social Responsibility: The Social Gospel in the Progressive Era, 1900–1920* (Macon, GA, 1988), 279–89.

2. Abrams, *Preachers Present Arms*, 55.

3. Reverend Sunday quotes and information in this and the next paragraph are from Roger Burns, *Preacher: Billy Sunday and Big-Time American Evangelism* (New York, 1992), 251–55; George M. Marsden, *Fundamentalism and American Culture, 1870–1925* (New York, 1980), 142.

4. *New York Times*, June 4, 1917; Burns, *Preacher: Billy Sunday*, 251–55. See also Michael Walzer, *Just and Unjust Wars: A Moral Argument with Historical Illustrations* (New York, 1977); Jean Bethke Elshtain, ed., *Just War Theory* (New York, 1992).

5. Dewey, "America in the World" (1918), quoted in Robert Westbrook, *John Dewey and American Democracy* (Ithaca, NY, 1991), 203; Lippmann quoted in David Kennedy, *Over Here* (Oxford, 1980), 39.

6. David Levering Lewis, *W. E. B. Du Bois: Biography of a Race* (New York, 1993), 553–54, also reports that Du Bois was willing to accept an appointment (it never came) from military intelligence.

7. *American Journal of Sociology*, July 1915, quoted in David Danbom, *World of Hope: Progressives and the Struggle for an Ethical Public Life* (Philadelphia, 1987), 199.

8. McAdoo, *Crowded Years*, 385.

9. George Creel, *How We Advertised America* (New York, 1920), 117–32. Advertisers themselves were quick to take credit for selling the war. The chairman of Eastman Kodak proclaimed advertisers to be "the cheerleaders of the nation," and the trade journal *Printer's Ink* boasted, "The war has been won by advertising, as well as by soldiers and munitions." Quotes in Jackson Lears, *Fables of Abundance: A Cultural History of Advertising in America* (New York, 1994), 222, 220.

10. Ads described in this and preceding paragraphs from Karetzky, *Mustering of Support*, 75, 71, 43, 68, 69.

11. Woodrow Wilson, April 2, 1917, Address, *The Papers of Woodrow Wilson*, ed. Arthur Link, et al., 41:524.

12. John Chambers, *To Raise an Army: The Draft Comes to Modern America* (New York, 1987), 148–49.

13. Chambers, *To Raise an Army*, 148–49; Benedict Crowell and Robert Wilson, *The Road to France*, 4 vols. (New Haven, CT, 1921), I:23–25.

14. James Harbord, *Leaves from a War Diary* (New York, 1925), 43; Heywood Broun, *Our Army at the Front* (New York, 1919), 51, 23.

15. James Harbord, *The American Army in France, 1917–1919* (Boston, 1936), 105. In an earlier visit to Les Invalides, Pershing had planted a kiss on the Emperor's sword. This was a kiss sent round the world by the wire services; Broun, *Our Army*, 22.

16. The YMCA and CTCA are discussed in Nancy Bristow, *Making Men Moral: Social Engineering during the Great War* (New York, 1996); Allan Brandt, *No Magic Bullet: A Social History of Venereal Disease in the United States Since 1880* (New York, 1987). Abundant primary source material on the CTCA is in Raymond Fosdick Papers, Mudd Library, Princeton University; Josephus Daniels Papers, Library of Congress; National Archives Record Group 165, Social Hygiene Division; American Social Hygiene Association Papers, Social Welfare Archives, University of Minnesota.

17. Brandt, *No Magic Bullet*, 97. Again, the Mexican border offered ample precedent. Social hygienists working for the U.S. military put Mexican towns and the Mexican quarter of American towns off limits. Raymond Fosdick, confidential memo to Newton Baker, August 10, 1916, Fosdick Papers, box 2; Bascom Johnson, "What Some Communities Have Done," reprinted from *Social Hygiene* (October 1917).

18. Brandt, *No Magic Bullet*, 66, 101.

19. "Reply to Simonin," in "Papers Relating to . . . Prostitution," Fosdick Papers, box 3, Mudd Library, Princeton University; see also Bristow, *Making Men Moral*.

20. Fosdick, *Chronicle of a Generation: An Autobiography* (New York, 1958), 171. A glimpse into the violent fury just beneath the highly controlled surface of social engineers like Fosdick is revealed in an incident that receives fleeting mention in his autobiography: in a "moment of manic violence," his wife killed

their two children before taking her own life. As if he had been the victim, Fosdick wrote, "I never dreamed such a catastrophe would overtake me" (249–50).

21. Brandt, *No Magic Bullet*, 119, 106.

22. Max Eastman, *Love and Revolution: My Journey through an Epoch* (New York,1964), 34.

23. Paul Boyer, *When Time Shall Be No More: Prophecy Belief in Modern American Culture* (Cambridge, MA, 1992), 101–3.

24. James Weinstein, *The Decline of Socialism in America, 1912–1925* (New York, 1967), 145–76.

25. After the war the Chicago Foreign Language Press Survey sampled opinion in the foreign language press, making sure to cull views from both nationalist and socialist/anarchist sources.

26. William O'Neill, ed., *Echoes of Revolt: The Masses, 1911–1917* (Chicago, 1989 ed.), 257–58.

27. Rebecca Zurier, *Art for the Masses: A Radical Magazine and its Graphics, 1911–1917* (Philadelphia, 1988).

28. See William Preston, *Aliens and Dissenters: Federal Suppression of Radicals, 1903–1933* (Cambridge, MA, 1963).

29. Editorials quoted in Mary Louise Degen, *The History of the Woman's Peace Party* (Baltimore, 1939), 200–201.

30. Jane Addams, *Peace and Bread in Time of War* (New York, 1922), 138–45, 150–51. Her spiritual crisis led her to question her own first principles. For the time being, she reverted to a pure idealism, deciding that the best way to hold out against the mass mind in times of crisis was by standing on the rock of "the categorical belief that a man's primary allegiance is to his vision of the truth."

31. The founder Carrie Catt was expelled from the Women's Peace Party. Jane Addams wound up working for Herbert Hoover's Food Administration. Women's Peace Party, *Resolutions Adopted by the Woman's Peace Party* (Chicago, 1917), pamphlet in WPP Papers, Swarthmore College Peace Collection.

32. Frederick Howe, *The Confessions of a Reformer* (Kent, OH, 1988, orig. 1925), 276–77.

33. Randolph Bourne, "The State," reprinted in *The Radical Will: Selected Writings, 1911–1918*, ed. Olaf Hansen (New York, 1992), part I, 355–81. Dewey not only failed to protest the firing of his antiwar colleagues at Columbia University, let alone resign along with Charles Beard, he connived to purge *The Dial* of his most astute and acerbic critic, Randolph Bourne.

34. Quoted in William Leuchtenburg, *The Perils of Prosperity, 1914–1932* (Chicago, 1958), 46.

35. Addams, *The Second Twenty Years at Hull House* (New York, 1930), 159.

36. Baldwin to Louis Lochner, August 21, 1917, in New York Lusk Committee, *Revolutionary Radicalism: Its History, Purpose, and Tactics*, 4 vols. (Albany, 1920) I:1057; Max Eastman, *Love and Revolution*, 14.

37. Stanley Lebergott, *Manpower in Economic Growth* (New York, 1964), 512; Florence Peterson, *Strikes in the United States, 1889–1936* (U.S. Dept. of Labor, Bulletin No. 651), 21; Valerie Conner, *National War Labor Board* (Chapel Hill,

NC, 1983), 24–26. See also David Montgomery, *Workers Control in America* (Cambridge, Eng., 1979), 97.

38. Abundant source material on the use of federal troops in domestic disturbances is available in the so-called Glasser File. Compiled in the mid-1930s by Justice Department lawyer Abraham Glasser, the Glasser File, located in Justice Department RG 60 in the National Archives, is an incomparable resource, in perennial danger of being closed by the FBI, as it was for 15 years in the 1960s and 1970s. William Preston, *Aliens and Dissenters: Federal Suppression of Radicals, 1903–1933* (Cambridge, MA, 1963), 106 and *passim*, has made the most extensive use of these files and is a definitive guide.

39. See Philip Taft, "The Bisbee Deportation," *Labor History*, 13 (Winter, 1972), 13. Evidence indicates War Department complicity in this vigilante action. The military intelligence officer on the scene recommended military detention of the strikers because "they do not want to work and influence others for the bad." Although three people had been killed on deportation day, this same officer had calmly cabled his superiors "everything orderly." Capt. James Hornbrook to War Department, July 12, 16, 1917, in Glasser Files, box 7, Justice Department, RG 60. In the case of Globe, Phelps Dodge refused to deal with the governor, and the Maicopa County Loyalty League threatened to keep the mines open "under protection of volunteer organizations." Glasser File, box 7, contains copies of AG 370.61, with all the relevant material, including: incoming correspondence of Newton Baker, July 2, 3, 4, 5, 8, 1917; Maicopa Co. Loyalty League to Commander Southern Department, July 20, 1917; Baker to Governor Campbell, July 24, 1917.

40. On unions in Butte and the lynching of Little, see William D. Haywood, *Bill Haywoods's Book* (New York, 1929), 298, 301, and Melvyn Dubovsky, *We Shall Be All: A History of the Industrial Workers of the World* (New York, 1969), 391–92;

41. Federal Revised Statutes, secs. 5297, 5298, 5300; Edward Berman, *Labor Disputes and the President* (New York, 1968, orig. 1924), 59–62. Prior to the war, the use of the army as a domestic police had been constrained by the "insurrection" doctrine; that is, the Constitution, federal statutes, and military practice all prohibited the use of the army unless state authorities could not "guarantee a republican form of government," as stipulated in Article IV, section 4 of the Constitution. In cases such as the Ludlow Massacre, a presidential proclamation to this effect was required before troops could be dispatched. Now such constraints were swept aside as army department commanders were authorized to supply troops directly upon request of the governor without any prior proclamation of danger to the republic.

42. The main source on troop use is National Archives RG 407, Decimal Files of the Adjutant General's Office, AG 381 and AG 370.6. War Department cables in the Glasser File, Box 8, June, July, 1917, reveal the "public utilities" doctrine and the emergency directive for direct response to governors' requests; this was modified Nov. 20, 1917, to have requests referred to the adjutant general, but the requirement for a presidential proclamation was not reinstated until June 8, 1922; cf. unfinished manuscript of Glasser Report, box 10; on federal troops, see General Liggett to Adjutant General, July 19, 1917, Glasser box 3;

Attorney General Gregory to Baker, Oct. 23, 1918, Glasser box 7; Preston, *Aliens and Dissenters*, 113–14.

43. Elliott Rudwick, *Race Riot at East St. Louis* (Urbana, IL, 1964), 16–19, 27, 217–18, 46, 50.

44. Lewis, *W. E. B. Du Bois*, 554–55; forum of Los Angeles to Wilson, July 8, 1917, *Papers of Woodrow Wilson*, vol. 43, 128–30; John Hope Franklin, *From Slavery to Freedom* (New York, 1969), 475.

45. Hasia Diner, *In the Almost Promised Land: American Jews and Blacks, 1915–1935* (Westport, CT, 1977), 77, 75; Urofsky, *American Zionism*, 74–75.

46. Arno Mayer, *Wilson v. Lenin: Political Origins of the New Diplomacy, 1917–1918* (Cleveland, 1967, orig. 1959), vii.

47. Jurgen Kocka, *Facing Total War: German Society, 1914–1918* (Cambridge, MA, 1984), 57–62.

48. The main primary source for the People's Council is the Papers of the American Conference for Democracy and Terms of Peace, located in the Swarthmore College Peace Collection. Other sources include Lusk Committee, *Revolutionary Radicalism*, I:1058–76; Irving Howe, *World of Our Fathers* (New York, 1976), 316–21, 325–30; Steve Fraser, *Labor Will Rule: Sidney Hillman and the Rise of American Labor (New York, 1991)*, 142–43.

49. Nearing and Hillquit speeches in People's Council, *First American Conference for Democracy and Terms of Peace* (New York, 1917), copy in Swarthmore College Peace Collection, Papers of the American Conference for Democracy and Terms of Peace.

50. One exception proves the rule. Vowing to forage on green corn as they marched on Washington, Oklahoma tenant farmers staged the colorful but short-lived Green Corn Rebellion. Their populist views were evident in a poster they put up: "Rich man's war. Poor man's fight. If you dont go J. P. Morgan Co. is lost. Speculation is the only cause of the war. Rebel now." James R. Green, *Grassroots Socialism: Radical Movements in the Southwest, 1895–1943* (Baton Rouge, LA, 1978), 259.

51. Mayer, *Wilson vs. Lenin*, 225–28; *Bulletin of the People's Council of America*, August 7, 16, 27, 1917.

52. *New York Times*, June 1, June 5, 1917.

53. Lusk Committee, *Revolutionary Radicalism*, I:1075. *New York Times*, Sept. 1–4, 1917; anonymous report on "The People's Council Convention," September 1917, People's Council papers, reel 3.1. See also, Frank Grubbs, *The Struggle for Labor Loyalty: Gompers, the A.F.G. and the Pacifists, 1917–1920* (Durham, NC, 1968).

54. Reed quoted in Granville Hicks, *John Reed: The Making of a Revolutionary* (New York, 1936), 259.

55. This and the description below are from John Reed, *Ten Days That Shook the World* (New York, 1967 ed.), 126–27.

56. Robins to Theodore Roosevelt, August 24, 1918, Robins Papers, State Historical Society of Wisconsin, box 14, f. 5.

57. Quoted in Mayer, *Wilson vs. Lenin*, 302–3.

58. *Bulletin of the People's Council*, Dec. 14, 1917. The *Bulletin* from February through May provides a running account of the unsuccessful effort of Americans to join the second inter-Allied Labor and Socialist Conference.

Chapter 6. World Leader

1. The idea of an American moment was first proposed by Arthur Walworth, *America's Moment, 1918: American Diplomacy at the End of World War I* (New York, 1977); the most illuminating account of progressive internationalism is Thomas Knock, *To End All Wars: Woodrow Wilson and the Quest for a New World Order* (New York, 1992).

2. Quoted in Arno Mayer, *Wilson v. Lenin* (New York, 1967; orig. 1959), 276.

3. The metaphor of a magic mirror is used rather differently to characterize Puritan ideology in R. H. Tawney, *Religion and the Rise of Capitalism* (New York, 1950 ed.), 175.

4. *Times* quoted in Knock, *To End All Wars*, 146; John Horne, "Re-mobilizing for 'total war': France and Britain, 1917–18," J. Horne, ed., *State, Society and Mobilisation in Europe during the First World War* (Cambridge, Eng., 1997); see also Andre Kaspi, *Le Temps des Americains 1917–18* (Paris, 1976).

5. Mayer, *Wilson v. Lenin*, 36–58.

6. Frederick Lynch, *President Wilson and the Moral Aims of the War*, quoted in Frederick Lynch, *The Christian in War Time* (New York, 1972), 5–8. The dean of Divinity at the University of Chicago believed "patriotism is an evangel of peace and justice;" Shailer Mathews, *Patriotism and Religion* (New York, 1918), 101, and 32, 36.

7. *The Survey* (March 9, 1918), 633. The quote went on, "We have always had a welcome for a Kossuth or a Garibaldi: we have stood for self-determination in South America and Mexico against armed debt collectors; we went to war for the revolutionists of Cuba."

8. *Bulletin of the People's Council*, Dec. 14, 1917; January 15, 1918. (The *Bulletin* from February through May provides a running account of the unsuccessful effort of Americans to join the second inter-allied socialist conference.) Crystal Eastman proposal to AUAM, June 15, 1917, in Blanche Wiesen Cook, ed., *Toward the Great Change* (New York, 1975), 26. See also American Union for a Democratic Peace, in AUAM Papers, reel 10.1.

9. Max Eastman, *Love and Revolution: My Journey through an Epoch* (New York, 1964), 104.

10. Knock, *To End All Wars*, 144–47; Robert Johnson, *The Peace Progressives and American Foreign Relations* (Cambridge, MA, 1995), 80.

11. Walter Weyl, *The End of the War* (New York, 1918), 71, 51.

12. Ibid., 298, 299–303.

13. Johnson, *Peace Progressives*, 86, 85.

14. Larry Duren, "An Experience," unpublished memoir, p. 25, p. 37, 4th Division, 58th Infantry, Company K, World War I Survey, Military History Institute, Carlisle Barracks, Pennsylvania; Ronald Schaffer, *American in the Great War: The Rise of the War Welfare State* (New York, 1991), 182–98. See also, Mark Meigs, *Optimism at Armageddon: Voices of American Participants in the First World War* (New York, 1997).

15. Clarence Mahan, "Hoosier Doughboy with the First Division World War One," World War One Survey, First Division, Carlisle Barracks, pp. 2, 33.

16. J. M. Winter, *The Experience of World War I* (New York, 1989), 244–45.

17. In the absence of figures for the occupational distribution of the entire American army, something can be gleaned about the background of the troops from information on the first draft held in June 1917. Of the 787,100 accepted for service, 52 percent (412,055) were from industry, broadly defined, a figure considerably higher than the proportion of industrial workers in the population at large; 26 percent (205,700) were from agriculture; and 22 percent (169,400) were from domestic service, trade, and other occupations. U.S. War Department, *Report of the Provost Marshal General . . . on the First Draft* (Washington, DC, 1918), 64–65, 34–35; "industry" is a composite of all employees in mining, manufacturing, and transportation, plus laborers; the participation ratio (accepted for service: total number in occupational category) for agricultural workers was 1.48, compared to 3.12 for coal miners and 5.90 for iron and steel workers.

18. U.S. War Department, *Report of the Provost Marshal General*, 34–35. On the draft, see John Chambers, *To Raise an Army: The Draft Comes to Modern America* (New York, 1987); Alexander Bing, *War-Time Strikes and Their Adjustment* (New York, 1921); Valerie Jean Conner, *The National War Labor Board: Stability, Social Justice, and the Voluntary State in World War I* (Chapel Hill, NC, 1983); Harold Tobin and Percy Bidwell, *Mobilizing Civilian America* (New York, 1940); Felix Frankfurter Papers, Box 192.

19. Frank Hayes, *United Mine Workers Journal* (January 17,1918), 24.

20. Crystal Eastman, *Work Accidents and the Law* (New York, 1969; orig. 1910), 11–15, 49–50, 65, 75, 93. Of the 526 fatalities recorded in Allegheny County in the 12 months beginning July 1906, deaths in the steel mills accounted for 195. In return for accepting risks, workers expected fair treatment. After a logger's head was smashed by a piece of runaway machinery, one lumberjack said, "Anybody's likely to get his leg, or arm, or neck broken at any minute. They take their chances on that, but we want to be treated like human beings, not like cattle"; Andrew M. Prouty, *More Deadly Than War! Pacific Coast Logging, 1827–1981* (New York, 1985), 88–89.

21. Eastman, *Work Accidents*, 93, 24, 231.

22. Robert Leckie, *The Wars of America*, rev. ed. (New York, 1981), 646.

23. Quoted in Ray Abrams, *Preachers Present Arms* (Scottdale, PA, rev. ed. 1969), 175–76.

24. Bok quoted in Joanne Karetzky, *The Mustering of Support for World War I by the Ladies' Home Journal* (Lewiston, NY, 1997), 35.

25. Conningsby Dawson, *The Glory of the Trenches* (New York, 1918), 138, 139; Willa Cather, *One of Ours* (New York, 1922), 420.

26. Ernest Hemingway, *A Farewell to Arms* (New York, 1957; orig. 1929), 184–85.

27. James B. Wharton, "Squad," in Eugene Lohrke, *Armageddon: The World War in Literature* (New York, 1930), 683.

28. Grosvenor Clarkson, *Industrial America in the World War: The Strategy behind the Line, 1917–1918* (New York, 1923), 3.

29. Clarkson, *Industrial America in the World War*, 331, 423, 442.

30. Clemenceau quoted in Clarkson, *Industrial America*, xxiii.

31. Paul Kennedy, *The Rise and Fall of the Great Powers* (New York, 1987), 244, 271, manufacturing ratio calculated with 1913 figures.

32. Weyl, *End of the War*, 29.

33. Clarkson, *Industrial America*, 173, 321–28.

34. Johnson, *Peace Progressives*, 86, 85.

35. Quote on strikes from Food Administration circular, in Harriet Laidlaw Papers, Schlesinger Library, box 5, folders 77. See also, Food Administration records, National Archives (NA), Record Group (RG) 287.

36. Harry Scheiber, Harold Vatter, and Harold Faulkner, *American Economic History* (New York, 1976), 325.

37. William G. McAdoo, *Crowded Years* (Boston, 1931), 378.

38. The idea that politics was, at bottom, the expression of conflicting social and economic forces was not, in itself, the result of the war. It had always been a central tenet of progressive thinking, as embodied in such landmark books as Charles Beard's 1913 *Economic Origins of the Constitution* and Walter Lippmann's *Drift and Mastery*. But the experience of war deepened the conviction. Perhaps the most fully developed analysis of the links between war and society appeared in the writings of someone only a few Americans, mostly those associated with *The Masses*, had ever heard of. Antonio Gramsci was an Italian communist best known for his leadership of the factory council movement in postwar Italy. More than anyone else, Gramsci took seriously the idea of a fusion of battlefront and homefront. He drew a contrast between two kinds of conflict. In the multilayered and increasingly democratic societies of the west (France, Britain, and the United States), dominant and subordinate groups fought a protracted war of position, just as their immobilized armies had to fight for every inch of ground along the trenches of the Western Front. By contrast, in the hierarchical and authoritarian societies of the east, landlord and peasant, tsar and subject, oppressor and oppressed fought a war of movement, sometimes through underground societies and secret police, at other times through open rebellion and violent suppression, just as the armies of the Eastern Front moved across great stretches of terrain. To Gramsci, the military collapse of Russian armies on the Eastern Front was part and parcel of the political collapse of the old tsarist regime.

39. Lippmann, *Drift and Mastery* (Englewood Cliffs, NJ, 1961; orig. 1914), 54.

40. Cookbook of the United States Food Administration (Washington, DC [1917]), 8–9; information on the pledge campaign and the cook book is in NA, RG 287, Y3 box Y772; RG 4, box 328.

41. Joanne Karetzky, *The Mustering of Support for World War I by the "Ladies' Home Journal"* (Lewiston, NY, 1997), 75, 71, 43.

42. Information on college women from Harriet Laidlaw Papers, Schlesinger Library, box 5, folders 77, 78.

43. John White, *United Mine Workers Journal* (January 17, 1918), 24.

44. Wilson quoted in *United Mine Workers Journal* (January 17, 1918), 24.

45. Lippmann quoted in David Kennedy, *Over Here: The First World War and American Society* (Oxford, 1980), 39.

46. Conner, *The National War Labor Board*, 25; David Montgomery, *Fall of the House of Labor: The Workplace, the State, and American Labor Activism, 1865–1925* (New York, 1987), 355.

47. Frank Walsh, Labor Day speech, 1918, Frank P. Walsh Papers, scrapbook 41, New York Public Library.

48. Bing, *War-Time Strikes*, 70, 108, 78–79; Conner, *War Labor Board*, 46–47; Harold Tobin and Percy Bidwell, *Mobilizing Civilian America* (New York, 1940), 125–26; "work or fight" order spelled out by Felix Frankfurter, Frankfurter Papers, box 192. In characterizing the WLB as an example of "voluntarism," Conner, *War Labor Board*, viii–ix, and *passim*, applies the same idea used by Robert Cuff, *War Industries Board: Business-Government Relations during World War I* (Baltimore, 1973); both stretch the term too far.

49. John F. Piper, *The American Churches in World War I* (Athens, OH, 1985), 78–85.

50. Melvyn Urofsky, *American Zionism from Herzl to the Holocaust* (Garden City, NY, 1975), 202, 213, 216–17.

51. William Tuttle, Jr., *Race Riot: Chicago in the Red Summer of 1919* (Urbana, 1970), 218.

52. David Levering Lewis, *W. E. B. Du Bois: The Biography of a Race, 1868–1919* (New York, 1993), 555–60.

53. Stephen R. Fox, *The Guardian of Boston: William Monroe Trotter* (New York, 1970), 216–19.

54. Du Bois quoted in L. S. Stavrianos, *Global Rift: The Third World Comes of Age* (New York, 1981), 513; see also Lewis, *W. E. B. Du Bois*, 551–52.

55. Stanley Weintraub, *A Stillness Heard round the World: The End of the Great War: November 1918* (New York, 1985).

Chapter 7. The Millennial Moment

1. John Dos Passos, *Nineteen Nineteen* (New York, 1979; orig. 1932), 344.

2. *The Nation* (October 25, 1919), quoted in *The Nation* (January 10/17, 2000), 12.

3. George Soule, "Hard-boiled Radicalism," *The New Republic* (January 21, 1931), 262.

4. See George Marsden, *Fundamentalism and American Culture, 1870–1930* (New York, 1980); Paul Boyer, *When Time Shall Be No More: Prophecy Belief in Modern American Culture* (Cambridge, MA, 1992), 101–3.

5. See Susan Kellogg and Steven Mintz, *Domestic Revolutions: A Social History of the American Family* (New York, 1988), 113–19.

6. Mary Dennett, *The Sex Side of Life*, pamphlet reprinted from the 1918 *Medical Review of Reviews*, 10; see also Freda Kirchwey, ed., *Our Changing Morality* (New York, 1924).

7. Dos Passos, *Nineteen Nineteen*, 369.

8. See Robert Sklar, *Movie-Made America: A Cultural History of American Movies* (New York, rev. ed., 1994), 78–79.

9. Soule, "Hard-boiled Radicalism," 262.

10. Dos Passos, *Nineteen Nineteen*, 390.

11. Vorse quoted in Dee Garrison, *Mary Heaton Vorse: The Life of an American Radical* (Philadelphia, 1989), 141.

12. Crystal Eastman, "In Communist Hungary," *The Liberator* (August 1919); reprinted in Blanche Wiesen Cook, ed., *Crystal Eastman on Women and Revolution* (New York, 1978), 328.

13. Manifesto of the Communist Party of America, September 1919, quoted in Theodore Draper, *American Communism and Soviet Russia* (New York, 1977), 9.

14. Interchurch World Movement, *Report of the Steel Strike of 1919* (New York, 1920), 137–41.

15. William Z. Foster, *The Great Steel Strike and Its Lessons* (New York, 1920).

16. Soule, "Hard-boiled Radicalism," 262.

17. Wilson speech in Des Moines Sept. 6, 1919, in *Public Papers*, ed. Ray Stannard Baker and William Dodd (New York, 1927), II:17.

18. William Tuttle, *Race Riot: Chicago in the Red Summer of 1919* (Urbana, IL, 1996 ed.).

19. On labor disputes in Panama, see Michael Conniff, *Black Labor on a White Canal, Panama, 1904–1981* (Pittsburgh, 1985), 52–61.

20. Randolph's *Messenger* editorial of May–June, 1919, quoted in Leon Fink, *Progressive Intellectuals and the Dilemmas of Democratic Commitment* (Cambridge, MA, 1997), 192.

21. Quoted in Steven Fraser, *Labor Will Rule: Sidney Hillman and the Rise of American Labor* (New York, 1991), 144.

22. Emily Rosenberg, *Spreading the American Dream: American Economic and Cultural Expansion, 1890–1945* (New York, 1982), 134.

23. The August 1920 UNIA Convention is extensively documented in Robert A. Hill, ed., *The Marcus Garvey and Universal Negro Improvement Association Papers* (Berkeley, 1983), II:476–673.

24. Garvey speech in Chicago Sept. 28, 1919, reported by British Military Intelligence to American Military Intelligence, Oct. 3, 1919, in Hill, *Marcus Garvey Papers*, II:50.

25. Hasia Diner, *In the Almost Promised Land: American Jews and Blacks, 1915–1935* (Westport, CT, 1977), 54–55.

26. Melvyn Urofsky, *American Zionism from Herzl to the Holocaust* (Garden City, NY, 1975), 131.

27. Urofsky, *American Zionism*, 128, 131; Jordan A. Schwartz, *The New Dealers* (New York, 1993), 118–19.

28. See Elizabeth McKillen, *Chicago Labor and the Quest for a Democratic Diplomacy, 1914–1924* (Ithaca, 1995), 170, 169, 171, 183.

29. Dos Passos quoted in Garrison, *Mary Heaton Vorse*, 135.

30. George Seldes, *The George Seldes Reader* (New York, 1994), 71.

31. Garrison, *Mary Heaton Vorse*, 126–27.

32. Quoted in Lloyd Gardner, *Safe for Democracy: The Anglo-American Response to Revolution, 1913–1923* (New York, 1987), 1.

33. Mary Drier, *Margaret Drier Robins* (New York, 1950), 142–45, 160–63; Papers of Mary Anderson, International Federation of Working Women, box 4, f. 80; "With the First International Congress of Working Women," *Life and Labor*

(December 1919); Mary Anderson, *Women at Work: The Autobiography of Mary Anderson* (Westport, CT, [1973, c.1951]), 125–27, 132–33.

34. Gertrude Bussey and Margaret Tims, *Women's International League for Peace and Freedom, 1915–1965* (London, [c. 1965]).

35. Wells quoted in Thomas Knock, *To End All Wars* (New York, 1992), 1.

36. Frederick Howe, *Confessions of a Reformer* (Kent, OH, 1988; orig. 1925), 308; Lincoln Steffens, *Autobiography* (New York, 1931), 778; Wells quoted in Knock, *To End All Wars*, 1.

37. Knock, *To End All Wars*, 71, 78.

38. Agnes Nestor, *Woman's Labor Leader* (Rockford, IL, 1954), 225.

39. Dos Passos, *Nineteen Nineteen*, 383.

40. Stephen Bonsal, *Suitors and Suppliants: The Little Nations at Versailles* (Port Washington, NY, 1969; orig., 1946), 56, 32.

41. William S. Graves, *America's Siberian Adventure, 1918–1920* (New York, 1931).

42. Lloyd George speech March 8, 1919, quoted in Herbert Hoover, *The Ordeal of Woodrow Wilson* (Washington, 1992; orig. 1958), 168; Lansing, October 28, 1918, quoted in Klaus Schwabe, *Woodrow Wilson, Revolutionary Germany, and Peacemaking* (Chapel Hill, NC, 1985), 139.

43. Lloyd George speech March 8, 1919, quoted in Hoover, *Ordeal of Woodrow Wilson*, 168.

44. Lansing quoted in Gardner, *Safe for Democracy*, 244.

45. Hoover, *Ordeal of Woodrow Wilson*, 72; Herbert Hoover to President Wilson, March 28, 1919, in Hoover Papers, box 8, Hoover Institution on War, Peace, and Revolution.

46. Dos Passos, *Nineteen Nineteen*, 248.

47. William McDonald, "The Madness at Versailles," *The Nation* (May 17, 1919), quoted in *The Nation* (Jan. 10/17, 2000), 12.

Chapter 8. Retreat from Reform

1. House quoted in Walter Russell Mead, *Special Providence: American Foreign Policy and How It Changed the World* (New York, 2001), 323.

2. Curiously, most of the historians who emphasize America's relentless expansion have been its critics, starting with William Appleman Williams, *The Tragedy of American Diplomacy* (New York, 1959), and followed by N. Gordon Levin, *Woodrow Wilson and World Politics: America's Response to War and Revolution* (London, 1968); Carl Parrini, *Heir to Empire* (Pittsburgh, 1969); Emily Rosenberg, *Spreading the American Dream: American Economic and Cultural Expansion, 1890–1945* (New York, 1982); Thomas McCormick, *America's Half Century: United States Foreign Policy in the Cold War* (Baltimore, 1989). The classic realist account is George Kennan, *American Diplomacy* (New York, 1951).

3. F. H. Brown to Irenee Du Pont, May 16, 1919, Acc. 1662, Hagley Library.

4. Ibid.

5. Secretary of War, *Annual Report, 1920* (Washington, 1921), vol. I; William Preston, *Aliens and Dissenters: Federal Suppression of Radicals 1903–33* (Cam-

bridge, MA, 1963), 198. For extensive documentation on the use of troops in domestic disturbances, see the report prepared in the 1930s by a Justice Department attorney and compiled in the so-called Glasser Files, Department of Justice RG 60, National Archives; these files duplicate much of the material in the main source on the use of federal troops, RG 407, Decimal Files of the Adjutant General's Office, AG 381 and AG 370.6.

6. Leonard Wood to Adjutant General, Oct. 7, 1919, copy in RG 165 370.6, Gary, Indiana, National Archives.

7. Leonard Wood diary (unpublished), entries for October, Library of Congress.

8. Gompers quoted in Stanley Coben, *A. Mitchell Palmer: Politician* (New York, 1963), 171.

9. Raymond Fosdick to Eric Drummond, November 25, 1919, Fosdick Papers, box 4, Mudd Library, Princeton University.

10. E. David Cronon, ed., *Cabinet Diaries of Josephus Daniels, 1913–1921* (Lincoln, NE, 1963), 444.

11. Charles Lydecker, press release, October 6, 1919, Elihu Root Papers, box 137, Library of Congress.

12. Burleson Papers, Library of Congress, vols. 19, 20. See also George Creel Papers, Library of Congress.

13. The main secondary source for this discussion is Keith Jeffrey and Peter Hennessy, *States of Emergency: British Governments and Strikebreaking since 1919* (London, 1983); see also Ralph Desmaris, "Lloyd George and the Development of the British Government's Strikebreaking Organization," *International Review of Social History,* 20 (1975), 1–15; Christopher J. Whelan, "Military Intervention in Industrial Disputes," *Industrial Law Journal,* 8 (1979), 222–34. The main primary source material on the Supply and Transport Committee is in Cabinet Papers (CAB 21, 24, 27), the War Office (WO 32), and other collections located in the British Public Record Office. Access to comparable French material is more difficult, but some material is apparently housed in the Archives de la prefecture de police, la commissariat de police, Paris.

14. Henry Wilson (Chief of the Imperial General Staff) to the Secretary of State, November 6, 1919, "The Employment of Troops in Industrial Disturbances," War Office 32/5467, p. 2.

15. Memo from Colonel Dunn, July 29, 1920, Record Group (RG) 165, Military Intelligence Division, 242-13.

16. Emergency Plans White, Third Corps Area, RG 165 MID, 242-13, p. 4.

17. Emergency Plans White, Third Corps Area, p. 6.

18. Emergency Plan White, Sixth Corps Area, RG 407, Adjutant General's Office 381, Appendix II (G-2), pp. 6–9.

19. Wilson address to the Senate, July 10, 1919, *The Papers of Woodrow Wilson*, ed. Arthur Link (Princeton, 1983), 61:436.

20. Reservations of the Senate Foreign Relations Committee, *Papers of Woodrow Wilson*, 65:52n3.

21. *Daily Jewish Courier,* August 1, 1919, Chicago Foreign Language Press Survey, reel 34.

22. Root to Lodge, June 19, 1919, Root Papers, box 161, Library of Congress.

23. Speech in Des Moines, Sept. 6, 1919, *Papers of Woodrow Wilson*, 65:77

24. Raymond Fosdick, *Chronicle of a Generation* (New York, 1958), 205, 202, 213.

25. Wilson speeches, Sept. 4–Sept. 26, 1919, *Papers of Woodrow Wilson*, 65:44, 47.

26. Walter Lippmann to Raymond Fosdick, August 15, 1919, Raymond Fosdick Papers, box 4, Mudd Library, Princeton University.

27. Ralph Stone, *The Irreconcilables: The Fight against the League of Nations* (Lexington, KY, 1970), 81–112.

28. For further discussion, see John Milton Cooper, *Pivotal Decades: The United States, 1900–1920* (New York, 1990), 354–55.

29. Thomas Bailey, *Woodrow Wilson and the Great Betrayal* (Chicago, 1963).

30. David Kennedy, *Over Here: The First World War and American Society* (Oxford, 1980), 256–58.

31. Holmes quoted in Allan Chase, *The Legacy of Malthus: The Social Costs of the New Scientific Racism* (New York, 1977), 315.

32. Questions reprinted in Allan Chase, *Legacy*, 245.

33. Cornelia James Cannon, "American Misgivings," *The Atlantic Monthly* (February 1922), 145–57.

34. Michael Guyer, "Eugenics," *Heredity* (Philadelphia, 1925), 242.

35. Part of the reason historians have had a field day in interpreting prohibition is that there were so many different social groups behind it. Thus there is no necessary contradiction between those who focus on urban social engineers' push for efficiency, such as James Timberlake, *Prohibition and the Progressive Movement* (New York, 1970); on rural evangelical distrust of the city, such as Paul Boyer, *Urban Masses and Moral Order in America* (Cambridge, MA, 1978); on spiritual uncertainty, such as Joseph Gusfield, *Symbolic Crusade: Status Politics and the American Temperance Movement* (Urbana, IL, 1963); and those who stress the gender component, such as Barbara Epstein, *The Politics of Domesticity: Women, Evangelism, and Temperance in Nineteenth Century America* (Middletown, CT, 1981).

36. "First Aims of the League of Women Voters," Proceedings of the Jubilee Convention of the National American Woman Suffrage Association, March 1919, p. 37, italics added.

37. Osborn quoted in Chase, *Legacy of Malthus*, 278.

38. Marion T. Bennett, *American Immigration Policies* (Washington, 1963), 48–49; Coolidge message to Congress, Dec. 6, 1923, U.S. Dept. of State, *Foreign Relations*, 1923, I:xviii.

39. Nancy McLean, *Behind the Mask of Chivalry: The Making of the Second Ku Klux Klan* (New York, 1994), 5.

Chapter 9. Progressive Rebirth

1. Jane Addams, *The Second Twenty Years at Hull House* (New York, 1930), 7.

2. Crystal Eastman quoted in Blanche Wiesen Cook, ed., *Crystal Eastman on Women and Revolution* (New York, 1978), 140.

3. Addams quoted in Robert Johnson, *The Peace Progressives and American Foreign Relations* (Cambridge, MA, 1995), 217; platform of the 1920 Farmer-Labor party.

4. Quotes in Mary Renda, *Taking Haiti: Military Occupation and the Culture of U.S. Imperialism 1915–1940* (Chapel Hill, NC, 2001), 191, 267.

5. Renda, *Taking Haiti*, 192; *LaFollette's Magazine*, August, September, October 1919, January 1920.

6. Moon quoted in Johnson, *Peace Progressives*, 231; Renda, *Taking Haiti*, 269.

7. Frederick Howe, *The Confessions of a Reformer* (Kent, OH, 1988), 320.

8. Du Bois quoted in Thomas Holt, "W. E. B. Du Bois's Archeology of Race: Re-Reading 'The Conversation of Races,' " Michael Katz and Thomas Sugrue, *W. E. B. Du Bois, Race and the City: The Philadelphia Negro and Its Legacy* (Philadelphia, 1998), 71–73.

9. Gregg Andrews, *Shoulder to Shoulder? The American Federation of Labor, the United States and the Mexican Revolution, 1910–1924* (Berkeley, 1991); Military Intelligence tracked the Pan-American Federation of Labor; as recorded in RG 165 War Department General Staff 10110-1237.

10. Anonymous author quoted in David Danbom, *"The World of Hope": Progressives and the Struggle for an Ethical Public Life* (Philadelphia, 1987), 215.

11. Paul Kennedy, *The Rise and Fall of the Great Powers* (New York, 1987), 280, shows Europe in 1920 at a manufacturing index of 77.3 compared to 100 in 1913, and at 103.5 in 1925. Meanwhile the United States roared ahead from its 1913 index level to 122.2 in 1920 and 148 in 1925.

12. Emily Rosenberg, *Spreading the American Dream* (New York, 1982), 123; Kennedy, *Rise and Fall*, 280.

13. Ron Chernow, *The House of Morgan: An American Banking Dynasty and the Rise of Modern Finance* (New York, 1990), 245.

14. Quoted in Kees van der Pijl, *The Making of an Atlantic Ruling Class* (London, 1984), 66.

15. Mary Borden, quoted in Modris Eksteins, *The Great War and the Birth of the Modern Age* (Boston, 1989), 269.

16. Quoted in Mary Nolan, *Visions of Modernity* (New York, 1995), 9.

17. Figures for 1914 from Kennedy, *Rise and Fall*, table 21, 243.

18. Quoted in Eksteins, *The Great War*, 269. The flivver was a Ford Model T.

19. Rosenberg, *Spreading the American Dream*, 100.

20. Antonio Gramsci, *Selections from the Prison Notebooks*, Quintin Hoare and Geoffrey Nowell Smith, eds. (New York, 1971), 277–318.

21. Artur Holitscher quoted in Nolan, *Visions*, 8.

22. Ludwell Denny, quoted in Frank Costigliola, *Awkward Dominion: American Political, Economic, and Cultural Relations with Europe, 1919–1933* (Ithaca, NY, 1984), 140.

23. For a discussion of the "independent internationalism" of the 1920s, see Rosenberg, *Spreading the American Dream*, 108–60, esp. 114–15; for "business internationalism," see Joan Hoff Wilson, *American Business and Foreign Policy, 1920–1933* (Lexington, KY, 1971).

24. Quoted in Frank Ninkovich, *The Wilsonian Century: U.S. Foreign Policy since 1900* (Chicago, 1999), 79.

25. George Norris, *Fighting Liberal* (Lincoln, NE, 1973; orig. 1945), 249.

26. Quote in Jackson Lears, *Fables of Abundance: A Cultural History of Advertising in America* (New York, 1994), 225.

27. Walter Lippmann, *The Phantom Public* (New Brunswick, NJ, 1993; orig. 1925), 5.

28. Walter Lippmann, *Public Opinion* (New York, 1922), 399; Lippmann, *Phantom Public*, 146, 162.

29. Dewey quoted in Robert Westbrook, *John Dewey and American Democracy* (Ithaca, NY, 1991), 309; Dewey, *The Public and Its Problems* (New York, 1927).

30. George Soule, "Hard-boiled Radicalism," *The New Republic* (January 21, 1931), 262–63.

31. Howe, *Confessions*, 323, 318, 325.

32. Ibid., 323, 325, 318.

33. Quote in Eugene Tobin, *Organize or Perish: America's Independent Progressives, 1913–1933* (New York, 1986), 186.

34. Martin, *The New Republic*, 32 (Sept. 20, 1922), quoted in Nancy Cott, *The Grounding of Modern Feminism* (New Haven, 1987), 173.

35. La Follette 1924 campaign cartoon, Peoples Legislative Service, Library of Congress.

36. Norris, *Fighting Liberal*, 248–49.

37. Blanche Wiesen Cook, *Eleanor Roosevelt* (New York, 1992), I:258, 273–74, 341, 358–59, 368.

38. Platform of the Farmer-Labor party, 1920, copy in Agnes Nestor Papers, Chicago Historical Society.

39. Kenneth MacKay, *The Progressive Movement of 1924* (New York, 1966; orig. 1947), 76; Tobin, *Organize or Perish*, 137.

40. On the 1924 Progressive party, see MacKay, *Progressive Movement*; Tobin, *Organize or Perish*.

41. *Citizen-Labor's Official Paper*, August 29, 1924, 8; cartoons in People's Legislative Service Papers, Library of Congress, box 1.

42. MacKay, *Progressive Movement*, 79.

43. Analysis of voting is based largely on MacKay, *Progressive Movement*, 274–75.

44. Quoted in Cook, *Eleanor Roosevelt*, I:341.

Conclusion

1. Quoted in Frederick Lewis Allen, *Only Yesterday* (New York, 1931), 303.

2. Walter Lippmann, *Public Opinion* (New York, 1922), 418.

3. Dashiell Hammett, *Red Harvest* (New York, 1927).

4. Quoted in Steven Fraser, *Labor Will Rule* (New York, 1991), 198.

5. George Soule, "Hard-boiled Radicalism," *The New Republic* (January 21, 1931), 262–63.

6. McKay and Kirchwey quoted in Cook, ed., *Crystal Eastman on Women and Revolution* (New York, 1978), 34, 36.

7. Eugene Tobin, *Organize of Perish* (New York, 1986), 192–93, 203–13.

8. Soule, "Hard-boiled Radicalism," 265.

Epilogue

1. Marc Bloch, *The Historian's Craft*, trans. Peter Putnam (New York, 1953), 28.

2. Truman quoted in John L. Gaddis, *Strategies of Containment: A Critical Appraisal of Postwar American National Security Policy* (New York, 1982), 62.

3. Arthur Schlesinger, Jr., *The Vital Center: The Politics of Freedom* (Boston, 1949).

4. Quoted in John Culver and John Hyde, *American Dreamer: The Life and Times of Henry A. Wallace* (New York, 2000), 452.

5. Whole histories of the 1960s have been written without even a mention of progressivism. For example, see Maurice Isserman and Michael Kazin, *America Divided: The Civil War of the 1960s* (New York, 2000). Historians writing in the 1960s and 1970s often emphasized the conservative aspects of progressivism; e.g., Gabriel Kolko, *The Triumph of Conservatism: A Reinterpretation of American History, 1900–1916* (Chicago, 1963).

6. Michael Tomasky, *Left for Dead: The Life, Death, and Possible Resurrection of Progressive Politics in America* (New York, 1996); E. J. Dionne, *They Only Look Dead: Why Progressives Will Dominate the Next Political Era* (New York, 1996).

7. Kennedy quoted in *The Philadelphia Inquirer*, August 16, 2000, A18; Arthur Schlesinger, Jr., "A Question of Power: Is the Time Ripe for a Progressive Revival?" *The American Prospect*, April 23, 2001, 26–29; Michael Sandel, *Democracy's Discontent: America in Search of a Public Philosophy* (Cambridge, MA, 1996); Robert Putnam, *Bowling Alone: The Collapse and Revival of American Community* (London, 2001 ed.); Robert Bellah, et al., *The Good Society* (New York, 1991); Alan Wolfe, *Whose Keeper? Social Science and Moral Obligation* (Berkeley, 1989); Michael Schudson, *The Good Citizen: A History of American Civic Life* (Cambridge, MA, 1998).

Index

Page numbers appearing in italics refer to illustrations.

Cuba, 78, 79, 82, 364n.4
Cubism, 149
Cummins, Albert, 284

Daniels, Josephus, 121
DAR. *See* Daughters of the American
Revolution
Darrow, Clarence, 322
Darwinism and race, 80, 86, 237
Daughters of the American Revolution
(DAR), 94, 111, 274, 286
Davenport, Charles Edward, 287
Davis, John, 327
Dawes Plan (1924), 307–8
Dawson, Conningsby, 196
Debs, Eugene: antiwar activities of, 156,
157, 168, 191; arrest/jailing of, 157, 158,
190, 191, 322; death of, 336; on the Four-
teen Points, 190; presidential cam-
paigns of, 15, 228, 323; Socialist party
leadership of, 15
Declaration of Independence, 184
Dell, Floyd, 51
DeMille, Cecil: *The Ten Commandments*,
223
democracy: dance of, 202–13, 243; industrial, 206, 209–10, 226–27, 336; making
the world safe for, 5, 143, 147; and race,
288; and state intervention in daily life,
203–6
Democratic Leadership Council, 356
Democratic party: Irish prominence in,
235–36; Ku Klux Klan's influence in,
293; liberalism of, 351; progressivism
of, 337–38, 342; on strikebreakers,
163–64
Dennett, Mary, 222
Depression, 9, 132–33, 214, 330, 341–
42
Dewey, John, 44, 116, 147, 286, 316–17,
338, 368n.14, 373n.33
Dewey, Tom, 350
Díaz, Porfirio, 30, 97, 100–101
Dillingham Commission (1911), 291
disarmament, 298, 299, 300–301
discontent, U.S. vs. British reactions to,
260–68, 336
dissidents. *See* discontent, U.S. vs. British
reactions to; leftists
Dodge, Mabel, 33
dollar diplomacy, 5, 22–23, 30, 32, 61, 92–
93, 313

*Dollar Diplomacy: A Study of American Im-
perialism* (Freeman and Nearing), 303
Dominican Republic, 79, 80–81, 102, 301
Dos Passos, John, 59; *Nineteen Nineteen*,
219, 222, 224; *Three Soldiers*, 197; on the
Versailles Peace Conference, 237, 246,
255, 256
draft, 120, 168, 194–95
Drift and Mastery (Lippmann), 42–43, 203,
378n.38
Du Bois, W. E. B.: "Close Ranks," 212–13;
on the double consciousness of African-Americans, 127; on Garvey, 233; on
the Great War, 147, 371n.6; NAACP
founded by, 52–53, 71; Pan-Africanism
of, 238, 304; progressivism of, 329, 353;
on race, 52–53, 82, 303–4, 353; socialism
of, 48
Duncan, Isadora, 53
DuPont, 263

Easter Rebellion (1916), 120, 156, 230, 235
Eastman, Crystal: American Union for a
Democratic Peace founded by, 190; antiwar activities of, 103, 117, 368n.15; back-
ground/reputation of, 49, 95; death of,
336; on democracy, 190; liberalism/so-
cialism of, 48, 49, 95; in the People's
Council of America, 167; on revolution,
225; on women's conferences, 300; in
the Women's Peace Party, 332; work accidents investigated by, 195
Eastman, Max: on the Fourteen Points,
190; on the peace movement, 155, 156;
on sexual freedom, 49, 52
East St. Louis riot (Illinois, 1917), 53, 160–
61, 163–64, 211, 261
Economic Origins of the Constitution
(Beard), 378n.38
economics: and American ambivalence toward commercial motives, 138; American vs. Mexican/Caribbean, 97–98,
366n.32; and the Great War, 199–200;
on the Great War, 107, 118, 132–34, 137–
38; trickle-down, 200; and U.S. world
leadership, 181–82, 186, 191, 259, 306–
11; and the Versailles Peace Conference,
248. *See also* capitalism
Eighteenth Amendment (U.S. Constitution), 57, 146, 289. *See also* prohibition
Eisner, Kurt, 224
Eliot, Charles, 25

POLITICS AND SOCIETY IN TWENTIETH-CENTURY AMERICA

༻✿༺